vabnf

378.1 SEG

W9-BWJ-967

Segal, Theodore D., 1955- author
Point of reckoning
33410017061476   03-26-2021

POINT OF RECKONING

Valparaiso Public Library
103 Jefferson Street
Valparaiso, IN 46383

THEODORE D. SEGAL

POINT OF RECKONING

THE FIGHT FOR RACIAL JUSTICE

AT DUKE UNIVERSITY

DUKE UNIVERSITY PRESS · *Durham and London* · 2021

© 2021 Theodore D. Segal
All rights reserved

Printed in the United States of America on
acid-free paper ∞
Designed by Matthew Tauch
Typeset in Whitman by Westchester Publishing Services

Library of Congress Cataloging-in-Publication Data

Names: Segal, Theodore D., [date] author.
Title: Point of reckoning : the fight for racial justice at Duke
    University / Theodore D. Segal.
Description: Durham : Duke University Press, 2021. | Includes
    bibliographical references and index.
Identifiers: LCCN 2020021181 (print) | LCCN 2020021182 (ebook)
    | ISBN 9781478010401 (hardcover) | ISBN 9781478011422
    (paperback) | ISBN 9781478012955 (ebook)
Subjects: LCSH: Duke University—Students. | African
    American college students—North Carolina—Durham—
    History—20th century. | Racism in higher education—
    North Carolina—Durham—History—20th century. |
    Racism—North Carolina—Durham—History—20th century.
    | Durham (N.C.)—Race relations—History—20th century.
Classification: LCC LC2803.D87 S443 2021 (print) | LCC LC2803.D87
    (ebook) | DDC 378.1/9829960730756563—dc23
LC record available at https://lccn.loc.gov/2020021181
LC ebook record available at https://lccn.loc.gov/2020021182

Cover art: (*clockwise from top left*) Policeman approach-
ing unidentified student, from *Chanticleer*, 1969; Allen
Building study-in, November 13, 1967; Allen Building
takeover supporters being tear-gassed, February 13, 1969;
Duke's first three African American graduates (*left to
right*: Wilhelmina Reuben, Nathaniel White Jr., and Mary
Mitchell Harris), 1967; Allen Building takeover, February
13, 1969. Photos courtesy of David M. Rubenstein Rare
Book and Manuscript Library, Duke University and Duke
University Archives.

We stood yester-morn on the campus of the great Duke University, amazed at its vastness and magnificence. We thought of the stupendous sum of money spent by the Dukes to make this one of America's greatest educational institutions. We thought of the tobacco industry and its rise to one of the largest business enterprises in the world.

We thought of the blood of Negro men, women and children that had gone into the buildings to make up Duke University, and we likened them unto the bodies of Chinese slaves thrown into the Great Wall of China when it was erected. Like a great panorama, this throng of our forefathers passed before us. . . . . . some with stooped shoulders, bowed heads and pinched brows made so in order, that a great institution of learning might come into existence. As they trod their weary way, the earth shook about us.

We thought of the great God who sits in judgment over the affairs of mankind and thought of questioning him about the justice of permitting the blood to be squeezed out of black bodies to build a university for white minds . . . only white minds.—"My Lord what a morning."

If white people have labored in the factories of the American tobacco industry for less than enough on which to live, they have had the satisfaction of knowing that their children may reap the benefits in a school that provides the very best training. If Negroes have done the same thing, it must pierce their hearts to know that Duke University has been built for every other race under the sun but theirs. Chinese, Japanese, Germans, Russians or any other foreign race may be admitted to the school; but the American Negro stands alone as the one human being on earth, too loathsome in the eyes of the American white man to share the benefits of Duke University.

Is this the price of humbleness? Is this the price of faithfulness? Where is justice? Where is right? Where is God?

We left Duke University at high noon. The sun had reached its zenith and was casting its brilliant rays upon the school's massive buildings. Everything was in contour and detail; but they tell us the sun went down and that there was darkness—black darkness. My Lord, what a night!

L. E. Austin, publisher
Carolina Times
May 6, 1939

FOR THE BLACK STUDENTS WHO FORCED DUKE

TO CONFRONT ITS JIM CROW PAST; AND FOR THOSE

WHO SUSTAIN THE STRUGGLE FOR RACIAL JUSTICE

AND INCLUSION AT DUKE AND BEYOND

CONTENTS

———

ABBREVIATIONS

—

A&AA · African and Afro-American

AAS · Afro-American Society

ASDU · Associated Students of Duke University

Endowment · the Duke Endowment

Indenture · the Indenture and Deed of Trust of Personalty establishing the Duke Endowment

MSGA · Men's Student Government Association

NCC · North Carolina College at Durham (predecessor to North Carolina Central University)

SAE · Sigma Alpha Epsilon

SDS · Students for a Democratic Society

SFAC · Student Faculty Administrative Committee

SNCC · Student Nonviolent Coordinating Committee

Special Committee · Special Trustee-Administrative Committee

UNC · University of North Carolina

UPPAC · University Policy and Planning Advisory Committee

WSGA · Women's Student Government Association

KEY ACTORS AND THEIR ROLES, 1963–1969

Name · Position   *Unless otherwise noted, all positions are with Duke University.*

William G. Anlyan · dean, School of Medicine, 1964–69

Brenda E. Armstrong · student; chair and member of AAS

Frank L. Ashmore · vice president, institutional advancement, 1963–73

Tony L. Axam · student; member of AAS

W. Waldo Beach · professor, divinity school

Charles L. Becton · law student; member of AAS

John C. "Jack" Boger · student; Vigil Committee of 10

Brenda C. Brown · student; member of AAS

Edwin C. Bryson · university counsel, 1947–71

Louis J. Budd · professor, English; chair of Budd Committee

Stokely Carmichael · chair, SNCC

William H. Cartwright · professor, education; chair, Academic Council

John W. Cell · professor, history

Claudius B. Claiborne · student; member of AAS

R. Taylor Cole · provost, 1960–69

Samuel DuBois Cook · professor, political science

Robert E. Cushman · dean, divinity school, 1958–71

A. Hollis Edens · president, 1949–60

Henry A. Fairbank · professor and chair, physics

Howard L. Fuller · director of community development, Operation Breakthrough

Dick Gregory · Black activist; comedian; author

William J. Griffith · director of student union, 1954–67; assistant to the provost in the area of student affairs, 1963–69; assistant dean, College of Arts and Sciences, 1964–69; assistant provost and dean, College of Arts and Sciences, 1969–79

J. Deryl Hart · president, 1960–63

Oliver Harvey · janitor; labor organizer

J. Lee Hatcher · law student; member of AAS

David M. Henderson · student; Vigil Committee of 10

Marcus E. Hobbs · vice assistant provost and dean of the university, 1960–62, vice provost and dean of the university, 1962–63; provost, 1969–70

Joyce A. Hobson · student; member of AAS

Charles W. "Chuck" Hopkins · student; chair and member of AAS

Bertie R. Howard · student; member of AAS

Charles B. Huestis · vice president, business and finance, 1966–85

Gene Kendall · student; one of "first five" Black undergraduates to attend Duke

Alan C. Kerckhoff · professor, sociology; chair, Kerckhoff Committee

Jonathan C. Kinney · student; ASDU president; Vigil Committee of 10

Douglas M. Knight · president, 1963–69

Harold W. Lewis · vice provost and dean, College of Arts and Sciences, 1963–69; vice provost and dean of the faculty, 1969–80

Michael R. McBride · student; chair and member of AAS

Stef McLeod · student; member of AAS

Mary Mitchell · student; one of "first five" Black undergraduates to attend Duke

Clarence G. Newsome · student; member of AAS

Rufus H. Powell · secretary of the university, 1966–81

A. Kenneth Pye · dean, law school, 1968–70

Henry E. Rauch · trustee; member, Special Trustee-Administrative Committee

Wilhemina M. Reuben · student; May Queen; one of "first five" Black undergraduates to attend Duke

Margaret "Bunny" Small · student; Vigil Committee of 10

Cassandra Smith · student; one of "first five" Black undergraduates to attend Duke

John H. Strange · professor, political science

Wright Tisdale · chair, 1963–68, and trustee, board of trustees

William C. Turner Jr. · student; member of AAS

Charles B. Wade Jr. · chair, 1968–71, and trustee, board of trustees; member, Special Trustee-Administrative Committee

Richard L. Watson Jr. · professor and chair, history

Nathaniel B. White Jr. · student; one of "first five" Black undergraduates to attend Duke

Janice Williams · student; member of AAS

Barnes Woodhall · vice provost and dean, School of Medicine, 1962–64; vice provost in charge of medical affairs, 1964–67; associate provost, medical affairs, 1967–69; chancellor pro tem, 1969–70

Bunyan S. Womble · chair, 1960–63, and trustee, board of trustees

ACKNOWLEDGMENTS

——

When I left graduate school in 1979, I promised my history professor Bill Chafe and myself that I would complete the master's thesis I had started on Black campus activism at Duke in the 1960s. After a break of more than forty years, this book is the fulfillment of that promise. Returning to a topic I had last looked at as a young man was fascinating, absorbing, disorienting, and surreal. Turning that experience into a book would never have happened without the assistance and support of many people.

Most important was Bill Chafe. In the decades since we had been in touch, Bill had become a renowned civil rights historian and author, respected department chair, mentor and adviser to multiple generations of graduate students, and one of the founders of the oral history program and the Center for Documentary Studies at Duke. As dean of the faculty of Arts and Sciences and vice provost, he spearheaded numerous significant initiatives that made Duke a more diverse and inclusive institution. Despite his preeminence, Bill readily agreed to supervise a retired corporate lawyer to whom he had not spoken in years who wanted to finish a history project left over from his distant past. Without Bill's generosity, extraordinary editorial suggestions, and friendship, this book would not exist. In the acknowledgments to my senior history honors thesis on the Duke Silent Vigil, I told Bill that because of his brilliance, he would always be my professor and due to his warmth, he would always be my friend. Those words are as true in 2020 as they were when I first wrote them in 1977.

Others have been instrumental as well. Valerie Gillispie, the Duke University archivist; Amy McDonald, the assistant archivist; and the staff of the Duke University Archives and the Rubenstein Rare Book and Manuscript Library have supported my efforts unstintingly over the past three years. They have made the archives easily accessible, answered myriad questions, and helped me locate missing information. The passion Valerie and Amy have for Duke history and for telling the university's many stories helped sustain me over weeks of research in Durham.

As a first-time author, I have been incredibly fortunate to work with Gisela Concepción Fosado as my editor at Duke University Press. Gisela has been a true advocate for my book, providing wise comments, kindness, and deep expertise in the publishing process. She has provided constant encouragement, kept me on track, and shared with me her passion for and deep insights into racial justice and inclusion. Gisela's associate Alejandra Mejía has been ever-helpful in spearheading aspects of the production process. Ellen Goldlust, my Duke University Press project editor, and copyeditor Sheila McMahon did a remarkable job taking my "finished" manuscript and turning it into a polished book.

Various individuals provided input on my manuscript, including Allison Alexander, Elizabeth Bausch, John Dienelt, Susan Fiester, Valerie Gillispie, Robert Korstad, David Patterson, Renee Roth Powers, Judith Sandalow, Rebecca Segal, Zelda Segal, Samson Shifaraw, Michael Wasserstein, Daniel Weiss, Melissa Wiley, and Gail Winston, and I am grateful for their ideas. I am especially indebted to William C. Turner Jr., who read and commented on the manuscript from the perspective of a participant in the events described and a longtime Duke professor. The comments I received were very helpful. Of course, any remaining errors of fact or judgment are entirely my own.

Wesley Hogan has been instrumental to this entire process. A brilliant historian, documentarian, and gentle deliverer of hard truths, Wesley encouraged me and provided input, direction, and inspiration at every turn.

Because I have tried to tell the story in this book in the words of those who lived the events described, interview transcripts have been a key resource. I am truly indebted to those activists and administrators who sat for interviews (with me or other researchers) and am hopeful that I have done justice to their story. Special thanks to Brenda Armstrong, Charles Becton, Brenda Brown Becton, and William Turner, who sat for interviews with me in 1979 and again in 2017.

Several talented professionals have helped with aspects of the book, including editor Lynn Lauber, bibliographer Christopher Catanese, cartographer Tim Stallman, lawyer Kevin Casey, and indexer Jason Begy. Benjamin Klein served as a research assistant and found great resources, particularly on the Silent Vigil. The efforts of these individuals have made this a better book.

One advantage of taking a forty-year pause in a research project is that this interval gave me the time to become father to Brenda Segal Bochner and Gregory Segal, see both grow into terrific adults and marry exceptional partners in David Bochner and Gabriella Meltzer, and benefit from the compelling insights of these four remarkable individuals. Over countless dinners and other family events, my children have been a source of great enthusiasm and interest for this project (not to mention patience).

Finally, I must thank my wife, Joyce Wasserstein. At every stage, Joyce has helped sharpen my ideas, improve my writing, and bolster my energy. Like all other good things in my life, this book would not have been possible without Joyce's wisdom, love, and support. Whatever I have accomplished we have accomplished together, and I am forever grateful for the life we have shared.

Introduction

A Historic Encounter

———

As they arrived on campus, Black undergraduates who entered Duke University in the early years following desegregation were busy with the tasks all new students face. There were boxes to unpack in too-small dorm rooms, roommates to meet, and tearful, proud parents to send on their way home. Soon orientation would be over, classes would begin, and extracurricular commitments would ramp up. Before they knew it, the first semester of their freshman year would be in full swing.

But although their daily activities tracked those of their white counterparts, these Black students experienced Duke very differently. Gene Kendall, one of the first five Black undergraduates, arrived on campus in the fall of 1963. He stood on the carefully manicured main quad and surveyed the magnificent gothic-style buildings surrounding him. "I was a wide-eyed kid who was fascinated when I looked up at the chapel for the first time," Kendall recalled. "I thought, 'What in the world am I into?'"[1] Brenda Armstrong was overwhelmed by the transition from the predominantly Black atmosphere of her childhood to Duke's "sea of white."[2] Chuck Hopkins recalled waking up one morning early in his freshman year and seeing "all these Black men raking leaves" outside his dorm window. "It was like a plantation," he recalled thinking.[3]

Kendall, Armstrong, and Hopkins were not alone in these sentiments. They were among a vanguard of talented Black youngsters who, in the early 1960s, gained admission to historically white colleges and universities (HWCUs) throughout the South.

The arrival of these Black students marked a profound change for these historically white institutions. For decades, Jim Crow and segregation had defined the organization and daily operations of these schools. For whites, segregation was a given—both entrenched and pervasive.

Hence, when desegregation occurred at HWCUs, it created immense challenges for all parties.[4] White administrators, faculty, and students, many of whom had never interacted with a Black person other than in a service capacity, were forced to learn how to relate to Black students. Likewise, these Black students, the vast majority of whom had never interacted with white individuals as equals, faced their own challenge: how to deal with white administrators and faculty, and white students as peers. This was a historic encounter.

How would they live and work together at Duke? Under Jim Crow, the academic and social opportunities offered by Duke were for white students only. The "Duke Experience" was a training ground for advancement in white America. Theoretically at least, desegregation meant that Black students now would have the chance to share in these opportunities. But how desegregation played out depended on whether Duke was prepared to invest the political capital, as well as economic and human resources, to allow Black students to realize their full potential at Duke. Would the curriculum be changed to reflect the rich history of African American life, culture, and thought, now that Black students were a part of the institution? Would the composition of the faculty and administration change to reflect the presence of Black students on campus? In sum, what resources was Duke willing to reallocate to create an inclusive environment that could serve the needs of all students—both white and Black?

By the end of the 1960s, college campuses throughout the United States were engulfed in Black student protest.[5] At Duke, significant white and Black student protests dominated the campus in the last years of the 1960s. As Black protest at Duke was accelerating, a group of primarily white students and faculty held a "Silent Vigil" in April 1968 in response to the assassination of Martin Luther King Jr. The vigil, with more than 1,500 students and faculty eventually occupying the campus's main quadrangle, demanded that Duke University take bold steps to show its commitment to racial and economic justice. The vigil was followed just ten months later by the takeover of key areas of the Allen Building, Duke's central administrative headquarters, by Black students. The Silent Vigil and the Allen Building takeover show the different ways white trustees, administrators, and faculty perceived—and reacted to—white and Black student protest. How persistent were the assumptions of Duke's Jim Crow legacy?

Looking back fifty years later, how should the actions of Duke trustees, administrators, and faculty be judged? The school's basic principles "have remained constant," Duke's bulletin for the 1963–64 school year declared. The school motto, "Eruditio et Religio," expressed "a fundamental faith in the union of knowledge and religion" and the values of scholarship, freedom and truth, tolerance, and service. Through "changing generations of students," the bulletin announced, the objective of the school has been "to encourage each individual to achieve to the extent of his capabilities an understanding and appreciation of the world in which he lives, his relationship to it, his opportunities and responsibilities."[6] It seems fair to ask to what extent Duke leaders were able to embrace those values and reach for those objectives as they confronted the reality of Black students in their midst. More simply, when Douglas M. Knight, Duke president during this period, and others said that they were acting in "good faith" to address the needs of Duke's Black students, did their actions meet that standard?

I started my study of Black campus activism at Duke in 1978, when I was twenty-three years old. After a thirty-five-year career in corporate law practice, I decided to return to the subject. As a retired lawyer who had spent most of his adult life in business and social settings shaped by white privilege, I saw Black student protest at Duke during the 1960s very differently. Having sat on many law firm "diversity" committees and task forces, I saw how ineffective these initiatives could be. Without substantial investment of resources by the law firm, little was accomplished to advance the hiring and promotion of people of color. Being a parent also shaped how I viewed events when I revisited them. "Black activists" I interviewed in 1978 when I was twenty-three became for me "kids" by 2016—youngsters who entered college with the same swirling mixture of excitement, aspiration, strength, and vulnerability that all children experience at this auspicious moment. As a result, I became fascinated by questions I never thought to ask in my twenties. When talking to Black activists—most of whom were now close to seventy—for a second round of interviews, I knew more and had different questions. I wanted to know about their families, schools, and communities and how parents and other relatives responded to their participation in campus protest. Among

Duke leaders, I wanted to understand the attitudes and institutional framework that blocked them from responding to Duke's new Black students with more empathy and professionalism. For Knight, the liberal Duke president, I wanted to explore why his progressive attitudes on race did not translate more forcefully into leadership on issues he claimed that he cared about. In essence, I wanted to come to terms with the human dimension of people and events that I had previously understood largely as abstractions.

This story challenges the comfortable narrative that has emerged over the decades about the role campus protest played in the history of Duke. That narrative focuses on change—the role Black and white student protesters played in successfully forcing a provincial southern school to confront its Jim Crow legacy. Although some aspects of this narrative may have merit, it overlooks the powerful shape-shifting resiliency of traditional racial attitudes at Duke. As this account shows, Duke deployed an array of strategies to resist change, even when faced with protest. Change, when it did occur, came very slowly because racial inclusion was never a core value of the university.

From the moment it was established, Duke University aspired to greatness. William Preston Few, the president of Trinity College when it became Duke University, told students that they would have an important part in "launching one of the great education establishments of the world." In its "aims," the new university aspired to "advance learning in all lines of truth; to defend scholarship against all false notions and ideals; to develop a Christian love of freedom and truth; to promote a sincere spirit of tolerance; . . . and to render the largest permanent service to the individual, the state, the nation, and the church."[7]

The events that followed desegregation at Duke expose the conflicting forces that converged as a segregated southern institution was forced to confront its long history of racial exclusion. They show that race and the struggle for inclusion stand at the center of the university's story—and the story of the nation. Indeed, Duke University could not approach its lofty aims nor achieve its national ambitions until it came to terms with a racial past defined by segregation and exclusion. The story tells us a great deal about Duke University in the 1960s as well as the dynamics that played out following desegregation at other HWCUs and the country at large. It also illuminates conflicts and challenges that continue to resonate at Duke, within higher education North and South, and throughout the country to the present day.

_____

CHAPTER 1

A Plantation System

Desegregation

_____

When the first class of Black undergraduates enrolled as freshmen at Duke University in 1963, less than forty years had elapsed since the gift from James B. Duke that transformed Trinity College into a prominent southern university. During that time, the university had made great progress in realizing James Duke's vision of creating a school that would attain "a place of real leadership in the educational world." A magnificent gothic-style "West Campus" had been constructed just over a mile from the location of former Trinity College in Durham, North Carolina. Trinity's campus had been reconstructed and a Woman's College established on the site. Graduate and professional programs in more than twenty disciplines had been added, the undergraduate college had expanded, and the quality of both the faculty and the student body was on the rise. One observer noted that Duke's graduate school "was considerably beyond that of any other institution in the south" and was ready to become a leader nationally in a number of areas.[1]

Despite these achievements, Duke's transformation into a prominent national academic institution was a work in progress. The school remained largely defined by its city, state, and region. In 1963 a significant portion of undergraduates were raised within two hundred to three hundred miles of the school. More than 400 out of a total of 1,199 freshmen came from North Carolina. Alumni were also concentrated in the South, and fully 75 percent of university trustees came from the region, mostly from North and South Carolina. President Douglas Knight recalled board meetings during the 1960s characterized by a "high degree of gentility" that was both "southern" and "courtly." Duke was the largest employer in Durham by a factor of two and a half. If Duke's place in the region's academic and business communities was changing, the school remained, in Knight's view, both "dominant and isolated."[2]

Duke's location in North Carolina gave it a strong geographic foundation but also meant that the university embraced the powerful racial codes that defined the segregated Jim Crow South. The arrival on campus of Duke's first Black undergraduates in 1963 marked the official end of segregation at the school. Although only five in number, the presence of these freshmen, who joined a small number of Black graduate and law students admitted a year earlier, meant that Duke's history of racially exclusive admissions was over. Still, this step marked barely a beginning if the university were to confront the Jim Crow attitudes and practices that infused campus life.

⋯⋯⋯⋯⋯⋯⋯⋯

The transformation of Trinity College into Duke University occurred in 1924 with the creation of the Duke Endowment by James B. Duke. The businessman rose to prominence in the "New South" as the region struggled to replicate the economic success of the northern industrial revolution and become more a part of the Union and world. President of American Tobacco Company when still in his early thirties, Duke and his family also had extensive holdings in the textile sector. By 1899 the Dukes began to develop water power as a means of generating electricity for their textile operations. As Duke developed his interests in electric power, he began to look for ways to combine his business and philanthropic activities. The Duke Indenture—which established the Duke Endowment and gave it control of Duke Power Company—was the realization of this ambition.[3]

The sums involved in creating the Duke Endowment were enormous. Securities worth $40 million, primarily in Duke Power Company, were turned over to the Endowment with a stipulation that 20 percent of its net income would be added to the Endowment until an additional $40 million had been amassed. The beneficiaries of the Endowment fell into four categories—hospitals, Methodist Church–related organizations, nonprofits established for the care of orphans, and educational institutions. By far the most substantial of the bequests—up to $6 million—went to the establishment of Duke University. James Duke provided in the Indenture that Trinity would receive this bequest, along with an allocation of fully 32 percent of the Endowment's annual net income, as long as the school changed its name to Duke University and amended its charter to provide for "perpetual existence." Duke hoped that his largesse would allow Trinity to be transformed rapidly into the first research university in the emerging New South.[4]

In less than three weeks, Trinity's trustees said yes. "We have found," the board declared after its historic meeting, "that the University is to be developed according to plans that are perfectly in line with our hopes for the expansion" of Trinity College. On December 30, 1924, the legal formalities required for the transformation of Trinity into Duke University were completed.[5]

Duke did not intend that the university he endowed become a haven for free thought or the exchange of radical ideas. During this time, historian John Egerton wrote, "a rigid orthodoxy of thought and opinion governed virtually every discipline and field of study" at southern universities. Like other New South business leaders, Duke believed deeply in hard work and success in industry as the pathway to a productive life. "There ain't a thrill in the world," Duke once said, "to compare with building a business and watching it grow before your eyes." His aspirations for Duke University were pragmatic. He valued education, he said in the Indenture, "conducted along sane and practical, as opposed to dogmatic and theoretical, lines," and considered it, "next to religion, the greatest civilizing influence." As for students, he sought only those "whose previous record shows a character, determination and application evincing a wholesome and real ambition for life." One writer at the time went so far as to comment that what Duke wanted "was a Babbitt factory, a mill for grinding out go-get-'em boys in the wholesale and undeviating fashion in which his Chesterfield plant across the way ground out cigarettes."[6]

A novel "dual-governance" structure established for Duke complicated matters. Under the Indenture, the Endowment trustees could withhold funds from Duke University if, in their judgment, the school was not "operated in a manner calculated to achieve the results intended." This created the risk that the independence of the university could be compromised if the Endowment trustees withheld funds from the school. Adding to this concern, Endowment trustees were required to provide oversight for Duke Power Company, the entity whose stock made up the bulk of the Endowment's assets. To ensure that they could discharge this responsibility, the majority of initial Endowment trustees selected by James Duke were directors or senior officers of Duke Power Company. Given this context, Knight observed that, for the Endowment trustees, "money rather than education was their primary concern." This structure meant that an Endowment board composed of Duke Power executives and other businessmen held significant leverage over what went on at the university.[7]

With the substantial Endowment funding, Duke grew rapidly. The school immediately undertook an ambitious building program. Between 1925 and 1927, eleven red-brick Georgian-style buildings were constructed on the original Trinity College campus. Soon this became the location for the Woman's College. In 1926 graduate schools of arts and sciences and religion were added to the campus, followed by professional schools in medicine, law, nursing, and forestry. Between 1927 and 1930, work was initiated on the new, Gothic-style West Campus. The School of Nursing was established in 1931 and the College of Engineering in 1938. Over the years, Duke's graduate programs expanded, with some gaining a national reputation. Construction of West Campus was finished in 1954 with the completion of the Allen Building, which became the center of the university's administrative operations. Faculty salaries and morale went up.[8]

As Duke was growing, the quality of its undergraduate student body also continued to change. During the late 1950s and early 1960s, William J. Griffith, who served as director of the student union during this period, remembered that Duke had "good students" but the women students "across the board were of a higher caliber than the male students." As a result, Griffith recalled, "men had an [academic] inferiority complex." Zoology professor Peter H. Klopfer was more candid. He remembered Duke's male students as predominantly southern, "not particularly bright," and "conformists to a fascinating degree."[9]

As the 1950s ended, however, the academic quality of undergraduates began to improve. In 1959 Duke president A. Hollis Edens reported "an intellectual groundswell . . . among the students." Barney L. Jones, assistant dean of Trinity College at the time, called the class entering Duke in the fall of 1959 "potentially the best ever." Still—despite these changes—Duke had not achieved the level of national prominence it aspired to. Even by the early 1960s, Duke had only three departments that were recognized as being in the top fifteen nationally. Its graduate programs had been placed, according to one report, in a "third group" behind twenty-two other schools.[10]

To help chart its path forward, the university formed a long-range-planning committee in 1958 to develop goals for the next ten years. At the university's

June 1959 board meeting, the committee presented its initial progress report. It identified three objectives—higher faculty salaries, improvements to buildings and facilities, and investments targeted to bolster the university's areas of strength. Taken together, the committee's recommendations would cost $76 million. "It would be difficult to exaggerate the importance" of the report, Edens commented. He called the ten-year plan "the most challenging dream presented for the University since the dream which created it."[11]

Edens was careful to point out to the trustees that the planning committee's conclusions were consistent with the vision of Duke's founders. "They did not set out to build a provincial University," Edens noted, "though they were in sympathy with the need to render special service to the South." Noting the "extraordinary educational developments" that had taken place in the postwar era, Edens cautioned that "universities are now more complex and the demands more pressing both as to the quality and the quantity of production." He warned that Duke could not "rest at this point without falling behind in the procession." "Duke University was born to lead," Edens concluded, and "not to follow."[12]

With all of Duke's progress, one area of university life that remained nearly unchanged since the school's founding in 1924 was race. Although the University of North Carolina at Chapel Hill—Duke's neighbor—had admitted Black students in 1955, Duke's board resisted desegregation, even given the *Brown v. Board of Education* decision by the Supreme Court in 1954 declaring segregated public schools to be unconstitutional. The board voted down a resolution in 1957 authorizing the admission of Black students to the Duke University Divinity School.[13] By the early 1960s, this failure to "lead" on racial matters threatened to derail the school's ambitious plans for national prominence.

....

Despite its progressive reputation, North Carolina was, as one author put it, "a full-blown Jim Crow state." Described by historian Leslie Brown as a "troubling set of racial codes" ultimately enforced by violence, Jim Crow "attempted to appropriate black life and labor by any means necessary." It portrayed Black people, Brown recounted, as "inhuman, irresponsible, and immoral" and "translated antiblack rhetoric into officially administered discrimination in the arenas of democracy—employment, education, and elections—and sustained it for over a hundred years."[14]

At the core of Jim Crow were numerous laws and customs that denied Black people social equality by imposing a strict separation of the races. One white officeholder described the dangerous "slippery slope" Jim Crow was established to prevent.

> If I sit side by side in the Senate, House or the judicial bench with a colored man, how can I refuse to sit with him at the table? What will follow? If we have social equality, we shall have intermarriage, if we have intermarriage . . . we shall become a race of mulattoes. . . . We shall be ruled out from the family of white nations. So, it is a matter of life and death with southern people to keep their blood pure.[15]

"The idea of social equality was so abhorrent," historian Leon Litwack wrote, "so weighted with fears of racial impurity and degeneration, that the very suggestion of such equality had to be rigorously rejected and punished." These attitudes were anchored in a racial creed based on religious teachings. "It is clear that organized religion in the white South was dominated by spokesmen," theologian H. Shelton Smith wrote, "who held firmly to the dogma of Negro inferiority, and who thus maintained that the system of black-white separatism represented the normal development of a divinely implanted instinct." William C. Turner Jr., a Black undergraduate who came to Duke in the mid-1960s, explained that those who embraced segregation had "imbibed the toxic nectars of white supremacy and even more of cosmic disaster [and] believed that you are engineering the disaster of the races when you mix them or exchange their proper place on the chain of being."[16]

Given the perceived "life and death" stakes involved, it is not surprising that in states living under Jim Crow—including North Carolina—legally mandated segregation permeated all areas of life where white and Black people might come into social contact. In Durham, segregation encompassed marriage, housing, public transportation, water fountains, public restrooms, restaurants, hotels, theaters, libraries, churches, hospitals, jails, swimming pools, public parks, funeral homes, morgues, cemeteries, and municipal services such as police and fire stations. Social customs created further separation. Black people were required to address white people as "mister," "miss," or "ma'am," while white people called Black individuals by their first names or "sister" or "boy," regardless of age. In commerce, Black patrons were required to enter white-owned stores and food establishments by the back door, and wait until all white shoppers had been helped. When shopping for clothes, white shoppers were allowed to try on items of clothing, while Black customers were required to make their purchases "strictly on sight."[17]

Growing up in Durham in the early twentieth century, Pauli Murray noticed that "the signs literally screamed to me from every side," "FOR WHITE ONLY, FOR COLORED ONLY, WHITE LADIES, COLORED WOMEN, WHITE, COLORED. If I missed the signs," she recalled, "I had only to follow my nose to the dirtiest, smelliest, most neglected accommodations. . . . The world revolved on color and variations of color." Murray continued, "It pervaded the air I breathed. I learned it in hundreds of ways. . . . The tide of color beat upon me ceaselessly, relentlessly." "These separate and inferior Black facilities," historian Ibram X. Kendi wrote, "fed Whites and Blacks alike the segregationist idea of Blacks being a fundamentally separate and inferior people."[18]

Segregated education was a cornerstone of the Jim Crow system. Although the North Carolina Constitution adopted in 1868 under Reconstruction gave all people in the state "a right to the privilege of education," it also required separation of the races in public education. Black schools operating under Jim Crow possessed only a fraction of the resources available to schools attended by white students. A review of Black rural schools conducted by white state agent Nathan C. Newbold in 1914 concluded that "the average negro school house is really a disgrace to an independent civilized society." According to Newbold, these schools revealed "injustice, inhumanity, and neglect." For Murray, her "seedy, run-down school" in Durham conveyed the message that if Black people "had any place at all in the scheme of things it was a separate place, marked off, proscribed and unwanted by the white people."[19]

Supporters of segregation believed that Black people were not only different from white people but also inferior. Between 65 and 70 percent of white survey respondents in Guilford County, North Carolina, in the mid-1950s believed that Black people were inferior to white people with regard to "responsibility," "morality," and "ambition." Fully 75.6 percent of respondents preferred segregated schools. "It remained unthinkable" to whites, according to historian Melissa Kean, "that any good could come from the breakdown of the strict bars that kept these threatening people away from whites, especially white youth."[20]

Because "inequality and pretense saturated all their interactions," historian Jason Sokol explained, "whites actually harbored a racial animosity [toward Black people] rooted in a lack of knowledge." The experience of southern novelist William Styron was typical. "Whatever knowledge I gained in my youth about Negroes," he wrote, "I gained from a distance, as if I had been watching actors in an all-black puppet show." Segregation was so pervasive in the Jim Crow South, Sokol noted, that it "inspired little reflection." If white people did notice segregation, one observer said, "it was in the way they noticed water flowing from a tap or hot weather in the summertime—it was unremarkable."[21]

All these Jim Crow rules, customs, and attitudes were in place at Duke University until the early 1960s. No Black students were admitted to Duke's graduate, professional, or undergraduate schools. When Black pastor R. Irving Boone asked President Edens in 1957 if he could complete coursework for a master's degree started at the Union Theological Seminary at Columbia University, the Duke president said no. "No doubt you are familiar with the traditional admissions policy of Duke University," Edens told Boone. As "there has been no change in this policy," Edens wrote, "I am unable to give you a favorable reply."[22] For as long as Duke's "traditional" admissions policy remained in effect, this response, with minor variations, was repeated each time a Black student asked about admission.

Duke had no Black faculty members. None served in university administrative or clerical positions, and none worked in the library. Black workers dominated the "unskilled" subordinate positions, such as working in the dining halls and hospitals or as maids for undergraduates in the dormitories. They also served as groundskeepers, janitors, and dormitory switchboard operators. But of 1,666 officials, managers, and professionals at Duke in 1964, only seven—.4 percent—were Black. In contrast, among 1,230 laborers and service workers, 1,059—or 86 percent—were Black. Labor organizer and leader Oliver Harvey, who came to Duke in 1951 to work as a janitor, summarized the situation. "You didn't have any equal employment opportunities, or anything like that," he recalled. "There were no black people in the office unless they cleaned it up. . . . We cooked the food served in the dining hall and, daggone it, can't eat in the dining hall."[23]

Segregation defined all aspects of campus life. Until 1962, dining facilities on Duke's East and West campuses were segregated. With no Black undergraduates, dorms were all-white, and the rare Black campus visitor was prohibited from staying on campus overnight.[24]

Duke Hospital had similar policies. The wards were segregated, and when Black patients and visitors attempted to sit in the main lobby, they were asked to move to a smaller, less attractive location. Medical Center Christmas parties were segregated. William G. Anlyan, dean of the medical school, recalled in his memoir that "there were always two water fountains and two bathrooms, and that this division even went so far as the morgue at Duke Hospital, which came with four subcomponents differentiating sex and color." "The same was true of the blood bank," Anlyan reported, "where there was a separate, recognizable stamp to mark blood that had come from black donors."[25]

Through the early 1960s, the Southern Conference of the Methodist Church, a key Duke constituency, was "overwhelmingly in favor of segregation," recalled divinity school professor W. Waldo Beach. As a result, Duke University Chapel was segregated. Seating for Black parishioners was limited to the south transept, and Black people were not permitted to preach or otherwise lead religious services in the chapel. After learning in Duke's student newspaper, the *Duke Chronicle*, that Black scholar and educator Benjamin E. Mays would be speaking on campus in Page Auditorium, James T. Cleland, dean of the chapel, wrote to Duke president J. Deryl Hart in November 1960, "I am doing a slow burn." He continued, "Sir: If Negroes may speak in Page Auditorium under University sponsorship, then, in the name of God and of his Christ, why cannot one preach in the Duke Chapel? I know that the Church does not give moral and spiritual leadership on great social issues. But may we not be allowed to catch up with the moral bandwagon?" Almost three and a half years would elapse before preacher and theologian Samuel DeWitt Proctor became the first Black speaker at Duke Chapel.[26]

Consistent with the power of Jim Crow, segregation also applied to campus activities. At the football stadium, a sign labeled "colored entrance" marked off a separate section—in the corner of the end zone—for Black spectators. A report prepared in 1962 explained that "the Negro section at the outdoor Stadium is predicated on the assumption that Negroes prefer to sit together and that such separation avoids 'incidents.'" No such "preferences" or "incidents" could be documented. The Duke golf course gave priority to Duke students, faculty, alumni, and staff—all of whom were white—and Black golfers had their applications to play denied. Journalist Barry Jacobs reported that when John McLendon, the Black basketball coach at North Carolina College who was later inducted into both the Basketball Hall of Fame and the College Basketball Hall of Fame, asked to see a game at Duke's indoor stadium, "he was told he could attend if dressed as a waiter." "Dixie," the de facto national anthem of the Confederacy, was routinely played at sporting events and the Confederate flag was displayed.[27]

Eleven fraternities and two sororities on the Duke campus had clauses in their national constitutions prohibiting Black students from joining. The constitution of the Kappa Alpha Order, for example, provided that "no infidel; no person of the religion of a Jew; no person of African or Oriental descent . . . shall be eligible to membership in the order." Even when there was no written policy excluding Black members, many Greek organizations required that each pledge obtain a "hometown" or alumnus recommendation as a condition of membership. Others required that the national chapter of the fraternity or sorority approve each member of the pledge class. Either by express prohibition or application of these requirements, the vast majority of fraternities and sororities at Duke were open to white students only.[28]

In Page Auditorium—Duke's primary performance space—tickets were sold to Black patrons only in a circumscribed mezzanine area. In 1955 the campus theater group sought permission to allow Black audiences to attend its plays at Page with racially mixed seating. Duke administrators said no.[29]

As a result, there was rarely if ever any official interaction between white and Black people on the Duke campus. Black academics visited only infrequently and, while on campus, were required to use scarce segregated toilet facilities and prohibited from eating in campus dining halls. Among those who had to work under these restrictions was John Hope Franklin, who became a preeminent Black historian and Presidential Medal of Honor winner. While researching his groundbreaking 1947 book *From Slavery to Freedom*, Franklin was not permitted to use the public restrooms on campus.[30]

Leading Black theologian J. Deotis Roberts learned of Duke's restrictive racial policies when, in 1951, he inquired about attending a summer research program on campus on the topic of "Christianity and the Law." Beach, one of the codirectors of the program, responded belatedly to Roberts, explaining that his delay was "due to the necessity . . . to clear with the University administration as to the policies which we will need to observe for you as a negro, should you still be free and able to come." Beach reported that while all the library facilities, carrel space, and research facilities would be fully available to Roberts, "the question of housing and dining facilities has represented an awkward point." Beach advised Roberts that, should he come to Duke over the summer, "it would be necessary to ask you to make your own housing arrangements in Durham," since the campus dorms were for white residents only. As to the "borderline question of dining facilities," Roberts was told that his campus dining options would be limited to "various snack bars around campus . . . open for general trade" and lunches in the faculty dining room. The segregated university dining halls would be off-limits. Beach concluded by assuring Roberts that the limitations "in no sense should inconvenience you or hamper your full participation in the program."[31]

Segregation also extended beyond campus. A "restrictive covenant" in the deeds for home lots in Duke Forest made available by the university to faculty and administrators prohibited the sale, transfer, lease, or rental of the parcel to "persons of Negro blood." The deed included a clarifying "proviso" that the restrictive covenant "shall not be construed to prevent the living upon the premises of any Negro servant or servants whose time shall be employed for domestic purposes only."[32]

Segregation in off-campus activities was an accepted part of university life. University organizations, including academic departments, fraternities, sororities, and student clubs, routinely held school-related functions at the segregated Hope Valley Country Club. Membership in Hope Valley, the premier country club in the area, was highly valued. A list published in 1967 showed that many Duke administrators and faculty belonged to the club; moreover, the university reimbursed some of its senior officers for membership dues.[33]

Consistent with all of this was Duke's treatment of its Black employees. The workers "were treated as sub-humans," Harvey recalled. "You worked there ten and twenty years [and] if the supervisor didn't like you, he'd tell you he didn't need you anymore. People were absolutely afraid. . . . I never worked at a place as bad as Duke or as racist. You talk about slavery, it was absolutely so at Duke because people almost had to beg to keep their jobs when they were the least little aggressive." Like many others, Harvey had a pointed way of referring to this paternalistic employment structure in which the university held unchecked power over the working lives of its nonacademic employees and paid, at best, subsistence wages. "It was," he said, "a plantation system."[34]

Duke's treatment of its all-Black housekeeping staff reflected this same mentality. Through the mid-1960s, Duke employed a team of maids responsible for "preparing" the rooms of undergraduate men Monday through Saturday during the semester. Work involved routine cleaning tasks such as making beds and emptying trash. "Maids would wash windows, get up on ladders and wash walls," Harvey recalled. In addition to moving dressers and turning mattresses, maids "would help carry light furniture and baggage from one area to another one." Working daily from 8:00 a.m. to 1:00 p.m., each maid was responsible for up to thirty-two beds, they were prohibited from eating or drinking on the job, and they had access to only limited restroom facilities near the various housekeepers' offices. These restrooms were marked with a sign stating "Colored Women." In keeping with Jim Crow codes of behavior, maids, as well as other Black workers at Duke, were required to address students as "mister" or "miss." Students, in turn, would call these workers by their first names.[35]

The workload was often overwhelming, especially after the findings of an "efficiency" study conducted for the university in 1966 were implemented. "Just too much work for any person to do in five hours time," one maid commented. "It rushes me too hard trying to do this work," another said.[36]

Even more problematic, Duke's maids, like the university's Black janitors and other service workers, received poor wages. There was a "plantation-type mentality in labor relations" at Duke, A. Kenneth Pye, dean of the law school, pointed out, where "people were terribly underpaid." The "old way of running Duke," he explained, "was you hired ten Blacks to do the job of two and you paid them a tenth of what they should be paid." Under this system, Duke's maids were paid $0.43 per hour in 1951. By the start of 1959, the hourly amount was $0.65 per hour, earning maids a paycheck of $19.50 for a standard thirty-hour work week. By 1965, wages increased to an average of $0.85 per hour, far below the federal minimum wage of $1.25. Maids "had to go from house to house and clean up for white folks to survive," Harvey recalled, "or else they went on welfare." Duke's all-Black janitorial staff fared little better. As of January 1966, Duke's highest-paid janitor earned $2,808 per year, almost $200 below the poverty threshold. "In addition to low wages," Harvey recalled, Duke's nonacademic employees "had hardly any fringe benefits at all. No holidays, no sick leave." Maids and janitors could be asked to work more than forty hours per week at their supervisor's discretion and received no increase in hourly wage for "overtime" hours. Making matters even worse, through the mid-1960s, Duke's service employees had almost no recourse to address job-related grievances. As the *Carolina Times*, Durham's Black newspaper, wrote in 1959, Black nonacademic employees at Duke effectively found themselves in "peonage."[37]

Given how entrenched Jim Crow segregation was at Duke, any change in the university's racially exclusive admissions policy would not come easily. At least through 1957, a majority of the university's trustees supported segregation. All but a handful of trustees were from the South, affiliated with the Methodist Church, and alumni of Duke. A substantial number had been serving on the board since the 1920s. Growing up in the Jim Crow South, Beach noted, many trustees had a "habit . . . of accepting the pattern of polite, not vicious, segregation in education, in political affairs, [and] in cultural affairs." Klopfer agreed, commenting that segregation was "consistent with the value systems many trustees grew up with." The university had "a long, inherited, established practice of accepting segregation," explained Robert E. Cushman, dean of the divinity school, and there was "an inertia that had to be overcome."[38]

Those who favored desegregation at Duke faced the challenge not only of changing the votes of trustees but of doing so under a decision-making process requiring civility and consensus. In his book *Civilities and Civil Rights: Greensboro, North Carolina, and the Black Struggle for Freedom*, historian William H. Chafe explained that civility—"courtesy, concern about an associate's family, children, and health, a personal grace that . . . obscures conflict with foes"—was the cornerstone of the "progressive mystique" that defined racial attitudes in North Carolina. For Chafe, civility was "a way of dealing with people and problems that made good manners more important than substantial action." Because of the importance of civility, North Carolina progressives believed that "conflict is inherently bad, that disagreement means personal dislike, and that consensus offers the only way to preserve a genteel and civilized way of life." Since conflict "will permanently rend the fragile fabric of internal harmony," Chafe explained, "progress can occur [on matters such as race] only when everyone is able to agree—voluntarily—on an appropriate course of action."[39] The requirement that a consensus favoring desegregation emerge on the board before any change in policy could occur shaped Duke's consideration of the issue over many years. It also gave those who favored the status quo a strong platform from which to resist change.

....

The 1950s saw no change in Duke's racially exclusive admissions policy. Approached by external constituencies seeking a change during this period, Edens simply counseled patience. When urged in 1953 by Methodist minister and Duke alumnus Bill Wells to desegregate "in the name of Jesus Christ!" Edens responded, "It is difficult to judge the proper timing in the hesitant steps of social progress." He cautioned that "a University is a highly complex organization and changes in pattern of thought and activity will have to come slowly." Alumna Helen Morrison also urged a change in policy in 1953. The Duke president replied, "It would be impossible for me to predict how soon a change will take place." Identifying himself as a "gradualist," Edens told Morrison that it was his "firm conviction that Duke University can and should admit negroes only when the community and constituency are prepared for it"—an example of the power of civility and the "progressive mystique."[40]

While Edens gave little indication to external constituencies that Duke's restrictive admissions policy was a topic of discussion, the gears on desegregation had in fact started to move. The issue was raised initially in 1948 when divinity school students presented a resolution asking that the school consider desegregating. Welcoming the "fellowship, stimulation, and fuller Christian cooperation" that would exist if "Negro students were to join us in our common Christian study," the students put forth a "request" that those in charge of the school give "serious consideration" to the admission of Black students to the divinity school "without affecting the general university policy." Other petitions, expressing what future provost R. Taylor Cole described as a "Christian concern for the segregation policy," were presented in 1949 and 1951.[41] Still, no action was taken.

Through the 1950s, trustee opposition to desegregation remained strong. Barney Jones recalled that "the generally conservative and provincial outlook of the Board was nowhere more evident than in its studied, southern-styled avoidance of the integration issue." The board, according to Jones, was "determined to keep Negroes out of the university—at least as long as possible." Edens shared this view of the board, telling Cole, after discussions with key trustees, that desegregation faced "the determined opposition of a large majority of the Trustees."[42]

In late 1956, a group of students wrote letters directly to board members advocating for desegregation. One such letter was written to trustee Edwin L. Jones by undergraduate Anne Corpening. She expressed the hope that Jones would "keenly feel the necessity of revising, as quickly as possible," racial policies that "speak of intolerance, retrogression and moral indifference." The response Jones sent to Corpening shows just how unimaginable he found the prospect of desegregation to be. Stating that Corpening's letter "could be answered intemperately," Jones instead responded by raising "a few questions."

1. Should the Trustees of Duke University permit conditions at Duke that are not permitted in the homes of the students who comprise the student body of Duke?

2. Do your father and mother practice social and racial equality with the Negroes in your home?

3. Why should Duke discriminate against the qualified white students who are clamoring to get into Duke University so as to admit Negroes who would create problems, probably impossible to solve?

4. Aren't the Trustees charged with the responsibility toward white students for whom the University was founded?

5. Why should the Trustees begin to practice discrimination against the white race?

In Jones's opinion, Duke had been founded to serve the needs of white students. Desegregation meant social equality between the races. This would be unthinkable in any Duke family home and amounted to reverse discrimination against the "white race."[43]

In early 1957, divinity school students published a petition addressed directly to the board requesting that the school's racially restrictive admissions policy be eliminated. Although he knew he did not have a consensus, Edens decided that the time had come for the trustees to go on record on desegregation. To buttress the case for desegregation, Edens provided the trustees with a letter from James Cannon III, dean of the divinity school at the time, who insisted that the "standing of the university" would suffer if Duke retained its racially exclusive admissions policy. It was an "embarrassment" for a national institution such as Duke to be "out of step" with its peer schools, Cannon argued, pointing out that its divinity school was one of only two in the South that had not eliminated segregation or announced plans to do so. "The problem of assimilating the few Negroes who would be eligible for admission to the Duke Divinity School," Cannon concluded, "is a minor one compared to the problem of further delay." On this basis, Edens asked for "discretionary authority . . . to admit negroes to the Divinity School if and when properly qualified applicants should apply."[44]

In response, the board voted to keep the divinity school segregated. When the newspapers reported the trustees' action, Edens received multiple letters. "I wish to commend you and your Board for the stand you have taken with reference to admitting negroes to the Divinity School," Whiteville, North Carolina, attorney J. Bruce Eure commented. "The races are separate and distinct and should stay that way." E. J. Burns, a member of the Duke class of 1927 and law school graduate in 1929, was "delighted" that "no Negroes will be admitted to Duke Divinity School." Again, racial mixing was the key concern. "It seems so unnecessary and unwise that our young white and negro students be mixed up socially and in our educational institutions," he commented, expressing his desire "to send my daughter to Duke . . . provided we can keep Duke for the white students."[45]

The volatility of the race issue became even clearer at the racially mixed North Carolina Mock Student Legislature meeting in November 1957. At the opening of the two-day session, the student delegation from Duke's Woman's College proposed to rescind laws prohibiting racial intermarriage in North Carolina. The bill passed the legislature, which drew harsh criticism from North Carolina congressman Harold Cooley. "I do not know of anything that has happened in the Student Bodies of the various colleges of this State that has aroused as much unfavorable criticism as that bill," Duke trustee P. Huber Hanes Jr. wrote to Edens. "I cannot conceive of any self-respecting young girl being a party to endorsing a bill of that kind." T. Conn Bryan, a double Duke graduate, told Edens that the resolutions, even if proposed in jest, "are abhorrent to everyone who has even a modicum of personal and racial self-respect." Another alumnus told the Duke president that several of his friends "who now have daughters at Duke have 'blown their tops' to me and have been so incensed that they have threatened to take their children out of school."[46]

In response to the furor, Edens wrote a low-key letter to the trustees and faculty to defuse the situation. While "sorry the incident occurred," the Duke president saw it as part of students with "immature and half-reasoned ideas and actions" growing up.[47]

After the February 1957 board vote on desegregating the divinity school, Edens ceased any further efforts to address desegregation with the board. Edens had concluded, Cole recounted, that "moral suasion . . . would not move [the board] toward gradual desegregation." He knew where the board stood and was, according to Barney Jones, "determined that a wedge not be driven between himself and his Board." In fact, Edens soon resigned from the Duke presidency following an internal power struggle involving the Endowment in February 1960. He was replaced on an interim basis in April 1960 by J. Deryl Hart, a respected member of the medical school faculty.[48]

Meanwhile, concern over Duke's racially restrictive admissions policies continued to crystallize on campus. The *Duke Chronicle* published regular editorials condemning segregation. Under the headline "Barbaric Tradition," the student newspaper declared in late 1955 that segregation "is anti-democratic, anti-Christian, harmful propaganda to the rest of the world and incompatible with the idea of a university." A growing number of graduate and undergraduate organizations and faculty joined the divinity school in pressing for a change in university policy. In 1959 the Men's Student Government Association and the students and faculty of the Graduate School of Arts and Sciences pushed publicly for desegregation; and in 1960 law students, students on West Campus, and incoming graduate students also made known their opposition to the school's racially restrictive admissions policy.[49]

When the Duke trustees finally voted to end the school's racially exclusive admissions policy in 1961, however, the decision was not made because of pressure from internal or external Duke constituencies. Rather, desegregation was approved only after a majority of trustees came to believe that the continuation of segregation at Duke would threaten the school's progress and block its path to national prominence.

In other words, the primary reason was money, not ideology. Increasingly, the federal government and national foundations were making clear to Duke and other southern universities that grants would stop if they refused to admit Black students. By the early 1960s, the federal government began to advise schools that to be eligible for future government contracts, private universities would be required to have in place nondiscriminatory admissions policies. The Ford Foundation and other national philanthropic organizations also made it known that they would limit grants to segregated schools.[50] Once fully implemented, these policies would destroy Duke's aspirations to become a leading national research university.

In 1961 Hart determined that opening the university's graduate programs to Black students was essential if Duke was to realize its national ambitions. To present the case most effectively, Hart directed three senior university officers to prepare a memorandum for the board outlining the impact continued segregation would have on Duke. The memorandum covered three areas: the perception of external constituencies, the impact on the medical school, and the consequences, especially on faculty morale, for the rest of the university.

In the memorandum, Cole argued that Duke's racially restrictive admissions policy had "created barriers to the fullest development of Duke University and . . . resulted in a decline in its prestige." The university's segregation policy, Cole concluded, "is a major barrier to attaining the national and international recognition which Duke University deserves." On the impact in the "Medical Area," Barnes Woodhall, vice provost, listed seven potential sources of federal financial support for Duke Medicine. This support—totaling $16 million over the "foreseeable future"—could well be jeopardized, he argued, if the university remained segregated. In the final section, Marcus E. Hobbs, vice provost, focused on "destruction of the general morale" that would occur if Duke failed to address segregation. He presented a detailed chart showing that the university received approximately $7 million in federal grants and contracts from 1959 to 1960, money that would be put at risk unless Duke changed its racial policies. Hart and the three university officials asked the trustees to allow Duke's graduate and professional schools to accept "the small number of obviously well-qualified Negro applicants."[51]

In response, on March 8, 1961, the trustees approved, with no discussion, a change in university policy to allow the admission of students to Duke's graduate and professional schools "without regard to race, creed or national origin."[52] In September of the same year, two Black law students matriculated at Duke.[53] In June 1962, after further education and persuasion, the trustees voted to desegregate Duke's undergraduate colleges. Duke's first Black undergraduates arrived in September 1963.

This decision achieved the results Hart and others anticipated. Just after the board voted to desegregate the graduate and professional schools, Thomas L. Perkins, Duke Endowment chair, wrote to the president of the Ford Foundation, the president of the Carnegie Foundation, and the vice president of the Rockefeller Foundation to notify them of the decision. All three responded with approval.[54]

More generally, the board's changes to Duke's racially restrictive admissions policies were widely praised. "The Board of Trustees deserves hearty congratulations for its action," the *Duke Chronicle* editorialized. It declared that in desegregating the graduate and professional schools, the trustees had "set a commendable example for other Southern institutions and increased the University's prestige from a national standpoint." The next year, A. T. Spaulding, one of Durham's most prominent Black leaders and chief executive of the Black-owned North Carolina Mutual Life Insurance Company, wrote the Duke president to say that the trustees' decision to desegregate the undergraduate schools "marked a monumental milestone along the highway of Duke's history." The step "will be looked upon as a reckoning point in the years ahead," he asserted, and "a point of reference in measuring Duke's future progress and achievement at an ever accelerating rate."[55]

....

Without diminishing the significance of the board's actions, three points about desegregation are important to note in order to understand what was to occur. First, as at other private HWCUs such as Emory, Rice, Tulane, and Vanderbilt, the decision to desegregate was not voluntary. While Bunyan S. Womble, university board chair, wrote at the time that the decision to admit Black students "did not come as a result of any pressure or petitions, but only after careful and intense consideration over the past few months," the reality was quite different. In fact, Womble himself wrote a fellow board member that "if we had been free to follow our own inclinations many of us would not have favored the change." After private meetings with a group of trustees in Charlotte and Winston-Salem discussing graduate school desegregation, Hart reported to Womble: "I believe they hated to see it come, . . . and although it was contrary to what they had hoped would be the case they would go along with it." One trustee told Cole of his profound concern over racial mixing by describing a medicine dropper and a glass of water. If one drop of ink passed into the water, the trustee told Cole, it would color it all. Cushman observed that for trustee Edwin Jones, it was "inconceivable" for Duke to seat Black and white students in one room. Again, the concern was racial mixing. Jones feared the "intermarriage of Black and white," according to Cushman, "more than anything else." Woodhall was told by a trustee that his wife would leave him if he voted in favor of desegregation.[56]

Second, desegregation was not approved because of moral or human concerns but due to the adverse consequences the university would suffer if segregation were maintained. While Cole on the one hand argued that any claim that the desegregation decision was based "exclusively on economic considerations" was "wrong," he nevertheless agreed that the "economic argument" was critical to achieving desegregation "at the earliest possible time." Noting that the board acted to desegregate "on prudential grounds," Barney Jones wrote, "Probably one would have to concede that integration at Duke was provoked more by economic than moral considerations. We integrated because it became necessary rather than because it was right." Indeed, Jones looked back with regret that Duke "did not base our action on higher ground."[57]

Finally, the board vote to desegregate did not mean that long-standing racial attitudes among white leaders at Duke had vanished. If an individual viewed white people as superior prior to the vote to desegregate, this attitude almost certainly continued after the vote. For example, when Womble wrote to reassure those upset by the desegregation decision, he pointed out that the relative abilities of Black and white students would mitigate the impact of the policy change. "On account of the very high standard of requirements for admission, I am sure very few Negroes will be admitted," he wrote. "With the thousands of white students being turned down each year for lack of space," Womble observed, "I shall be surprised if any Negroes applying will possess qualifications entitling them to be admitted any time soon." An unnamed faculty member struck a similar note, predicting in the *Duke Chronicle* that "the search for a qualified Negro applicant may be more difficult than convincing the Trustees to admit Negroes."[58] Contending with these attitudes would remain a profound challenge.

With the decision to desegregate, Duke had finally removed a major obstacle to realizing its national ambitions. With financial support solidifying, a strategic plan in place, and the morale of most university constituencies improving, Duke's leaders had good reason for optimism. Only one further step remained to position Duke for rapid growth—selection of a new president to lead the university into the future. The November 1962 choice of Douglas Knight illustrated how far the board was prepared to go to realize its national vision.[59]

....

Chosen to be president when he was only forty-one, Douglas Maitland Knight brought to Duke qualities of mind and spirit that had helped propel his rapid rise to the highest levels of academia. By the time he reached Duke, Knight's career had already combined scholarship, teaching, and college administration. Although some might wonder whether he was ideally suited to lead a large, southern university, none could claim that Knight was not an accomplished individual of presidential stature.

Born on June 8, 1921, in Cambridge, Massachusetts, Knight did not have an easy childhood as an only child whose father died when he was five years old. Stability was hard to come by for the Knight family. They moved several times a year; indeed, by the time Knight entered junior high school, he had attended thirteen different elementary schools. Pushed ahead by school administrators who recognized his academic aptitude, Knight entered junior high school at age ten.[60]

By the time Knight turned fourteen, a wealthy family friend arranged for him to attend the prestigious Philips Exeter Academy in New Hampshire. At Exeter, Knight found a "sense of intellectual community [he] had never experienced before" and within a few months he was "hopelessly in love with the place." Finding that Washington DC, his home at the time, had no "magic" for him, Knight cut short his first vacation from Exeter and returned to school early. The elite private school had become the place where Knight felt most comfortable.[61]

College and graduate school at Yale University soon followed. Knight earned his PhD in English in 1946 and was immediately appointed to the Yale faculty as an English instructor. Soon his first book appeared, a scholarly study titled

Pope and the Heroic Tradition. Within a couple of years, he was promoted to assistant professor of English. A score of scholarly articles soon followed and, by the age of thirty, Knight's career in academia was well established.[62]

In 1953 Knight's professional life changed dramatically when he was chosen to become president of Lawrence College in Appleton, Wisconsin. At thirty-two, he was the youngest college president in the nation. The position at Lawrence was important, not only for the experience it offered Knight but because of the college's reputation as the training ground for major university presidents. Lawrence boasted a remarkable statistic: in the thirty years prior to 1953, eleven of Knight's predecessors had gone on to hold the presidencies of prominent universities, including Brown and Harvard.[63]

Knight spent almost ten years at Lawrence, a school he recalled fondly as "that wonderful little place." This was a happy time for Knight and his family. He recalled his tenure at Lawrence as "a golden few years in which everything seemed to work." A college with around 1,100 students and 100 faculty members, Lawrence suited Knight perfectly. "There was the simplicity of the administrative structure," he recalled, "which allowed problems to be met intimately and immediately." In addition, the college's small size "allowed working intimacies of every sort—often evolving into increasingly close friendships." Although Knight kept up a frenetic pace, he still found time at Lawrence "to rejoice in the excitement of all of it, and time to enjoy that texture of activity in all its richness."[64]

Knight's tenure at Lawrence proved to be a great success. During his presidency, the book value of the college's physical plant increased by 100 percent and the value of the school's endowment by 150 percent. Six major buildings were constructed, and Knight secured the two largest gifts in the 150-year history of the college. In the course of his tenure, he also built a national reputation. He served on more than a dozen national committees for education and religion, often traveling up to eighty days a year. Given these accomplishments, it is not surprising that by the early 1960s, Knight was one of the two or three college presidents most major universities considered when their presidencies came open. After more than nine years in Appleton, Wisconsin, Knight was ready to move on. He expected it of himself, and others expected it of him.[65]

In 1962 Knight was offered jobs at Duke *and* Cornell almost simultaneously. With a strong sense that there was "something fated and inescapable about the choice," Knight accepted the Duke presidency. Knight found the chance to be a transformational figure at Duke compelling. "Duke, it seemed to me," Knight recalled, "had always played under its feet rather than over its head. It had opportunities . . . to be much more of a place than it was. . . . And the opportunity that I saw was for the university to push as hard as it could and then find out what would happen."[66]

Knight's selection as Duke president was announced in November 1962. But having committed to remaining at Lawrence until a successor was found, he did not arrive in Durham until August 1963. One can only imagine the sense of limitless possibility that Knight—soon to be inaugurated as a major university president at only forty-two years of age—must have felt as he and his family "stepped in by station wagon [to Duke] late one August morning, to find an official house crammed with our boxes and furniture."[67]

In Knight, Duke had a president with youthful vigor, an Ivy League pedigree, and a national reputation that personified its aspirations. Knight's selection as Duke's fifth president was met with almost universal acclaim. Wright Tisdale, chair of the trustees' Presidential Search Committee, predicted that under Knight's "warm and inspired leadership . . . Duke will attain an ever higher and more distinguished position in the educational world." The *Duke Chronicle* saw Knight as a man who could bring greatness to the university. Observing that there are those who believe "there is too much nostalgia and resistance to change for the South to take the lead in intellectual spheres," the *Duke Chronicle* found that "the selection of a man so obviously dynamic, who at 41 already has behind him nine years at the helm of a distinguished college, is the greatest single step taken in recent years toward enhancing this university's position." Combined with other factors, Knight's selection gave Duke the ingredients for a "juvenescence which will soon lead this university to new heights of achievement." Perkins and Tisdale suggested that copies of the *Duke Chronicle*'s glowing write-up on Knight be forwarded to all alumni.[68]

Knight, in fact, did bring an array of strong qualities to the Duke presidency. He had passion, vision, intellect, tremendous energy, the humanism of an English professor, and administrative experience gained from his successful tenure at Lawrence. Lost in the excitement over Knight's selection, however, were aspects of his background that made him, in retrospect, an unlikely pick to lead Duke in the early 1960s. For one, Knight was hardly an ideal cultural fit for a southern university that had only recently desegregated. In 1963 Duke was still very much a conservative southern school and Knight was a northern liberal. He was Duke's first president from outside the South and almost everything about him—including dress and personal style—spoke of the Ivy League, not the Atlantic Coast Conference.[69]

Knight recalled his mother telling him "I knew you were in for trouble" when she saw the Durham paper's headline describing the new Duke president as "Yankee Born and Yale Educated." Knight wrote, with at least some overstatement, that "when the Duke trustees decided to look outside their own region for a president . . . they were taking a step as new and controversial as the admission of Black students had been. It called forth some of the same reservations, and it would have some of the same disruptive consequences in the turbulent years to come," he observed.[70]

Alumni reaction to Knight reflected how geography shaped people's perceptions. Although "looked upon pretty generally in [North Carolina] as a villain," Roger L. Marshall, director of alumni affairs during Knight's tenure, recalled, "he was looked on as a great leader in other areas," such as New York and California. A fellow guest at a faculty wedding reception at Hope Valley Country Club told Knight how one southerner viewed the Duke president. He "stood there in the middle of a social gathering," Knight remembered, "and said, 'I just wanted to tell you that from the first time I met you I knew you weren't one of us.'" Knight found it deeply frustrating that because he was a northerner, some at Duke considered him lacking sufficient commitment to traditional values like family and community. "New Englanders have as much a sense of tradition as most folk in the South do," Knight explained. "I was not . . . in a mood to accept the idea that I would be regarded as an uprooted interloper, in short, as a carpetbagger of the 1960s."[71]

Some also saw Knight's religion as an issue. He was a Congregationalist leading a school with long-standing ties to the Methodist Church and a board of trustees composed almost entirely of Methodists. "It was suggested to me by the then chairman of the board that I [change my religion]," Knight remembered. "He just said, 'It's perfectly easy to do.' I had to say, 'But Bunyan, I don't do that.'"[72]

Given suspicions about Knight's northern, liberal background, the timing of his arrival on campus—just weeks before the university's first Black undergraduates enrolled—could hardly have been worse. Feelings on racial issues at Duke remained extremely unsettled following the board's decision to desegregate. The arrival of the first Black undergraduates guaranteed that race would remain a complex problem for the university for years to come. "I was joining a university with great potential stature and a major role to play both nationally and in its own quadrant of the country," Knight explained. He continued, "[Duke] was *not* equipped, by nature and location, to absorb sudden change of any kind, let alone disruptive challenges. Its admission of the first Black undergraduates had not yet been digested, nor had the complexity of doing justice to their needs been faced."[73]

National and local events also kept race in the spotlight. In the thirteen months between Knight's selection as Duke president in November 1962 and his inauguration in December 1963, George Wallace became governor of Alabama; civil rights protests in Durham escalated dramatically; Medgar Evers was assassinated in Jackson, Mississippi; Martin Luther King Jr. delivered his "I Have A Dream Speech" to the March on Washington; and President John F. Kennedy was assassinated. When racial issues emerged, Knight's background deepened the concerns of some that he was not sufficiently aware of white southern racial attitudes and practices. Knight "was not sensitive, he was not aware of the real attitudes and ideas and values of the people in this part of the country," Marshall recalled. Marshall also thought that Knight misread—and misunderstood—southern character. "He could see rednecks and lynching parties in every thicket," Marshall remembered.[74]

If Knight lacked experience dealing with white southerners on racial issues, he also had limited experience engaging with Black people. At the start of World War II, Knight remembered watching a Black platoon in Glenn Miller's Air Force Band perform on the Yale campus. Tremendously impressed by the group's "dance-march drill," Knight deemed onlookers like himself, as well as members of the white platoons who performed, "earthbound clods by comparison." But the point of the story for Knight lies in what he did not say, think, or even consider—"that this was a segregated unit. . . . I felt myself thoroughly emancipated in the matter of color," Knight wrote, "while in fact I was merely blind to all it meant in barriers or limitations." Once ensconced in university life, Knight's view of race, like others in his cohort, remained detached and limited. Knight recalled:

> It would be pleasant to write that the American academic community was aware of a great need to educate blacks in the country's universities and that we were busily devising programs to that end. Of course, such was not the case and never had been. . . . Most of us in northern colleges were not opposed to black students—if they appeared in the normal course of things and were qualified. We were not blocking anyone's entry; we felt comfortable about our racial attitudes and the way we implemented them—or not, as was the case for most of us.[75]

Knight's tenure at Lawrence provided little opportunity to advance his thinking or sensitivity on matters of race. While the school admitted its first Black students since the 1920s during his tenure, there were few conversations about them other than a brief encounter with a couple of senior trustees who asked, "Why here and why now?"[76]

Duke's size may have also challenged Knight's leadership skills. For one thing, although he had developed a national profile as a successful college president, Knight had only nine years of administrative experience when he became president of Duke. Because he made the leap directly from his Yale professorship to the Lawrence presidency, Knight never served in lesser academic administrative positions, such as dean, provost, or even department chair. Knight's career had offered him the chance to think a great deal about the nature of liberal education, and he wrote that his convictions on this important topic "had reached a high level of coherence during the Lawrence years." Knight's training and experience were "based in a concept of the university and of liberal education totally grounded in mediation, critical discourse, civility and the restraint of uncontrolled dogmatism." He saw universities as "places of civility and debate rather than insult and confrontation." While these words may have described Lawrence during his tenure there, they did not describe Duke. Knight did not fully appreciate the difference, and he worried some of his new Duke colleagues with his pronouncements that the administrative problems at Duke "would not be different [than those] at Lawrence."[77]

While Lawrence may have been only a fraction of the size and complexity of Duke, it had been a perfect fit for Knight's analytical approach. "I had treated my Lawrence and Duke relationships in a highly committed and totally personal way," Knight recounted. "I ignored the political issues once I had made up my mind about the best course of action for myself as the servant of the place," he wrote.[78] But Duke, when he arrived, was "a university under stress and also in inevitable transition."[79] Leading a large institution with many competing constituencies would require a new and different kind of political skill than he needed at Lawrence. In this context, Knight's approach to Duke was too passive. Knight wrote later that when conflict erupted at Duke in the 1960s, he sought to be "evenhanded" in his treatment of issues and movements, not to "attempt at leading and guiding them. As a result," Knight observed correctly, "the issues themselves provoked extreme responses [and] our own attempts to avoid these extremes were largely misunderstood."[80]

One person who found Knight's approach unacceptable was history professor John W. Cell. Knight was "the wrong man for that time," Cell contended. "He was a leader for an intellectual community [but had] tremendous insecurity, [and] lack of confidence, and inability to face a crisis situation. Knight wanted to do the right thing but was indecisive." Hobbs agreed. Knight "tended to be a very agreeable person," he explained. "Unfortunately, major administrators, sometimes . . . have to say 'no' either pleasantly or indirectly. . . . That is a degree of political sensitivity" Knight did not have. Robert Ashley, managing editor of the *Duke Chronicle* during the late 1960s, was most succinct. "Tragically," he commented, Knight "had none of the skill set to deal with the seismic changes that were shaking society, particularly universities, and particularly Duke."[81]

Griffith, by 1967 the assistant dean of the College of Arts and Sciences, who found Knight "good to work with," wondered if Duke's president was not simply too sensitive to succeed in the rough and tumble of university administration. "His happiest moments, I think, were sitting out under a tree with a class," Griffith observed. "Doug was . . . a humanist," Anlyan commented, and "was too gentle a person to deal with the turbulent Sixties."[82]

Whatever challenges Knight would face, he brought great confidence to his work at Duke. He had a bold vision for the school. The university, Knight told a large Founders' Day audience days after being elected president, faced an unprecedented opportunity. It could, in the years ahead, move from being a leading southern educational institution to becoming a premier national university. Three reasons made the attainment of national greatness a possibility. One was the "tradition of responsible freedom in the university. . . . This we do not have to create," Knight stated, "and we have the rare chance to extend it, to use it in the service of great causes and high ambitions." Another was the enormous resources Duke had to call upon. "No great university ever has everything it wants," Knight acknowledged, but "the fact remains that much has been given us, and much will be expected." For Knight, Duke's vast financial resources also offered a challenge: "we dare not be satisfied," Knight proclaimed, "until we are a national force in every field which legitimately concerns us." The third reason offered by Knight was perhaps the most significant. It captured the central contradiction facing Duke and its president and mirrored the challenge facing the entire southern region. "It is rare," the president-elect stated, "for a university to be able to draw upon so deep a traditional knowledge of the humane life and at the same time to be a focus for the emerging national strength of a whole region. . . . It will be our privilege . . . in the years ahead," Knight told the Duke community, "to make tradition new as no university in the south has done it before."[83]

Appropriately, Knight's vision for Duke encompassed both an emphasis on bold new initiatives and a deep respect for tradition. But many questions remained unanswered. How amenable to change was Duke, given its traditional ways? How would the arrival of Black undergraduates and the persistence at Duke of long-standing racial attitudes and practices complicate the university's efforts to expand its sights? And could it do so without slighting the region with which it was identified? How effective would Knight be at handling this transformation? Answers to these questions would begin to unfold even as Duke's first Black undergraduates stepped onto campus in the fall of 1963.

CHAPTER 2

———

Like Bare Skin and Putting Salt on It

First Encounters

———

When five Black freshmen entered Duke University in the fall of 1963, it represented a profound change for the university. For the first time, Duke would have Black undergraduates as participants in all aspects of campus academic and social life. Significant in its own right, desegregation also required the university to address aspects of its racially exclusive past, especially if the school were to move toward a future of multiracial equality, acceptance, and respect. "You have a Southern way of life," Black undergraduate William C. Turner Jr. explained, "where everybody has their place [and] where everything [is] tiered." For Turner and many others, the key question was whether, following desegregation, people would come to Duke to "learn how to . . . perpetuate this Southern orthodoxy and tiered society. Or," as Turner asked, would Duke become a place "where people can come and participate in the opening of society?"[1] The HWCUs that were desegregating throughout the South at this time all confronted this central issue.

The first encounters between Duke and its new Black students thus loomed large in defining the school's racial future. Would these initial contacts lead to greater communication and acceptance between white administrators, faculty, and students and the new Black students on campus? Or would they serve to reinforce, or even accelerate, historic antagonisms? What factors would determine the path the school would follow? A careful look at how Black and white students perceived and interacted with each other as they made this historic step helps illuminate these important questions.

....

Called the "chosen few" by some members of Durham's Black community, the Black students who came to Duke during the early years of desegregation shared a common background. Almost all were from the South. Born in the 1940s and early 1950s, these students had spent their childhoods in segregated communities. As Turner noted, the first Black students at Duke "grew up in an all-Black setting. . . . We came up in all-Black churches, all-Black schools, all-Black communities—all-Black everything," he said. Growing up in this environment, family, school, and church helped determine one's sense of self-worth and advancement. In rural Ayden, North Carolina, "the entire Black community was united," law student Charles L. Becton recalled. "It was a family. People would always call your mother or your parents if you were not doing what you were supposed to be doing. The teachers would spank you and call your parents and you would get spanked again. People were looking out for each other because no one in the white community at that time . . . cared much about Black youth."[2]

The first Black students at Duke grew up in "protective Black communities," Brenda E. Armstrong explained, "that had [an] incredible history [and people who] demonstrated by example the dignity that our ancestors had been able to call on to . . . convince themselves that they were real people and they were good people." Armstrong learned that history from her father, Dr. Wiley "Army" Armstrong, a prominent Rocky Mount, North Carolina, physician and civic leader. Driving to the country to see patients, Dr. Armstrong would take his daughter along. Only three generations removed from emancipation, he taught his daughter during these long car rides about Black history in North Carolina and shared stories about the courage, resiliency, and faith of their family. He told "these stories with such passion," Armstrong recalled. "Even though I was young, I never forgot them." When she talked to her friends at Duke, Armstrong found that "they had the same experiences." Almost all had learned about their ancestors and their people through powerful stories communicated by family members.[3]

Janice Williams, a Black undergraduate at Duke in the late 1960s, learned of the courage and stoicism of her great-great-grandmother: "My grandmother told us the story [of] her grandmother. She had been a slave. Because she would not cry when she was whipped, the slave master cut her thumb off. So what she did, was slung her thumb, and the blood, and walked off, and *still* did not cry." "The moral you got," Williams remembered, was "'You're gonna be beat, you're gonna be strong, and you are not gonna cry.'" For Michael R. McBride, hearing the price his father paid for refusing to follow dehumanizing Jim Crow codes of behavior had a powerful impact. McBride's father was a county agent for the segregated farmer's extension service in Alabama. "I resented that my father had to flee Alabama when my mother was pregnant with me," McBride recounted, "because he wouldn't say 'Yes Ma'am' to a white woman who handed him his checks. I came to Duke with that resentment." While in college, Turner was told by his father about the brutality his great-grandfather suffered based on the false claim that he had violated Jim Crow social norms. He was lynched in Person County, Turner was told, after being accused of consorting with a white woman. "Social mixing was not a thing to be done in the pre–Civil Rights South," Turner explained, "on pain of losing your life."[4]

When learning about their ancestors, Duke's first Black students heard about the paramount importance these men and women placed on the value of education. This focus became apparent immediately following emancipation. "Virtually every account by historians or contemporary observers," historian James D. Anderson commented, "stresses the ex-slaves' demand for universal schooling." "To a school official in Virginia, trying to convey his thoughts about the freedmen's enthusiasm for education," historian Leon F. Litwack wrote, "the phrase '*anxious* to learn' was insufficient; 'they are *crazy* to learn,' . . . as if their very salvation depended on it." "Few people who were not right in the midst of the scenes," Booker T. Washington observed, "can form any exact idea of the intense desire which the people of my race showed for education. . . . Few were too young, and none too old, to make the attempt to learn." "If I nebber does do nothing more while I live," one freedman declared, according to Litwack, "I shall give my children a chance to go to school, for I considers education next best ting to liberty."[5]

The passion felt by freed slaves for education did not arise externally from white philanthropists, northern missionaries, or federal government largesse. In fact, as historian Herbert G. Gutman observed, "the ex-slaves' educational movement was rooted deeply within their own communal values." Ex-slaves "have within themselves," Freedmen's Bureau superintendent John Alvord wrote in July 1866, "a vitality and hope, coupled with patience and willingness to struggle, which foreshadows with certainty their higher education as a people in the coming time." Even as early as 1866, Alvord could see "that the incipient education universally diffused as it is, has given these whole four millions an impulse onward never to be lost. They are becoming conscious of what they can do, of what they ultimately *can* be. . . . Self reliance is becoming their pride as it is their responsibility."[6]

Passion for education in the Black community endured, even as Jim Crow policies and practices became entrenched throughout the South. "When the lights went out in the 1890s," theologian Samuel DeWitt Proctor wrote, "when the political currents swirled against black progress, . . . hope still bloomed within the black community. We learned that the key to the future was education. Somehow we believed that we, too, could bloom, darkness notwithstanding." Faith was the key. Proctor's grandmother, who was born into slavery, possessed "intrepid confidence," he said, that "rested on a simple uncomplicated notion: God created all people; any inequalities among us were due to unequal opportunity." From his grandmother, Proctor learned that "hatred and vindictiveness were always destructive. 'No use fretting or crying,'" he recalled her saying. "'If you do your part, God will do the rest.'" Elders "spoke to us children in the subjunctive mood," Proctor recollected. "Not what is, but what *may be*, when our faith flowered into reality."[7]

The values embraced and transmitted through the generations by their forebears were reflected in the communities where Duke's first Black students grew up. Education was of primary importance. We were fortunate, Armstrong wrote, to attend "strong but segregated primary and secondary education systems" defined by "caring, protective, high-achiever teachers." Teachers were "always supportive and encouraging," Becton remembered. "Every teacher I had cared about us and what we could become." Many of the schools these students attended covered grades 1 through 12 and traced their roots to private academies established for Black students during Reconstruction throughout the South. Even in the 1950s, Turner explained, "these schools operated in the shadow of Reconstruction."[8]

Mary Mitchell Harris and Nathaniel White Jr., two of the five Black students in the first class after Duke desegregated, attended Hillside High School in Durham. Tracing its roots to the Whitted School, founded in 1887, Hillside was the only Black high school in Durham. Parents, grandparents, other relatives, and members of the community had also attended the school. "The people in my church, the people in my community," Hillside alumna Minnie Forte explained, "were all Hillside graduates. My dentist, my doctor and my pediatrician were all Hillside High graduates. [Hillside was] intertwined with everything I knew." "There was not a Black student in Durham who did not know everybody," Hillside graduate and language teacher Jeanne Lucas remembered: "We knew every community, every student, every neighborhood, most of the families. . . . We knew everybody who went to every church, so there was the community neighborhood. . . . The teacher, the church, the community and the home [were] so connected that you couldn't fail."[9]

Despite the fact that Hillside used hand-me-down books from the all-white Durham High School and lacked the financial resources of other schools, its students never doubted the quality of their education. "I never felt inferior," Forte recalled. "I knew that I was getting the best education that was available to me. . . . I wasn't worried about going to college and I wasn't worried about the SAT exam. . . . I knew that I was well equipped to do whatever I wanted to do." This confidence came from the Hillside teachers. To ensure that they knew every student and every family, Hillside teachers visited the home of every student before the school year began. "If they had 150 kids," Lucas explained, "they would visit 150 homes." The message that Hillside students received from these teachers, according to Forte, was that "you could be all that you wanted to be, there were no limits. . . . There were people [at Hillside] that would help you gain and rise to whatever level you wanted to go, regardless of your resources and your background." Hard work was the key. "One of the things [the teachers] said," Jacqueline Williams, a 1965 Hillside graduate, recalled, "is that the white man's skin color was going to get him over so you as a Black person had to work twice as hard."[10]

Teachers taught students, Hillside graduate Sterlin Holt recounted, that "as African Americans, we come from a long history of achievements . . . against a lot of odds and a lot of adversity." Lucas explained that Hillside "protected, educated, nurtured, prepared, groomed—oversaw—the total growth of students." Because the pastor in her church was committed to seeing Hillside students in his congregation go to college, virtually all did so. Doing so required great sacrifice. "Even though our parents were maids and dry-cleaning people," Lucas recounted, "worked for the university professors, [were] factory people, they borrowed money from the bank to educate us." "We were all poor," she reflected, "but we knew that we were going to have a college education."[11]

The teachers in the schools these Black students attended were extraordinary. "We grew up in segregated times," George Creed, a childhood friend of White, explained. "The big advantage for students was [no matter] how much education a person had, about the best you could do was be a teacher. Because our smartest people could not do anything else," he described, "they taught us." "You've got folk all over the South with PhDs and master's degrees [teaching] in the Black high schools," Turner recalled. "So you have the best teachers in the Black schools." These teachers, Williams explained, stressed not only strong academics but also a specific life philosophy. "That philosophy," she recounted, "was that in order to be Black and to achieve, you've got to be better than the next person."[12]

Armstrong, who came to Duke in 1965 as a member of the third class of Black undergraduates, attended Booker T. Washington High School in Rocky Mount, North Carolina. Tracing its history back to the Rocky Mount Graded School for Colored Children that started in 1901, Booker T. Washington High School opened as a separate high school facility for Black students in 1927. Although its resources and regular weekday curriculum were not on a par with the white high school in Rocky Mount, Booker T. Washington students knew they were getting an excellent education. The tone was set at the start of the school day. "The teachers met us as we walked into school," graduate Otis Cooper described. "They were there to help and set the tone each morning when we arrived." Because school board rules required that courses in Black schools be taught at only a basic level, teachers found ways to compensate. Most remarkable was a "Saturday Academy." Armstrong explained:

> What we could not be legally taught Monday through Friday, we were taught on Saturday. . . . Living about 70 miles from Raleigh, [we would pool our money so] we could go to the state capitol, museums, concerts. We even went over to the University of North Carolina campus to see what the possibilities were. . . . Even though the school board wouldn't let them teach the things we needed during the week, they taught us on Saturday. And nobody complained.

"Who would ever think," Armstrong asked, "that people who worked five days a week in a substandard facility would come back on Saturday to create . . . a Saturday Academy?"[13]

Teachers at Booker T. Washington were deeply involved in their students' lives. "They were part of our life at home," John H. Perry recalled. "They knew our parents and they knew us outside of the classroom." "Teachers visited our houses," graduate Tolokun Omokunde remembered. "I would go home and the teachers would be sitting at the kitchen table—eating up my peach cobbler!" This caring was expressed in myriad ways. If a daily assignment was not finished, Guion C. Davis would meet his teacher at her house and together they would complete the work. "She would feed me just to make certain that I was cared for," Davis recalled. "The teachers did what they had to do." Another teacher would give any needy student money and send them "downtown to buy whatever you needed." Teachers were role models. "They built a strong family among us," Delores Battle Powell explained. "We respected them and they respected us." Being a "family" meant students looked out for each other. "If there was a student who was not doing well, [fellow students] would come together as a group to help," recounted Helen Mercer Dixon. "And while we were helping one another, we were learning from one another."[14]

Booker T. Washington High School had a lasting impact on its students. Teachers communicated that Booker T. Washington students were as good as anyone. Although "some said our education was 'substandard,'" Armstrong pointedly recalled, "we knew our education was *not* substandard . . . because of the adaptations that the communities we came from made. . . . The kids in the public and private schools that were segregated—we had the same education, we just had to go about it a different way."[15]

What was not addressed at school were the increasingly dramatic challenges the civil rights movement was making in the South to segregation and other aspects of Jim Crow. Otis Cooper recalled that while his teachers certainly knew what was happening in the United States, "they couldn't speak out against the system for fear of losing their jobs." Instead, teachers "worked within the system" teaching students to navigate a segregated world." The teachers instilled strength," Cooper remembered. "We knew of the injustices and were prepared to face an unjust society." One teacher told Omokunde that education "would get [him] through anything—even Jim Crow." Looking back, Omokunde said, "she was right."[16]

It was at home that the most direct discussions of social injustice and social change occurred. Lenora Bradley's teachers did not talk about segregation much in class, "because we learned that at home. Our parents were teaching us what to do out in society. The teachers and parents were working together." For Armstrong, home was a place of intense focus on civic matters. Deeply involved in the voting rights movement, unions, and the Black churches in Rocky Mount, her parents made the civil rights movement a constant topic of conversation. And Armstrong's exposure was not limited to family discussions, however frequent and intense. "Everything they did, and everywhere they went, they took the children."[17]

On November 27, 1962, Martin Luther King Jr. visited Rocky Mount and spoke to a crowd of almost two thousand people in a packed Booker T. Washington gymnasium. At the time, Armstrong's father was vice president of the Rocky Mount Voters and Improvement League—the organization sponsoring King's visit to Rocky Mount. In the late afternoon, Armstrong's father told her, "'I've got a meeting to go to, and I want you to come with me. I want you to sit and listen.'" The meeting was with King and a handful of other attendees. At the meeting, King's speech that evening and the upcoming March on Washington were discussed. Armstrong had a chance to shake King's hand. "This is history," her dad told her. She told her mother later in the evening, "I'm never going to wash my hand again."[18]

Armstrong's father was seated on the dais behind King during the speech. Before going on the platform, he found the tallest person he could and asked if his daughter could sit on his shoulders. King's speech that evening—"Facing the Challenge of a New Age"—was notable because it was among the early times he used "I have a dream" as a cadence in his talk. In the speech, King noted the many young people in the audience and implored them to be ready to take advantage of the changes happening around them.

> Opportunities are coming to us, today's young people, that did not come to our mothers and fathers. The great challenge is to prepare ourselves in order to be ready to face these challenging opportunities. . . . We must work hard. We must realize that because of conditions of oppression . . . we may have to work a little harder than other people. . . . A challenge comes to us to do a good job. And to do that job so well that the living, the dead, or the unborn, couldn't do it better.

For Armstrong, propped on a man's shoulders, the speech was a "transformative moment." Even at thirteen, her family, her church, her school, and her community had prepared her to take in King's words. Looking back, Armstrong realized that she grew up "in the presence of geniuses, people who figured out how to compensate for the viciousness of racism. And not to be so angry that it made us angry. It made us proud. Because they were able to use their genius to make things available to us. Everything they said to us was couched in 'you're going to have opportunities that we didn't have and you are not going to waste those opportunities.'"[19]

Five years later, Armstrong was off to college. Like the other Black students at Duke, she was sent to college by her family, teachers, church, and community to take her place as one of the "most successful, well-exposed, ambitious, and focused group of people to benefit from the earliest successes of the civil rights era."[20]

The Black students matriculating at Duke in the early 1960s benefited richly from the strong families, schools, and communities that produced them. All were among the most gifted students at their schools, each with excellent grades, strong SATs, and impressive records of leadership. Many were National Merit or Achievement scholars. "The [Black students] who came . . . were go-getters," Becton recounted. "They were all hard workers. There were no 'legacy admits'—people who came because their parents went [to Duke] and think they can just sail through." R. Taylor Cole, the Duke provost, told the board that the five Black undergraduates admitted for the fall of 1963 "would have merited admission to almost any college or university in this country." A good example was Wilhelmina M. Reuben, who arrived at Duke as one of the first Black undergraduates in 1963, having completed high school ranked at the top of her class. Her father was the president of Morris College in Sumter, South Carolina, and her mother was on the faculty. Gene Kendall was recruited by MIT and Princeton but came to Duke because he got a full scholarship. Kendall's community was "ecstatic" when he chose Duke. A superb student, Brenda C. Brown was one of the first Black students to desegregate the public high schools of Greensboro, North Carolina, in 1963. Brown came to Duke because her high school guidance counselor advised her not to. "He had a fit," Brown recounted. "He said, 'If you go, you'll flunk out.'" Brown, who graduated from Duke after only three and a half years, responded, "If I flunk out, I'll have done what I could do, so I'm going." Turner attended high school in Henrico County, Virginia, where he was a standout student and athlete. Although Turner had planned on attending a historically Black college like Howard, Morgan, or Virginia State, he ended up at Duke, he explained, because the math teacher and football coach who had "cultivated and trained" him "put the application in my hand. He got it. He had it. And he told me to fill it out," Turner remembered. "And he had made such an investment in me I would do anything he told me to do." Armstrong, who arrived at Duke in 1966, was a National Merit Scholar and a finalist for the university's prestigious Angier B. Duke scholarship. Accepted at Michigan and Radcliffe, her first preference was to go to a historically Black university such as Shaw or Meharry. She came to Duke because it was her father's preference and to be close to home.[21]

Duke's first Black students arrived at the school having prepared for a unique historical moment. "You . . . had a generation of elders around you [that] . . . were uncanny in their prescience, their knowledge of the times," Turner explained. "They knew that things were going to change—had to change. . . . They had a sense of what time it was in history." Turner and his colleagues were among a cadre of young men and women from segregated communities in the South who were ready to take advantage when doors started to open. "It was in the atmosphere," Turner recalled, "the way you were nurtured and trained and counseled and advised. It's not something that we sat around and talked about," he remembered. "It's just the way we had been groomed . . . just been formed, developed, and shaped that way." These students entered college under the weight of great expectations. "When I went to Duke," Joyce A. Hobson described, "I went with the blessing and the responsibility of the whole community. Personal advancement was what I sought to do," she recalled, "but it was very closely linked with advancement for my entire race." "We were there," Constance Jackson Carter recounted, "to allow students after us to go to schools wherever they wanted to." Asked why he and other Black students chose to come to Duke in the first wave of desegregation, Turner explained that it had to do with the notion of "responsibility to your race. . . . You do it for your mother, your father, your people, your community, your church. This is your duty." These talented students arrived at Duke, Armstrong observed, "with the purpose to take our places as the next generation of Black leaders."[22]

....

For most of the Black students arriving at Duke in the early 1960s, the adjustment to campus life was extremely difficult. Turner recalled going from the all-Black setting of his precollege years to the "complete antithesis" at Duke as "almost as complete a shock as you can encounter." Even though he grew up in Durham just four miles from Duke, White had no frame of reference once he got on campus. "There was no relationship," he said. "It was complete discovery. I can't express . . . how much the town that I lived in as Durham and the town that I moved to as Duke were such separate enterprises." "The experience was surreal," Mary Mitchell Harris, another Black student who grew up in Durham, explained. "It was like another world altogether."[23]

This is not to say that every Black student arriving at Duke in the early 1960s experienced campus life in the same way. Some students, including many matriculating in the first years following desegregation, had little problem adjusting. Reuben, for example, came to campus in the fall of 1963 feeling a "responsibility to create the environment you desire" and quickly became involved in an array of academic and social activities. "Duke made [this engagement] a comfortable possibility for me," Reuben remembered, "and it was fun!" Mary Mitchell Harris, also a member of the first class of Black undergraduates, remembered being treated as a "curiosity" upon arrival. "It wasn't unnerving at all," she recalled. "It was great receptiveness." Having been among the first Black students to attend a desegregated high school in Greensboro, Brown quickly acclimated to life on campus. "I had people threaten [me] in high school," she recalled. "Duke . . . was a real big step up from what I had experienced. . . . My expectation was for a lot worse." White saw the small number of Black undergraduates immediately following desegregation as a reason that fewer problems occurred. "The numbers were so small, we were fairly negligible," he recalled.[24] Despite such positive experiences, however, the vast majority of Duke's small number of Black students in the early years following desegregation faced a difficult transition. The reason was the Jim Crow racial attitudes and practices that continued to pervade Duke.

Encounters with faculty and deans over academic matters presented an initial challenge. "Some teachers were hostile, overtly so," Turner remembered. "Some were more subtle with it, but there was a tension you could feel in almost every class." During his freshman year, Michael LeBlanc encountered a political science professor who was openly racist. The professor would talk, LeBlanc recounted, "and he would say, 'the "nigra" over there, what do you think?'" For the first two or three classes, LeBlanc, the only Black student in the class, "took it." The next time, however, he confronted the professor. With sweat pouring down, LeBlanc stood and said, "Excuse me Professor Simpson, . . . I'm a Negro." The professor responded, "Nigra, sit down." LeBlanc again said, "No, I'm a Negro." "We had a battle . . . for the whole semester every time he said 'nigra,'" LeBlanc recalled. "To be seventeen years old, that was not easy."[25]

Charles W. "Chuck" Hopkins recalled one episode in a freshman composition course that illustrated "a stereotype of Black students that they weren't supposed to be able to write." The professor had been open with Hopkins that, in his opinion, "Black people are not smart enough to be successful at a school like Duke University." Hopkins recounted that after he produced a strong paper in English class, this professor accused him of having his roommate do his essays. "He just couldn't believe I could write," Hopkins recalled. Bertie R. Howard had a similar experience. Her freshman English teacher "would be surprised when I wrote a good paper, but would never find a reason to give me an A. . . . At one point [when] I wrote what I thought was a *very* good paper, he was really surprised [and asked], 'Did I go to a tutor?'" For Clarence G. Newsome, one of Duke's first Black scholarship athletes, his English literature professor's comments required no interpretation. As Newsome was leaving class one day, the professor stopped him. Looking directly into his eyes, the professor told Newsome, "Blacks can't write. And especially Black males." "It was an attempt to pierce my spirit and my soul," Newsome thought. Armstrong remembered that she got her first freshman English paper back marked with a D+. Devastated, she sent the paper to her mother, asking, "Mom, is this right?" Armstrong's mother, an English teacher with graduate degrees from Columbia University, saw the quality of the paper, telling her daughter, "You didn't write this well when you were with me!" Marguerite Armstrong wrote to the Duke administration on her daughter's behalf, demanding an apology and a revised grade and threatening legal action. Armstrong never got the requested apology, but she did get an A on the paper.[26]

Discriminatory grading practices were so common that Brown tended to steer toward science and math classes, where "either you could answer a question or you couldn't. I definitely felt the professors, especially English and history . . . graded us differently," she remembered. Yet sometimes, even courses with a quantitative focus provided no protection from overt prejudice. As a freshman, Claudius B. "C. B." Claiborne and three of his fellow Black students took an engineering class together. Uncertain about the homework assignment, they asked the professor for clarification, telling him, "We want to get an A on the assignment." "I'll never forget it," Claiborne recounted. "This guy who was an old professor . . . said, 'Don't worry about it, you won't get an A.' He didn't know anything about us. . . . We all came from [strong academic] backgrounds; we were expecting to do well."[27]

White also experienced grade discrimination. In one case, a professor went so far as to change the grading system for the entire class to justify giving White, the only student to earn a perfect score on the midterm, a C. Turner recalled that some students even devised ways to test the integrity of the grading process: "They would write a paper in one night, then write another paper and spend a week or two on it. No matter what paper they wrote, what the quality of the paper was, they got a C. Always. One friend of mine said he actually took a paper from a white fellow who had received an A on it. He turned that paper in and got a C." Discriminatory grading "happened to all of us," Armstrong remembered. Soon, a consensus evolved among Duke's Black students: "If you're Black, you're a C student."[28]

"Most of my professors were indifferent," Hopkins remembered. "They had not been sensitized to the special needs of the Black students." Samuel DuBois Cook, Duke's first Black professor, shared this perception. White professors "can often be unwittingly insensitive," he observed. "They can't empathize, they can't see what Black students have gone through, [and] what they have experienced." Because of this lack of empathy, these professors do things that are "utterly insensitive," according to Cook, "because Blacks are just outside the orbit of their experience. And often [outside] of their compassion." Without empathy, Cook explained, "they just can't reach out, just can't perceive what it means to be Black and the kind of hurt that Blacks may have."[29]

Academic deans and other university personnel exhibited similar attitudes. In the early weeks of her freshman year, for example, Armstrong went to her dean. She explained: "My English achievement scores should have allowed me to place out [of freshman English]. But when I found out, it was too late. So I went to the dean and asked if it was still possible to place out. Her comment was, 'Well, you *need* to be in first-level English.'" Because of her plan to attend medical school, Armstrong also sought "guidance and counseling [from her dean] on being a premed." Her attempt met with frustration. "I was virtually written off," Armstrong recalled, "as possibly being a premed." White's interaction with an athletics administrator communicated a similar message. When White urged the administrator to start recruiting Black athletes to Duke, he received a lecture about how Duke had high academic standards. "I told him," White remembered, "I didn't think I'd gotten in without meeting those academic standards."[30]

Years after graduating, Armstrong described the attitudes Black students faced.

> We were the objects of the worst kind of racism in the classroom, where we started out at a deficit. It was incomprehensible to have been considered smart enough for "A" work, especially when subjective grading of essays or term papers, or theses were concerned. The few of us in science battled the results of that isolation even in areas where subjective grading would have been harder. We were not given the benefit of old tests, or the lab assistant's

tutelage. We were thought of as "dumb" when we asked for help. The white students were characterized as "competitive" for the same request.[31]

These academic issues contributed to one of the biggest problems faced by Duke's Black students—a chronically high attrition rate. Armstrong recalled that during the years 1966 through 1968, almost 50 percent of Duke's Black students left school after one or two semesters. Of the fifteen Black men in Armstrong's freshman class, for example, only ten remained after the first year. Given their academic performance in high school, the academic difficulties these students faced at Duke were a shock. "Everyone was under real pressure to do well," Howard remembered. "I just didn't realize that everyone here was from the top of the class and that somebody was going to be on the bottom," Brown explained, "and most likely it was going to be you." Students came to refer to dismissal from school as having been "punched out." For some, departure from school had life-or-death consequences. Brown remembered her close friend Warren Franks, who lost his student deferment when he dropped out of Duke after his sophomore year. "He was killed [in Vietnam] a month before our graduation," Brown recalled. Because of the likelihood that they would face the draft, Armstrong recalled feeling "awful terror" when male students left Duke.[32] Despite these problems, the university initially created no programs to prepare Black students for the academic challenges they would face and provided little support when they encountered academic difficulties.

Contacts with Duke's campus security added to the picture. Black students were frequently stopped on campus and asked by campus security to produce university IDs. This often happened in the university gymnasium. "Apparently it was just assumed," Turner explained, "that anybody Black down there playing was not a Duke student and should be asked to produce an ID on the spot."[33]

The contempt certain members of campus security had for the Black students is reflected in a memo from W. C. A. Bear, the chief of campus security, to Cole. While the purpose of the memo was to transmit to the provost a report on a campus altercation involving a Black student, Bear used the exchange as an opportunity to express his feelings toward Black students at Duke generally. Stating that the report pertains to a "negro student," Bear told Cole that he wanted the provost to see the report so that he may be familiar with "what our men must put up with from these people."[34]

Other encounters with university personnel were also problematic. "I know of instances," Becton reported, "where you would go into the Dope

Shop [the campus snack bar] and the people there would go out of their way to wait on everyone else except the Black kids." Howard recalled times when she was first in line at the Dope Shop but sixth to be waited on. As a result of these practices, Becton remembered, "you go into the [Dope Shop] and it takes you twenty minutes to eat because they're serving everybody else first." Becton did not take this treatment passively. At the cafeteria, when the cashier would attempt to help a white student behind him in line, Becton would say, "No, no, no, I was in line first, I'm giving you money." "I was six-four and I wasn't menacing in any way," Becton recalled, "but I would just simply speak up. And the person would typically defer."[35] The absence of a Black barber was another issue. Although the university maintained a campus barber shop, no one there was able to cut hair in the styles popular among Black students. Consequently, they went into Durham if they needed a haircut.

Certain university practices were also deeply disturbing. Among these was the long-standing tradition at Duke athletic events of playing "Dixie." White remembered that "Dixie" was "practically like the national anthem because everyone would stand up [and sing along]. People went wild over that song." White refused to participate. "I never stood for 'Dixie' at any time, anywhere," he recounted. In fact, White, along with other students, "would organize sit-downs." White recalled that eventually they had "a whole section that wouldn't stand when it was played." During a football game in 1968, the Georgia Tech marching band started playing "Dixie." When the music started, Turner recalled, "two Black students had a Confederate flag that they unfurled [and] set it on fire. One man decided that this was an affront to him, so he came down and jumped in the flames and put it out. Some white students joined him. It was a little altercation. When the police arrived, only the Black students were removed." "If there was something going wrong between white students and Black students," Turner recounted, "it was assumed . . . the Black students were at fault."[36]

Howard's reaction to tangible symbols of racism at Duke like the playing of "Dixie" and displays of the Confederate flag is typical. While she understood them as "part of accepting going to a white school in the South," she found them to be "repulsive." Ernie Jackson was a consensus All-American football player at Duke. But the thing he recalled "more than anything else," he said, was walking "through the dorms on the way to practice every day." "Most of the football players," Jackson recalled, lived in fraternities. "When you saw the Confederate flag hoisted out of their dorms all the time," Jackson remembered, "it was extremely difficult to have to go to war with those guys and play with them from a teammate perspective."[37]

Duke's practice of holding school-sponsored events at local facilities with racially restrictive policies, such as Hope Valley Country Club, was also problematic. Many Duke administrators and faculty were members at Hope Valley and campus organizations had, for decades, hosted events at the segregated club. But as the Black student population at Duke grew, this practice would become increasingly controversial.

Social and cultural issues confronting Black students at Duke added to the problems. The most dramatic issues involved overt physical harassment. "Once [fraternity men] found out that Black students were sensitive," Hopkins reported, "it was fun for them to provoke stuff. [You'd] walk past dorms and somebody would throw a plastic bag full of water—drop it on you. . . . Silly stuff like that."[38]

But other interactions were not at all "silly." "I was in the laundry room one night," Hopkins remembered, "and something moved in the corner of my eye. I turned toward the window, and just as I turned . . . this big rock came and hit me in the chest." "I had friends," Turner reported, "who told me there were incidents in which they would literally be told . . . 'All right, Nigger, let me see you run. Somebody pull out a switchblade. Make him run.'" Occasionally, these incidents would escalate into fights. "There were almost little mini-wars," Turner noted. "Black students and white students against each other and they'd be armed."[39]

For Turner, attempts at physical intimidation did not create serious problems because of his size and the aggressive stance he adopted. "If somebody bothered me, I'd let them know something right quick," Turner recalled. "I'd have people [slip] up and call me 'boy.' I'd say, 'You see a boy, you slap him.' And it wasn't likely they were going to do it. Back during those days I bench-pressed over three hundred pounds, and anyone who saw me could tell it. That was just my way of taking up for myself."[40]

But not all students had Turner's physical strength to fall back on. Asked how others responded to intimidation, Turner responded, "With knives, with screwdrivers, staying together in groups. Literally fighting." Duke's female Black students felt especially vulnerable in the face of the overt hostility they encountered from some segments of the campus. "We needed the brothers to literally escort us to the basketball games to protect us from the racial slurs that effused from the [Kappa Alphas] as we walked by their house on the way to the indoor stadium," Armstrong remembered. "Those were some crazy people" who lived on Animal Quad, Howard recalled. "The rednecks of Duke were in [Kappa Alpha]—and they made threats. There had been lots of intimidation of Blacks by those people. . . . I had a lot of people proposition me, or [make] a lot of lewd remarks."[41]

Other interactions with the Duke community were less overt but communicated an equally clear negative message. Armstrong recalled what it "felt like when we sat down at a table in the dining room and everyone else got up. On the bus and even in the classroom everyone else moved over." Cassandra Smith had similar experiences. "Some of the students would cross the quad rather than speak to me," she recounted. "Or they would look the other way when they walked past." Like other Black students who attended Duke, Smith had grown up in a "very sheltered environment." "It really hurt," she recalled. "I hadn't ever been treated like that. For a long time, I put it out of my mind because it was so unpleasant."[42]

The dormitory provided no respite. "The dormitory life . . . was the worst part of my experience at Duke," Armstrong explained. "I had a Black roommate my first two years. She and I clung to each other because I couldn't talk with anyone else. No one else understood anything," she remembered. "They had . . . decided that my . . . experiences . . . were so different from them that they looked on us as unusual people."[43]

In the dorm, Black students were the objects of stares, giggles, offensive name-calling, and unimaginable isolation. So many dorm mates stared at Armstrong and her roommate "going about their business" that "you got the feeling that something was wrong with you." Overt acts of racism were also not uncommon. Armstrong explained, "Some of us came back to our dorm rooms to find Confederate flags on the doors with 'nigger go home' written over it." On her first day of classes, Armstrong was in her dorm bathroom, washing her face and brushing her teeth before class. A white dorm mate approached and, touching Armstrong's face, announced, "This is the closest I have been to a colored person, and I wanted to see if it came off." Armstrong was deeply offended. "If you put your hand on me," Armstrong warned the young woman, "one—it's assault; and two—you are going to have a hard time getting up off the floor because I'm going to hit you." Turner recalled verbal harassment. "Football players and fraternity men would get drunk out on the quad," he remembered, "and just holler: 'Ahhhh you niggers, cut out the lights.'" Harry DeMik, a white student, remembered a heckler at a basketball game shouting, "'Get out of the game you dumb Nigger'" to a Black Duke player who was having an off night. Hopkins recalled that he and two other

Black students were approached one evening by a "white guy living down the hall from us. He came to us," Hopkins recounted, "and asked us to procure a Black woman for a fraternity party he was having." We said, "'Wow, that's crazy.' We almost got in a fight with the guy."[44]

Other dorm interactions highlighted the racial insensitivity of many white students. "The woman who worked downstairs at the desk [in our dorm] was Black," Armstrong recalled, "and they always called her by her first name. After three months of that we finally revolted and said at one of the house meetings: 'That person is old enough to be our mother. You have no right to call an older woman "Mildred" when she is Mrs. Jones. She is someone's mother. She is someone's wife.'" Armstrong remembered that her fellow students responded, "We didn't think we were insulting her" and "She likes it that way." But when Armstrong and her friends asked their dorm mates if they had ever asked Jones her preference, the question was met with silence. "It was patronizing," Armstrong explained. Maybe they let you get away with that in your neighborhood, she told her dorm mates, "but if I called [an adult] by their first name, my mother would stop the conversation and beat me. We were always taught to respect adults." "You could see them turn pale," Armstrong remembered. Hopkins was shocked to discover that older Black women were employed by Duke as maids to clean dorm rooms. "Duke is an upper-class southern gentleman type thing," he recalled. "You had all these old Black women waiting on these white male students hand and foot. . . . Some of us—those were the kinds of things our mothers were doing back home."[45]

Even when friendships developed between Black and white students, issues of race could intrude. Once, Armstrong was invited to dinner with a friend and her family. After meeting Armstrong, the family "made some excuse for not being able to go." Armstrong learned later that it was because the group had planned to go to a restaurant or to visit friends at Hope Valley Country Club, where segregationist policies would not allow her to attend.[46]

Duke's dynamic fraternity and sorority scene—a key social avenue for many students—provided no such outlet for the university's Black students. Even those fraternities and sororities that did not expressly prohibit Black members found ways to ensure that they remained segregated. In the case of fraternity Sigma Chi, for example, there was no express legal prohibition in the organization's charter documents on admitting Black members. Still, according to Barney Jones, the fraternity's "Grand Proctor" "made clear . . . that race is an absolutely decisive criterion for membership." To enforce this prohibition, the Grand Proctor required that racial data, along with corroborating photographs, be submitted to the national office for all prospective members. Many national sororities prevented Black students from joining local chapters by requiring that each prospect obtain a "favorable" recommendation from a sorority alumna. In the event of a negative recommendation, there was no right to appeal or to learn the basis for the rejection. Several years after desegregation, a Pi Phi representative told Mary Grace Wilson, dean of undergraduate women, that "several Negroes in this year's freshman class . . . were 'good sorority material'" but that no sorority chapters on the campus "could get the necessary (required) clearance as to recommendation."[47]

While not publicized, these exclusionary policies were known by Duke's Black students. "When it came to [sorority] rush," Armstrong reported, "we obviously weren't wanted." To Howard, it was clear that there was no reason for her to participate in sorority rush, and she told the woman in charge of the selection process that she did not think "there is any sorority that is willing to admit a Black." Howard recounted that the woman encouraged her to participate, telling her, "It's a great way to get to know people, you never can tell." After going through two or three days of sorority rush, however, Howard was told by the woman that "everyone really likes you, but we can't get references so there is no way to admit you." Understandably, Howard came away from the experience feeling that many Duke people she encountered would say, "We really welcome Black people to Duke" but that "you take step one and then there is no room for advancement."[48]

In the background of these racially charged experiences was the significant socioeconomic gap that existed between Duke's Black students and their colleagues. White students at Duke were generally affluent. "We were a totally different sort from the average Duke student," Turner explained. "Most of us were kids from the South . . . from very modest financial and social backgrounds. . . . And we had a totally different mentality and a totally different approach both by virtue of being Black and by virtue of our background." Marcus Hobbs, who was appointed provost in January 1969, saw little "commonality of interest or background" between the Black students and their white colleagues. "After all," he commented, the Black students "hadn't spent the summer at Newport or whatever the hell have you." Besides inhabiting different worlds at Duke, most Black and white students had no significant interracial contact before college. "We didn't grow up together," Turner explained. "The only contacts we had with white youngsters was in fights" or the occasional football or basketball game. Even then, Turner remembered, "the white boys would come to your community; we wouldn't go to theirs."[49]

Compounding all these issues was the profound isolation most Black students experienced. Not only did these students stand apart from the mainstream of the university but, during this period, they remained largely cut off from each other. Until the fall of 1966, the main reason for this was lack of numbers. Five Black undergraduates enrolled at Duke in 1963, eleven matriculated in 1964, and fourteen joined the freshman class in 1965, a miniscule number on a campus with almost five thousand undergraduates. Making matters worse, Duke was divided into two campuses located about a mile apart—West Campus for men and East Campus for women. Further, the small number of Black students was spread out in various dorms. "Duke thought the best way to bring us here," Hopkins recounted, "was to keep us isolated from each other." "To this day," he said in 2019, "I don't know why that was their policy."[50]

"Seems like you could go on for months without seeing another Black person," Brown recalled. "I never had a class with other Black students," White remembered. Turner felt "loneliness and isolation at every point" and likened the experience to "being cast into a foreign, alien world." "I was the only Black student in my dormitory," he explained. "There was nobody to go to. No Black staff, no Black faculty. . . . And [there was] the frustration of a college undergraduate in the first couple of years with no one to turn to. . . . If you have another Black student in a class with you, it's strange and unusual. . . . That's an experience that almost defies description. It's more than you can describe."[51]

Before college, Williams recalled, she could always find refuge by coming back to "a Black community, and a Black home, and very familiar cultural surroundings." At Duke, she explained, "the difference was I never left. I never went back and got recharged. I could never let my guard down. I never could just relax and be myself and not worry about what [I] said or what [I] thought or . . . what [I] did." Intensifying these feelings was the fact that undergraduates at Duke, like every other college student, were still young. "If you are talking about dealing with adolescents—which is what you are—there are certain identity needs, certain cultural needs, certain emotional needs that you have," Williams explained, "in addition to the intellectual enrichment they were trying to provide." To Armstrong, her experience at Duke was "like bare skin and putting salt on it. We were there in the middle of a whole bunch of white folks," she explained. "We weren't ready for them and nobody had any idea how to deal with it."[52]

These experiences at Duke led most Black students to conclude, as Hopkins did, that Duke "was not ready to have Black students here. They didn't realize that integration meant they had to make some changes, too." According to Hopkins, the administration's view was that "bringing us [to Duke] was like bringing the natives into civilization." For Turner, the university's attitude was "Look—we have granted you the privilege of coming to this great school. You are on scholarship, financial aid, whatever. What else do you want? What else can we give you?" Brown's view was similar. She saw the administration's stance toward the Black students as "Shut up. Don't make waves. And get out. . . . You're here because we need some Black spots on campus to make things look right. Other than that, we don't want to hear from you."[53]

In the depths of her freshman year, Armstrong called her mother to talk through her college experience. Hearing her daughter's despair, yet knowing from life experience how difficult it would be to change Jim Crow at Duke, Marguerite Armstrong encouraged her daughter to take the long view. "Somebody has to do this," she told her child. Alienated from Duke and likely wishing she had ignored her father's wishes and instead gone to an all-Black school, her response was brief—"Why us?"[54]

....

Duke's Black students were correct that the university was not ready for them. Although undergraduate desegregation may have marked in some ways a significant turning point in the history of Duke, the university made only limited efforts to plan for the arrival of these students or to understand and anticipate their needs. As William Griffith, who by 1963 served as assistant to the provost, recalled, there were planning meetings over the arrival of Black students "but not in a really in-depth kind of way." Duke, he said, "didn't make a lot of changes."[55]

This university failure extended to Jim Crow policies and practices that remained in place at Duke even after the Black students arrived. Although the classrooms, dorms, dining halls, and football stadium were desegregated, separate wards for white and Black patients remained in place at Duke Hospital. No effort was made to require fraternities and sororities to eliminate provisions in their charter documents prohibiting Black members. University organizations remained free to hold off-campus events at segregated facilities. The university continued to use racially restrictive covenants for its Duke Forest homesites.[56]

In the view of President Douglas Knight, the university's failure to plan was due to the deep ambivalence many felt about desegregation. According to

Knight, many at the university believed that "once we have admitted Blacks, what more do they want?" Administrators also felt that by admitting Black students, Duke's primary work on race had been accomplished. "We had worked fairly hard to get the decision" to admit Black students made, Griffith explained. "There was a feeling—'we've climbed that mountain, you're over it, now you can rest a little' . . . having accomplished what seemed to be the main goal."[57]

The fact that significant relationships did not exist between Duke officials and Black professionals made it possible for this attitude to persist. In 1963, Duke had no Black faculty or administrators and just one Black secretary. As a result, Waldo Beach noted, "Blacks had no part in the academic life of the school," and faculty contacts across the color line "were limited to those between [white] faculty and their wives and Black help." Off-campus, administrators lived segregated lives. "Housing [in Durham] was entirely segregated," Beach recalled. "There were no Blacks in the all-white neighborhoods." As a result, the men who ran Duke had no one in their immediate professional or social circles to call on for insight into the needs of Black undergraduates. Although Durham had a thriving Black business community and since 1910 had been home to the all-Black North Carolina College at Durham (NCC), no effort was made to reach out to local Black leaders for insight on the needs of Duke's new students. The university approached desegregation passively and without preparation. "I'm not sure that anybody here . . . knew what to expect," Griffith remembered. "There was no one in the Black population to call on," Griffith noted incorrectly, and "we did not know what the Black experience was or what problems they would face—except everyone knew . . . for a Black student who came from a predominantly Black school it would be quite a different experience." "In retrospect," Griffith reflected, "one of the things one might have wanted to do was to go to some institutions that had already been through" desegregation.[58]

Having failed to educate themselves on issues and challenges likely to be faced by Black students arriving on campus, Duke's leaders simply assumed that the new enrollees would adjust to campus life. After the board's decision to desegregate, William L. Brinkley Jr., director of undergraduate admissions, visited a number of Black high schools in the South scouting for solid candidates, talking about Duke, and attempting to communicate the school's "sincerity of purpose." At Atkins High School in Winston-Salem, North Carolina, Brinkley met with six top-ten students who raised frank questions with him about "integration in the first year." Brinkley was unequivocal in his response, giving the students "complete reassurances concerning the climate at the University and that we anticipated very little difficulty with the matter." Griffith had the same view. "There was a general feeling," he recalled, that the Black students would "go right into the student body." Many in the administration felt that Duke was not "going to set up specialized situations because a person is a different color. We're integrated now." It was expected, according to Griffith, that Black students would take their place as members of the Duke community through a "natural kind of amalgamation." We thought it was "a great opportunity for that student to get a good education and [we] lost contact with the . . . problems that student would face." These assumptions carried significant consequences. "You don't just accept Black students . . . without trying to sit down and think about what effect it is going to have on them and . . . on the university," Brown explained. "I remember feeling . . . that with a little bit of forethought, Duke could have avoided most of what happened."[59]

Once Black students arrived on campus, Duke neglected to establish *any* internal mechanisms to elicit feedback from them on how they were managing. Initially, the Black students did not come forward with concerns. They "did not raise a lot of questions," Griffith recalled, and Robert Cushman, dean of the divinity school, said there were "no problems" after desegregation. "The Black students came in," he recounted, "they were received, and they were part of the community." From the university's perspective, Griffith recounted, these years were the "easiest as far as not being challenged by any problems."[60]

As with the decision to admit Black graduate and undergraduate students initially, Duke evaluated the success of desegregation only from its own perspective. Because few problems were articulated publicly by the students, the university assumed that desegregation was proceeding smoothly. With respect to graduate and professional school students, Cole reported to the board of trustees soon after their arrival: "So far, there have been no reports of any major problems which have been created by the presence of negroes in the graduate and professional schools. They have rather melted into the ranks of the student body, as we had hoped and expected they would."

The university's attitude was also reflected in a memo written in February 1964 by the assistant dean of Trinity College reporting on the first semester of one of Duke's Black undergraduates. After reviewing the student's academics, the assistant dean advised that the student "has been a good citizen" and that "to this point there is no evidence of any problem connected with [the student's] residence in the College." The assistant dean concluded that the student's "affairs have gone so smoothly that it has required a special effort on our part to remember that the student is here as [one of] our first Negro[s]." History professor Richard L. Watson learned how little he knew about the Black students' experience when he commented once to a group of these students that "you certainly did not experience any overt antagonism or hostility on campus." "I made that as a kind of affirmative statement," Watson recalled. "And the [Black students] who were there laughed when I said that."[61]

Even when potential problems came to light, no follow-up occurred. Griffith remembered that he was "aware of [episodes of physical harassment] only from what they told me. I never saw things going on. . . . But there were problems of harassment, some subtle and not so subtle." Griffith heard of students carrying screwdrivers for self-defense but was not "physically aware" of such behavior. "Nobody ever pulled out something and said, 'Hey, look— this is what I am carrying to protect myself.'" Even these reports, however, prompted no administrative action. If the Black students "had problems, I was certainly unaware of them," recalled Marcus Hobbs.[62]

"We looked at it from a white perspective," Griffith explained. "We didn't know what the black experience was or what the problems that they would face were." "We were . . . far too simplistic about [the Black students'] presence," Knight wrote. "We tended to feel that once we had . . . overcome the admissions hurdle, the rest would be easy. In making this assumption," he explained, "we were . . . saying 'Come in, be white,' and that was not what these young people wanted." In Knight's view, "much too much was expected from the simple act of admitting relatively few Black students, and much too little thought was given to what it really means to have black citizens of this country be part of the institution."[63]

....

Because of their isolation from teachers, administrators, fellow students, and each other, Duke's Black students searched for connections elsewhere. A first source of comfort was Duke's Black nonacademic employees. For Joyce Hobson, Oliver Harvey and his wife, "Mrs. Louise," a maid in Hobson's dorm, became her "parents away from home." Hobson remembered spending "many hours in [the Harveys'] home and attending church with them on Sundays." Armstrong had the same experience. "The people who treated us with any respect," she remembered, "were the people who worked in the cafeteria, worked in the dorms, kept up the grounds. They had that quiet pride [in us] that we could detect . . . that, for many of us, kept us going." "My Daddy told me, 'Son—find your people,'" Turner remembered. "In the [men's dorms] you had maids. And I remember this one in particular . . . Beatrice Spencer. She belonged to West Durham Baptist Church between East and West Campus. And she'd just say, 'Be ready Sunday to go to church.' [I'd say,] 'Yes Ma'am.' These are people like your mother, your aunt—the same kind of people you had grown up with and are accustomed to. So they treated you just like that," Turner recalled fondly. "They would just take you to church."[64]

The "vast city of Durham," as Turner described it, offered a second critical connection as Duke's Black students came to know the city's vibrant Black community and storied history. Drawn by the opportunities to work in the flourishing tobacco—and later, textile—industries, thousands of Black people had migrated to Durham between 1890 and 1930. Over half of these new arrivals settled in the Hayti neighborhood, an all-Black community. By the first half of the twentieth century, Hayti had more than one hundred independently owned Black businesses, including theaters, beauty parlors, restaurants, and stores. North Carolina Mutual Life Insurance Company, which became one of the largest Black-owned companies in the world, was established in 1905 and provided capital for significant business and residential development in the city's Black neighborhoods. Because of its level of commercial activity, Hayti came to be known as the Black Wall Street, and by the mid-1920s, a leading sociologist had designated Durham the capital of the Black middle class.[65]

Although Hayti's best days were over by the early 1960s, the neighborhood remained a hub of activity for the Black community. It was there that Duke's Black students were able to escape the alienation they felt on campus and obtain needed services. Turner remembered an area that was "teeming, thriving, full of life." If you got over there, he recollected, "you're back home."[66]

Hayti's churches were also an important touchstone. White Rock Baptist Church was organized in 1866, holding prayer meetings in homes, a cotton gin, and a warehouse before a permanent structure was completed around 1877. In 1891 the cornerstone of a brick structure for St. Joseph's Church was laid. From 1965 to 1976, St. Joseph's was led by the Reverend Philip R. Cousin, a towering figure active in the civil rights movement. When we got to church, Turner recounted, "we found out that the people who were there had children just like us and they understood us implicitly." Howard remembered church as a group activity. "That's a thing a lot of people did together," she recalled: "go to church together, go to the community meeting together."[67]

Another magnet was NCC. Everyone had "homeboys or homegirls" over at NCC, Turner explained. Claiborne, who was from Danville, Virginia, counted eleven people from his graduating class attending NCC. "I used to go over there every day," Claiborne recalled. "It was like going back home for me." Claiborne even had a payment card in the NCC cafeteria and would eat there regularly. Turner went to NCC "every weekend." Social life was a draw—he would go for parties and to take girls out. Because the Black students had no "space [they] controlled" on Duke's campus, Turner explained, "whenever we socialized, essentially we had to leave campus." Because Duke had done so little to accommodate the needs of its Black students, heading into Durham was essential. "The world was still segregated," Claiborne explained. "There were two Durhams. Once you caught that bus and headed out toward Duke, you were entering a different world."[68]

Given the many contacts Duke's Black students developed in Durham, it is not surprising that they became involved with community organizations. One that became particularly significant for Duke students was Operation Breakthrough, an affiliate of the North Carolina Fund. Incorporated in 1963 and established by then governor Terry Sanford, the fund represented an innovative approach to attacking poverty and educational deficiencies in North Carolina.[69] Operation Breakthrough, an antipoverty program located in Durham, was one of the first initiatives undertaken by the fund.

The North Carolina Fund and Operation Breakthrough became important to Duke's Black students for a number of reasons. At the suggestion of Sanford, the fund established a domestic service corps composed of college students called the "North Carolina Volunteers." Operation Breakthrough also established a program in which Duke students on financial aid could satisfy work-study requirements through employment in the Durham community. Through these programs, Duke students were provided the opportunity to work in Durham's poorest neighborhoods and to develop organizational skills. Perhaps most significantly, these activities allowed volunteers to wrestle with "issues of meaning in their personal lives" while "making direct connections to the civil rights movement and struggles over the nation's values and moral purpose."[70]

The impact of Operation Breakthrough on its student volunteers was magnified by Howard Fuller, who was hired in May 1965 to coordinate the program's community organizing efforts. Fuller's physical presence was, according to historian Christina Greene, imposing. He was "tall, dark, and handsome," Greene described, and his "six foot four inch frame . . . made a lasting impression on Durham." Sally Avery was among those inspired by Fuller. Meeting Fuller for the first time in the spring of 1966, Avery recalled that he was "one of the most charismatic people I have ever met."[71] Because he was the leader of Operation Breakthrough, many of Duke's Black students came to know and work with him. A powerful local and national voice on Black empowerment, over time Fuller became an important sounding board and adviser for many of Duke's Black students.

Although isolated and alienated from the university, Duke's Black students spent the first few years following desegregation developing deep personal connections with members of Durham's Black community and gaining exposure to social and political activities in the city. "Durham was unique in the United States at that time," Hopkins commented, because it had "one of the most conscious and well organized Black communities. So as a young person . . . we immediately had older people who we could lean on, learn from, who were interested and supportive of what we were doing. . . . Looking back," Hopkins reflected, "we were lucky that we ended up in Durham." Their experiences during these years provided a crucial context for the actions Duke's students would take in the coming years.[72]

....

The racial attitudes held by Duke faculty and administrators were not altered when Black undergraduates arrived on campus. Beliefs about Black inferiority persisted in some and were expressed in behavior toward Black students that ranged from passivity to overt hostility. Those who did not hold these beliefs operated in an institutional context that narrowly defined acceptable modes of relating to the new Black students. One former dean and college president described university communities as "like country clubs—interdependent, intentional communities, characterized by autonomy and a shared value system." Proactive outreach, engagement, and follow-up with Black students were not part of that "shared value system." As a result, Black undergraduates, while physically present on campus, experienced a racial climate that left them isolated from each other and alienated from the university. Although Duke had joined the ranks of desegregated southern private universities, Black students, as a group, almost immediately became psychologically resegregated. Because of this separation, many Duke administrators and faculty ignored the new Black students, for the most part dismissing them. With few exceptions, they avoided developing personal relationships with these students and made no attempt to understand the values, expectations, and needs they brought to campus.

According to historian Jason Sokol, white southern author William Styron hoped that the civil rights movement would make it the "moral imperative of every white southerner . . . 'to break down the old law' and 'to come to *know* the Negro,' his real desires and fears, in fact rather than myth." Those who ran Duke did not meet this moral imperative. The Black students who arrived at Duke were the best and the brightest in their communities with remarkable records of achievement. Turner observed, however, that the university "didn't really know who they had admitted." Turner believed "that a lot of people [at Duke] thought they had just gone up and down the street and just snatched some street urchins."[73]

University leaders were unable to move beyond their entrenched belief in "white exceptionalism." They could not fathom that Black students did not come to Duke hoping to assimilate into white culture. "One of the biggest problems during this time," Turner commented, was the presumption among Duke administrators and faculty "that whites had the best thing going, [and that] once we've [created] opportunities for others, they will be glad to come in to this superior thing that we have already fashioned. They did not have a clue," Turner explained, "of how much [Duke's Black students] enjoyed our life. . . . It's not like we don't have brilliance, excellence, intellectual, culturally, etc. It ain't like we don't enjoy our churches and our singing. No, none of that's true. So you are dealing with people," he concluded, "who had no clue as to who we were."[74]

Viewed from the perspective of the escalating conflict that followed, the university's failure to relate empathetically to its new Black undergraduates was at best a lost opportunity. It was also a grave mistake. Perhaps the prospect of engaging with Black students as equals—in the classroom, in the dorm, in the dining hall, on the athletic field—was too threatening at a university where many continued to view Blacks as inferior and segregation as a necessary part of the social order. In this context, it is possible that the psychological isolation imposed on Blacks following desegregation was a way for the university to mitigate the perceived threat these students represented.

Whatever the explanation, the absence of meaningful contact between white Duke administrators and faculty and the school's Black students was a significant contributing factor to the events that followed. Without the personal relationships that could result from such interactions, racial issues at Duke became increasingly difficult to resolve. "I was naive," Knight remembered. "I believed that the university had made its way toward a time of multiracial acceptance of the world, toward a triumphing over the past that the War Between the States represented. I honestly underestimated the force that [race] could still have when the pressure was on."[75]

CHAPTER 3

—

Rights, as Opposed to Privileges

Race and Space

—

The Black students who came to Duke and other historically white colleges and universities in the early 1960s did not arrive on campus intent on launching a movement. Like their white peers, they arrived at college hoping to benefit from positive academic and social experiences and to use their undergraduate years as a springboard for personal and professional growth. The product of families, schools, and communities that had groomed them for success, Duke's Black students looked forward to entering a professional world where opportunities were expanding dramatically.

Like all freshmen, each of Duke's Black students arrived on campus with a set of unique experiences, skills, and aspirations. Some had participated in the civil rights movement. For Bertie Howard, the movement had been a part of her childhood. "Many days my grade school was interrupted," she recalled, "as we stood and applauded students from a local historically Black college as they marched downtown to picket local stores that would not hire African-Americans." Howard's sophomore homecoming football game was canceled, she remembered, "because most of the [football] team was in jail for boycotting segregation." "I have what is now a tiny little scar," Michael LeBlanc recounted in 2019, pointing to his forehead. "As a 135–40 pound thirteen-year-old, I got beat by the police for sitting down at Woolworths back in 1963 or 1964."[1]

However, even with these experiences, few of Duke's first Black students were focused on protest or confrontation when they arrived on campus. Some arrived with feelings of gratitude toward the university for the chance to attend Duke. "We came in as the most benign, ineffectual people they could possibly bring in," Brenda Armstrong recalled. "People who were so afraid and so frightened by Duke, that we'd be overwhelmed by it. Thankful for being allowed to come there." C. G. Newsome described the Black students entering Duke in the early years following desegregation as "the model kids in the communities they came out of. These were not troublemakers," he stressed. Looking at matters from the administration's perspective, William Griffith, appointed vice provost and assistant dean of Arts and Sciences in the mid-1960s, also sensed that these students did not come to Duke as activists. "I don't think we were really getting the militant student—out of the ghetto," he recalled. "We were getting the middle-class Black who almost had to discipline himself or herself to be a militant."[2]

By 1966 several Black student leaders had emerged at Duke. One was Chuck Hopkins, who had arrived at college having been politically active in high school. "I was really influenced by stuff that was happening at other places," Hopkins remembered. "Before I even got active dealing with the Black issues, some of my white friends [and I] were going downtown for vigils against the war. . . . And the incidents right here at Duke—all of those things were having an impact and making me say to other students, 'Hey—we need to be doing something.'"[3]

Law students Charles Becton and J. Lee Hatcher were also leaders. Both had been undergraduates at predominantly Black Howard University and "knew the kind of camaraderie that was there." They saw "none of that on Duke's campus." "Not only were there few of us," Becton recalled, "but [the Black students] did not . . . associate together . . . to any great degree." Duke's Black undergraduates, in Becton's view, "faced the danger of being assimilated into a society without thoughts of their roots. . . . I thought at least they needed to start meeting as a group to discuss common problems." Stef McLeod also assumed an early leadership role. Studying to be an electrical engineer and, in the fall of 1966, president of the sophomore class in the School of Engineering, McLeod was seen by colleagues like Becton as someone who "had a good handle on things" developing on campus.[4]

Starting in 1966, these students, along with a handful of others, tried to organize a meeting of Duke's Black students. Although Black student groups had already formed on other campuses, these initial organizing efforts at Duke were unsuccessful. Duke's Black students were simply not ready to meet as a group. "Chuck Hopkins, Stef McLeod, Charles Becton—they all had their heads at a place it took us all a year to get to," Armstrong explained. "They had already decided that Duke didn't want us at Duke. . . . They had found that although Duke was willing to accept us, they had in no way changed the socialization process that goes on in college to accommodate Black students. . . . They had already seen that Duke had no intention of changing to meet what we thought were our needs. We had to get to that point," Armstrong said.[5]

The first group meeting of Duke's Black students occurred in March 1967. By that time, circumstances had converged to make the students ready for such a gathering. One key factor was a controversy over "race and space" that began in the fall of 1966 and focused on Duke's long-standing practice of using segregated off-campus facilities for events sponsored by administration, faculty, student, and alumni groups.[6]

In the early years following desegregation, President Douglas M. Knight had been able to convince the Duke University board of trustees to eliminate certain vestiges of Jim Crow such as segregation at Duke University Hospital and a racially restrictive covenant in newly granted deeds to property in Duke Forest. Even these changes, however, had not been easy. "I think the feeling [among board members] was that they had made a major concession in permitting Black students to come to the university at all," Knight recounted. "But these other matters were not of a piece with that. The question of mixed wards, the question of housing—take the whole list." The view was, according to Knight, "'we've let them in, now what's the matter?'"[7]

Despite this incremental progress, by 1966—four years after Black graduate students first enrolled at Duke—the university had still not issued any policy restricting or otherwise addressing the use of segregated off-campus facilities by university groups. Focused initially on university events hosted at nearby Hope Valley Country Club, the dispute soon broadened to include demands that Knight resign his membership in the segregated club. The segregated facilities controversy provided both a backdrop and an initial focus for the emerging Black student movement at Duke. It also reignited the fears of many at Duke and in the Durham community that the admission of Black students to the university would inevitably disrupt the privileged social order existing outside campus. For decades, Hope Valley Country Club had been a haven for Durham's white academic, business, and social elites. Members relished the chance to mix business with pleasure by hosting events at *their* club. They believed, director of alumni affairs Roger Marshall explained, that as members of a private club, they had the right to determine the membership policies and guest criteria "on any basis we want."[8] For them, the segregated facilities controversy represented a challenge to this "right."

....

By any measure, Hope Valley Country Club was impressive. Founded in 1926, its clubhouse was constructed in a "classic Tudor design," today encompassing fifty-two thousand square feet of recreational facilities, including dining, swimming, and tennis. Noted architect Donald Ross designed a championship eighteen-hole golf course for the country club. The Hope Valley residential district, Durham's first "full-fledged country club suburb," was developed with the course as its centerpiece. The country club and community sought to attract the young white professionals who, in 1926, were thriving in Durham's tobacco, textile, and health-care industries, as well as faculty members and administrators from recently endowed Duke University and the rapidly expanding University of North Carolina (UNC).[9] Hope Valley also turned out to be a perfect fit for the young physicians recruited to Duke following the completion of the Duke hospital in 1927. As the growth of the surrounding community accelerated, hundreds of Durham's business and academic leaders joined the country club and enjoyed its many privileges of membership.

Established only two years after Trinity College had become Duke, Hope Valley Country Club essentially served as a social and recreational "annex" for the university. Duke administrators, faculty, students, and alumni took full advantage of the many resources at the club, located about four miles from campus. As early as March 1928, for example, a Duke "junior social" was planned at the club. When Duke's academic school year began in the fall of 1928, the *Duke Chronicle* noted that horseback riding would now be offered as a hobby for the school's coeds at Hope Valley Country Club. In 1931 the club was the site for Kappa Kappa Gamma's sorority social and Delta Delta Delta's installation ceremony. At least as early as 1932, the Duke golf team used Hope Valley's golf course for practice and tournaments. Over the years, university events such as commencements and alumni reunions routinely included activities at Hope Valley.[10]

Despite the variety of events at Hope Valley Country Club, all had one thing in common: participation was open to white people only. "Only persons of good character and reputation who are of the Caucasian race shall be qualified for membership in the Club," its by-laws stated. As membership was limited to whites, so too were guest privileges. The only Black people on the grounds were those providing landscaping, caddy, housekeeping, porter, kitchen, and other services to white members and guests. Black service workers accessing the majestic Hope Valley clubhouse were required to enter through a back door.[11]

Given the club's close connections to Duke, it was natural that Knight would become a member of Hope Valley. His application for membership proceeded smoothly. After he was admitted, Knight told the club president that he and Mrs. Knight "look forward very much to the privilege of membership." Duke reimbursed Knight for his $600 membership fee and paid his annual dues.[12]

Neither the school's practice of holding events at segregated off-campus facilities nor Knight's membership in Hope Valley drew much comment.[13] Until 1966, the contradiction posed by a desegregated university holding off-campus events at a segregated location went largely unnoticed, at least by white administrators, faculty, and students.

C. B. Claiborne, Duke's first Black basketball player, came to the university in the fall of 1965. Growing up poor in Danville, Virginia, Claiborne was a star player on a high school basketball team that rarely lost. He performed well on precollege standardized tests and began to receive interest from schools around the country, including the Ivy League. "C. B. could have gone to any school in the country," his high school coach Hank Allen commented. "Whether he played anything or not, they still wanted him academically because he was a brilliant kid." Recruited by Duke basketball booster Al Newman, Claiborne received a National Achievement Scholarship for Outstanding Negro Students as well as financial support from Duke. "None of us ever thought about going to a white school," Claiborne recalled. "I was the first one in my community to go." Still, choosing Duke "wasn't a hard decision," Claiborne explained, "because this is what I was expected to do. . . . No one had ever had this opportunity before. . . . You don't say no to it."[14]

Claiborne performed well both academically and on the basketball court. His play as a freshman earned him a "letter," to be given out at the athletic department awards banquet scheduled for the spring of 1966. At the time, Eddie Cameron, Duke's director of athletics, had just completed a term on the Hope Valley Country Club board of governors. Given the club's close relationship with Duke, Hope Valley must have seemed ideal when it was chosen as the location for the awards banquet. Not for Claiborne, however. There were no exceptions to Hope Valley's segregation policy. Actively recruited, a standout on the basketball court, and a fine student, Claiborne was prohibited from attending the awards banquet. "I couldn't even go to receive my letter," Claiborne recalled. "One of my teammates, Fred Lind, had to bring my sweater and my letter to me. But it wasn't just me. Duke University still had a bunch of functions at Hope Valley when it was still segregated." Becton recalled this episode as a "catalyst" for many Black students on campus.[15]

Duke's nursing school had also decided to hold its annual Christmas dance at Hope Valley in 1966. According to the *Duke Chronicle*, the committee was not aware of Hope Valley's segregation policy when plans for the dance were finalized. At almost the same time that the nursing school was making its plans, the Women's Student Government Association (WSGA) was looking for a venue for its 1966 winter coed ball. Also unaware of the club's segregation policy, the WSGA reserved Hope Valley for its upcoming party.[16]

As the fall 1966 semester began, racial matters continued to attract attention on campus. In September the school announced the appointment of visiting political science professor Samuel DuBois Cook as its first Black faculty member. Soon, Cook was offered a permanent teaching position in the department, despite concerns expressed by Knight. When told by department chair John H. Hallowell that the department wanted to keep Cook at Duke, Knight responded, "Oh no, we can't have Sam here." As reported to Cook, Knight said, "It hurts fundraising," among other things. When Hallowell persisted, telling Knight that the political science department "unanimously and enthusiastically" wanted to keep Cook at Duke, the Duke president was unmoved. Hallowell was then very direct with Knight. "Well, you tell him," he said. "I'm not going to tell Sam we don't want him here because we do." Cook never heard from Knight and soon became a permanent member of the Duke faculty.[17]

In early October 1966, the *Duke Chronicle* reported that a white Duke student protester had been attacked and injured at a local Ku Klux Klan rally. The episode occurred after imperial wizard Robert Shelton urged that "subversive elements" be purged from the crowd.[18]

Perhaps most significant, the Duke community learned in early October that Knight had sent a letter to Duke's fraternities and sororities directing them to eliminate all racial and religious restrictions to membership by September 1, 1967. The groups were also asked to sign a nondiscrimination pledge. In his letter, Knight appeared to take the high ground, explaining that Duke could not permit the use of university property by any organization that, through its organizational documents or practice, bars members based on "race, creed or color." Left unsaid by Knight was that the university acted to end discriminatory requirements only when the federal government threatened to cut off funding if it failed to do so. Therefore, even as the nondiscrimination requirements were announced, the university sought to reassure those concerned. "Above all," university vice provost Frank T. de Vyver stated, "this does not require integration at the local level." The vice provost also declared that the university had no plans to monitor whether sororities and fraternities had, in fact, met the new requirements.[19] Thus, while Duke seemed committed on one level to a nondiscriminatory policy, on another, more basic level, it refused to follow through with direct action.

At almost the same time, final arrangements were being made for WSGA's coed winter ball. To confirm that Hope Valley's segregation policy would not be challenged, T. F. Brovard, manager of the club, contacted the WSGA, informing the group that a Black band could not play at Hope Valley and seeking assurances that no Black students would attend the dance. Having now been made aware of Hope Valley's segregation policy, the WSGA decided to move its coed winter ball to another location. The *Duke Chronicle* commented on the development, urging "President Knight and the other members of the faculty and administration who are members of the club to work to have the rules of the club changed." The paper wanted university club members to "assure that there is never another such affront to the University community."[20]

However, predictably, another "affront" was not long in appearing. As the nursing school was making final plans for its Christmas dance, it too was advised by Brovard that the dance could not be hosted at Hope Valley if any Black people attended. At the time, no Black students were enrolled in the nursing school and it was considered unlikely that a Black person would be invited to the dance as a guest. Still, the Nursing Student Government Association considered whether the dance should be moved to another location. Significantly, the university remained neutral on the question. "Our student government association is in a position to make decisions," Mary Jane Burch, assistant dean of the nursing school, commented, "and it is their responsibility." When the association's Executive Council met to consider whether to move the Christmas dance, it decided not only to relocate the upcoming event but also to prohibit the use of segregated facilities for all future social events. The student body of the nursing school quickly voted overwhelmingly to affirm these decisions.[21]

Stef McLeod wrote about the nursing school's actions in an article published in the *Duke Chronicle* titled "The Half-Student." Perhaps the first widely distributed commentary on the racial climate at Duke published by a Black student, McLeod's article detailed that the situation confronting the nursing school had served to point out "how . . . the Negro student [at Duke] suddenly finds that he is a 'half-student,' discriminated against and offended daily in several aspects of this institution." Calling the idea of using a segregated facility "pathetic," McLeod expressed relief "that the nurses, as a whole, were . . . committed enough . . . to stand firm against" segregation. McLeod condemned the "hypocrisy and discrimination" that would allow a segregated facility to even be considered as the venue for a dance sponsored by a Duke college.[22]

The controversy over segregated facilities continued to gain momentum during the final weeks of the fall 1966 semester. Just after the action by the nursing school and the publication of McLeod's article, the Men's Student Government Association (MSGA) came out against the use of segregated facilities for off-campus events. It also asked Robert B. Cox, dean of undergraduate men and associate dean of Trinity College, to remove five facilities known to be segregated from Duke's "approved" list of off-campus venues.

Focus then shifted to a Duke-Durham Alumni Association dinner at Hope Valley planned for December 1. Although invitations to the dinner had already been sent to all "local alumni and friends of Duke," the Hope Valley location precluded Black "alumni and friends" of Duke from attending. Questioned by the *Duke Chronicle* about the choice of location, M. Laney Funderburk, executive secretary of the Department of Alumni Affairs, informed the paper that the question of race probably never entered the minds of those organizing the dinner. What would happen if a Black person tried to attend? he was asked. "We'll cross that bridge when we come to it," Funderburk responded. In an editorial, the *Duke Chronicle* expressed embarrassment that the Department of Alumni Affairs was unconcerned about an "affront" to Duke's Black graduate school alumni and friends and called on Marshall to issue a statement of policy regarding "the use of segregated facilities for any alumni function."[23]

The Department of Alumni Affairs served as the front line of communication between Duke and its thousands of alumni, a segment of whom were vocal in opposing recent changes at Duke. Many local alumni were members of Hope Valley Country Club. Getting an alumni group to consider restricting its use of Hope Valley would be extremely difficult. As Knight observed, the people working in alumni affairs "took on the color of the alumni."[24] Accordingly, even with segments of the university moving to a more progressive stance on race, alumni affairs continued to be very sensitive to the conservative racial attitudes of former Duke students, particularly those in North Carolina.

Compounding this dynamic, Marshall appears to have harbored attitudes toward Black people that made him resistant to changes in Duke's racial policies. These were highlighted in a January 1966 exchange of letters with William M. Werber, a standout baseball player at the university who was also the first Duke basketball player to be named an All-American. In December 1965, the *Duke Alumni Register*, the school's alumni magazine, published an article titled "Reason against Racism." In response, Werber wrote a letter to the editor to put forth certain facts regarding "the coming clash between the white and colored races." He said that he embraced "love thy neighbor" and similar concepts "in theory," but not in the case of race relations where your Black "neighbor happens to be your dedicated enemy" who has "sworn to bury his hatchet in your skull whenever you turn your back." "Blacks, wherever found, . . . have a demonstrated inability to compete in any society," Werber wrote. "Wherever you find them in numbers you will find illiteracy, poverty, disease and crime." "You most certainly have my permission to publish this letter," he told the editor, "for I believe it to be an expression of convictions held by the vast majority of Duke alumni."[25]

Marshall responded to the letter. "I know that you have all the courage in the world," he told Werber, "and that you are not reluctant to set forth your opinions firmly and emphatically, but I think always fairly." Marshall wrote Werber that he had vetoed publication of his letter to the editor, however, because he was worried about the reaction it would "excite among people who, in their attachment to the opposite side of the cause, are perhaps less tolerant and more vituperative." "Criticism of the Negro race, or even the toleration of such criticism, at the moment is most unfashionable on virtually every college campus in this country," Marshall said. "I don't mind admitting," Marshall concluded empathetically, "that I think it is most unrealistically unfashionable!"[26]

As the alumni dinner approached, a committee of students and faculty was formed to coordinate picketing at the event. The University Caucus, an ad hoc group of undergraduates, graduate students, and faculty formed in October 1966 to consider campus issues outside the existing student government structure, endorsed the protest. While some caucus members worried that a public stand on the segregated facilities issue could cost the fledgling group support, one student saw the Hope Valley issue as a bellwether for future controversies. "Those who are alienated by taking a stand on this," Randy Shannon declared, "will be alienated by our taking a stand on anything."[27]

On November 30, the WSGA joined the MSGA in opposing the use of off-campus segregated facilities by campus groups. Like the MSGA, the WSGA sought to implement the policy by asking Cox to remove segregated facilities from the approved "social list" maintained for the Woman's College. At the same time, the WSGA passed a resolution urging that all university events be held at desegregated facilities and "remonstrated" the Duke-Durham Alumni Association for hosting its upcoming dinner at Hope Valley. These views were communicated to Marshall.[28]

On December 1, the day of the alumni association dinner, Marshall responded to the student newspaper's demand for a statement of policy. Suggesting that the *Duke Chronicle* had implied that members of his department and Durham alumni "keep pointed hoods in the deeper recesses of their closets," he assured students that "this is scarcely so." Marshall pointed out that the permissive stance of the alumni affairs department on the use of segregated facilities was "entirely consistent" with that of the university. Like others who resisted change, Marshall characterized the segregated facilities issue as one involving "freedom of choice," not discrimination. "I should think that anyone so concerned with the philosophy of *in loco parentis* on the campus," Marshall patronizingly told the students, "would . . . be entirely sympathetic with the opinion that it is neither practical nor desirable for the University to select the meeting places of all of its various groups of alumni and friends." Most Duke alumni are "sane, balanced, and considerate people," Marshall explained, who can be depended upon to "move quickly and gracefully in the right direction when circumstances become awkward." Thus, it was up to Duke's alumni and "well-intentioned . . . Durham friends" to make a change "when, in their good judgment, conditions make their occasional meeting place of more than twenty years inappropriate."[29]

The *Duke Chronicle* called Marshall's explanation "unsatisfactory." In an editorial, the paper explained that protesters at Hope Valley that evening were there to demonstrate that "many within the University . . . do not agree with those practicing or supporting discrimination by attending the dinner."[30]

A group of almost two hundred Duke students, with some faculty, picketed outside Hope Valley Country Club to protest the alumni association dinner. Both Black and white students joined the protest, including the leaders of the MSGA, WSGA, and a number of other student groups. One protester carried a sign stating simply "There ARE Negro Alumni" to communicate the contradiction posed by holding a Duke alumni event at a segregated club. Inside, attendees saw the co-captains of the football team honored and all graduating seniors on the team receive wrist watches. When reporters tried to enter the club, Brovard turned them away. Afterward, protest organizers called the demonstration a success. "Our public rejection of racial discrimination will, hopefully, restrain further participation in segregated situations by any organizations associated with Duke," Harry Boyte and Clint Wilson declared.[31]

The nursing school, MSGA, and WSGA had gone on record opposing the use of segregated facilities by campus groups. The protest at Hope Valley Country Club had been well attended and had generated considerable local publicity. Thus, it is easy to see why some believed that the controversy over the university's use of segregated facilities could well be moving toward resolution.

But such optimism was premature. In January, a local paper ran a picture of W. P. Budd, president of the Blue Devils Club, and basketball coach Vic Bubas at a club luncheon at Hope Valley, the *Duke Chronicle* observing that "it is disappointing that Bubas . . . would be a party to embarrassing the University in this way." Clearly no change in policy or practice had occurred. The MSGA and WSGA were similarly distressed to learn that their request to Cox that segregated facilities be removed from the university's "approved list" for off-campus events would have no practical impact. Cox explained that while the university maintained a list of "suggested" facilities for off-campus events, it was not binding on campus groups. "I couldn't say, you can't go here, you can't go there," Cox explained. "We do not want to be put in a position of being paternalistic."[32] As the fall 1966 semester ended, the segregated facilities issue remained unresolved.

....

Given his role as university president and his hands-on management style, Knight almost certainly would have signed off on actions taken by Marshall, Cox, and others in his administration on the segregated facilities issue. He likely knew that he would eventually be drawn into the controversy—not an inviting prospect. Knight risked badly damaging his relationship with whatever side of the dispute he ended up disappointing. Complicating matters further, Knight believed that much of the controversy was being "fabricated" by internal factions "who saw that there were fascinating games to be played." "There was as much push on one side as the other," Knight recalled, "to try to get the university into a situation where it would have to make great political noises that would be very happy noises for one group and very unhappy noises for another." Students, Knight believed incorrectly, "went out of their way to pick a facility that would pose an issue."[33]

Initially, Knight looked for a practical solution to the problem. He asked his senior management team to collect, on a very confidential basis, "information about the restrictive regulations of private clubs which the University may want to use for meetings from time to time." Knight believed that the administration could "avoid a good bit of trouble if we know this beforehand and quietly get the information out to groups that are likely to have large meetings here." Knight understood that he was dealing with an "extremely delicate matter." "We could be construed as supporting the restrictive policies of the clubs," he told his colleagues, "while on the other hand private organizations must continue to have a right to select their own members." Knight had "no desire," he said, "to be backed by the *Chronicle* into a reactionary position on this one."[34]

William Anlyan, dean of the medical school, responded to Knight's request in a letter dated the following day, telling the Duke president that neither Hope Valley nor the Tobac Club admitted Black people as members or guests. Anlyan also shared his view on the use of these facilities. "It is, indeed, a shame," Anlyan told Knight, "that the occasional Negro guest makes it necessary not to use these two facilities." For the dean, the issue was a pragmatic one. "The message we need to get across to any critics," he explained, "is that we have to get along with all segments of our society, and we cannot please everybody all the time." In a handwritten note, Anlyan added, "We have to maintain our 'access' to all people." Knight agreed with Anlyan's view, responding, "Absolutely."[35]

In December, university secretary Rufus H. Powell provided Knight with detailed information on the racial restrictions at local clubs. Powell's report confirmed Anlyan's information on Hope Valley and the Tobac Club; neither allowed Black members or guests. As to whether Asians could be admitted as guests at the two clubs, Powell noted in his comments about

Hope Valley: "Orientals? Dr. Luke Lee, Chinese, attended Dean Latty's reception, held there." He also told Knight that the Ambassador Club "probably will accept Negro guests," the Elks Club allowed use of its hall on an unrestricted basis but would not rent the facility to "all-Negro groups," and the Key Club at the Holiday Inn would only allow Black people if they were "guests of the Inn."[36]

There is no record of whether Knight tried to use this information to direct university groups to the few desegregated Durham clubs. In any event, campus groups continued to use Hope Valley and other segregated facilities as 1967 arrived.

At the same time that pressure was building on Knight to clarify Duke's policy on segregated facilities, he was challenged over his personal membership at Hope Valley. The first communication came in a letter from undergraduate Doug Adams, described by the *Duke Chronicle* as a "clean-shaven midwest Republican with deep religious convictions" who is both "a serious scholar and a committed activist." "I know many Negroes (students and employees) and Jewish students and faculty," Adams wrote to Knight, "who are greatly hurt by your continued support (however minimal) of a segregated club which has upon several occasions insulted members of the Duke community." Although acknowledging that resigning from the club "will cause difficulties in your relations with the Durham community," Adams argued that the action would "greatly improve [Knight's] relations in the Duke community."[37]

Soon thereafter, the University Caucus presented Knight with its own resolution. While the resolution acknowledged that Knight's membership in Hope Valley "may be valuable to the University in terms [of] community relations," it nevertheless called on him to resign. "We believe that, because of his office," the resolution stated, Knight "uniquely represents the University in the community, and his underwriting of the policies of this Club jeopardizes the seriousness with which the stated policies of the University can be taken."[38]

Knight knew that he would have to respond. The challenge to his *personal* membership at Hope Valley was even more problematic for Knight than the related dispute over the university's use of segregated facilities. If forced to resign, Knight knew that his relationship with the many Duke and Durham leaders who were Hope Valley members would be severely damaged. In responding to Adams, Knight tried to buy time by warning about the need to avoid publicity. "If I were put under any public pressure to resign," he wrote, "I would then be in a situation where I'm afraid I couldn't do a good job of discussing the problem, let alone finding a constructive answer to it."[39]

Shortly after the adoption of the University Caucus resolution, two student representatives of the Council of the Methodist Church at Duke University weighed in as well. Emphasizing the university's religious roots, the students wrote that "Duke University has a unique responsibility in as much as its motto is 'Erudito et Religio.'" The students asked how this tradition was manifested in its present life. They recognized that "too often the distinction is blurred between Dr. Knight, the President of Duke University, . . . and Dr. Knight, the man." Regretting "the conflicts this blurred distinction must often bring," the students told Knight that they felt "in this situation, Dr. Knight the symbol should take precedence."[40]

Before the semester ended, Knight tried to organize his thoughts on the resignation demand by scribbling notes on the back of an envelope. He was clearly attempting to rationalize his continued membership in Hope Valley. First, he rejected the argument that his position as university president required that he limit the choices he made in his "private" life. "What about referencing other restrictions," he asked testily. "Should [the] president belong to a particular church, or no church (since his membership is offensive to some)[?]" "Should he live by the codes of others?" More broadly, Knight did not accept the argument that his membership in a segregated club meant that Duke University, *as an institution*, practiced discrimination. "The university is not *as such* the espouser of this or that cause," Knight wrote, "unless the cause stands at the *center* of human freedom or the center of the university's *own* action." Knight apparently did not see Hope Valley's "Caucasian only" membership policy as "standing at the center of human freedom." Although the school paid his Hope Valley dues and Knight routinely used the club for university business, the Duke president did not view his connection to Hope Valley as standing "at the center of the [university's] *own* action." Clearly, Knight seemed ready to engage in elaborate mental gymnastics to avoid taking the politically costly step of resigning from the club.

Notably, Knight's analysis did not account for the rights or needs of the school's Black students. His approach was more tactical than substantive. Concerned that a backlash could tie his hands, Knight wrote, "The cause in question would be damaged by the action called for."[41] Knight was clearly frustrated, and he saw the Hope Valley issue as increasingly perilous. This was an accurate perception. By the spring semester, Duke's Black students would emerge as a powerful voice in the controversy.

....

Although by 1967 a number of long-standing traditions at Duke had been set aside, the annual practice of crowning a "May Queen" endured. Selection of the queen was a centerpiece of popular May Day celebrations, a holiday whose origins date back to the ancient world. Villagers throughout Europe would collect flowers and participate in games, pageants, and dances throughout the day. It became customary to crown a young woman May Queen to oversee the festivities. During the early twentieth century, selection of a May Queen became common at women's colleges in the United States and had acquired a special meaning in the South. "The crowning of the May queen as the ritual incantation of Southern society's ideal of femininity," historian Christie Anne Farnham wrote, "was a traditional event at Southern female schools. . . . The queen was usually elected by the students on the basis of 'sweetness' and beauty," Farnham explained, "although the father's status often played a role."[42]

May Queen traditions at Duke dated back to 1921 when the school was still known as Trinity College. The *Trinity Chronicle* reported that two thousand spectators attended May Day festivities that first year and that the two-day celebration was spent "in gaiety and amusement." Undergraduate Martha Wiggins was crowned May Queen that year. The school newspaper wrote that she "wore a lovely costume of shimmering white, bearing a corsage of white roses with her golden hair cascading in waves down her back, making a charming picture of perfect grace and absolute loveliness."[43]

Given this context, it was newsworthy when Wilhelmina Reuben, a member of Duke's first class of Black undergraduates, was selected as the Woman's College's May Queen in the spring of 1967. As runners-up in the voting, white coeds Mary Earle and Jo Humphreys were designated to serve as Reuben's "court." The Associated Press picked up the news, reporting that "Mimi, as she is known to her friends, is a Negro—the first of her race to receive the honor at the women's college of the university." Chosen for her character, leadership, campus service, and beauty, Reuben had been selected May Queen by a vote of students in the Woman's College. A fact sheet on Reuben prepared by Mary Grace Wilson, dean of women, described her as "warm, friendly, perceptive and sensitive to the feelings of others." Wilson called her "one of the most admired and highly respected students on the campus." Reuben was a member of the freshman honor society and was elected to Phi Beta Kappa as a junior. A student intern at the State Department, she was listed in "Who's Who Among Students in American Universities and Colleges." For her part, Reuben was pleased by her selection. "I'm still trying to adjust to it," she told the Associated Press. "I've been walking around in a delightful haze of disbelief and excitement."[44]

Many at Duke were pleased with the news. Randolph C. Harrison Jr., an alumnus from Richmond, Virginia, wrote to Knight that the "undergraduates' choice of Miss Reuben as May Queen attests once more to Duke's greatness. What a step towards inter-racial accord."[45]

If Reuben's election represented progress to some, however, the prospect of a Black May Queen flanked by two white members of her "court" felt like a violation of the established social order to others. Jonathan C. Kinney, president of the Associated Students of Duke University (ASDU), the unified student government, saw the reaction when he had the responsibility of "crowning" the queen and her court. "I kissed all the rest of the panel," he recalled, "so I kissed [Wilhelmina Reuben]. There were a lot of boos in that stadium at that time." An anonymous alumnus sent the Duke president pictures of the "pretty May Queens chosen at Peace, St. Mary's, and Meredith Colleges," all of whom were white, along with a picture of Reuben, "a colored girl who was chosen May Queen at our Dear Ole Duke University." The alumnus noted the "deplorable contrast between the May Queens of other colleges and the stunning representative from Duke." He told Knight that "Duke Alumni everywhere were stunned and several in South Carolina had strokes." One correspondent, identified as a "lifelong, respected citizen of Wilmington, North Carolina," outlined with exasperation the problems that Reuben's election was creating at the city's annual Azalea Festival where May Queens from throughout North Carolina were invited to attend: "The Sprunt's annual garden party at Orton [Plantation] for the college queens (held for the past 20 years) has been cancelled; the Coastguard Academy, which was supposed to furnish her escort, says they don't have a colored boy available; the private home in which she was supposed to stay is not now available; and there are all sorts of complications. The crowd who elected her has done a *disservice* to her," the writer opined, "and placed a no doubt nice girl in an embarrassing situation."[46]

Finally, two trustees weighed in. C. B. Houck told Knight that he liked and respected "the colored people" and wanted them to have "every opportunity that the white people have." Still, he thought Reuben's election was in "bad taste" and that the "East Campus girls were leaning over backwards to be nice." For Houck, the symbolism was deeply troubling. "To select a colored person for May Queen and have white maids of honor flanking her on either side," he concluded, "makes for poor and critical relationship [*sic*] among many people, particularly in the South." Trustee George M. Ivey Jr. was also deeply concerned. Writing from Bangkok, Thailand, he called Reuben's selection "very upsetting to me." Even if the selection was by Duke's coeds, Ivey regretted "that the University has attracted the type of students that would vote for a Negro girl as a 'beauty' to represent the student body. It is nauseating to contemplate."[47]

Although Knight responded to almost every letter, he was not unaware that the May Queen episode damaged him politically in the eyes of some board members and alumni. Knight later wrote that Reuben "became known among board members as 'Doug's dusky beauty queen,'" and he believed that George Ivey, among others, held *him* responsible for Reuben's election. "Black undergraduates were new at Duke," Knight wrote, "and a strong minority of the Trustees had been opposed to their admission. The same, alas, turned out to be true of the alumni during these troubles; each critical event compounded those before it, and I found myself riding a historic wave, which—according to my constituents—I should have been able to control."[48]

Knight viewed such opinions as "an absolute bit of mythology" but acknowledged that "there was no way to free myself. If I had not chosen her myself, I had created a climate in which she could be chosen." From that point forward, Knight explained, Ivey was always disaffected: "He had been troubled enough before, but that just finished it off."[49]

The attitudes expressed in the letters to Knight about Reuben's election are also important. To Knight's credit, by the spring of 1967, Duke had eliminated most of the school's de jure discriminatory policies and practices. Reuben's election as May Queen could be seen as another positive sign of racial progress. But the episode also shined a spotlight on the depth of attachment some still had to traditional racist ideas. These attitudes would become even more pronounced as Black students at Duke began to assert themselves.

By the spring of 1967, a core of self-conscious and effective Black student leaders like Hopkins, McLeod, Becton, and Hatcher had emerged on Duke's campus. While Duke's Black students were far from monolithic, many were now developing a deeper understanding of the consequences of the university's failure to fully acknowledge—and prepare for—their presence on campus. William Turner recognized that Duke had not "come to terms with what it meant, practically speaking, to have a significant Black student population on campus." Janice Williams came to see that Duke was trying to "mesh two cultures and actually negating one." The university did not, according to Williams, realize that Black and white students "truly do come from a different background." Duke's Black undergraduates, in addition to seeking a good education, had "certain identity needs, certain cultural needs, and emotional needs" that could not be forgotten. Armstrong put it most simply: "We came in thinking we should be thankful. Around about February, we didn't know what we should be thankful for."[50] Clearly, any feelings of gratitude Duke's Black students felt for the chance to attend the university were disappearing.

Until the fall of 1966, the small number of Black undergraduates at Duke, and their isolation from one another, made establishing a cohesive group difficult. In September 1966, however, eighteen Black freshmen enrolled at Duke. As Armstrong described it, this established a "critical mass of 'us'" sufficient to forge a collective identity.[51]

Just as Duke's Black students were increasing in number and gaining insight into their situation at the university, a long-simmering generational schism in the civil rights movement exploded into the open. Martin Luther King Jr. had offered Black and white citizens a miracle born of nonviolent protest that held the promise of ending racial inequality in America and integrating Black people into mainstream society. But ever since the sit-in movement of 1960, a younger generation of leaders had started to see the prospects for change very differently. Frustrated by the slow pace of change in the civil rights movement and assaulted by the deaths of civil rights workers like Andrew Goodman, Michael Schwerner, and James Chaney in Mississippi in June 1964; the assassination of Malcolm X in February 1965; and the widely covered carnage of "Bloody Sunday" on the Edmund Pettus Bridge in Birmingham, Alabama, in March 1965, new, more militant leaders began to emerge. These new leaders had found, according to one historian, that "history could not be eradicated so easily, nor could the central significance of race to all American institutions and culture be rooted out simply through warm feelings." These young leaders "concluded that white institutions and white people could not be trusted, and that their promises were simply another effort to control and define what black America was all about."[52]

The most prominent of the new leaders was Stokely Carmichael, a graduate of Howard University who was elected head of the Student Nonviolent Coordinating Committee (SNCC) in May 1966. "A striking thinker and speaker,"

Ibram X. Kendi wrote, "the courageous, captivating, and charismatic Carmichael embodied the new defiant young Black generation that Malcolm X had seen approaching around history's corner." After his arrest at the June 1966 March against Fear in Mississippi, Carmichael injected the words *Black Power* into the national conversation. Speaking to a crowd in Greenwood, Mississippi, Carmichael told his audience that "the only way we gonna stop them white men from whuppin' us is to take over." For Carmichael, taking over meant "Black Power." "We been saying 'freedom' for six years and we ain't got nothin'," Carmichael exclaimed. "What we gonna start saying now is Black Power!" "Almost immediately," historian William Chafe observed, the Black Power "slogan became a rallying cry for blacks as well as a justification for a white backlash against the civil rights movement."[53]

In *Black Power: The Politics of Liberation*, Carmichael and political scientist Charles V. Hamilton described Black Power as "a call for black people in this country to unite, to recognize their heritage, to build a sense of community. It is a call for black people to begin to define their own goals, to lead their own organizations and to support those organizations. It is a call to reject the racist institutions and values of this society." Carmichael and Hamilton saw group solidarity as the key. For them, the fundamental premise of Black Power was that "group solidarity is necessary before a group can operate effectively from a bargaining position of strength in a pluralistic society." As Chafe explained, Black Power "required that blacks—not 'good' whites—control their own institutions, their own programs, their own demands." It also rejected the integration of Black people into a nation dominated by white values and institutions as the appropriate goal for the civil rights movement. Significantly, Black Power questioned the view that nonviolence was the only acceptable strategy in the Black freedom struggle. "Black Power spokespersons," historian William L. Van Deburg wrote, "felt that a beleaguered minority could hope to survive in the violent milieu of late-twentieth-century America only by developing the will and the ability to retaliate against outside attacks." As Carmichael explained, "nothing more quickly repels someone bent on destroying you than the unequivocal message: 'O.K., fool, make your move, and run the same risk I run—of dying.'"[54]

On September 27, 1966, under the front-page headline "'Black Power' Interpretation Due," the *Duke Chronicle* announced that community organizer Howard Fuller would be speaking on the Duke campus that evening. Hopkins was struck by the description of Fuller in the article as a "moderately militant Black Power advocate." "That blew my mind," Hopkins recalled. "I said, 'Who is this guy?' . . . In 196[6], to be a Black Power advocate was enough to make you a radical, if not a revolutionary. And here was this guy who was supposed to be a 'moderately militant Black Power advocate.' So I went to the seminar."[55]

That evening, Fuller addressed ideas at the center of the evolving concept of Black Power. Fuller told his audience that "integration at this time cannot be the answer when all of the power is in the hands of the white people." He identified organized Black political and economic strength as a necessary prelude to meaningful integration. Fuller derided the incremental progress toward integration achieved by the civil rights movement and emphasized that for Blacks to achieve an equal share of power, "the black man must begin to be proud of his blackness." He also rejected the contention made by some in the white and Black communities that Black Power had led to violence. "You don't get people to come out and burn things unless they see . . . nothing but dead roads ahead," Fuller explained. His talk impressed Hopkins. "After that we got together," Hopkins remembered. "We became good, good friends."[56]

Fuller was not the only speaker on Black Power at Duke during this period. As the most prominent Black Power advocate in the country, Stokely Carmichael spoke at dozens of community rallies and as many as twenty-five college campuses during the 1966–67 academic year. In March 1967, Carmichael visited Duke at the invitation of Lee Hatcher, who had known the SNCC leader when both were undergraduates at Howard University. Carmichael spoke before a packed crowd in Page Auditorium. Hatcher introduced him, calling Carmichael a "historic figure" who has "made a great, great impact on American Black people and . . . is destined to bring our people to freedom."[57]

In his prepared remarks and the question-and-answer session that followed, Carmichael used trenchant political analysis, provocative rhetoric, and wit to challenge long-standing assumptions held by both Black and white members of the audience. Carmichael critiqued the tactics and goals of the civil rights movement while arguing that the development of independent Black culture and institutions was essential to achieving change. Carmichael argued that "to bring about changes in the status quo, one needs power—not love, not non-violence, or morality—that's when you are developing a religion. When you want to bring change, you need power." "I'm not a pacifist," Carmichael explained. "If somebody tries to kill me, I'm going to shoot them before God gets the news. Dr. King would be willing to die to prove his point," Carmichael observed. "I would rather live and prove my point."[58]

Carmichael rejected integration as the goal of the Black freedom struggle. Integration was based, Carmichael argued, on the "assumption that there was nothing of value in the Negro community and that little of value could be created among Negroes." The civil rights movement was not seeking, according to Carmichael, to achieve progress for Black people as a group. Rather, "its goal was to make the white community accessible to 'qualified' Negroes" so that "each year a few more Negroes armed with their passport—a couple of university degrees—would escape into middle-class America and adopt the attitudes and lifestyles of that group." Instead of integration, the focus of the Black freedom struggle, Carmichael said, should be to "return to the ghetto to organize these communities to control themselves."[59]

Carmichael also challenged the white educational system. "I do not believe that the educational system in this country is perpetrated to help Black people," Carmichael noted. "It is perpetrated to help white people and reinforces white supremacy without even many of the white people noticing it. . . . It reinforces and gives validity to the values and institutions of this society. . . . That is the problem with education. One is given technical skills but one is [also] given an ideology . . . [that] warps the mind of Black people in this country." More broadly, Carmichael argued that white people should have no direct role in the Black freedom struggle. Instead, whites should return to their communities, organize poor white people, and attack institutional racism "so that Black Power become[s] a reality without bloodshed."[60]

Carmichael's critique of the civil rights movement, institutional racism, and the contradictions faced by Black students attending a white university resonated powerfully with Duke's Black students. "Stokely Carmichael just . . . brought it home," Armstrong recalled. "All of a sudden, there was someone who knew nothing about Duke who came in and just . . . described in a very graphic way exactly what was happening to us [on campus]. Things that we had tried to neglect." Armstrong's reaction to Carmichael was not uncommon. After Carmichael spoke at Tougaloo College outside Jackson, Mississippi, the student newspaper reported "a new awareness in the minds of the students. There has been a lot of thinking going on since he left, and these have been profound thoughts about US Black people." Aaron Dixon commented after hearing Carmichael speak at his Seattle high school that "the way I looked at myself and America changed."[61]

Carmichael's visit to Duke reignited discussions about organizing Duke's Black students. Charles Becton remembered a conversation with Lee Hatcher, campus visitor Samuel Shoots, and undergraduates Stef McLeod and Charles Hopkins after Carmichael's speech at the law school. We were "walking out . . . talking about the need to get together as a group and stay together as a group,"

Becton explained, "and Samuel was telling us there was an [organized Black group] at Tennessee State [University]. Almost simultaneously we said, 'Why don't we do that here at Duke?'" With that, Becton and Hatcher asked Hopkins and McLeod to round up Duke's Black undergraduates for a meeting. Now, when Hopkins approached his colleagues about getting together, their response was positive. Within a week of Carmichael's visit, the first group meeting of Duke's Black students was held. That meeting, Becton observed, "was the beginning."[62]

Virtually all Black students at Duke attended the first meeting, although some came with misgivings. Armstrong, for example, remembered "being awfully afraid." For her, the meeting "represented . . . a real revolutionary move . . . because I always associated it with a certain form of militancy." Becton remembered one student speaking out against the formation of a Black student group. "He came to the first meeting saying," according to Becton, "'we've got to all live together. We can't be holding separate meetings. What can you accomplish? You can't live in a separate society.'"[63]

With Becton, Hatcher, McLeod, and Hopkins leading the conversation, Duke's Black students got to know one another. "There were Blacks on campus we didn't know were on campus," Becton recalled. "Basically, studying by themselves." "Some of the people that the undergraduates thought were . . . janitorial staff," Brenda Brown remembered, "turned out to be graduate students." A key step at the first meeting was the decision to establish the Duke Afro-American Society (AAS). In so doing, Duke's Black students joined counterparts at other colleges and universities who had formed similar organizations. Scholars have recognized the key role these Black student organizations played in the Black activism that developed on many campuses. Sociologist William Exum described such student groups as "exclusively black in membership, monolithic in appearance, highly self-conscious, and motivated by sociopolitical concerns." Education professor Joy Ann Williamson noted that such groups "worked towards providing Black students with a structured and legitimate power base from which to force change at their institutions." While some student leaders at Duke viewed the AAS in these political terms, most students, at least initially, had more practical goals in mind. "We decided to make some formal structure," Brown recalled, "to make sure we didn't all get scattered and out of contact with each other." Accordingly, the initial focus of the AAS was to foster interpersonal connections. "The political evolution of the Afro-American Society came after the social evolution," Armstrong observed. Looking back, she remembered "a tremendous amount of needing to be with Black people on campus." The first project undertaken by the group was the preparation of a Black student directory listing the names, addresses, phone numbers, and major areas of study of all Black students on campus. With that contact information, "we had a couple of parties," Becton remembered, "just to get together."[64]

The early meetings of the AAS were not expressly "political." "Helping each other out—that's what it was all about at first," Becton recalled. Once Black students started to interact, individual experiences started to emerge as pieces of a broader pattern. "We talked about things that concerned us," Becton remembered. "We realized that a lot of things were happening that we just didn't know about." These interactions were crucial because they eased the isolation many Black students were experiencing. Isolation was "disorienting," Chuck Hopkins explained. "You were at Duke, but before something happened to you [personally], you knew something was wrong but you had no overt experience of [it]. When you finally got to know another Black student and you sat down and talked about experiences—it was a relief."[65]

As personal connections multiplied, a sense of community began to emerge. Common experiences, Armstrong explained, "served as the impetus for making the Black students who were at Duke at that time a very cohesive group." "We . . . became family," Janice Williams explained. "You needed someone to catch you, someone to fall back on, someone who understood all those little things."[66]

The initial student leaders remained highly visible during the early AAS meetings. Becton, Hatcher, Hopkins, and McLeod "were such strong individuals," Armstrong explained, "that they provided a protective umbrella for all of us." "We spent a great deal of time just talking to the kids," Becton recalled, "letting them know there was no reason they were being treated this way." Discussions also focused on the changes needed at Duke. "Once we started talking to people, we found out all sorts of problems—we needed tutors, we needed all sorts of things," Becton remembered.[67]

In April, Hopkins was elected the first chair of the AAS. "It was a consensus," Armstrong remarked. "Chuck was . . . elected because he was the most vocal, he was the most visible, he seemed to have the politics right, and he seemed to be much more familiar with the 'ins and outs' of Duke than we were." Hopkins embraced his leadership role. "It was something that I thought was right, it was something I felt strongly about," Hopkins explained. "I wanted to move people to [a higher] level of thinking."[68]

Just as regular AAS meetings began, the segregated facilities controversy reignited. Sigma Alpha Epsilon (SAE) fraternity decided to hold its pledge formal at Hope Valley Country Club on April 8, 1967. The *Duke Chronicle* reported the location and time of the dance and publicized plans by an ad hoc committee to picket the event. The ad hoc committee explained that the purpose of the picketing was to "protest and to express the insult to black students . . . brought about by the University's lack of clearly stated policies concerning the patronage of segregated facilities by [university] groups." One member of SAE described matters very differently. In a letter to the editor of the *Duke Chronicle*, he asserted that the choice of Hope Valley had nothing to do with race. Describing Hope Valley as a "nice establishment," he explained that several members of the SAE pledge class had fathers who were members of Hope Valley. The fraternity had simply "decided to take advantage of the opportunity to have our formal there." In an editorial, the *Duke Chronicle* compared SAE unfavorably to the nursing school and WSGA: a year earlier, they had "had the guts to say no to Hope Valley Country Club which they realized would discriminate against fellow students." Sarcastically, the paper urged SAE members to "hold your heads high, men."[69]

On the same day as the SAE formal, the *Duke Chronicle* published a list of Duke administrators and professors who were members of Hope Valley Country Club. The list was extensive—in addition to Knight, it included Duke's president emeritus, vice president for business and finance, provost, vice provost, university counsel, university librarian, director of physical education and athletics, head basketball coach, dean of the law school, and five law professors. The *Duke Chronicle* also noted that more than fifty members of the university's medical school and hospital staff were members of the segregated club.[70] Some noted that the list of Hope Valley members included many of the Duke senior administrators directly involved in setting university policy on the use of the facility by campus groups.

The renewed attention to the segregated facilities issue soon became a topic of discussion at AAS meetings. "Without those meetings, we wouldn't have known where fraternities had their parties," Brown remembered. "I wasn't even interested that they had them." Armstrong explained how the perception of the issue evolved. "It wasn't until the end of my freshman year [in the spring of 1967] or the beginning of my sophomore year," she recounted, "that we could understand what Hope Valley was. To condone Hope Valley and yet take in Black students was an obvious contradiction. Mutually exclusive views."[71]

Aware that the school year would be ending in a few weeks, AAS leaders were seeking an issue that could be used as a catalyst for group action while publicizing that Duke's Black students had gotten organized. With the SAE pledge formal and a roster of Hope Valley members now attracting publicity in the *Duke Chronicle*, AAS leaders decided to publish an "open letter" to the many Duke administrators and faculty members who were members of the club. "It was definitely an organizational tool," Chuck Hopkins remembered. "We had just started so we wanted to present ourselves in some form. . . . It was a chance to get out and do something active."[72]

Drafted by Hatcher and published in the *Duke Chronicle* on April 25, 1967, the open letter was signed by thirty-eight of the university's approximately fifty-two Black students. While recognizing "the right of any individual at [Duke] to belong to any private organization," the letter highlighted the conflict presented when a university publicly committed itself to racial equality yet allowed dozens of its administrators and faculty to participate in a private segregated club. "It is one thing," the letter asserted, "for the Administrators of this institution to say that we accept you Negro students here at the University on the same basis that we do other students, and quite another to smack us in the face by indicating in your private lives that you will not treat Negroes equally with others. The two are directly contradictory and must be considered irreconcilable."[73]

The open letter cast the Hope Valley memberships as part of a broader pattern of indifference to the needs of Black students at Duke. "We, as a group of Negro students, are fairly convinced," the letter explained, "that our sole purpose here at the University is confined to that of being conspicuous." In support, the letter cited Duke's failure to act in the interests of its Black students in areas such as graduate school housing, social life, and the hiring of Blacks in administrative positions. "For the school to continue sanctioning the use of segregated facilities by the various groups in the University community," the letter stated, "is an arrogance so flagrant as to suggest contempt for our well being." Despite using strong language, however, the letter made no express demand that Duke's Hope Valley members resign from the club. Rather, the open letter simply expressed "dismay" at Duke administrators and faculty who were Hope Valley members. It ended by warning these individuals that they would "receive ample rewards for your misdoings."[74]

That thirty-eight of Duke's Black students signed the open letter reflected the organizational strides the group had made by April 1967. The letter also displayed an advancing level of political analysis about the university's use of segregated facilities as well as other significant issues faced by the Black students at Duke. Still, the open letter demonstrated caution and restraint. Armstrong characterized the tone of the letter as "strongly pleading." The message, she said, was "please do this so we won't have to do something else." "That's not to say there weren't people who felt much more strongly. . . . It reflect[ed] the over-whelming majority Black student view," she explained, "that we ought to be a little more conservative about approaching this type of problem." Even so, sign-ing the letter was not taken lightly. "All of us came from pretty sheltered types of environments," Armstrong noted, "and most of us were really afraid of what this represented. We knew this was just a first step—all of us realized that."[75]

Knight was coming to the end of a very difficult school year. His leadership was under increasing scrutiny, not only by students. The "Fifth Decade Plan," Knight's ambitious roadmap for transforming Duke into a leading national uni-versity, had been announced to wide acclaim a couple of years earlier. Now, the $187 million plan had started to generate opposition, especially from Endow-ment trustees. Race played a role. "Trustees who otherwise would have stepped up to the plate [to support the Fifth Decade Plan] were so . . . bothered by racial issues," Knight reflected, "that one could no longer keep the lines clear."[76]

Traveling constantly, the Duke president was exhausted. "Every day in the later sixties," Knight wrote in his memoir, "I was burning more energy—more of myself—than I could replenish. . . . I was using up the capital of my mind and body, with no reasonable hope of protecting and restoring either one. Life had become relentless and I could do nothing to change it." When Duke students returned for the fall semester, they learned that Knight had been hospitalized over the summer with a case of hepatitis and faced a "lengthy period of recuperation."[77]

....

In the fall of 1967, the sense of community among Duke's Black students con-tinued to grow. Their exploration of the cultural and political aspects of Black Power deepened, and the AAS began to develop strategies to force change at the university.

One important development was the arrival of forty Black freshmen. The larger number of Black students in the fall of 1967—now sixty-seven undergraduates—made fostering connections easier. "Once there got to be more and more of us there," Brown observed, "you felt like there was someone there to reach out to." "You couldn't very well [develop your own society] with twenty people," Howard explained. "You needed numbers."[78]

With the influx of Black students, recruiting freshmen to join the AAS now became a priority. Beginning with the fall of 1967, Armstrong recalled, "we took it upon ourselves to meet all of the new Black students . . . and to get them interested in what we were doing." As a result, "it didn't take six months for all of us to find each other." Social events played a key role in the process. "I can remember distinctly," Armstrong commented, "some kind of get-together in back of my dorm, the first week of my sophomore year [in September 1967]. From that time on, everybody knew everybody."[79]

As they got to know the incoming freshmen, upperclassmen learned that these students were markedly different from those who had come before them. For Hopkins, who matriculated at Duke in 1965, the process of becoming politicized had been gradual and organic. "I was . . . indifferent to the whole thing [when I arrived at Duke]," Hopkins explained. "Duke's racism and oppressiveness assaulted me and made me respond." "The two or three classes that came in after me," he recounted, "came to Duke angry . . . because stuff was happening by then." Brown agreed. "The class that came after me was just a more militantly minded class than some of us who were ahead of them. They got here and they encountered some of the frustrations we had encountered . . . but they were [quicker] to react to them than we were." One reason is that these freshmen arrived at Duke after searing national events, like the Watts Rebellion in 1965 and the Newark uprising in 1967, had drawn intense national attention. These members of the class of 1971 also came to Duke after the AAS had been established. "When they came in, all of these issues had accelerated so rapidly," Armstrong explained. "They came in at a time when the slope of the curve was going up exponentially. . . . We came in at a time when things were brewing."[80]

With more Black students on campus, better methods of intragroup communication were necessary. One approach was to schedule more frequent get-togethers. "There were regular meetings by the time the classes after us came in," Brown recounted. "Kids just had the chance to sit down and really make an effort to talk about what this place was like, what was going down, and what we could change to make things better for the people who came after us." Meetings were not the only setting for group interaction. "The classes that came after us," Howard remembered, "were more socially oriented. They were into having a lot of parties so we saw each other more. That helped a lot," she explained.[81]

As the pace of events accelerated, ways of sharing information between meetings and other gatherings were also needed. One approach was to establish a simple but highly effective communication network, the "Drum." "You know what the grapevine is," Armstrong explained. "We called it the Drum."

Through the Drum, information could be passed among Duke's Black students with remarkable speed. "No one could understand how all of us knew about each other . . . and could get word to each other in such a short period of time," Armstrong recalled.[82]

In addition to communicating through the Drum, Black students created a meeting place called the "Block." "Between classes, . . . where the [student] union is," Armstrong recounted, "there is a block of cement next to the garbage can. We used to call it 'the Block.'" As Armstrong described it, "all of the Black people would congregate there in between classes and around lunchtime. It used to be like a magnet. . . . That's how word got passed a lot of times." Meals were also an opportunity for group interaction. Continuing a practice started in the spring, Duke's Black students ate a majority of their meals together, meeting daily at the same designated table in the dining hall.[83]

As hostility over race seemed to increase both at Duke and in the country at large, Duke's Black students looked increasingly to each other for support. "We were frightened" when we came to Duke, Armstrong recalled. "There is no question about it. But it frightened us into a collective sense of needing each other. We needed each other more than anyone needed each other. We were such a cohesive group. . . . We were a community within a community," Armstrong described, "and we were a very separate community."[84]

This sense of collective separateness—of "community"—led directly to the development of the Black student movement at the university. In addition to providing friendship and emotional support, closeness afforded these students the psychological and emotional space needed to achieve, as historian Lawrence Goodwyn described in *The Populist Moment*, a "heretofore culturally unsanctioned level of social analysis."[85] As they adapted the ideology of the Black Power movement, Duke's Black students began to challenge assumptions not only of the dominant white culture at Duke but also of their parents and the communities that had raised them.

An interview with Hopkins published in September 1967 illustrates how the AAS had adopted key elements of the Black Power program. Emphasizing the need for "self respect" among Black students, Hopkins stated that the purpose of the AAS was to develop and maintain "Black consciousness" on campus. Hopkins argued that Black students at Duke "by and large [were] obtaining a white education" and cited as evidence the many history classes at the school where Black contributions to society were "noticeably neglected" and "black people are not emphasized." The purpose of the AAS, according to Hopkins, was to promote "Afro-American history and culture" as well as a closer connection between Duke's Black students and the Durham community, especially in the area of open housing. Hopkins described the Black student at Duke as facing a choice between preparing to "'go north,' get a job and settle down into a comfortable living" or going back to his or her home community to "help his people." The AAS hoped to encourage Duke's Black students, Hopkins explained, to work in their own communities.[86]

Racial issues continued to be at the forefront in the fall. In September the university took action to eliminate segregation in off-campus housing. Duke required that the owners of all off-campus housing units listed by the university as available for students sign a nondiscrimination pledge. As was the case with the decision to desegregate and the requirement that fraternities and sororities eliminate discriminatory membership requirements, the immediate cause of the policy change was pressure from the federal government.[87]

In October 1967, the segregated facilities issue moved rapidly to the fore, with Duke's Black students playing a pivotal role. Soon, the issue divided the campus. Initially, ASDU was the primary actor. On October 17, 1967, after "long, sometimes heated debate," the ASDU legislature voted 27–15 to prohibit the use of segregated facilities by all university-related organizations. Debate focused on whether ASDU had the jurisdiction to prohibit private groups—such as fraternities and sororities—from holding events at segregated facilities. According to a report in the *Duke Chronicle*, most legislators who voted in favor of the resolution agreed with one student who said that ASDU had to "accept responsibility for the moral issue at hand." Although two motions demanding a student-wide referendum on the resolution were defeated, ASDU legislators asked that Duke undergraduates be informed of their right to force a student vote on the action.[88]

Immediately following passage of the resolution, Hopkins and McLeod issued a statement on behalf of the AAS "emphatically demand[ing]" that the university publish a clear policy on the use of segregated facilities. "The era of toleration of . . . lack of re-affirmation of policy is over," the statement read. "We as black students in this integrated community await a clear affirmation . . . from the University administration on this vital issue."[89]

Yet not only was there no statement of policy by the university, but different opinions arose among undergraduate constituencies. Almost immediately, two petitions calling for a student referendum on the ASDU resolution began circulating on campus. As petition signatures were being collected, the MSGA, voting 6–2, adopted a resolution proposed by Interfraternity Council representative Bob Pittman condemning ASDU's segregated facilities ban.

Pittman's primary concern, he said, was to affirm the "basic right of the individual organization to decide for itself on the matter." Days later, the WSGA cabinet voted 11–0–2 to support ASDU's stance and to prohibit the use of segregated facilities by all Woman's College groups.[90]

Other groups also weighed in. The Interfraternity Council voted 13–4 against banning the use of segregated facilities by its constituent members. The Men's Freshman Council voted to condemn the ASDU resolution as well, concluding that "while segregation is morally wrong, it is up to individuals and individual organizations to address the situation." Sigma Nu fraternity objected to the ASDU action as legislative overreach but also voted to prohibit the use of segregated facilities for future Sigma Nu events.[91] Women were generally more progressive than men and fraternity members more conservative than those men who lived in independent groups.

Meanwhile, university leaders seemed more indecisive than ever on the issue. In September the school released a policy that only confused matters further. The new policy, adopted by the University Policy and Planning Advisory Committee (UPPAC), prohibited the use of segregated facilities in connection with "official activities sponsored, financed, and controlled by University personnel and campus organizations." University administrators then seemed to contradict themselves, with the university Administrative Council stating that the policy was applicable only to Duke administration, faculty, and staff and not to students "except where there is overlap." Unable to answer questions on the precise scope of the new UPPAC policy, Cole explained that his public comments had been left "purposefully vague." When asked if the policy could be understood to prohibit student groups from using off-campus segregated facilities, Robert L. Price, dean of Trinity College, responded opaquely, "It may be interpreted that way."[92]

The segregated facilities issue had now taken center stage. Various student groups, citing, among other arguments, "freedom of choice," "moral considerations," and "legislative overreach," had come down on different sides of the issue. The administration had issued a seemingly expansive prohibition on the use of segregated facilities but excluded student groups from its reach. The final twist occurred when advocates for a student referendum on the ASDU ban announced that they had collected the seven hundred student signatures needed to force a campus-wide vote. The referendum was scheduled for November 7.

Faced with the upcoming student referendum, the AAS voted to boycott the vote. In a resolution addressed to the university, the AAS declared that it would refrain from participating in a process "designed to determine whether the black student on this campus should be recognized as a human being." As ballots on the referendum were being cast, twenty-five of Duke's Black students stood in front of the voting table on West Campus in silent protest. At 1:20 p.m., they ripped up their ballots and walked off. "We oppose the fact that students are trying to decide something that is our inherent right as members of this University," an AAS spokesperson commented.[93]

When the votes were counted, fully 60 percent of students voting came down *against* ASDU's resolution prohibiting the use of segregated facilities by student groups. Asked for a comment, Kinney stated that the "vote was revealing to many people, and in many ways." He also commented on the decision by the AAS to boycott the vote. "The fact that some Negroes did not vote is to be respected," Kinney said, "yet is a potential sign of danger."[94]

....

The AAS met soon after the referendum. The segregated facilities controversy had now been escalating for twelve months with no clear statement of policy by the administration. With their fellow students having now rejected ASDU's prohibition, there was little confidence that the university would make a policy change in the near term. Also, the AAS had by then been meeting for more than seven months. Interactions at these meetings caused a fundamental change in how Black students perceived the segregated facilities issue. The meetings of the AAS, Becton explained, had led to the "increased realization that . . . things [like a change in the segregated facilities policy] were things that were due us, rather than things we ought to be requesting." As Becton described it, the changes sought were "rights, as opposed to privileges."[95] With this perspective, Duke's Black students decided to take action to force a policy change.

In Becton's view, the Black students had more power than they realized. To illustrate his point, he described how university housing office personnel had reacted when he and Hatcher sought their help in finding suitable off-campus housing. Because almost all rental units near campus were available to white tenants only, Becton and Hatcher decided that "the university had an *obligation* to find us some housing." Their approach was simple, Becton explained. "We walked into the housing office one day and . . . told them that we had spent two days down here looking for a house. . . . We indicated that we were [prepared to go public with the university's failure] to find housing for Black kids." The results were dramatic, Becton recounted. "In one hour, we got a phone call and got a house right behind East Campus . . . just a great place to live." This story helped the Black students "realize that the power was there," Becton noted. Soon, most AAS members agreed with his assessment that "the more active we were, the more likely we were to have some of our demands met."[96]

The students considered three strategies to put pressure on the university. "One, [we could] take over [a] building," Armstrong remembered, "two, [we could] go and ask for a meeting with Dr. Knight; and three, [we could] do something that would not obstruct justice but would bring attention to the university." The first option—a building takeover—was quickly dismissed. "At that time, we did not feel that the issues were sufficient to prompt that kind of action," Armstrong explained. "We [also lacked the] political savvy to be able to pull that off. And most of us were scared at that time." The second option, a meeting with Knight, would allow the students to convey the urgency of the issue directly to the Duke president. Such a meeting, however, would represent little more than "strongly pleading" for a policy change, a course that had already been attempted without success in the "open letter" published in the spring. Discussion turned to direct action. Armstrong remembered "everyone talking about the fact that Duke hated bad publicity." The students began to consider forms of protest, she recalled, that would "bring attention to Duke without being violent." In the end, the group settled on a "study-in" in the anteroom directly outside President Knight's office as the "most politically expedient way" to accomplish these objectives. "We needed to bring some national attention to our demand," Becton explained. "Basically, power concedes nothing without a demand. . . . That is what it was about." Brown held a similar view. "We felt that this was the only thing that would have some impact," she recalled.[97]

The strategy also garnered support from AAS members because it was seen as less threatening to the university than other options. Since the students would be studying, the protest would be orderly and quiet. "To 'study-in,'" Armstrong explained, "meant in the process of us getting our education we were also trying to be heard. It was an acceptable thing because Duke students ought to be studying."[98] The students came from families that had taught them to follow the rules. Notwithstanding agreement that direct action was necessary to force a policy change, they settled on a strategy that would apply pressure to the university while causing as little disruption as possible.

Before initiating the protest, Hopkins, Joyce Hobson, McLeod, and Becton presented the university with a resolution demanding that it clarify its policy on the use of segregated facilities and threatening disruption if it failed to do so. The resolution framed the segregated facilities issue as part of a broader pattern of university disregard for the needs of its Black students. "It is now obvious that a true sense of . . . responsibility towards us . . . as a part of this University community is lacking," the resolution declared, "and that a willingness to defend our rights here . . . is even more lacking." On behalf of Duke Afro-Americans, the resolution demanded that "our administration *IMMEDIATELY* announce and explicitly institute a policy of total prohibition of patronization of segregated establishments by *ANY* official University organization." If the demand were not acted upon on or before 6:00 p.m. on November 12, the resolution concluded, "we . . . will enact . . . plans to disrupt the functioning of the University until our demands are met!" Looking back a decade later, Hopkins remained impressed by the urgency of the resolution. "Boy, I was crazy in those days," he commented. "The sky was the limit evidently. . . . Telling people we were going to disrupt the university."[99]

Knight's response was unequivocal. In a memorandum dated November 12, the Duke president made it "absolutely clear that the University will accept no ultimatum" and threatened "major disciplinary action" if the Black students disrupted the campus. Knight also dismissed the demand for immediate action, noting that a review of the university's use of segregated facilities was in process and "cannot be resolved hastily." Making clear that Duke would not circumvent established decision-making channels, he suggested that the Black students express their "opinions to the appropriate deans," so they may be given "consideration during discussions of the issues."[100]

Knight was now precisely in the situation he had hoped to avoid. He had concluded months earlier that he "could never have approved of university groups using segregated facilities." Yet attempts to resolve the issue without a confrontation had failed. Faced with the threat of disruption, Knight almost certainly recognized that any opportunity to resolve the issue without conflict was now gone.[101]

On Monday, November 13, at 8:30 a.m., thirty-five members of the AAS walked into the Allen Building and sat down just outside Knight's office for a "study-in." Photographs of the event show smartly dressed student protesters sitting closely together on the floor. Some smoked, and a handful of the men wore dark sunglasses. All read quietly or did other homework. "People really did work," Howard remembered. "We were all reading something about Black history. I remember in the press picture, Stef McLeod had *Black Power* by Stokely Carmichael." Brown recalled "a very good sense of group cohesiveness." A poster propped against the wall declared, "We Are Studying In For: Human Dignity," and another said, "Black Sisters Together with Our *Soul Men* to the *End*." The students asked to speak to Knight but were told that he was in New York.[102]

Members of the administration talked to student leaders both before and during the protest to prevent a physical confrontation. "I was very interested in keeping some semblance of egress and ingress in the situation which then kept us from having to impose any kind of sanction," Griffith commented. "We didn't want to move on it," he remembered. "We were looking for excuses *not* to move on it in a hard-line kind of way." Although access to the president's office was completely blocked for almost three hours, no direct confrontation occurred. The administration, however, was prepared for any contingency. Nine Durham policemen equipped with helmets and nightsticks were "on-call" in the campus security office throughout the protest.[103]

Around midday, a group of white students arrived and asked to join the protest. The offer was rejected, and when several white students refused to leave voluntarily, they were forcibly carried out. "I think most of us felt like we had to go inside and stand up on our own, first," Becton explained. "At that point, it had to be about *us* getting together." "We always had a strong thing with the liberal white students," Hopkins recounted, "who just wanted to come over and support us. . . . We were uncomfortable with that. . . . We were saying, you got problems too. So let's all deal with our [own] problems and come together on that." For participants in the early civil rights demonstrations, the move away from multiracial protest was stark. "It was not 'Black-and-white together,'" movement veteran and Duke professor Jack Preiss recalled. "It was a self-identification by Blacks that was exclusive. Whites were not accepted as part of it."[104]

Students remained outside the president's office for seven hours. Discussions between the university and the AAS took place on and off throughout the day. An audio recording of internal AAS deliberations makes clear that the substance of Duke's segregated facilities policy was never addressed in the course of these discussions. Instead, the talks focused exclusively on the university's demand that the Black students suspend their protest until UPPAC had the opportunity to meet and consider a policy change. The university explained that UPPAC was not scheduled to meet for nine days and Knight would need two additional days to consider any policy change the committee recommended. The university asked for suspension of the protest for eleven days.

On a divided vote, the protesters initially decided to accept the university's request for additional time. Just as they were notifying university representatives of their decision, however, the students learned that another significant university committee—the Student Faculty Administrative Committee (SFAC)—was scheduled to meet that very afternoon. Believing that SFAC should be able to make a definitive policy recommendation on an issue that had been in the spotlight for almost a year, the students reversed their earlier decision to stand down for almost two weeks. They demanded an answer from the university within two days. In a response that only a bureaucrat could comprehend, the students were told that their proposed timetable was unworkable, and the SFAC only had jurisdiction to make policy for Duke's undergraduate colleges. To change the segregated facilities policy for the entire university, the students were told, UPPAC action would be necessary. Why an emergency UPPAC meeting could not be convened in less than nine days was never explained.

The students met to consider a response. They found the university's rigid stance unacceptable. Recalling the decision by the AAS to refuse participation in the undergraduate referendum on segregated facilities, one student argued that "this is the same thing as . . . boycotting the polls. . . . No one has the right to vote on whether you are human." A change in the university's segregated facilities policy, one student argued, would never happen if considered under the school's normal decision-making procedures. "It's like Stokely Carmichael says," he explained. "We are hoping the university will act in good faith. But when push comes to shove, there is no such thing as good faith. They will give us the run-around as long as they can. You can put it off 10 days from now, you can put it off 20 days from now, you can put it off 'ever' from now."[105]

In the end, all agreed that the university's request for an additional eleven days to consider a policy change was unacceptable. "Why should we have to wait for SFAC or UPPAC or any kind of 'FAC'?" one student asked. "I'd like to hear a justification," another declared, "for why UPPAC, in a matter of emergency—and this is obviously an emergency—cannot get themselves together in less than eleven days." "These people can act when they get ready to act," another student insisted.[106] Clearly, the university's efforts to use bureaucratic procedures as a way to delay action on a moral issue was no longer acceptable.

By a unanimous vote, the students decided to suspend further protest until 6:00 p.m. on Wednesday, November 15. This would give Duke two days to respond. The scheduled SFAC meeting could convene later in the day, and Knight would have twenty-four hours to consider any recommended policy change.[107] The AAS representatives left to advise the university of the students' position.

As they prepared to disperse, the student protesters checked the radio to see whether reports of the study-in had been picked up by local or national news outlets. Within moments of turning on the radio, they heard, "Protesting Negro students lay down in the hallway today in the office of Duke University President Douglas Knight. They said they were protesting a student body referendum which supported the patronization of segregated places."[108]

The goal of creating pressure on Duke to act by generating unfavorable publicity for the school had been achieved. Before leaving, the protesters had one additional matter to attend to. "Let's leave this place just like we found it," one student admonished. Although participants in the study-in would now be seen as "militants" by many in the university community, their parents had clearly taught them to never leave a mess behind.

Soon after learning of the students' position, a university representative delivered a prepared statement. Formal in tone and substance, the statement spoke only to "process" issues and failed entirely to communicate any sensitivity to the feelings of hurt, frustration, and urgency that had prompted the students to protest. "The University cannot and will not take action under the threat of an ultimatum," the statement said. "Serious efforts were made today by appropriate officials of the University and by spokesmen of the group of students here today to agree on a procedure" for the university's reconsideration of its segregated facilities policy. "Unfortunately," the statement concluded, "agreement on these questions of procedure could not be reached."[109] Thus, the university's statement made clear that the school—not the students—would determine how and when any change in the segregated facilities policy would occur.

The SFAC met that afternoon. The segregated facilities issue consumed the entirety of the committee's four-hour meeting. Working with SFAC representatives to craft the resolution to be voted on at the meeting, Knight had competing goals. He wanted to show movement by the university on the issue while avoiding the appearance that the study-in had forced him to act. To downplay the impact of the protest, Knight wanted any change in the university's stance on segregated facilities to be framed as a "clarification" of the current policy, not a new pronouncement. The SFAC did as the president desired. The committee recommended that the university "promptly" reiterate its existing policy with respect to segregated facilities and, "if indicated, rephrase the statement so as to include student organizations and groups." With this recommendation, Knight concluded that he had the internal authorization to announce a policy change, even without UPPAC input.[110]

Between his strong letter to the Afro-American students on Sunday night and the university's refusal to make any policy change in the face of an ultimatum, Knight could fairly claim by Monday evening that the university had gotten the better of the student protesters. Local papers the next day carried headlines like "Defeat of Sit-In" and "Dr. Knight, Not Protesting Group, Still President of His University." Responding to a story on Knight's strong actions in the *Charlotte News*, trustee Edwin Jones wrote, "This is wonderful and is the sort of stand I have been hoping you would take. . . . Congratulations!"[111]

But events had yet to play out fully. On Wednesday evening, Hopkins took the step Knight had insisted upon. He withdrew any AAS ultimatum. "At this point we have not planned any further action," the AAS chairman announced. "We are waiting peacefully for a couple of days for a statement from the administration."[112]

Now that the threat of protest had been removed, at least temporarily, Knight felt that he could announce a new policy without violating his pledge "to accept no ultimatum." On Friday, November 17, less than four days after the study-in ended, Knight announced that Duke's "stated practice on discrimination and the use of segregated facilities, which has applied to faculty and staff organizations since late September, will in the future apply also to student organizations." Knight said that the announcement would have been made "in the normal course of events," even claiming that the consideration of the ASDU resolution, along with the "threat of disruption" made by the AAS, had delayed action. "To have accepted such an ultimatum would have been a major step toward anarchy," Knight said, "and it is now clear . . . that decisions cannot be based on ultimatums and disruptive action, rather than . . . principle." A few days later, the Duke Alumni Association announced that it would no longer hold events at segregated facilities.[113]

For the moment, the AAS was satisfied. The policy gives "Negro students something that should have been there" all along, Joyce Hobson commented, "something necessary." Hopkins saw significance in the policy change. "The action of Dr. Knight has shown that Duke has accepted its role of responsibility to all members of its community," he commented. "The statement means that black students can now have a meaningful identity with Duke as their school." In private, members of the AAS saw the study-in as a major victory. "It made us realize the power we had," Becton recalled, "because it was the first massive thing . . . that produced some action. [It] showed the kids what coming together was all about." "What it represented to us wasn't the end; it was the beginning," Armstrong remembered. "We felt like if we could get them to listen to us on that issue, then it was time to get them to listen to us on other issues."[114]

Some trustees and many alumni reacted to the events on campus with anger and dismay. For them, the study-in showed that Black Power had made its way to the Duke campus. They feared that the racial violence engulfing many parts of the country would soon follow. Perhaps even more concerning, trustees and alumni saw the change in the university's segregated facilities policy as capitulation to Black student protesters. Trustee Edwin Jones, who had written initially praising Knight for his strong stand, was not happy about Duke's "clarification" of the segregated facilities policy. "Regardless of prior statements in the newspapers the Administration of Duke University gave in to the Afro-American students and gave them all they asked for," he wrote. "I suppose they are to be criticized for not asking for more. This, of course, shows who is running the University." Board member George V. Allen particularly rejected the "revolutionary methods" used by the protesters. Other alumni were equally critical, urging Knight to expel the protesters, calling the study-in "repugnant," and warning that support for Duke was fast diminishing "in light of the apparent appeasement attitude of Duke officials . . . in allowing the continued actions by these ilk."[115]

Knight responded to every letter. He defended his actions by explaining that he had successfully established two principles: "1) to settle the question of ultimatums, which we did, and 2) to verify the University's position on non-discrimination." To those who said he had given in to the students, he countered that "only after the threat of destructive action on campus was retracted did we take our firm position against discrimination." The university had "no intention of giving in to any group of students," he said, "no matter what their color, if they try to make their point by disrupting the operation of the University."[116]

Despite these explanations, Knight knew that the segregated facilities controversy had further damaged his standing with conservative elements of the university community. "People on both sides were getting so strenuous on these issues that there was no way to get to any kind of reasoned position that wouldn't be assailed," he explained. During the entire period, Knight saw a "series of alternations between the pressure on the 'left' and the unyielding resistance of the 'right.'" "The left delivers the ultimatum, the right ignores it," the Duke president explained. "And then if you happen to be caught in the middle where you have to make real decisions in what the computer people call 'real time,' why you are faced with impossible issues." Asked if he tried to resolve conflicts by moving those with widely divergent views to more reasonable positions, Knight responded soberly: "with everybody, and unsuccessfully all the way around."[117]

Knight was certainly correct in believing that the segregated facilities controversy presented him with an impossible political dilemma. His political capital would be diminished no matter what course he took. Hence, he saw himself as the victim of larger historical forces playing out at Duke in the late 1960s. Caught in the middle of colliding parties that would not act "reasonably," the Duke president became a lightning rod for fear, anger, and mistrust. But in fact, Knight himself was a key actor in the segregated facilities controversy. Indeed, the actions he took—or failed to take—reveal a great deal about his capacities as a leader when faced with racial conflict.

Knight knew that Duke's continued use of segregated facilities was untenable. "If you forced yourself to the ultimate issue," he said, "there was no doubt about where the university would need to be." Yet he did everything he could for as long as possible to avoid taking a principled public stand on the issue. "I hoped for some months," he recounted, "that we wouldn't . . . be forced to the ultimate issue . . . because, frankly, I didn't think that [was] good enough ground to do real battle on."[118] Despite escalating protests by Duke's Black students and expressions of deep concern by others in the university community, Knight concluded that it was not worth investing his political capital in a battle over the university's segregated facilities policy.

How did he reach these conclusions on an issue where his view of the "ultimate issue" was clear and required a change in university policy? One answer lies in how Knight viewed his role as the leader of an academic community. For him, the university was a place defined by mediation, critical discourse, and civility. In such a setting, disputes are resolved through rational discussion with the "leader" gently pressing opposing sides to reach consensus. This approach had worked spectacularly well at Lawrence. In a controversy such as the one over the use of segregated facilities at Duke, however, Knight confronted a dispute that was considered "existential" by both sides. For Black students, Duke was either committed to embracing them as equal members of the university community or it was not. For conservative elements, on the other hand, Duke was either committed to the right of white members of the university community to exercise "freedom of choice" in deciding where to socialize and with whom or it was not. There could be no consensus reached on these opposing positions. As Knight acknowledged, "reason and moderation no longer defined the forces you were working with." He came to feel that "whatever you did was wrong" in such a situation "because the constituents were so divided among themselves."[119]

Knight's approach to leadership was rooted in his personality. "Doug always wanted to go to bed at night thinking that he had pleased 100 percent of the people he had dealt with during the day," Anlyan commented. "Unfortunately, this was not possible in that era (or in any other)." Knight was also accustomed to deference. "He was completely unprepared by background and temperament," Bob Ashley, managing editor of the *Duke Chronicle*, commented perceptively, "to have his authority challenged."[120]

Knight was not passive on all issues. Indeed, where leadership was required to protect a value he considered "core" to the university, he could act with alacrity. Academic freedom was one such core value. In 1966, for example, trustees and alumni were highly critical when Marxist historian and political activist Herbert Aptheker was permitted to speak on campus. Knight was unapologetic. To one trustee, he wrote: "At the level of principle we have to defend the unpopular opinion; at the level of politics we have to be smart enough to expose gentlemen whom we would make more attractive if we denied them the chance to speak." Knight saw the exploration of unpopular ideas or political positions as "an essential university duty" and not an issue that can be avoided when raised. In addition to communists, he defended the right of Black Power leaders, antiwar activists, and atheists, among many others, to speak on campus.[121]

Unlike academic freedom, however, Knight saw the segregated facilities issue as one that could—even *should*—be avoided when raised. He did not see racial inclusion as a value that was "core" to the university. This was because of his attitudes on race. The Duke president held racial views that some would call "progressive," but he did so without deep personal conviction. He was fine with Black students attending historically white universities as long as they were "qualified" and played by Knight's notion of the "rules." But he did not see it as his responsibility to investigate, understand, and address the problems Duke's Black students encountered on campus. Hence, the Duke president could not grasp the growing outrage Duke's Black students felt about the school's strong connections to Hope Valley, including his own personal membership in the club. "Country club issues and the like couldn't have been less important to me," Knight said in 1988. "I looked on [the students'] point as very well taken. [But] politically [resignation] was a very unwise thing to do because it offended a lot of people in the community."[122]

Whatever the cause, Knight paid a huge price for his failure to lead on the segregated facilities issue. Not only did his passivity prolong the controversy, but it also impaired his ability to lead on controversial issues that would arise in the future. Perceived as reactive on all sides, and challenged over a myriad of issues, he was increasingly marginalized in future decision-making.

By the end of 1967, Duke had been desegregated for more than four years and the first class of Black undergraduates had graduated in the spring of 1967. Against the backdrop of national events, even a benign protest like the November study-in was deeply threatening to conservative elements of the Duke community. The gap in perception on racial issues was growing, not narrowing. Two differing views on the segregated facilities issue illustrate the point. "Once they decided to have Black people there, they should have known they didn't need to be having things at segregated facilities," study-in participant Brown reflected. "What are they going to do with their Black students if one of them belongs to one of these [organizations] and they want to have something at a segregated facility? That's just common sense, but nobody thought about what it meant to have us [at Duke] and [nobody] cared."[123]

Knight, of course, saw matters differently. Asked if the men who ran Duke "should have known" that the continued use of segregated facilities following the arrival of Black students was an obvious contradiction, Knight responded, "I'm not sure they are quite right to say, 'They should have known.' . . . That's too simple."

> If they would say instead, "How tragic that they didn't know. How sad that they didn't know. Why don't human beings understand these things?," I would agree. I don't think they can say, "They should have known." Because . . . you've got to remember where these . . . folks were coming from. . . . It would be quite unrealistic to assume that . . . the university, in that location, with those characters playing their roles, could remotely have understood that if you meant to admit Black students you meant there should no longer be segregated facilities related to the university, and no longer a president that belonged to that [segregated] country club.

According to Knight, "People didn't remotely think of that." He acknowledged that these failures of insight are "no exoneration."[124]

By the end of 1967, Knight finally recognized that any hope of finding a path forward for his administration and the Black students required opening a direct line of communication with them. Just a week after the segregated facilities controversy was resolved, Knight wrote to Griffith, asking, "When would it seem wisest to you to try to sit down with that group of Negro students? I am sure you have a good many thoughts about it, and I'll welcome your judgment."[125]

CHAPTER 4

We Were Their Sons and Daughters

Occupation of University House

In the spring semester of 1968, student activism at Duke sharply intensified almost as soon as the semester began. In late November 1967, Douglas Knight had asked William Griffith for suggestions on the best time to "try to sit down with that group of Negro students." Griffith must have recommended "very soon" because, on January 9, Knight met for the first time with representatives of the AAS. At the meeting, Knight asked for a list of Black student "problem areas." Although no specific time frame was set, the students agreed to provide him with their list.[1]

During the same week, the university issued, for the first time, regulations on pickets and protests. The new rules sought to distinguish between "legitimate forms of picketing and protesting" and "illegitimate" protests that "disrupt the orderly operations of the institution" or "jeopardize public order or safety." In the event that "proper University authorities" determined that an "illegitimate" form of protest was underway, they were instructed to direct protesters to "cease and desist" within a specified period of time. If the protesters failed to do so, they would be subject to discipline by the university as well as possible arrest and prosecution under applicable criminal laws.[2]

Through the mid-1960s, Duke was hardly known as a hotbed of student activism. Indeed, until April 1968, one observer noted, "white students had not been motivated to demonstrate en masse over any issue." In a March 1968 *Sports Illustrated* article on the student climate at Duke University, sociology professor Jack Preiss went so far as to label students at the school as members of the "timid generation." If activism was not widespread at Duke, however, by this point, the university had a core group of thirty to forty student activists who considered themselves part of the New Left. Members of this group immediately began to test the new pickets and protests regulations. Small demonstrations were held when army recruiters came to campus on January 9, navy recruiters on January 11, and representatives of Dow Chemical Company in early February. Although one student was found guilty of violating the new rules, the pickets and protests regulations proved difficult to enforce. Most problematic was the "waiting period" provided for in the regulations. These were being "abused," Knight said, "in such a fashion as to aggravate congestion and disorder." After a couple of months, Knight announced that the "waiting period" in the regulations was "suspended."[3]

As members of the New Left protested against the war, the AAS held elections for new leadership. Although Chuck Hopkins sought reelection as chairman, his candidacy turned out to be controversial. He faced opposition from those who favored a less confrontational approach to the administration. "There was one faction," Brenda Armstrong explained, "that had a very acute sense of how Duke was mistreating . . . and acting against Blacks. [They] wanted to do something about the things that were going on. Then there was a faction," she described, "that felt as strongly, but was not willing to [take] action. [They] wanted to talk about it, . . . to give the administration a chance."[4]

As the election approached, Hopkins and his supporters worried that control of the AAS might be lost to the more conservative group. Faced with this possibility, Hopkins withdrew his candidacy and threw his support behind Armstrong; she then became a consensus candidate. "We had reached a point," Hopkins recalled, "where I was over here, Stef was over here, somebody else [was over] there. . . . Brenda had a lot of respect from everybody. She was voted in to pull everybody together." When the votes were counted, Armstrong prevailed. In her, the AAS had a leader who could bring the group together. "I was [conciliatory] to the conservative faction that couldn't fight me," Armstrong recalled, "as well as acceptable to the more radical element." Hopkins agreed. "She did a good job," Hopkins said. "She held people together."[5]

On February 8, 1968, national events rocked Black students at Duke and throughout the nation. State highway patrolmen fired on a crowd of students on the campus of South Carolina State University in Orangeburg, South Carolina, following a protest to desegregate a local bowling alley. Three students were killed and twenty-seven other protesters wounded in what came to be known as the Orangeburg Massacre. Forensic reports showed that many of the victims had been shot in the back. The Orangeburg Massacre "hurled legions of students to the left," historian Ibram X. Kendi observed. Soon, a wave of sympathy protests by Black college students swept the country.[6]

With racial activism increasing, the assassination of Martin Luther King Jr. had a profound impact on the university and the country. King, who had spoken at Duke in 1964, was in Memphis, Tennessee, at the time of his assassination, supporting Black city sanitation workers who were striking to protest unequal wages and working conditions. His murder intensified all the racist terror the civil rights movement had been fighting against for years.[7]

The night after the tragedy, a group of 250 Duke students—almost all of them white—occupied University House, Knight's official residence. They remained for almost two days. After leaving, the group reassembled on Duke's main quadrangle. With their number increasing eventually to more than 1,500, they held a four-day sit-in that brought the university to a virtual standstill and came to be known as the "Silent Vigil." Participants demanded that Duke respond to the King assassination with immediate, concrete actions that would clearly demonstrate the institution's commitment to racial justice. They called on the university to grant its nonacademic employees a significant wage increase and, even more importantly, the right to bargain collectively. Further, the students demanded that Knight resign from the segregated Hope Valley Country Club.

The events at Duke following King's assassination illuminate the racial dynamics in place at the university in the spring of 1968. Caught between stasis and change, they show how far the university was willing to go to dismantle the "plantation system" that had circumscribed employer-employee relations at Duke for decades. Occurring just five months after the AAS study-in on segregated facilities—and only ten months before the Black student takeover of the Allen Building—the April 1968 protests highlight the different ways that Black and white Duke students experienced protest. They also expose the role that race played in how the university perceived—and responded to—demands for change. In the end, the University House occupation and the Silent Vigil dramatized how a white institution struggled with its racial past even as it aggressively continued to pursue its dream of national prominence.

....

Martin Luther King Jr.'s assassination on Thursday, April 4, 1968, sent a country already reeling from conflict to a new level of crisis. "In Chicago," historian William Chafe observed, "twenty blocks of the downtown business area burst into flame, set afire by rioters, as Mayor Daley ordered police to 'shoot to kill' arsonists. More than one hundred American cities witnessed violence. Soldiers garbed in battle gear set up a machine-gun emplacement atop the nation's Capitol. More than 5,500 troops were finally required to quiet the weeklong expression of screaming fury."[8]

For Duke's Black students, the assassination was a stunning moment of truth. "I remember that evening so well," Armstrong recounted. "It was 6:30 and I was studying on the floor of the dormitory. The girl who lived next door came in and said, 'Did you know Dr. King was killed?' and I laughed at her. I thought she was being funny. And then I turned the TV on." Soon, Armstrong's shock turned to anger. "No one could understand how I felt," she explained. "That was the angriest I've ever been. . . . I hadn't gotten to the point," Armstrong recalled, "where I [believed] that there were people who didn't like me because I was Black or [who were] unwilling to give me a chance. . . . There were people in my dorm that just said, 'Somebody would have shot him anyway' and 'He deserved to be shot.' Then I knew," Armstrong remembered.[9]

Other Black students responded with similar rage. In a political science class on the morning after the assassination, a Black student said that she was "sickened" by liberal white Americans who "never did more than talk about how liberal [they] are." Bertie Howard, like other Black students at Duke, experienced fear when she heard the news. "I was babysitting at [political science professor John H. Strange's] house the night King was killed," she recollected. "I just remember being afraid, because Strange had done a lot with people in the Black community. If the Klan would get anybody, they would come and get John. I remember locking the doors." For many, the feelings of grief were overwhelming. One Black student attending class the morning after King's death "began crying as he tried to explain how he felt when he saw his mother come home after working all day scrubbing people's floors and cleaning up after a white family."[10]

Like so many of her colleagues, Armstrong knew that King's death would alter the struggle for civil rights. "They just killed the spirit of anything that Black people wanted to do peacefully," she remembered thinking. "They took our prince." These deep feelings of anger and loss led many Black students to turn inward. "Our initial reaction," Hopkins explained, "was to separate ourselves from what was happening."[11]

Among white members of the Duke community, reactions varied. Some were unfazed by the news. "There were a great many members of the Duke constituency who didn't care whether Martin Luther King lived or died," Knight recounted. "They felt he was disruptive." The *Duke Chronicle* described "students who clapped or yelled from their windows in ecstasy at the news of Dr. King's death." Others, like the Duke president, showed more concern. Knight was on his way home from a dinner in Winston-Salem, North Carolina, when his Black driver, George Gilmore, shared the news. "Dr. King has been shot and I'm afraid," Gilmore told Knight. Knight knew that Gilmore was concerned not only about how the Black community in Durham would respond but also how white people would react. "He knew better than I that, even as we drove, there were a good many white people rejoicing over that violence," Knight wrote. "I was as worried as he." Griffith focused on how the Black community in Durham would react. "The assassination of Martin Luther King was traumatic," he explained. "There was concern that the Black community would go berserk."[12]

The assassination had a powerful impact on many white students. King's visit to campus in 1964 loomed large in their minds. "Martin had spoken in Page Auditorium a few years earlier," David M. Henderson recalled. "Many of us who heard him . . . knew we were in the presence of a godly man. We were touched by his life and his death." John C. "Jack" Boger remembered the speech as "one of the most prominent events of our freshman year." Boger was attending the symposium "The Theology of Hope" when he learned that King had been shot. "The theology of hope seemed instantaneously irrelevant," he wrote later. "I left, stunned at the news." But even those who had not seen King were deeply moved. "I wept. I was afraid," one student remembered. "I don't think I could capture the atmosphere of those days," observed another student, who was a freshman in 1968. "There are no words to describe . . . how it felt to try and face a black student and look him in the eye in those first hours after the assassination." David K. Birkhead, former editor of the *Duke Chronicle*, summarized the feelings of many: "The world just did not seem the same after the death of Dr. King."[13]

A small coterie of members of the New Left at Duke saw the King assassination as a call to action. This was a chance to recruit other students to join their movement. Around midnight on Thursday, a group met in Birkhead's dorm room to discuss their response. "It was the hard core," Henderson commented. "We would have been the ones who said, 'We're going to do something. If other people come along, that's fine.'"[14]

Soon, the group in Birkhead's room learned that individuals active in the University Christian movement were meeting separately to discuss how to respond to King's murder. At around 2:00 a.m. the two groups began meeting jointly. The University Christian movement had already planned a Memorial Vigil for King at noon on Friday and flyers for the event had been distributed. They agreed that a candlelight march on Friday evening would be held, with the details for the march announced at the Memorial Vigil the next day.[15]

Discussion then turned to the destination for the march. After much debate, it was decided that the march would head to Hope Valley, what Henderson called "the symbol of wealthy white dominance" in Durham. While in Hope Valley, marchers would split into groups, canvasing the area to ask residents to sign a "statement of concern" that was being drafted.[16]

The Memorial Vigil at noon the next day lasted only a short time due to rainy weather. Soon, discussion turned to plans for the evening. At this point, both Griffith and Strange joined the discussions. Griffith was trusted by many of the student leaders, while Strange had become an informal adviser to many of the protesters. Henderson described him as "liberal," not "personally radical, just effective." Both were uneasy about the planned march to Hope Valley. Griffith's primary concern was safety. "At that time," Griffith recalled, "citizens in Hope Valley and other areas were making sure they had guns and ammunition in their houses." Learning of plans for students to go door-to-door in Hope Valley to solicit signatures, Griffith worried that these residents "weren't about to have people come off the streets into their homes. They were afraid."[17]

Griffith suggested that the march should instead head to Duke Forest, a neighborhood populated by many Duke faculty members and administrators. Griffith even suggested University House as a possible destination. "I felt that if they were going to carry any message," Griffith explained, "they ought to carry it to the Duke community." Strange suggested that students obtain signatures in Duke Forest for a petition on racial justice as well as an advertisement scheduled to appear in the *Durham Morning Herald* supporting racial equality and progress. Once Duke Forest was settled upon as the destination for the march, Griffith provided the group with a map of the area and pointed out the location of faculty residences and University House.[18]

Because it continued to rain, a group of about ten students and faculty went inside to discuss the evening's plans. They were joined by Peter Brandon, the Durham organizer for Local 77, the union that had been seeking to represent Duke's nonacademic employees in collective bargaining with the university. The group then decided that the destination for the march would be Knight's house. The demands would be framed as "an approach to Knight for a 'positive action'" and would ask the Duke president to take specific steps to advance the cause of racial justice at Duke. Brandon suggested that the demands focus specifically on the plight of Duke's nonacademic employees and his proposal was quickly accepted. Support for these workers had been slowly growing among Duke students and faculty since the mid-1960s. A Student-Faculty Committee had formed in late 1966 to support the nonacademic employees and, in April 1967, two hundred students joined the workers on a picket line to pressure the university to accept impartial arbitration of employee grievances. A number of students and faculty actively supported early efforts by the university's nonacademic employees to unionize. There was "very much a pro–working class sentiment among the core group" of activists, Henderson commented. "As soon as we started formulating demands, those demands regarding the workers were among them." The group also agreed that marchers who wanted to do so would sit-in at Knight's house until their demands were met.[19]

By evening, the students had crystallized around four demands. The first requested that Knight sign a *Durham Morning Herald* advertisement that would be circulated for additional signatures in Duke Forest that evening. The ad said, in part, that the murder of King had presented each citizen a stark choice "between the promise of America the Free or a harvest of death and inhumanity which is the result of continued oppression of black Americans." It stated that "we are all implicated" in allowing a society to flourish that "could take the life of a man who asked only for the freedom of his people" and outlined specific steps it urged white Americans to take to support racial progress.[20]

The next two demands took aim at the "plantation system" at Duke. The first of these supported the nonacademic employees in their ongoing struggle to gain the right to bargain collectively with the university. It asked Knight to establish a committee of students, faculty, workers, trustees, and administrators to "consider" collective bargaining and union recognition for these workers.

The second of these two demands asked Duke to establish $1.60 per hour as the base level of compensation for Duke's nonacademic employees—the national minimum wage for "for-profit" organizations. It requested that Knight make finding the funds for these raises a first priority for the university—ahead of any building programs.

The final demand was directed at the university's continuing relationship with the segregated Hope Valley Country Club. It called on Knight to resign his membership in the club. Knight, of course, had heard this demand before.[21]

Identifying negotiators for the group was the next step. Margaret "Bunny" Small, Birkhead, and Jonathan Kinney were chosen by a vote of the group. All three were active in campus politics, held leadership positions in student organizations, and were well known to Duke administrators. Kinney was the president of ASDU, Birkhead had served as editor of the *Duke Chronicle,* and Bunny Small had been elected president of the Pan-Hellenic Council before resigning soon after the start of her term.[22]

In the late afternoon, a flyer for the 7:00 p.m. memorial procession to Duke Forest was distributed on campus. To emphasize the solemnity of the occasion, students were instructed to "wear clothes appropriate for mourning" and "bring candles to carry."[23]

Until Friday evening, April 5, Henderson noted, the core group of politically active students at Duke had found it "extremely difficult to organize a demonstration of any size." "When we did decide to go to Knight's house," Henderson recalled, organizers thought, "'Well, we might get 20 people to go.'" Therefore, they were "ecstatic" when 450 students and faculty converged on the Alumni Lounge on a rainy night to receive instructions for the procession. The emotions aroused by King's assassination, plus the fact that "the issues were not new ones," explained the turnout, Henderson recounted. Seeing the size of the group, he "knew we had seized a moment in history." Whatever the cause—especially given the small number of politically active students at Duke—the large turnout meant that most of the marchers had little, if any, prior protest experience. Many were also unaware that a sit-in at University House was planned.[24]

Strange addressed the marchers before they headed out. He sought to forge a connection between the predominantly white protesters and the life and work of King. Describing the slain civil rights leader's commitment to nonviolence, Strange spoke of King's belief that the "Black man cannot be free until the white man is free." He recalled King's "regrettable conclusion" that "the white moderate who is more devoted to order than to justice" posed "the

Negro's great stumbling block in his [d]rive towards freedom." King called for "you and me, who probably are moderate," Strange told the marchers, "to walk in the rain for a long distance—past dark woods—to present a list of grievances to the president of the university. . . . We are gathered here tonight," Strange said, "to express our conviction that [King] shall not have died in vain. . . . Let us stand and act now," he concluded.[25]

It took about forty minutes for the procession to reach Knight's house. Given that King, a minister, had preached the power of Christian love as a weapon for social change, it is not surprising that the march had a strong religious dimension. "It was like a pilgrimage, a crusade," Henderson said. "We could have as easily been singing 'Onward Christian Soldiers' as whatever it was we were singing." Small observed that many of the leaders came from religious backgrounds. "The whole development," she explained, "came from a circle of people who [had] religious affiliations—the University Christian movement, the YWCA—so there was a shared framework."[26]

While the vast majority of protesters were white, some of Duke's Black student leaders joined the march, including Armstrong (the chair of the AAS at the time), Hopkins, Stef McLeod, and Howard. If Duke's white students felt passion born from protest for a noble cause, Black students experienced the march differently. According to Armstrong, these students were still reeling from the assassination of King. They remained confused about the motivations and commitment of their white colleagues. On the march, Howard wondered whether the planned sit-in at Knight's house would actually occur. "I remember . . . saying," she recounted, "'Well, let's see what they are going to do 'cause we don't think they're going to do it.'"[27]

When the marchers arrived at Knight's driveway, Henderson wrote, "Dr. Strange announced that some of the group would stay and that he would take those who would not stay to canvass the neighborhood for signatures and contributions for the advertisement." Griffith had called Knight to warn him that the students were marching to his house. "Mrs. Knight and I went to the door of University House to meet them," Knight wrote later. "I started to try to talk with them, but it was dark outside and both of us invited them in." A few marchers had trickled into University House before the Knights issued their invitation. Soon their numbers increased and, eventually, about 250 students entered the house. "It was dusk" when we reached the house, student Peter Neumann recalled, "and he couldn't see the crowd. The news that he had invited us into his house went like lightning to the back of the line. We couldn't believe our luck, but . . . Knight's beginning road to hell was paved with his good intentions." Neumann saw the shock Knight was experiencing. "By the time I entered his house," he reported, "Knight, standing at the door, was in a state of near catatonic immobility." Another student observed that Knight was "speechless" when he came through the front door of his house and found 250 "students sitting quietly in his living room." The moment was powerful. Sally Avery remembered entering Knight's house as "the moment I became a radical."[28]

Knight later acknowledged "what a wild thing it must have seemed" to open his house to the marchers. His reasons for doing so were complicated. For one thing, the Duke president viewed University House, completed under his direction in 1966, as both his personal residence and as a university building constructed to entertain large groups. Because the students did not attempt to enter the Knight family's living quarters, the Duke president saw them as occupying public—not private—space. A second reason may have been that Knight, always confident in his powers of persuasion, thought that talking with the protesters might bridge differences and defuse an emotional situation. Perhaps most importantly, Knight knew a number of the protesters personally, having worked with them on university matters. He felt empathy for the others. Knight hoped that hospitality and conversation could ease the pain he knew the students were experiencing. "We did not see these distraught young people as demonstrators," Knight wrote, "nor did we—even at moments of great tension as the evening wore on—see them as invaders of our privacy." Knight explained later that he felt "very close" to the students and "wanted as little distance as possible between them and [himself] when the important questions turned up." "There were a lot of [students] who were hurting," Knight emphasized. "On a rainy night, if there was a possibility of getting in out of the rain to talk, why then let's do it."[29]

Knight's empathy for the students and sympathy for their cause would be sorely tested as the evening wore on.

....

The 250 students occupied a large living room. "I had never seen a living room so big," student Avery wrote: "brand-new, very modern, with almost no furniture on the . . . plush beige carpeting." One student commented that the room "looks like a Howard Johnson's Motor Lodge." Designed to accommodate large groups, "the living room stretched out the full width of the back of the house," Avery recalled, "with a glass wall rising two stories high." Even this grand space, however, soon became cramped. "The crowd at Knight's house got very large," one student remembered. "We really covered the floor."[30]

Kinney, Small, and Birkhead told Knight that they wanted to discuss the four demands. The three joined Knight in his private study, where negotiations went on for several hours, without progress. Throughout his Duke tenure, Knight had always been equivocal on the sensitive racial and political issues underlying the demands. "Birkhead would ask a point blank question, like 'Do you believe in collective bargaining?'" one student described, "and Knight would respond in typical fashion that the question couldn't be answered except in the 'proper frame of reference.'" Asked to add his name to the signatories for the *Durham Morning Herald* ad, Knight refused because the text said that "we are all implicated" in the King assassination. Knight explained that he could not make such a statement on behalf of the university since "some of [Duke's] trustees . . . did not feel implicated." Knight also felt that he could not agree to a wage increase for Duke's nonacademic employees. "I had to explain that I could not take such a step even if I would, and . . . why the option was not available to the university in any case." Looking back, Knight acknowledged that his "earnest efforts to make both of these points . . . were guaranteed to be baffling and frustrating to the negotiators."[31]

Every fifteen minutes or so, one of the student negotiators would emerge from the study to brief the larger group on the status of discussions. According to Henderson, "this was a pre-arranged signal [for protest organizers] to lead the cry that we were not leaving until we got the four items." Henderson reported that at one point, when the group started shouting, "Hell no, we won't go," the house "shook" and Knight was "visibly shocked." As to the four demands, every update was essentially the same—the Duke president was being "absolutely intransigent."[32]

Despite the lack of progress, the protesters remained upbeat. They sang protest songs throughout the evening, including "We Shall Not Be Moved," the American folk song that was a standard in the labor and civil rights movements. "There was a great deal of camaraderie," student Steven Burke recalled, and "pride that a gesture had been made." Along with these reactions, however, Burke also remembered "anxiety resulting from the continual whispers that Knight had decided to call in the police—which seemed unlikely."[33]

During the evening, some of the participants watched television coverage of the violence erupting in scores of American cities. At these times, exhilaration gave way to concern. "We were all sitting there with the TV on," Boger recalled, "watching buildings burning in Washington and rioting in cities and there was a real feeling that this was an apocalyptic age." "We heard reports that were frightening," Jeff Van Pelt wrote later: "riots in city after city, violent police response, machine gun emplacements on the Capitol steps." "The effect of watching the nation's capital burn," Henderson wrote, "intensified our determination to make the 'system' work."[34]

Armstrong had a different reaction to the television coverage. She could relate to the actions of the rioters. "I watched the riots on TV," she recalled. "People were saying how they couldn't understand how people could do that. I thought, 'How could they not?' I want to do that. But I don't have enough guts; or, I'd been socialized to believe that's just not the appropriate way of expressing your anger."[35] Despite violence in many other American cities, Durham remained quiet on Friday night.

Negotiations continued until 11:00 p.m., when Mrs. Knight interrupted to insist that her husband eat something. At this point, Knight spoke to the students. Introduced by Kinney over shouts of "Hell no, we won't go" and fidgeting with a matchbook, he addressed the protesters from a balcony overlooking the living room. Any hope that the Duke president would simply accept the four demands quickly evaporated. While Knight expressed sympathy for the goal of advancing racial justice, he told the protesters that he lacked the authority and willingness to make concessions in such a polarized environment. "If you think I can, sitting here, make many sorts of promises for an institution," Knight explained, "all I can say is that I simply don't have that power." For Knight, caution was the mode of the day, even in the face of a racial crisis that was exploding across the country—not to mention in his own living room. Acknowledging the need to "keep our society together," Knight nevertheless refused to make concessions under duress. "I don't think pushing one another is the answer," he commented. "I'm not setting out to push you, [and] I don't want to feel that I myself [am] pushed."[36]

Knight was scheduled to address a memorial service for King the next day in Duke Chapel. He told students that he planned to use these remarks to "suggest some concrete things that I feel that we have been doing in the university [and] some of the things we can do beyond it." He continued: "If we don't try to meet the frustrations of this world with violence . . . I still believe there are some things we can do," but "we've got to have enough order so that we can accomplish them."[37]

By now, the students in University House were insisting on immediate action. They were unsympathetic to Knight's plea for "order" and his request for time to pursue unspecified further steps. Would progress have been made in the civil rights movement after Selma, one student asked, if not for pressure from people who were willing to "get up and say, we're not going to take this any more? That's what we're saying," the student insisted, "and you don't seem to understand it!" Knight felt that he had supported racial progress at Duke. "One thing that I regret more than any of you know," he told the students, "is that . . . you don't really believe that I have fought for some of these things that you are talking about." Knight wrote later that the students "couldn't imagine how much I agreed with them." "I trust that you fought for these things," Boger responded, "but I think that there comes a time when we can't temporize, when we can't wait, when we have got to take a stand now."[38]

"What about your country club?" a student shouted. Despite demands that he resign from Hope Valley as early as November 1966, Knight seemed not to get it. Instead, he told the students that he "hadn't looked upon [Hope Valley] as the important issue." Knight argued, as he had previously, that he preferred to "work with members of *my* community who may not see the matter of country club membership as you do." Knight didn't consider it "wise" to cut himself off from the chance to work for change from *inside* the club.[39]

For Boger, however, time had run out on Knight's gradualist approach. "Tonight, tanks are in Washington; machine guns on Capitol Hill," he said. The country was "polarized" and Boger feared that without decisive action by men of good conscience, it would become even more divided. "When you say that you must stay in this country club to deal with interests in this community," he argued, "it may be that we have come to the time when we are going to have to start working in opposition to . . . some of the aims of some of these people in the community." "That is not a fair representation," Knight responded, once again not seeming to comprehend the urgency of the students nor the national moral crisis to which they were responding.[40]

Asked by graduate student Huck Gutman if the university would be willing to make a wage increase for nonacademic employees a higher funding priority than Duke's aggressive building program, Knight objected. Salaries for non-academic employees had increased by 50 percent in the past five years, Knight pointed out, and "the money for the buildings doesn't come from the same sources" as the money for wages. Knight acknowledged twenty years later that his comments were not helpful. "That's the sort of rational response that's not appropriate to that evening," he said. "It didn't have any impact."[41]

Boger spoke for the entire group when he described the urgency of the moment. "I really feel that an old order has changed in the United States of

America," Boger declared. "I think that the tanks that are right now rumbling down the streets of Washington [are] witness [to] this change." Boger continued:

> One of the things that we as young people will not allow in the future are institutions that remain . . . immoral. Good men involved in all levels of Duke University somehow cannot take moral stands because of various forces seemingly beyond anyone's control. . . . In this new order we have to stand up morally as institutions. We have to make stands . . . that meet the situation at hand. We cannot [face] a situation in which the country [is] falling apart with "maybes," "might happens in the future," and, "we're very concerned."

"I have no doubt of your deep concern," Boger told Knight, "but we have come here non-violently, as students of this university, to say we must do something important now. Duke University, we must do it now. We are non-violent, but we will not be moved." After Boger spoke, the *Duke Chronicle* reported, students "exploded into cheering and applause." "We'll stand behind you if you take a stand," they shouted at Knight.[42]

Although the "reasonable middle ground" Knight had tried to claim at Duke was disappearing before his eyes, he persisted. When students began another chorus of "hell no, we won't go," the Duke president responded, "I don't think we're going to settle the questions that torment us and tear us apart by your operating as though you were a mob, which I don't believe you are." Knight repeated that he could not act in response to a "mandate" or a "demand." "I think you have to understand," he told the students, "how we try to do our best in light of the other things we have to do in the University. I'm not trying to pussyfoot with you," he said. "I'm just telling you the truth about it."[43]

Knight's interaction with the students totally failed to have the calming effect he hoped for. In fact, his remarks only exacerbated an already tense situation. "He has a way of talking down to students that can be most antagonistic," Henderson commented. "Knight was terribly inept," another student observed, "and was rudely harangued by the crowd." Knight saw the disconnect. "Communication just went to hell in a hat," he observed later.[44]

After the confrontation with Knight, the protesters began to discuss whether they would stay overnight. Birkhead argued that remaining at Knight's house was a small sacrifice given events occurring in the country. Kinney was concerned about the impact that leaving might have on the Black students at Knight's house. Van Pelt had a somber recollection of why students stayed. "In a collapsing world," he wrote, "holding together in the name of what was right seemed the only sane thing to do." Ultimately, approximately 90 percent of the 250 students who entered University House Friday evening chose to remain overnight.[45]

Learning that the students were discussing the overnight occupation of University House, Knight told them he thought it was counterproductive. "My reaction . . . is that this very much limits my freedom to do the very thing that you are asking that we do together," he said. "It's as simple as that." Asked by a WDBS radio reporter what he would do if the protesters refused to leave, Knight made clear that he would not initiate a confrontation. "I certainly don't feel that removing them by force is an answer to our problems," he commented. "Yes, they may stay."[46]

The women who wished to occupy Knight's house overnight faced a problem—in April 1968, female Duke undergraduates who planned to spend the night off campus were still required to sign out of their dorms to a specific location. In a contradiction that captures the ambiguity of the protest, a substantial number of coeds were concerned about violating this rule. To applause from the students, Knight gave permission for Duke women to sign out to University House for the night.[47]

Meanwhile, negotiations resumed in the kitchen. Knight had an antagonistic relationship with Birkhead dating back to his time as editor of the *Duke Chronicle*. Knight asked that Birkhead be removed from the negotiating team. This request was accepted and Strange took his place. Still, no progress was made. According to Knight, by around 1:30 a.m., the group "could at least agree that nothing more would be accomplished that night." Exhausted, Knight went to bed. Avery remembered the Duke president "on his way to his bedroom, carefully stepping over the sleeping bodies, followed by his basset hound." Bob Ashley recalled Knight "looking beaten."[48]

By the end of the evening, protest leaders realized, according to Small, that Knight "was not going to negotiate with us; he wasn't going to do anything. That's where he was really a 'wuss,'" Small reflected. "He should have done something. [But] it wasn't in his character to step out on a limb."[49]

Both the atmosphere and the physical set-up in University House made sleep difficult. It was "a pretty tense situation," the student narrator of a Silent Vigil audiotape commented. "It was hard to stay calm and cool about the whole thing." The excitement also made sleep elusive. "There was a party atmosphere in that there was a bunch of people who were doing something that felt good," Burke remembered. Henderson called it a "festive atmosphere." Another student described the mood as one of "exhilaration" and "uncertainty."[50]

Black students in University House had mixed reactions to the unfolding events. Armstrong was concerned that Knight was setting a "trap" for the students and worried that police might still be called to evict the demonstrators. Deeply grieving King, she felt disconnected from the "festive atmosphere" she saw around her. Howard doubted whether the demonstration would succeed. "I don't think there were a lot of people who had any experience with activism in that group," she remembered, and "I'm not clear the sense of 'groupness' was there." Howard was also concerned about the level of commitment of the white students. "Part of it was 'stick-to-itiveness,'" she explained. "Even after they bedded down, I didn't think they were going to stay. . . . It was just a fun thing for a lot of people there."[51]

Griffith came by University House around 2:00 a.m., relieved that the students were safe. Griffith agreed with Knight's decision to allow the protesters to stay through the night. Knight "very carefully, and rightfully so," Griffith recalled, "never said 'leave,' which would have been a mistake. . . . He would have had to produce—[either to] have them leave or be reversed." Support for the president's decision, however, was far from unanimous. "The trustees, general public, and alumni felt" that allowing the protesters to stay "was a weak response," Griffith recounted, many people believing that Knight "should have kicked them out." "People were calling us from the University community and outside," Knight remembered. They were saying, "Now, do you want us to get force to put them out?"[52]

Pressure on Griffith and other administrators to end the occupation would build rapidly once morning arrived. To cover any contingency, a security force was stationed near the house.[53]

⋯⋯⋯⋯⋯⋯⋯⋯⋯⋯

Before leaving for campus on Saturday morning to speak at the memorial service for King, Knight spoke to the protesters for about twenty minutes. He again stated that he had not realized how important a symbol his Hope Valley membership was. He told them he would do something about it "not today, but certainly not in 18 months." Knight claimed credit that Duke was the first white southern university to prohibit the use of segregated facilities by campus groups, not mentioning the role the study-in by Black students had played in forcing the policy change. Reiterating that he could not respond under pressure, he told the students that he would form a committee consisting of administrators, faculty, students, and trustees to discuss the labor situation at Duke.[54] Taking no questions, he then left for campus.

At around 10:00 a.m., a group of senior Duke administrators, all white men, met to discuss the rapidly unfolding events. Presided over by Cole, attendees included Griffith, vice president Charles B. Huestis, vice provost Barnes Woodhall, director of information services Clarence E. Whitfield, vice president for institutional advancement Frank L. Ashmore, and university counsel Edwin C. Bryson. This group formed the core of an "administrative working team" that would participate, according to Cole, in a "continuous and expanding meeting of administrative and faculty colleagues . . . to decide on an appropriate course of action."[55]

When Knight joined the working team on Saturday morning, four courses of action were under consideration. Among them, according to Cole, was "the use of force for removal." The final decision was left to Knight. He decided against the use of force. Instead, the Duke president would proceed with his planned chapel remarks, which, he hoped, would help resolve the crisis. Knight told his fellow administrators that, in his talk, he would commit "the university to certain efforts to improve relations in the Duke community and to appoint a committee composed of both Black and white members to examine problems in the Duke community."[56]

The students spent part of the morning cleaning up the public spaces they had occupied in University House. Throughout Saturday and the days that followed, the protesters were careful to present themselves as a moderate, respectful group motivated by morality and conscience. They were not extremists ready to use violence to force changes at the school. "We didn't see ourselves as radical," Bunny Small explained. "We weren't destroying property or burning cities; we were a moderate voice of reason. We weren't challenging the university's power; we were challenging the university to play the role universities in liberal societies are supposed to play." This message was received. "Even in their times of vigorous protest," Knight wrote, "they were a surprisingly polite and civilized group. . . . They were at one level antagonistic because they were determined to make demands . . . yet they were restrained and disciplined along with their passionate sense of outrage."[57] Cleaning up University House reinforced this perception.

Knight spoke at the King memorial service in Duke Chapel just after 1:00 p.m. In remarks he later called "an outburst against the violence and social injustice of our society," Knight talked about the need for healing while cautioning that change would take time. Noting that he and Mrs. Knight "are probably the only ones here with 200 guests in their house at the moment," the Duke president said he hoped that the student protesters were listening to him. "The mixture of feelings and emotions among those of us here and among the men and women of this country are beyond rational description at this moment," Knight said. "To be honest with you, I cannot say either to you or to my friends at home that all of the losses, tragedy, [and] bafflement of this moment can be resolved in a weekend."[58]

Knight alluded to only one of the four student demands in his speech—the establishment of a committee to study labor issues. Acknowledging the importance of the university's treatment of its nonacademic employees, Knight said that, in the next two or three days, he would speak about bringing together members of the board of trustees, faculty, student body, employees, and administrative staff to look "in common purpose . . . at those developments which will serve us best in this great University." In all of this, Knight was intentionally unspecific. Rather, he spoke of the need for each individual and institution to assume their share of the "burden" for the violence and destruction in the world. He suggested that the protesters in University House were attempting to absolve themselves of guilt by making demands on others. "If I have one criticism . . . of the righteous indignation of some of my young friends of the moment," Knight observed, "it is that they have felt that somehow we could pass the burden of responsibility to others. No man is guiltless," he argued. Knight ended with a call to work together to find solutions to common problems.[59]

While acknowledging in general the dimensions of the crisis Duke and the country were facing, Knight failed to respond to the issues that had motivated the protest. Having been told by Knight that he would address their concerns at the memorial service, the protesters were disappointed with what they heard. Not only had just one of their four demands been mentioned, but the Duke president had characterized their attitude as one of "righteous indignation." Henderson described Knight's decision not to take a dramatic stand on the issues as a "drastic mistake." He cited Knight's attitude as pivotal in contributing to the "determination" of the protesters. Once again, Knight knew that his efforts at communication had failed. He wrote later that his speech had "satisfied no one—including myself."[60]

After the memorial service, Knight went to Cole's home. Later in the afternoon, William G. Anlyan, dean of the School of Medicine and Knight's personal physician, stopped by to examine him. Anlyan concluded that the Duke president was near collapse and seemed at risk of suffering a relapse of his recent hepatitis. Anlyan ordered Knight into seclusion for forty-eight hours. "He and the provost looked at me," Knight recalled, and said, "'You're not going back to your house. You're going out to the lake and you're going to be away from this.' They meant it," Knight remembered. Although he later wrote that "part of me felt like a draft dodger," Knight did not protest. "There comes a time when the physical self just comes apart," he remarked. With Knight sidelined, board chair Wright Tisdale designated Cole acting chief executive officer of the university.[61]

As Saturday passed, demands to end the occupation grew ever stronger. "Calls were flooding in from alumni," according to Griffith, and they were saying, "Get those damn people out of the house. How can you allow them to stay in there another minute?" Over and over, according to Griffith, members of the administration heard the same refrain: "Why are they in Douglas Knight's home? We've lost control. The university has no leadership."[62]

These reactions were, of course, colored by perceptions of Knight. At board meetings, Griffith recounted, the Duke president would try to make sense of the student activism emerging on campus to the trustees: "He interpreted why they were doing things and what they were doing." After a point, however, a number of board members had heard enough. "Those people would say," Griffith remembered, "'Doug Knight's been making excuses for those students for five years and we're no longer [wanting] to hear any more excuses, it's time to get them under control.' . . . Many people eventually said he's just an apologist for the students. . . . He can't control [them] so he's trying to validate what they are doing."[63]

Thus, Knight found himself in an impossible position. He was perceived as a "wuss" by the student protesters because of his refusal to agree to their demands and as weak by trustees and alumni because of his inability to control the students.

Members of the administration's working team "were very concerned," Griffith recalled. "We were sensitive to what was taking place. We knew we had a limited amount of time. . . . The pressure [from the general public] was tremendous." Even some on the working team questioned whether the university's moderate course of action was the right one. "I disagree with the position taken by President Knight," Cole wrote later, that people in University House could be considered "guests . . . rather than . . . uninvited occupants. . . . Had the president given his approval," Cole commented, "I was prepared, together with Ed Bryson, to . . . use force . . . to try to dislodge the occupants."[64]

Ultimately, force was not used. One reason is because the situation in Durham made such a move risky and difficult. "It was continually feared that an explosion in Durham would be sparked by events at Duke," Cole wrote later.

"The Durham Police force at the time was over taxed and over extended." Cole believed that "this fact was never appreciated by those . . . who demanded a policy of throw the rascals out."[65]

A second reason, however, was equally important. Although the 250 students in University House were perceived as an occupying force by many trustees, alumni, and faculty, members of the administrative working team continued to view them sympathetically. "Those of us who were here . . . knew the people involved," Griffith recounted. "These were people who had leadership responsibilities. Many of them we had gotten to know very well." Ashmore described the leaders directing events as "people . . . with whom we have worked, and for whom we all had a great deal of respect." Administrators, Griffith explained, felt that "we should attempt to work in a reasonable kind of fashion with people who were our students, they weren't our enemies. They were part of our . . . University family. . . . You don't kick your family out of someplace, you try to understand," he explained. Kinney described the connection between administrators and protesters much more succinctly. "We were their sons and daughters," he explained.[66]

Griffith remained in regular contact with Strange by phone throughout the day. Around 8:00 p.m., Griffith and Anlyan visited University House to brief Kinney, Small, and Strange on Knight's health. They told them that the Duke president was exhausted, would not be returning to the house, and would be incommunicado until 4:00 p.m. on Monday.[67]

The news that Knight would be sidelined until Monday afternoon presented the leaders with what Henderson called the "first real crisis" of the protest. "Not only did we not know where to direct the demonstration," he wrote, but "we did not know if we could hold the demonstration together." The students were also genuinely concerned about Knight's health. "We were afraid that he might really be sick," Henderson remembered.[68]

Unable to decide what to do next, the three leaders asked the students to designate seven additional representatives for consultation. Known collectively as the Committee of Ten, this group would lead the protest going forward. All were white.[69]

After further discussion, the expanded leadership group decided that the best course would be to move the demonstration to Duke's main quadrangle in the morning. Griffith was approached about the idea and he was very supportive. "My feeling was that there was not a whole lot of room in that house for more people," Griffith explained. To gain additional support for the four demands, Griffith believed, "it was important to take [the protest] to the Duke community." Moreover, Griffith believed that the Duke campus was the right place for the four demands to be addressed. "I guess my feeling . . . is that Duke is a family, and if you want to change things, you should try to work with your family first before going externally." Protest leaders asked Griffith if Duke women who joined the protest would be allowed to sign out of their dorms to the quad overnight. He "immediately jumped at the idea," according to Henderson, "and called the deans to tell them about it."[70]

If Griffith quickly embraced the prospect of a move, many of the protesters camped out in Knight's living room were wary. Even before the plan could be fully explained, "dissension spread," according to Henderson. Although most of the students in University House had little experience participating in demonstrations, the prior twenty-four hours had made a strong impact. "A number of people who had never questioned the authority of the university before," Henderson explained, "suddenly found themselves in an occupying force in the house of the university President. They were pleased with their boldness, and many did not want to give up the position of power." Writing later, one student commented that for him, the sit-in at Knight's house had been a turning point. He said, "I had asserted myself for the first time in my life."[71]

The group discussion that ensued was highly charged. Some students were concerned that a sit-in by two hundred or so students on the main Duke quadrangle would get lost, with the protest seen as "nothing but a joke." Local 77 organizer Peter Brandon argued vehemently that the protesters should remain at University House. He said that preliminary discussions were underway for a strike by Duke dining hall workers but that any planning was predicated on Duke students having seized "a key installation on the Duke campus." Leaving University House, he told the demonstrators, "will be judged a retreat by . . . Duke employees." Bunny Small, who favored a move to the quad, worried that Knight's illness would cause those on campus who were already skeptical about the occupation of University House to become even more antagonistic.[72]

As discussions dragged on, tempers flared. Late in the evening, the increasingly tense discussions were interrupted by a student who told the group that Durham was imploding. "The police station reports police cars are burning in the police garage lots," the student reported. "Marcels supermarket is burning, condemned houses all over Durham are burning, cabs started burning when the police changed shifts." "Right after that," a student described, "there was the most tremendous hush I've ever heard that fell across the whole place." By Sunday, a 7:00 p.m. curfew had been declared in Durham and the sale of explosives, firearms, ammunition, gasoline, alcoholic beverages, and other items considered dangerous was prohibited. The National Guard was mobilized to keep the peace. Tension at University House increased with news of the evacuation of Aycock Hall on the Duke campus following a bomb threat.[73]

Sleep was again difficult for those occupying University House Saturday night. By Sunday morning, however, a consensus had formed around the plan to move to the main quad. When a vote was taken, 90 percent of the protesters supported the move.[74]

Saturday evening, Brandon had suggested that a strike by Duke's nonacademic employees was under consideration. Early Sunday morning, he confirmed that planning for a strike had begun. The leaders of Local 77 saw the student protest as a way to gain student and faculty support for higher wages and collective bargaining. News of the potential strike raised the stakes for the students. "If the protest failed," Gutman warned, "some people . . . may get fired and find it very difficult to get work in Durham. . . . By involving the [workers and the Durham] Black community, we're giving them expectations," he explained.[75] The protest was no longer just a statement by Duke students and faculty to their university. Now events had real-world consequences for Duke workers.

Howard had been at University House since Friday night and was concerned. On Sunday morning, with the protest about to move to the quad, she commented on the "generally festive atmosphere" at Knight's house during the sit-in. Having participated in the AAS study-in outside Knight's office in November 1967, she was "quick to point out the difference in the organization and discipline of the two demonstrations," Henderson wrote. He recalled Howard pointing out that "whites put so much store in individuality that they were almost incapable of self-enforced unity and discipline." If the group went to the quad with the same attitude, Howard predicted, they would be "ridiculed for being so poorly disciplined." "It was too loose for me," Howard remembered. "I didn't think they cared. It was like 'how cute, here we are spending the night at Dr. Knight's house.' And I didn't think there was a seriousness of purpose." Howard was direct with the group. "This ain't going to be worth nothing," she remembered telling the group, "because you just don't have it—unorganized, undisciplined people just don't seem to be serious about it at all."[76]

Howard's comments made a difference. Through a process of "collective decision making" but based largely on Howard's remarks, the decision was made that the protest on the quad would be a "Silent Vigil." No talking would be permitted, except during breaks and at mealtime. In addition, a group of monitors would be established and instructed on how to keep the group together. Reminded that her comments gave rise to the idea for a "silent" vigil, Howard was surprised. "I would have never thought that silence was a part of it," she commented wryly, "because that ain't me." As for the monitors, "of course they were there for discipline," Howard recalled, "but the whole business about the monitors was a safety feature." "The lessons of my youth participating in demonstrations were applied to the vigil," she recalled, "as much for survival (how not to get beaten by the police) [as to provide a] recipe for a successful protest."[77]

With "trepidation" and no sense of how they would be received, the protesters started marching to West Campus around 10:30 a.m., accompanied by a police escort. Henderson's thoughts were racing as he left Knight's house. He recalled questioning "if we had made the right decision, wondering if Knight was sick, thinking that we had lost our power base, [concerned that the] struggle would get very diffused." A small "cleaning crew" of students remained behind at University House.[78]

Griffith and other members of the administrative working team were relieved that all but a handful of the protesters had vacated the president's home. By labeling the students as "guests" and treating them as "family," Duke administrators were able to end the occupation without using force. Oliver Harvey wondered, however, whether race had played a role in the administration's restraint. "Naturally, 250 white students, the university is going to respond to," he commented later. "Had we as Black people gone to Knight's house, they would have tear-gassed us out, gone in and drawn injunctions on us. That's law. But with 250 or 260 white students, no. Black students saw that as well as we did. . . . Duke is going to respect their whites, not us. They respect nobody Black, students or employees," Harvey remarked.[79]

When they arrived on the quad, the protesters assembled in rows. Churchgoers leaving Duke Chapel on Sunday morning were "somewhat surprised" at the reception waiting for them when services were over.[80] The Silent Vigil had begun.

CHAPTER 5

———

Hope Takes Its Last Stand

The Silent Vigil

———

The 250 students who had occupied University House arrived on Duke's main quadrangle on Sunday morning and made essentially the same four demands of Douglas Knight that they had been insisting on since Friday. One asked Knight to sign a newspaper advertisement committing the university to pursue racial justice. The second asked that the Duke president resign his membership in the segregated Hope Valley Country Club. Two demands pertained to Duke's nonacademic employees; one requested that Knight "press for a $1.60 minimum wage for all Duke employees" and the second asked him to "appoint a committee . . . to make recommendations concerning collective bargaining and union recognition at Duke." Eventually, the demand for collective bargaining became the paramount issue for the vigil. While protesters accepted that the mechanics of any arrangement would have to be finalized later, they insisted that the university accept in principle the right of Duke's nonacademic employees to bargain collectively.

Collective bargaining was crucial for these employees. As matters stood in 1968, Duke management set wages for workers with no input from labor: the terms of employment were set forth in a personnel handbook prepared by the university. While Duke permitted its workers to join voluntary employee groups, it refused to bargain with these organizations or to enter into any legally enforceable collective contract. As described by the faculty committee established during the Silent Vigil to investigate collective bargaining, "the provisions of the Personnel Handbook [are] subject from moment to moment to unilateral revision by the university," and the university alone.[1] As the largest employer in Durham, this gave the university almost unfettered power to dictate wages and working conditions for its employees.

Under collective bargaining, this situation would be transformed. Labor-management issues at Duke would be resolved through negotiations between representatives of the nonacademic employees and university executives. Terms of employment would be set forth in a legally binding agreement between the workers and the university. While collective bargaining can take many forms, at its core, this right would require the university to cede at least some of its power to unilaterally establish the terms of employment for its nonacademic workers. Duke employees had been pursuing the goal of collective bargaining since 1965. They saw gaining this right—in some form—as essential to ending the paternalistic "plantation system" that had prevailed at Duke for so many decades. With the students at the Silent Vigil supporting this demand, Local 77 hoped to accelerate progress toward this key goal.

The Silent Vigil had multiple dimensions, but the university's nonacademic employees were central to the entire effort. What limits, if any, would the university accept on its unfettered power to establish wages and working conditions for these workers? In the fraught climate following the assassination of Martin Luther King Jr., who had made the rights of the poor pivotal to racial equality, the university could either respond to the crisis by taking meaningful steps to advance the cause of economic justice or it could stick to the "plantation system." Duke's response would reveal how willing it was to move beyond attitudes that had shaped its Jim Crow past to become a leader in the quest for social and economic justice.

·······················

A flyer signed on behalf of "the 200+" circulated through campus Sunday morning. "JOIN US on the West Quad in Front of [the] Chapel" for a rally at 2:00 p.m., it announced. "Those students and faculty sitting in at the President's residence," the flyer declared, "have decided . . . we will continue our vigil on the University campus. . . . The American crisis demands that all institutional leaders . . . demonstrate moral commitment to eliminate racial dissensions and inequities." Another flyer emphasized the connection between King's work for economic justice and the goals of the Silent Vigil. "Dr. King died in Memphis as he was preparing a march on behalf of striking garbage men," the flyer stated, that is, "workers whose union was ignored by their employers. We protest on behalf of Duke's non-academic employees, whose wages are far below the poverty level and whose union the University refuses to bargain with."[2]

The Sunday rally was attended by 1,100 students, faculty, and other members of the Duke community. Logistics for the event were improvised and organized on the fly. "Can anyone here play the guitar?" a student leader asked. "We are looking for someone who can play 'Blowin' in the Wind.' This is your last chance to sing and we've got to make our presence felt with our voices so that the whole darn community and the whole darn world can hear us!"[3]

None of the Committee of Ten leading the vigil had ever directed a protest of this size. They were being carried along by events. It was "a period of radicalization for those of us who were radicalizing others," David Henderson observed. As for participants, a survey found that fully 77 percent of those who joined the vigil were taking part in their first "demonstration," including political rallies. As a result, participants in the Silent Vigil were not jaded about their prospects for success. "American society is much more cynical today," Bunny Small commented many years later. "It's much harder for people to believe in their own actions; they get discouraged before they even try." But this was not the case for these Silent Vigil participants. "We had an optimism," Small reflected, "in that we believed if we worked together we could change things."[4]

Small told the rally what an "amazing," "really fantastic" experience the sit-in at Knight's house had been. "We didn't know if we would be booted out, arrested, [or] suspended," she explained, "but we felt we had to commit ourselves. . . . If white America, those of us who come from nice middle-class homes, could not make the 'system' work for us," she asked, "what chance would our Black brothers have?" Small made clear that the purpose of the Silent Vigil was to compel concrete action by the university. "Everyone is for freedom, everybody is for justice," she shouted, "but we're gonna get something [done], we're gonna get it here, and they ain't gonna move us one inch until we get it!"[5]

Black students at Duke and members of the Black community in Durham were skeptical of white leadership, another speaker said. "Many Blacks have already decided that there is no hope for this society," he explained. One reason for the Silent Vigil was to restore that hope. Black people were looking to see if white students could cause an institution like Duke to make "the important, the dramatic, the meaningful changes," he said. If Black people did not believe such changes were possible, the speaker warned, "they will be in the streets in guerilla warfare and they will try to bring the country down."[6]

Watching events on the quad, William Griffith thought the demonstrators were pursuing worthy goals while behaving respectfully. "I'm just very impressed with the manner in which those who are participating are expressing themselves," he told wdbs radio, "and I'm very moved by the expression myself." Although many in the administration agreed with Griffith, the trustees were another matter. University and Endowment board member Marshall Pickens spoke for many when he wrote to two students: "My reaction to the so-called vigil is that it is a form of blackmail which should not be used in a civilized community." With Knight sidelined, board chair Wright Tisdale decided that he would come to Durham to be closer to events.[7]

On Sunday night, five hundred people, the vast majority of them white Duke students, slept on the main quadrangle of the university. "We expect no trouble," Kinney told the protesters, "and we are being protected by both the Durham and the campus cops." Still, there was no way to know what nightfall might bring. There were rumors, according to Henderson, "of trouble from some of the more reactionary [students] including some of the football players." Of greater concern were outsiders intent on disrupting the protest. "We are watching for firebombers," W. C. A. Bear, chief of campus security, commented. "There have been lots of threats. We have been having men standing by . . . in case there is any outside interference."[8] Other than a few firecrackers going off, Sunday night passed uneventfully.

Meanwhile, once Tisdale arrived in Durham on Sunday, he started meeting with members of the administrative working team immediately. The board chair told the team that he did not favor the hands-off approach taken toward the protest thus far. "Let's straighten this out," Tisdale told them. "Let's not have this going on at Duke University." Tisdale had his own idea of how to proceed. "When Wright Tisdale flew in," Charles Huestis recalled, "his first announcement was that he was going to close the university down. That really got us tied up in knots."[9]

....

"I still have a feeling of awe when I think about waking up that first morning on the quad," Bertie Howard recalled years later. "I did not believe the number of students who had joined the vigil during the night. It was incredible how the amount of space we used up had multiplied."[10]

As the Silent Vigil grew in size, it also became more highly organized. Upon joining the vigil, participants were seated in rows of exactly fifty people. They were provided with printed "Ground Rules for Those Participating in the Vigil." These rules were strict. They included "No talking. . . . No eating except at group snack and meal breaks. . . . No sunbathing" and "No singing except at specified periods under the direction of the song leader. . . . The monitors are in charge so please listen to them."[11]

As instructed, protesters sat in silence. "They have a break every 45 minutes," Small told a reporter on Monday, "to stand and sing." "We are a self-regulated bunch," history professor Thomas Rainey commented. "Before joining us," he explained, "all students agree to abide by the rules." In case of rule violations, monitors were quick to respond, although some thought these efforts at maintaining order went too far. Hutch Traver, among the more militant students at Duke, remembered the monitors saying, "'Please be quiet, Stay in your Vigil lines' over and over again. 'Raise your hand if you need to go to the bathroom.' I thought it was very stupid," he recalled.[12]

Other aspects of the vigil were also well organized. By Monday, monitors had been recruited, a sound system set up, and a press operation was running around-the-clock. Information tables were set up for those who had questions. A lost-and-found center, transportation pool, trash pickup, and banking service were all quickly established. The protest even had a poet laureate—activist John Beecher—who was elected early in the demonstration. Bertie Howard remembered "discussions about our bank account—we had raised $6000 or so for the union strike fund in a few days, and suddenly there was talk about a tax ID number and investment strategies." The vigil had "superb organization," one researcher commented accurately, that was put in place with a speed that was "truly impressive."[13]

The elaborate structure of the vigil emerged organically. "The organization [was not] planned out beforehand," political science professor John Strange commented. "It was serendipitous," he reflected years later. "As it evolved it was magic, it was beyond any of us." "The vigil was a classic case of middle-class college kids using the skills they had to organize something," Small recalled. Griffith shared the same sense. "If you look at pictures, it was so regimented. They had cleanup detail. . . . They had people to walk the gals to the restroom facilities at three o'clock in the morning." Marveling at the organization, Griffith described the students running the protest as "potential technocrats, potential presidents of business concerns."[14]

Cleanliness was a priority. Monday morning, the small cleaning crew left behind at University House was, according to Strange, "polishing it from top to bottom." They were "sweeping down the [rugs], scrubbing the garbage cans, vacuuming all the floors."[15] Out on the quad, trash was collected and hauled away at regular intervals.

Although operating on little sleep, vigil leaders even found time to send a note to the Knights. "Please accept our sincere thanks," Small, Strange, and Kinney wrote the Knights on Monday, "for your welcome and hospitality and our apologies for any inconvenience during our stay over this weekend."[16]

The nonviolence, order, and good manners so evident at the vigil served multiple purposes. One was to garner support from those who viewed the student protest with concern. "We wanted to give the impression that we were . . . responsible," the student narrator of a Silent Vigil audiotape commented. At every turn, "the idea of making a good impression held sway. . . . We were trying to not only affect people on campus but outside of it," he explained, especially "the moneyed, respectable middle class of Durham. We felt that being neat and clean was very important in this respect."[17]

A second purpose was more strategic. Demonstrators hoped to pressure the school to meet their demands while communicating to trustees and administrators that they remained loyal members of the Duke "family." "I do give us credit for being smart enough to [be] not threatening," Kinney recalled. "To try to be effective and [non]threatening is a very hard needle to thread."[18]

This disciplined approach also helped recruit new vigil participants. "The order that we were able to maintain," Henderson wrote in his journal, "undoubtedly contributed to . . . the support we got from faculty and other students." Another student described the dynamic in a more personal way. "We were cautious," Serena Simons commented. "There was a real feeling of moderation in our radicalism. It was a very culturally controlled event in that we were all 'good' kids."[19]

Vigil participants also hoped that their tactics would send a message to Black students at Duke and in Durham. "Almost to the individual," a researcher who interviewed participants after the event reported, "the members of the Vigil view their action as the last opportunity to [show] the Black Community that peaceful means can . . . bring about results." Strange made that point at a Monday press conference. "The militant Black community was probably somewhat amused by the tactics which were being used" at the vigil, he commented. Both students and the broader community "have been amazed by the support which we have garnered both from faculty and students by a very deescalated type of approach" and "are reassessing their attitudes about the ways in which you approach these problems." However well intentioned, these comments by white protest leaders were not always well received. Brenda Armstrong recalled later that at least some of the Black students found them "condescending."[20]

Meanwhile, little contact between vigil negotiators and the administrative working team was occurring. Monday afternoon, the Committee of Ten was informed that Knight would be remaining in seclusion "for several days or longer."[21]

At the same time, Local 77 was moving forward with a strike. At a 5:00 p.m. Monday meeting, Duke dining hall workers voted to strike, effective at 12:01 a.m. Tuesday morning. They approved two demands: the right to collective bargaining and an end to "poverty wages" through the establishment of a $1.60 per hour minimum wage for all Duke workers. Significantly, the vigil participants asked *only* that the university establish a committee to "consider collective bargaining and union recognition for Duke's non-academic employees." Local 77 demanded specific action. "The University must recognize that Local 77 represents Duke workers," a flyer for the strike meeting asserted, "and that Duke will negotiate a contract that will be voted on by the union membership and signed by both the union committee and the Duke administration." While vigil protesters supported recognition for Local 77, Small explained, "our goal was to get the university to do anything that would be [a move] in [that] direction."[22]

For Local 77, recognition as the "exclusive bargaining agent" for Duke workers was essential. Agreement by the university only to the "principle" of collective bargaining could allow other unions to compete with Local 77 for the right to represent segments of Duke's nonacademic employees. Should such a competition result in more than one union representing different groups of Duke workers, the negotiating leverage nonacademic employees were seeking could have been significantly reduced. Still, when told about the strike, vigil participants voted overwhelmingly to support the workers.

With King's funeral to be held the next day, vigil leaders announced a class boycott starting at 8:00 a.m. on Tuesday. The school canceled third- and fourth-period classes, "as a part of the university's participation in the memorial to Dr. Martin Luther King."[23] The university wanted to acknowledge the sense of loss felt by many on campus while maintaining, to the extent possible, normal university operations.

Starting on Sunday, vigil participants had declared a boycott of the West Campus dining facilities. While the boycott continued, vigil organizers were responsible for feeding the growing number of protesters. A distribution system staffed by faculty wives, nonacademic employees, and East Campus coeds was quickly established. Claiborne Tapp, manager of the Chicken Box, an iconic Black-owned restaurant in Hayti, proved instrumental in feeding the protesters. On Monday, the Chicken Box provided five hundred meals for vigil participants at its cost of fifty cents per plate. "If you need anything," Tapp told protest organizers, "just call me. We're with you all the way. We appreciate what you're doing for us." "Good meals . . . from the Chicken Box," Howard recalled, opened up "a whole new world to white students who had not ventured into the world of African-American cuisine."[24]

Meanwhile, faculty support for the vigil continued to grow. Some joined students on the quad while others helped with food service. Faculty also showed support in other ways. At their regularly scheduled meeting on April 8, for example, the faculty of the divinity school voted unanimously to suspend any annual increment in faculty salary. They requested that "the resultant savings be transferred to the budget of the non-academic employees for the raising of their minimum wage."[25]

"It was obvious from the beginning" of Monday, Henderson reported, "that support for the Vigil was growing." Not only were more students joining the protest, but the campus had become "polarized" between those who supported the demonstration and those who opposed it. "One of my students told me," Samuel DuBois Cook recalled, "that his fellow students had to 'justify' to themselves their nonparticipation. How interesting and significant!" "An atmosphere of decency, morality, civility and social, racial, and economic justice permeated the campus," creating a "great and proud moment in Duke history," Cook remembered.[26]

The hundreds of students who joined the vigil did so for a myriad of reasons. Some were moved by the assassination of King. For other students, the vigil was a direct way of responding to racial problems at Duke and in American society. "Eulogizing Martin Luther King did not seem enough," one student recounted. "For me, the main issues were recognizing the rights of workers and recognizing that the University had a responsibility to the community." Others joined for reasons that had nothing to do with politics or the "four demands." Asked why she joined the vigil, Simons said that she was "wildly in love with this person who was real political. . . . I was dating him at the time." Most participants joined the vigil for a combination of these reasons. "The Vigil attracted me," a student recalled, "because it embodied many of the values I find important—democracy, [the] right to assemble, human justice, and dignity, and equality. . . . I also remember I had a big paper due," he continued, "and the Vigil gave me an extension because the class didn't meet (All motives are mixed!)."[27]

Whatever their reasons, by Monday, vigil participants had created a *separate* community on the main quadrangle of Duke University. This community operated outside the cultural and social norms of the school. Students sang together, slept together, and ate together. Once classes began to meet on the quad, they studied together. Security, banking, transportation, and medical care were all provided. Jeff Van Pelt described the "separateness" experienced by the vigil community. "One by one our numbers grew," he wrote, "but only in one way: only as each person stepped onto the quad, stepped over the line that divided our ranks from the world as it had been before."[28]

The vigil community offered participants the social space to reflect on their values, politics, and goals in a new way. "You have levels of understanding, intellectual and emotional," history professor John Cell explained, "and an experience like [the vigil] deepens, intensifies, focuses. It's not that you hadn't thought about these things, hadn't known these things, or maybe hadn't even understood these things," he said. "But you understand them [now] in different ways and they become personal." For many, the experience was transformative. "The Silent Vigil was a noble event and a sacred or divine experience," Cook commented on the thirtieth anniversary of the protest, reflecting that it was "historical, institutional, symbolic, existential, and personal." Cook remembered the protest as "one of those supreme and unforgettable mountaintop experiences in which the 'Word was made flesh.'" It was "a magical moment," Huck Gutman recalled, "when you think the world can be transformed and you can be a part of it." "I was transported in a way unequalled for me either before or since," another student explained. "I suppose it was as close as I ever came to a religious feeling."[29]

The dozens of letters written to Provost Cole by vigil participants on Monday expressed the passion and moral clarity that many at the vigil were feeling. "We do not want trouble," one student warned, "but we are sick of apathy, sick of injustice. We want equality and we want peace NOW, at any cost to our personal futures." Another student wrote poetically about the powerful sense of rebirth and renewal he was experiencing, calling it "a new Genesis. It is my sole hope," this student wrote, "that Duke University can, in like manner, arise to the renaissance which it has undergone."[30]

Cole and others in the administration were receiving a very different message from alumni. Despite efforts by vigil participants to present themselves as moderate, many alumni viewed the protesters as out of control. Letters from alumni called participants "hoodlums," "mob-like," "impressionable adolescents," "complainers," "malcontents," and "beasts." Almost all alumni urged the university to take a hard line against the protesters. "This is not the time to let the animals run the zoo," an alumnus wrote, urging the administration to "take a firm stand against these misguided youths." Letters "poured in like the snow," Roger Marshall recalled. "At one point, I had 3,000 unanswered letters on my desk."[31]

Alumni were not alone in opposing the vigil. Many students also did not approve of the protest. "The Vigil could have only occurred in the scholastic environment," one student wrote critically, "a totally artificial arena where the participants can devote themselves to idealism with no concern for the mechanics of existence—food, shelter, birth, death." Christopher Edgar, an economics major, opposed union recognition and a wage increase for nonacademic employees: "I felt that the administration had a duty to its students to provide the highest quality education at the lowest possible cost."[32]

As time passed, Wright Tisdale became increasingly concerned about events. By Monday evening, the board chair had been in Durham for twenty-four hours. Almost all that time had been spent in intense discussions with the administrative working team. Cole, Huestis, and Griffith, among others, were trying to explain to Tisdale "what the students were trying to say to us" and "that it was a peaceful demonstration and not out of control." But with the protest growing in size by the hour, dining hall workers heading out on strike, a class boycott scheduled for the next day, and at least some faculty rallying to the cause, Tisdale was not persuaded. Noting that "feelings ran high at times," Cole wrote that on Monday evening he was "*ordered* [by Tisdale] to dismiss summarily from the University a number of the leaders of the Vigil under threat of his resignation in case I failed to do so. I gave my strong reasons for refusal," Cole explained, and "answered by promising my own resignation if the action by administrative fiat were taken." The dismissals never occurred because, as Cole recounted, "cooler counsels eventually prevailed." Still, Cole's relationship with Tisdale became irrevocably strained. "The Chairman always considered me to be too sympathetic in my dealings with the students," Cole wrote, "and I in turn felt that he was emotionally unpredictable and too far removed . . . from the 'firing line' . . . to make responsible judgments."[33]

Tisdale then proposed even more aggressive action. On Monday night, Huestis reported, "Tisdale said he'd heard enough and was going to close down the university." His intent, according to Huestis, was "simply to . . . demonstrate that Duke was . . . not going to put up with this kind of [nonsense]. We argued vehemently [with Tisdale] on that," Huestis recalled. "I remember saying, . . . 'Wright, will you explain to me why it is necessary that Duke University be the first university in the United States to close in the face of a student protest, especially when it's a peaceful student protest?'" Huestis also played for time. "You don't have the authority to close this university," Huestis told Tisdale. "At a minimum, you've got to take it to the executive committee [of the board of trustees]." Tisdale then deferred action. The executive committee was summoned to Durham for an emergency meeting on Wednesday, April 10.[34]

Griffith was relieved at the decision to call in the executive committee. He had his resignation "in his hip pocket," he recounted, "if force was used against the demonstrators." Huestis was exhausted. "I don't know any time that I've felt as emotionally, and physically, and spiritually drained as I felt that night," he remembered. Huestis told his wife, "'We've been through this now for a day and a half and I just don't know how I can do it all over again . . . from scratch with the executive committee.'"[35]

Monday evening on campus was taken up with a rally that featured a previously scheduled appearance by antiwar activists Joan Baez and David Harris. When Baez and Harris tried to connect the issues in the vigil to those in the antiwar movement, some people raised objections. "We appreciate your speaking to us about the resistance," one student told Baez and Harris to loud and prolonged applause, "but this is not our main focus." "I want to remind you," another student said, "that this vigil is not a draft resistance vigil. . . . Our main object here is for the employees of Duke."[36] On Monday night, more than one thousand students and faculty slept on the main quadrangle of Duke University.

⸻

Early Tuesday morning, Cook, Kinney, and Howard Wilkinson, chaplain of the university, boarded a flight to Atlanta to attend Martin Luther King Jr.'s funeral. Cook and King had been friends for decades. Classmates growing up, the two entered Morehouse College in 1943 at age fifteen. Their friendship blossomed in college and they became allies in the civil rights movement.

As Cook and his Duke colleagues traveled to Atlanta, picket lines went up around campus dining facilities in the West Union, East Union, and Graduate Center. Labor organizer Peter Brandon estimated in the *Duke Chronicle* that by Tuesday, the student boycott of the West Campus dining facilities was "90% effective." On Tuesday afternoon, maids and janitors on West Campus voted to strike, effective as of Wednesday morning. The class boycott also began on Tuesday, and a vigil spokesperson estimated 80 percent of students stayed away from classes.[37]

There was no contact between vigil leaders and Duke administrators on Tuesday morning. A memorial service for the civil rights leader was held in Duke Chapel at 10:30 a.m., timed to coincide with King's funeral in Atlanta. Throughout Tuesday, "rumors were flying," according to Henderson, "that Mr. Tisdale was running the university and that the students were going to be removed from the quad with fire hoses and police." A WDBS reporter commented on the pending confrontation between the trustees and the students. "It becomes possible, in a very real sense," he said, that "some of the students . . . may be putting themselves on the line not just bodily but in terms of their standing with the university."[38]

Meanwhile, some of the national press broadcast news of the vigil, and statements of support from national leaders started to arrive. "By your action in support of the employees of the university who seek recognition for their bargaining rights," Senator Robert F. Kennedy told the protesters, "you set a standard that all should emulate." Civil rights leader Benjamin E. Mays, who delivered a eulogy at King's funeral, commented on the redemptive power of the protest. "As long as students like you are interested in racial justice and are determined to carry on [King's] noble work," he told participants, "he will not have died in vain."[39]

Howard Fuller's appearance at the vigil on Tuesday was one of the most powerful events of the day. As the most visible Black leader in Durham, Fuller lent credibility to a civil rights protest composed almost entirely of white students and faculty. "We have an administration at this university that is out of touch with the needs of those Black people who toil every day to see to it that food is right, the grass is cut, and all of the other things that need to get done . . . are done," Fuller told the crowd. "With your support," he stated, Duke workers have "taken a stand" against "inferior wages and bad working conditions." Fuller challenged the protesters to ask themselves, "'Are you really serious?'" To thunderous applause, he said, "If you're really serious . . . that means that a lot of us are going to be out here for a long time." "Any . . . people who don't believe that everybody can be free," Fuller told the group, "should be here today to see all of these people." "I'm proud to be a Black man and I'm proud to be here today!" Oliver Harvey was amazed at the power of Fuller's speech. "Howard Fuller . . . really moved things up," he remembered.[40]

Duke's Black students were at best equivocal in their support for the vigil. The AAS did not officially endorse the protest, although members were free to participate as individuals if they chose to do so. "The Blacks were clearly not as active in [the vigil] as they were in their own things," Charles Becton explained. "It was mostly a white vigil." "I think the white students were very committed to the Vigil," Hopkins observed, "but I . . . was not committed to that type of protest. . . . I personally would not sit out on the quad for days." "It was absolutely unnecessary for us as Negro students to say we supported the Vigil," Black student leader Stef McLeod commented. "To ask a black student if he is for the goals of this demonstration," he said, "is like asking a Jew in the heights of Hitler's reign if he was for the termination of the torture, oppression and extermination of the Jews."[41]

Many Blacks saw "white guilt" as a primary motivating factor for the protest. The vigil, according to Armstrong, was seen "as a way for many whites to exonerate themselves from their guilt at being tied [to the King assassination] by the fact that they were white." Hopkins agreed. "Black students did not feel this guilt and thus many did not support the Vigil." Griffith had the same sense. Black students, he remembered, "were not very much involved [after King's death] that I could perceive." "Those few that I talked to said, 'This is whitey's thing—if he's got a guilt trip, well he can take his guilt trip.'"[42]

To the extent Black students did participate in the vigil, they did so primarily to support Duke's Black maids, janitors, and dining hall workers. Janice Williams recalled that "to us these people represented our parents." Given these deep personal connections, the university's treatment of its nonacademic employees was "one of the most significant politicizing things" for the Black students, according to Hopkins. "I did not participate in the Vigil," Brenda Brown explained, "except to the extent we were helping the non-academic employees on the picket lines. . . . Any involvement on my part would be picketing, rather than sitting on the quad." "Black students wasn't too happy all the way through the vigil and the strike," Oliver Harvey recalled, "but they did participate with us."[43]

Significantly, one of the reasons Black students were ambivalent about the vigil was the failure of the protesters to demand that Local 77 be recognized as exclusive bargaining agent for the nonacademic employees. The Black students, Oliver Harvey recalled, "told the white students . . . 'How far are you going? You don't mean what you are doing.'" For the Black students, collective bargaining, without recognition of Local 77 as exclusive bargaining agent, was not enough. "'You people are talking about compromise, and grow as you go,'" Harvey remembered the Black students telling vigil participants. And the Black students "were saying the same thing we were saying. 'People want exclusive recognition. They want it now.'" One Black student was also concerned that white students did not fully appreciate the importance of the workers' demand for a union. "I became . . . exasperated," she said, "when I saw that the vigilers could not understand that the union, as a tool through which the workers can approach employers in a dignified and adult manner, was far more important than a raise in salary."[44]

Another concern for Black students was whether a protest so firmly committed to "working within the system" could succeed. "While I did not question the ends," McLeod observed, "I did question the means by which they were to be accomplished." Henderson noted the same thing. "Most of the black students said all along that [the vigil's] tactics would not work," he wrote, "and refused to participate."[45]

It was ultimately a personal decision whether a Black student joined the vigil. Armstrong recounted,

> I didn't participate in the vigil. I think I appreciated the fact that a lot of the white students and faculty and other people really felt deeply moved by it. I just didn't feel that they understood. I was just too angry to do that. . . . I can remember walking onto campus and there were all these people sitting around in the rain. And I couldn't understand what they were doing. And I wasn't sure what it meant to me. I thought it was just another world and I didn't feel like I belonged.[46]

The working team of university administrators spent Tuesday in meetings with Tisdale. They kept stressing the moderate nature of the protest and the caliber of the students involved. Cole described the "typical participant" in the vigil as "a highly motivated person of respectable middle-class background, with a creditable academic record . . . who was idealistic, concerned with the goals of equal rights and social justice for others." The administrative team was also trying to persuade Tisdale that events were "moving in the right direction" and that force was not needed to resolve the protest.[47]

During the late afternoon on Tuesday, Tisdale was joined in Durham by trustee Henry E. Rauch, chairman of the board of Burlington Industries in Greensboro, North Carolina, and a member of the powerful Executive Committee of the university board. Discussions among Tisdale, Rauch, and the administrative team could not have been easy. Tisdale and Rauch, both staunchly anti-union, saw Duke facing a protest where the central demand was collective bargaining for Duke employees. By Tuesday, according to the *Duke Chronicle*, the vigil was "on the verge of virtually shutting down the entire university." "One can imagine no greater pressure on an administration negotiator," the paper commented, "than to realize that the students are in control of the University."[48]

Around 8:00 p.m. Tuesday evening, Griffith told vigil leaders that the university would issue a statement the next day. He told them that they could see the statement before it was released but cautioned that there was little likelihood that any changes would be made based on their input. Griffith also said he saw little possibility that the university would agree to collective bargaining.[49]

Despite Griffith's cautionary statements, vigil participants continued to believe that the demonstration could achieve its demands. "Participants sincerely felt," Henderson wrote, "that the university had a great opportunity to take a significant step forward in race relations and in progressive labor practices in the South." "In hindsight," Henderson wrote in his journal for Tuesday, "it seems rather naive to think that we could appeal to the moral consciences of men, on the issue of collective bargaining, who had been fighting unions and organized labor all their lives."[50]

Hope prevailed, however, even in the face of discouraging feedback. Early in the protest, Small had characterized the vigil as an "act of faith." The "spirit and faith" of vigil participants was "just overwhelming," she said. Asked by a reporter why so many at Duke participated in a nonviolent protest while campuses around the world were seeing violent confrontations, Small explained that "sometimes hope takes its last stand."[51] It was this hope that drew more than 1,400 Duke students and faculty to sleep on the quad Tuesday night.

Maids and janitors on West Campus went on strike on Wednesday morning. As vigil participants woke up, picket lines were forming around dormitories, the divinity school, and the engineering, physics, and biological sciences department buildings. Rain drenched the protesters.[52]

The Executive Committee of the board of trustees started meeting early Wednesday morning. The meeting lasted most of the day. "It really took a long time to hammer out some of these things," Griffith explained. He described the discussion on the minimum wage demand. "Trustees were focused on how are we going to find that money," he recounted, "where is it going to come from, was it the right thing to do, could we do it under the pressure of the vigil, is the university caving in? It was a very politicized situation," he recalled.[53]

In the afternoon, 160 Duke law students assembled on the quad to show support for the vigil. Much more significant, Howard Fuller, community organizer Benjamin S. Ruffin Jr., and 100 leaders of the Black community in Durham marched to campus. Looking back years later, Bertie Howard said that seeing the group from the United Organizations for Community Improvement and the Durham Black community arrive on campus and join the protest was one of the "things about the Vigil [that] will always remain with me."[54]

Around 3:00 p.m., Cook, just back from King's funeral in Atlanta, spoke to the vigil crowd. "Just as it is hard to believe that Martin Luther King is dead," he told the protesters, "it is equally difficult to believe that a movement for social justice and equality . . . is alive at Duke." Cook echoed King's last speech, in which the civil rights leader spoke of having seen the "Promised Land." "My eyes, physically now," he told the protesters, "have some vision of the glory of the coming of social justice to this University and country, because of you."

Cook then spoke of King's funeral:

As I saw, from afar, the casket containing his lifeless body, I was sustained by the knowledge of a thousand or more bodies, full of life, vision, and integrity, here carrying on his legacy in the spirit and in conformity with his ideals and methods. I was uplifted by the fact that you had made his mission your very own. And I am sure that Martin Luther King would be proud of you—mighty proud of you. Your vigil wiped my tears and helped to sustain me. *You provided, at a tragic moment, roses for my soul.*

Continued Cook, "A few minutes after the assassination of Dr. King the other night, a great soul, Dr. John Strange, came to our house." Strange asked, "How much more can you take? Can you take any more? Haven't you had enough?" According to Cook, "In a split second, my mind roamed over the tragic pilgrimage of my people since 1619. I wanted to give a religious answer—in the tradition of the faith of my fathers. I couldn't. How could I say anything in the name of God when Martin Luther King, a good man and great soul, had been assassinated? I struggled over alternatives. But they did not satisfy me. I have been haunted by John's probing question."[55]

"I think I have the answer now," Cook told Strange and the other two thousand listeners:

I can go on affirming life; and I and other Negroes can go on hoping and believing in the promise of America; we can go on believing that we are going to be free someday because of people like you and all other members of this magnificent vigil. This provides hope and succor for my spirit. You are helping to create that kind of community, where, in the days ahead, after this long and tragic night of racial separation and misunderstanding, you and I, white and black together, can shout from the mountain top and the valleys of our innermost being and say what is inscribed on Martin Luther King's grave: "We all are free at last. Free at last. Thank God Almighty, we are FREE at last."[56]

The emotional climax of the Silent Vigil, Cook's speech prompted loud cheers and was replayed often in everyone's memories. By connecting the vigil to the life and work of King, Cook had embraced the tactics and goals of the protest while validating the efforts of the demonstrators to advance the cause of racial justice at Duke.

Shortly after Cook's speech, vigil negotiators were summoned to the university development office, where they received a very different message. The Executive Committee had finished meeting and Tisdale was ready to share a copy of the university's official response to the vigil. Although Tisdale was described as "cordial," he would not consider changes or offer any interpretations of the written text. Tisdale told the students that he was prepared to deliver the statement to the vigil participants in person.[57]

Reading Tisdale's planned remarks, negotiators saw immediately that the university's response to the four demands was unacceptable. They also noted, however, that the chairman's statement contained no threats to clear the quad by force or to close the university. The administrative working team had succeeded in persuading Tisdale to respond to the Silent Vigil with restraint. At the executive committee meeting, "Bill [Griffith] and I hardly had to say a word," Huestis recounted. "Wright explained what the students were trying to say to us, emphasizing that these were our best and brightest students. He did a beautiful job explaining it." Griffith remembered that Tisdale "used the same arguments that we had used." Among other points, Tisdale told the executive committee, according to Griffith, "'These are our kids, they are part of our family . . . You basically work with your family.'" He was "just very eloquent," Griffith recalled. Huestis, for one, was surprised. "Here was a man I'd been fighting for forty-eight hours."[58]

In his brief statement on the quad to vigil participants, Tisdale acknowledged the protesters' "deep concern with respect to the human issues which have now so intensely been brought into focus" and told them he "personally share[s] this concern with you." Tisdale recognized that "Duke University has its own responsibilities" in addressing the "great trouble" the nation is facing. Tisdale then responded to the demand for a $1.60 per hour minimum wage for all Duke workers. While not willing to act immediately, Tisdale committed the university to achieving the $1.60 minimum by July 1, 1969—two years before the legally mandated deadline. Further, Tisdale said, the university would make a "significant step" toward this goal by July 1, 1968. Tisdale said nothing about collective bargaining. He characterized the final two demands—that Knight sign the newspaper ad and that he resign from Hope Valley—as personal to the Duke president. A response to those demands would await Knight's return.[59]

After Tisdale finished, the crowd began to sing "We Shall Overcome." Asked to join in by a student, Tisdale "gave a long, level, cold stare," according to Huestis, "and said, 'I'm not sure I can do that.'" However, as Tisdale started to walk away, Oliver Harvey recalled, a "white student grabbed him and had him rocking." Standing just feet from the board chair, Huestis became "suddenly aware" that Tisdale was "booming out the song in his baritone voice, and he knew the words! He got caught up in the emotion of the moment," Huestis thought. Criticized later for joining the protesters, Tisdale said that he had done so only because "there would've been a real disturbance" if he refused. "If you saw the picture" of me singing, Tisdale told an alumni group, "you'd know I wasn't happy about it."[60]

In his journal, Henderson credited Griffith and Huestis for the "intense education" they gave Tisdale and for their role in persuading the trustees "not to use force to clear the quad, not to get rid of the leaders, to speak to the issues, to answer them positively, and for Mr. Tisdale to make his statement directly to the Vigil." Henderson believed that if force had been used, "there is no doubt that the University would have been destroyed, possibly with violence, undoubtedly by instant attrition by professors and students."[61]

If total catastrophe had been averted, however, the protesters were far from satisfied. The statement from the board of trustees was "totally unacceptable," the student narrator commented. "There is no mention made of collective bargaining. . . . The only people they talked to about this was faculty. They didn't talk to any students, they didn't talk to any workers."[62]

It is not surprising that the university refused to address, let alone concede, the issue of collective bargaining. "Duke was nervous about unions and collective bargaining," board member Mary D. B. T. Semans commented later, "and there was much apprehension about them during the Vigil period." Griffith also recognized the power of the anti-union sentiment on the board. "I think the trustees were very much opposed to collective bargaining," he commented. "I think a lot of them were . . . textile people [who had] successfully fought the union situation." These trustees were aware that any concession Duke made to its nonacademic employees could set a precedent in labor negotiations for other companies in the area. "I hope the union isn't recognized," Tisdale told a Detroit alumni group in May 1968. "I don't think it is good for the individuals involved."[63]

Because it was still raining, more than one thousand vigil participants moved into Page Auditorium to discuss the next steps for the protest. "In Page Auditorium," Henderson reported, "there was unanimous discontent with the statement from the Trustees." The meeting of vigil participants lasted nearly six hours and was, by all accounts, chaotic. Kinney called it "democracy run amok." According to the *Duke Chronicle*, Silent Vigil leader Jack Boger and other speakers were interrupted "as hundreds repeatedly jumped to their feet shaking their fists and four fingers, and shouting in solidarity 'Four, Four.'" "The dissension Saturday night at Dr. Knight's house was nothing compared with this," Henderson wrote.[64]

A meeting of the Academic Council attended by approximately four hundred faculty members concluded just as Tisdale was delivering his remarks to the vigil. At its meeting, the council unanimously adopted a resolution supporting the goals of the vigil, urging amnesty for all striking workers and asking all faculty and students to "return to their classrooms, libraries and laboratories." Students and faculty could have the assurance, the resolution stated, "that those . . . issues that generated the [vigil] will receive the continued attention of the faculty, students, and administrative authorities of the University." The council also established a committee, chaired by economics professor John Blackburn, to "determine the adequacy of the university's relationship with its non-academic employees." Early in the evening, the Executive Committee of the Academic Council arrived at Page Auditorium to tell students about these developments.[65]

The discussion in Page Auditorium continued with no consensus. With the Silent Vigil having failed to obtain meaningful concessions from the university, many students pushed for more militant action. "[We] absolutely entertained" the idea of occupying the Allen Building, Henderson remembered. "It was widely discussed. . . . We assumed we couldn't pull it off." He continued,

"Given what we had built, it was impossible to move more than twenty-five or thirty people into Allen Building. There were large numbers of people who would have felt set up and sold out. They were there peacefully—that was the whole theme."[66]

Eventually the protesters adopted a series of proposals put forth by Strange. The vigil would be suspended for a ten-day moratorium. During this time, students would continue to honor the dining hall boycott and staff picket lines while raising monies for a strike fund. In addition, the *Duke Chronicle* reported, participants would "carry the argument of the Vigil to the classroom" to convince people to support the goals of the vigil and to "take advantage of the support [the vigil had] received, in Durham and nationwide." Finally, a committee of students, workers, and faculty would be created (Vigil Strategy Committee). This group would meet regularly to plan strategy for the protest and to investigate the implementation of collective bargaining at Duke.[67]

Although the vigil had failed to achieve a single one of its four demands, some students and faculty began to characterize the protest as a success. "We have realized our great end already," religion professor John Sullivan told the gathering in Page Auditorium. "You have transformed the university." An editorial in the *Duke Chronicle* echoed this theme. It described the Silent Vigil as more than a means for gaining the four demands and memorializing King. "More essentially," the paper wrote, "it was a call for a change in spirit, a call for the University . . . to take a position of leadership in the community, a call for recommitment by whites to the principle of non-violence, and to working together to help Blacks. This, we feel, was to a large extent accomplished." "We have seen things happen here," the paper concluded, that would have "seemed inconceivable less than a week ago."[68]

The workers and their allies in the Black community had a very different view of events. They were not ready to suspend their protest or to declare the Silent Vigil even a partial success. "I was very impressed by the number of people they got to sit on the quad," Howard Fuller commented. "They felt they had achieved a victory by sitting on the grass. To me, the victory has not been won until the union gets everything it has asked for." The strike would continue, the *Duke Chronicle* reported, because "Local 77 felt that they were given no satisfactory answers on the $1.60 minimum wage and collective bargaining." "I don't know what anybody else's plans are, but we're striking," Brandon said. Harvey emphasized the importance of collective bargaining. "We appreciate what you have done very much," he told the students. "You have helped us live a decent life." For Harvey and the workers, however, the path forward was clear. "We're going on if you decide to go back. Sink or swim, live or die, we're going on."[69]

On Wednesday night, vigil participants slept in Duke Chapel, Page Auditorium, and the West Campus Union. Well after midnight, Tisdale announced to Griffith that he wanted to visit Duke Chapel. Tisdale "had a strong feeling for the chapel," Griffith explained. It "was very important to him, to his faith." Griffith cautioned the board chair that if he appeared on campus, he might "need to speak to people." Despite this warning, Tisdale went to the chapel, accompanied by Griffith and Ashmore. Student David Roberts who was in the chapel to "dry out" remembered seeing "an older man" who "looked up at the ceiling and bowed his head." Although no one disturbed the board chair as he prayed, a student identified Tisdale on his way out. "They gathered around and they really put the pressure to him," Griffith recounted, "just like a beehive." Tisdale was, according to Henderson, "absolutely adamant that Duke would never have collective bargaining." The *Duke Chronicle* reported that the board chair "reiterated the determination that he will not recognize a union because 'a union can't get nothing for these workers that we will not give them.'" Alarmed that Tisdale's remarks were making an already volatile situation worse, Griffith and Ashmore pulled him out. "We were just anxious to get him out of there," Griffith remembered, "and he was anxious to leave."[70]

....

Thursday morning began with another mass meeting of vigil participants in Page Auditorium. Many students were angry when they learned of Tisdale's chapel remarks the prior evening. Nevertheless, the decisions made the prior evening to declare a ten-day moratorium on the vigil and continue the dining hall boycott retained majority support. In addition, the Vigil Strategy Committee would meet regularly to plan strategy and investigate the implementation of collective bargaining at Duke.[71]

Midmorning, vigil protesters reassembled on the main quadrangle. To mark the suspension of the Silent Vigil, the group marched to East Campus. A rally at 7:00 p.m. on the quad in front of Duke Chapel was planned.

Later Thursday, the university learned that Knight had been hospitalized. Although William Anlyan commented that further testing was needed to predict how long Knight would be on leave, he told the *Duke Chronicle* that initial indications were that Knight faced a recovery period that "may be a few weeks."[72]

Almost three thousand people attended the 7:00 p.m. rally on the main quad, the largest such gathering in the history of Duke University. Professor Charles Tanford told the protesters exuberantly, "You have wrought a revolution!" Not everyone was persuaded, however, that significant progress, let alone a revolution, had been achieved. "A large segment of the crowd," the *Duke Chronicle* reported, "decried the observation . . . that the Vigil had won important victories."[73]

The ten-day vigil moratorium was taken up by "rallies, strategy meetings, and planning sessions." Dining hall workers remained on strike. The student boycott of the West Campus dining halls continued. According to Theodore Minah, Duke's dining hall director, the boycott was 75 percent effective on West Campus. Minah also said that as many as one hundred Duke students had crossed the picket lines to work in the dining halls.[74]

On Monday, April 15, the full university board met in an all-day session. In response to a request from Griffith, vigil leaders prepared packets of information on the protest for board members. Included was a written statement strongly advocating for collective bargaining. Given the anti-union attitude of many of its members, however, there was little chance that the university board of trustees would agree to *any* form of collective bargaining. Rather than make its position on collective bargaining clear in mid-April, however, on the advice of Cole and other administrators, the board remained silent on the issue.[75] In doing so, the board delayed the strongly negative student and union reaction that would inevitably follow the announcement of its final position on the issue. Such a strategy worked to the university's advantage, the trustees likely thought, because it would be difficult for students to reignite substantial protest at the end of the semester.

Although the board might have avoided inflaming protesters on collective bargaining, the statement it released Tuesday was hardly conciliatory. Stepping back from Knight's commitment to form a committee of students, faculty, administrators, trustees, and workers to address employment-related issues, the board established a Special Trustee-Administrative Committee (Special Committee) to "look into . . . the adequacy of the relationship between the university and its non-academic employees." In a powerful statement of the real intent of the trustees, neither students nor any nonacademic employees were included on the committee. In what the board may have regarded as a concession, the statement "invited" striking workers to return to their jobs "with full standing." Finally, the statement announced that the July 1 raise for nonacademic employees promised by Tisdale would be spelled out "as soon as information is available [on] University resources [for] this purpose." The statement ended by cautioning that the resolutions to the open issues "will not advance further for some time."[76]

The composition of the Special Committee was also problematic. While the committee was not precluded from considering collective bargaining, Tisdale populated it with trustees whom he knew would oppose any such arrangement. Henry Rauch, CEO of Burlington Industries, would be the chair. Charles B. Wade Jr., vice president of R. J. Reynolds Tobacco Company, P. Huber Hanes Jr., president of Hanes Corporation, and Walter M. Upchurch, senior vice president of the Shell Company's foundation, would serve as members. Rauch, Wade, and Hanes, professor Peter Klopfer wrote, "are associated with companies whose reputations in the area of labor are notorious, to say the least." Their personal opposition to the principles of collective bargaining and fair grievance procedures was, according to Klopfer, "unremitting." As for Upchurch, he had been personnel director at Duke "at a time when the exploitation of Duke's nonacademic employees was at its height."[77] Although there would be other members of the Special Committee, it was unthinkable that senior executives of Burlington, R. J. Reynolds, and Hanes and a former director of personnel at Duke would allow a collective bargaining recommendation to come out of the group.

Both the students and the union reacted to the April 15 board's action with anger and disbelief. At a Tuesday night rally of 2,500 students and faculty on the main quad, Boger called the statement "disappointing and inadequate." He explained, "They have not so much as mentioned in their statement collective bargaining." Edward L. McNeill, president of Local 77, was even more direct. Rejecting the statement "even before he had heard it," McNeill said the trustees could have done something better with their time. Still, the previously announced ten-day moratorium on student protest would continue.[78]

More than two thousand people attended a vigil rally on Wednesday night featuring folk singer Pete Seeger. Harvey assured the crowd of his unshakable determination to continue the fight. "I want to let you know," he told the protesters, "we're not going to give up." Harvey told rallygoers that the striking workers needed $2,000 to $3,000 per week to remain on strike. He asked them to continue their efforts to raise money and to boycott the dining halls.[79]

Despite his strong statement at the rally, with the strike by dining hall and housekeeping workers nearing the end of its second week, Harvey was aware that time was running out to resolve the labor action. "The University had almost won," Harvey remembered, "because our employees had gotten . . . worried about getting back on the job. They were fixin' to leave me." Harvey was "very, very worried" because he knew "we would lose at Duke if we walked back in there," he recalled. "But by the help of God," he recounted, "on the thirteenth day . . . my wife called me and said that the Trustee board wanted to meet with me." Harvey had been seeking such a face-to-face meeting with the trustees for years. He considered the chance to speak directly to Duke's governing body a significant accomplishment.[80]

Harvey appeared at a Special Committee meeting held on campus on April 20. The nonacademic employees "didn't get anywhere" at this meeting, Harvey remembered, "because my main point was what we had struck for was exclusive recognition. But they talked all around that." Instead, the Special Committee proposed that "another type of organization" be set up. "They pleaded to us to go back, to call off the strike, and no person would be penalized," Harvey said. Faced with this response, the workers decided to go back to their jobs. "So we come to the conclusion to end the strike," Harvey explained, "by promises from the Trustee board that we would work with an organization that we'd agree on together that would [have] the same meaning to us as a union, and that everybody would be brought up to a $1.60 minimum."[81]

Student representatives also met with the Special Committee, stressing the importance of collective bargaining. The *Duke Chronicle* reported "that the students were pleased at the receptiveness of some of the committee members to their proposals." Rauch told the students, according to the student newspaper, that the committee "wanted to provide personal dignity and integrity in the decision-making process of the University." Despite the facade of amiable give-and-take, however, students had almost no negotiating leverage in the meeting. "We did not have the strength or the organizational ability to be determining what would go on in the negotiating sessions," Henderson explained. "We were negotiating from a position of threat, not strength." "I think we got a little seduced," Gutman said decades later. "We were sitting down with the trustees and we had the vigil on our shoulders. . . . I think the firmness we showed when we planned the vigil, the firmness we had out on the quad, I don't think it was [there] quite as much . . . in that room."[82]

During their meeting, the members of the Special Committee also reviewed a university study comparing the wages of Duke's nonacademic employees with compensation levels at state universities in North Carolina. The findings were stark. The study found that the minimum wage paid to employees at state universities was $1.45 per hour, more than 20 percent higher than the $1.15 per hour minimum wage at Duke. In addition, wages paid to employees at state universities with more than five years of experience were "substantially higher" than those paid to comparable employees at Duke. Finally, the study considered how the university's payroll system was administered. Confirming a claim that Duke workers had been making for years, the study found that the administration of the wage structure at Duke was "extremely poor." Actual wages paid to nonacademic employees at Duke, the study found, were "in most instances at substantial variance with the approved rate ranges for each job classification." This meant that many employees at Duke were not even being paid the amount applicable to their job classification.[83]

The wage study was central to the Special Committee's recommendation that "prompt action . . . be taken to bring Duke wages more nearly in line with those currently paid by the State Universities." Armed with a study showing wages at Duke "grossly out of line" with other schools, Huestis explained, "we were able to lay in front of [the trustees] the figures. They didn't hesitate." "We didn't feel like our conscience could be cleared before we took care of" the wage disparity, Special Committee member Wade recalled. "We were grateful to the students. We were just sorry the students had to go to the length they did." Huestis emphasized that this was not "a decision to break up the Vigil." Rather, Huestis noted, "it was a statement by the trustees that this was something they felt was the right thing to do."[84] The fact that Duke administrators had not previously provided this compelling and readily available market data on wages to the board speaks powerfully to how little concern they had for the economic circumstances of the university's nonacademic employees.

On Saturday, April 20, at 9:00 p.m., following what Cole called a "long and soul-searching deliberation," the Special Committee released a statement. The committee acknowledged that "inadequacies in the relationship of the University and its non-academic employees do exist" and expressed its intent "to work as rapidly as possible to remedy them." The minimum wage for Duke employees would be raised from $1.15 per hour to $1.45 per hour on May 6, 1968, bringing it to the level at state universities. On June 3, 1968, "additional appropriate adjustments" would be made for employees earning more than $1.34 per hour. Finally, the statement reaffirmed the university's commitment to reach a $1.60 minimum wage by July 1, 1969. Huestis advised the Special Committee that the annual cost of these wage adjustments was approximately $2 million.[85]

Although the Special Committee once again made no reference to collective bargaining, students, faculty, and workers still reacted positively. "There was an atmosphere of general elation in the strategy session following the release of the statement," Henderson reported, and "everyone seemed to feel that we had won a significant victory." The workers were similarly encouraged, commenting that "they never would have believed that things would have worked out to this point . . . so well." The "statement changed everything," the student narrator observed. In its response to the Special Committee, the Vigil Strategy Committee said it looked forward to "the establishment of structures that will allow effective employee participation in decisions affecting their relationship with the University." At least some students continued to believe that these "structures" could include some form of collective bargaining.[86]

The striking workers met on Sunday afternoon and voted to return to work for a "trial period" of three weeks. The Local 77 president declared that this suspension of the strike was to "allow time for the students, faculty, and trustees to consider and act upon the issues and conditions which have arisen from the strike."[87] In addition, returning to work was a financial necessity for the striking workers. Most could no longer sustain the loss of income from being out of work.

At this point, Huestis and Griffith, among others, urged the students to refrain from further protest. In their view, any escalation would jeopardize support for the vigil's demands among faculty, administrators, and trustees. Vigil leaders accepted this advice. Further protest activities would be low-key and the dining hall boycott was suspended. Given the arc of events, however, the student narrator—among others—was starting to doubt the trustees' good faith. "My only concern," he said at the time, was that "I'm not so sure that the trustees are playing fair with us. They could very well just be leading us down the garden path. . . . We'll just have to keep our fingers crossed and hope that they deal with us in good faith," he concluded.[88]

A nighttime rally attended by four hundred students and some faculty was held on Sunday, April 21. It was, according to Henderson, "a victory celebration." "Participants felt that the University was finally moving in the right direction," he wrote. "Our methods had worked; we had proven that people with concern could effect rapid, progressive change."[89]

Rauch also thought that things were heading in the right direction. He wrote to the board of trustees on April 22, reassuring them that "only about 400 students, faculty members and employees" participated in the rally the previous night. This was only a fraction of the more than two thousand who had attended the final vigil rally and Seeger concert only ten days earlier. "While our statement did not go as far as [faculty and student groups] would have liked," Rauch told the trustees, "they accepted it as evidence of good faith and exerted their full influence on the faculty, students and employees on Sunday to accept it as evidence of definite progress."[90]

With all the celebration, however, the central issue of collective bargaining remained unresolved. The *Duke Chronicle* reported that McNeill told the Sunday night rally crowd that workers would return to their jobs for three weeks, "while the faculty, trustees, and committees had time to make constructive movement toward collective bargaining at Duke." "We'll be right back" on strike, Harvey told the rally, "if constructive progress towards collective bargaining is not made within three weeks." Vigil leaders agreed. "This thing might not be over," vigil leader Bob Creamer told the rally. "The trustees have made a few statements but certainly have not instituted collective bargaining. We've got to let the trustees know we're still here." "We cannot return to normalcy," Strange told the rally crowd. "The effort to build the beloved community is long and difficult [and] we have only begun."[91] In the days leading up to the end of the spring semester, students and workers would learn just how "long and difficult" the effort would be.

....

By May 5, two weeks had passed since the first encouraging statement from the Special Committee. No word had yet been received from the committee on the issue of collective bargaining. With the end of the three-week moratorium approaching, vigil leaders were becoming increasingly aware that their key demand might not be achieved. "Things are very much up in the air," Creamer commented.[92]

Several days later, on May 9, the Vigil Strategy Committee issued a statement expressing its growing concern "about the progress of the special committee . . . toward creating a collective bargaining system for Duke's nonacademic employees." It called the absence of any communication from the Special Committee "disappointing" and declared its support for a complete boycott of the university dining halls on May 10.[93]

On Saturday, May 11, one day before the three-week moratorium was set to expire, the Special Committee finally released a brief statement. The committee proposed establishing a "council of non-academic employees" at the university. It also indicated that it was looking into forming a "Duke University Employee Relations Advisory Committee" composed of administrators, faculty members, and nonacademic employees. Neither proposal addressed collective bargaining in any form. The statement also said that the Special

Committee would be reconvening on Wednesday, May 15, and hoped to meet at that time with faculty representatives, students, and workers.[94]

In a final attempt to apply pressure to the Special Committee when it met on May 15, the Vigil Strategy Committee decided to reconvene the vigil at 2:00 p.m. on May 14. "It is with despair and disappointment that we return to the quadrangle," a Vigil Strategy Committee statement explained. "We believed that the Trustees were acting in good faith. . . . It is now obvious that there was no good faith and no understanding. . . . We must be on the quad to demonstrate that we expect collective bargaining and will not accept less."[95]

The workers were also deeply disappointed by the Special Committee's statement. Oliver Harvey told the *Duke Chronicle* that while employees would report to work on Monday, May 13, representatives of the different departments would meet on May 14 "to determine if and when the non-academic employees union members would begin striking again." Harvey's message to the Vigil Strategy Committee was somewhat different. He told the committee that a strike during the waning days of the spring semester was unlikely because students would be leaving for summer vacation and many nonacademic employees would be furloughed during that time. Anticipating his upcoming meeting with the Special Committee, Harvey told the *Duke Chronicle* that collective bargaining is the "main issue" and that the workers "are not planning to commit ourselves to anything else."[96]

On May 14, students and faculty marched from East Campus to West Campus to reconvene the vigil. In contrast to early April when nearly 1,500 protesters slept on the quad, now just over two hundred joined the march. Because of a downpour, participants in the May vigil moved inside the chapel around 6:00 p.m. and remained there overnight. Student protesters and their faculty supporters were "disillusioned with the Board of Trustees," Creamer commented. "We are here out of sadness and determination." Leaders announced that the vigil would remain on the quad until after the Special Committee meeting the next day.[97]

In Duke Chapel, many vigil participants were busy working on end-of-semester projects. To understand why the turnout was so small, the *Duke Chronicle* conducted a "random sampling" of participants in the Silent Vigil who did not join the vigil when it reconvened. Some were uncomfortable that the protest now focused exclusively on collective bargaining. Most Silent Vigil participants who did not participate in May, however, cited pragmatic reasons. One "typical ex-Vigiler," the student newspaper reported, commented,

"I have too much damn work to do, finals and papers are . . . approaching, and being out there tonight just doesn't stack up."[98]

When they met with the Special Committee on May 15, the students' fears were confirmed. The Special Committee would not be recommending collective bargaining in any form. The scene was confrontational. Collective bargaining "has gotta happen," Small declared. "The time has come. Duke's not a plantation." At this point, according to Small, "Henry Rauch started shaking—literally shaking. He said, 'There will never be collective bargaining at Duke University.'" Instead, the Special Committee identified seven areas that would be the focus of efforts to enhance employer-employee relations at Duke.[99]

The Special Committee delivered this same message to the workers. Harvey was direct in his response. According to the *Duke Chronicle*, he asked the committee whether the trustees were totally against collective bargaining. While trustee Brantley Watson responded, "We have not said we are against collective bargaining," Rauch interjected, "I am!"[100]

Rauch also made his position clear when he transmitted the Special Committee's recommendations to the full board. He expressed the group's desire to improve relations between the university and its nonacademic employees and described the nonacademic employee "council" that the Special Committee recommended be established by the university. Rauch made clear to the board, however, that the creation of the employee council did not mean any change in who controlled the labor-management relationship at Duke. Employee participation, he assured the board, "is [not] intended in [any] way to transfer decision making responsibility to employees."[101]

As the Special Committee was meeting on May 15, a group of about eight members of the small Duke chapter of the Students for a Democratic Society (SDS) decided that they no longer had any choice but to escalate the protest. The group entered the Allen Building, then staged a brief sit-in in the lobby on the second floor. Hutch Traver, the group's leader, saw the tactics of the vigil as too moderate. "Like the Afro-Americans have realized in past weeks," he said, "most of us realize the ways of the liberals don't work now." Once the SDS members entered the Allen Building, Traver tried to persuade those in the larger vigil group on the quad to join the sit-in. He was unable to do so. After about thirty minutes, the SDS members left the Allen Building. Traver later called the attempt at escalation a "disaster." "For some reason it just died," he recounted. "We got upstairs, sat down. . . . There weren't even enough of us to block traffic in the lobby."[102]

The Special Committee did not make its specific recommendations public. Instead, the committee issued only a brief general statement saying that it intended to work on spelling out the details of the program that had been outlined. "We don't expect you to be happy with this," Huestis said to the students when he handed the statement to them.[103]

Huestis was right. The *Duke Chronicle* reported that vigil leaders responded to the statement with "resigned disgust" and that a "sense of frustration seemed to grip many participants." The Vigil Strategy Committee said it was "extremely disappointed" that "little progress [had been made] on collective bargaining." The students were getting "increasingly disillusioned" about the prospects for working with the Special Committee, the *Duke Chronicle* editorial board wrote. Noting the committee's "intransigence" on the issue of collective bargaining, the paper correctly stated that students saw "no hope of dialogue with a group which delayed its discussion as long as possible so as to make demonstrations academically difficult."[104]

The nonacademic employees were also very disappointed. As they understood it, the proposed employee council could not enter into a binding agreement with the university and would not be independent. Accordingly, the employee council could do little, if anything, to improve the employees' negotiating leverage with the university. "The trustees don't want to negotiate with a union," a flyer for a meeting of nonacademic employees stated, "but instead want to sit and talk to workers from a council. What's the difference?" the flyer asked. "Power!!!!!!!!!!"[105]

The vigil soon disbanded. "It looks pretty hopeless," Gutman told vigil participants. Small told the *Duke Chronicle* that "many students are considering transferring." "By the end of the vigil," Henderson said later, "we hadn't won anything."[106]

Given that the Silent Vigil failed to achieve its objectives, it is striking that Duke trustees, administrators, faculty, and students now broadly consider the protest as having been highly successful. For many, memories of the vigil have taken on a reverential glow. Cook called it a "transcendent moment and indelible memory." Trustee Mary D. B. T. Semans recalled "golden moments" during the protest, calling the vigil "a special chapter in the life of Duke." "It was," she commented, "a collaboration of students and faculty acting for the betterment of the total university." Students exhibited a "new maturity" and "elements of unselfishness," Semans recounted, "and the administration plus trustees listened and acted." Professor Alan C. Kerckhoff recalled the event as a "beautiful example of people trying to effect change through nontraditional means." The vigil had been "inspirational," he said. "We did this one right," Kinney recalled. "It showed me the value of a small cadre of people making committed decisions."[107]

What explains this positive view of a protest for racial justice that, in April 1968, nearly shut down the university and ended with leaders feeling "resigned disgust"? One answer is that the vigil had, in some instances, a transformative impact on both Duke University and those who participated in it. Before the vigil, one student wrote in the *Duke Chronicle*, the university was a "peaceful, quiet bastion of Christian morality . . . , a pleasant, sheltered place inhabited by bright, but unconcerned people; where 'nice kids' came for four years of beer, basketball games and studying." After the vigil, that changed. "I use the metaphor of the tree," Cell reflected in describing the impact of the vigil on Duke. "When the tree is shaking, [you don't know] what's going to come down. And it did shake the tree." Cell saw a "new intensity" at Duke following the Vigil and he was very excited by it. "I told the students the morning of [April] 11 in Page," he recalled, "that it was the first time I had been really proud of the university." "I think the vigil made a difference in the institution," he said later. "It marked the beginning of the changeover from a board comprised of mostly conservative, North Carolina businessmen [to a more progressive board]. The image Duke had of itself," Cell commented, "and the kind of people who were in positions of power changed." Small, among others, dismissed the view that the vigil itself caused any fundamental change in the university. "That's a bunch of crap," she said. "As long as people like Henry Rauch are in charge of an institution, it's going to stay exactly the same."[108]

Students had also been affected. For one thing, the vigil challenged the Cold War mindset that many students had brought with them to college. "It is hard for people today to envision," Van Pelt later commented, "a time when virtually every American believed without question that we . . . always had been good guys, which is why we were a wealthy nation that never lost a war; that our leaders and law enforcement officials were on a mission from God." The vigil challenged these assumptions. "For five days we made common cause with one another and the workers," student David Roberts recalled. "Many of us found ourselves in growing realization that the world might not be so predictable, that our lives might not progress from comfort to comfort, that we would not have the luxury of ignoring or merely observing the anguish and misfortune of Black Americans." Campus activists had found a new momentum. "Many white people," according to McLeod, "have been forced to think for the first time." "'Activist' will no longer be regarded as an epithet" at Duke, the student newspaper commented.[109]

For a number of students, the vigil had a profound personal impact. One alumnus writing on behalf a group of Duke graduates living together in California years after the vigil found that "the days of protests seem naive now."

> Yet the Vigil was a true and important beginning. We learned on the sodden and trampled grass of the quad that people can live and work together, and that ordinary people possess within themselves the power to change the world. Yes, I remember panty-raids, blue jeans, drugs, making love (Duke Gardens!). I even remember Freddy Lind's great play to beat UNC in overtime. But most of all, I remember the Vigil. The spirit of it lives on here.

Another participant wrote that "those four or five days when I participated in the Vigil, and my two days of sitting on the quad is very important in my life. Participating in an . . . active show of support for something I very much believed in," she said, "gave me a foundation for later active participation in my academic and work communities. None so dramatic or meaningful as the Vigil, but all stemming from my experience then." "I was never the same" after the vigil, student Clay Steinman commented. "I was now someone who saw my life as being interconnected with the lives of others. I can't tell you what a change that was."[110]

The vigil also had a positive impact on Duke's nonacademic employees. Responding to one of the vigil's demands, the university agreed to a significant increase in the minimum wage for Duke workers, bringing it up to the level paid at state universities. In September, Huestis announced that the university would meet the $1.60 per hour minimum wage by October 7, 1968. The cost to the university for these increases was not insignificant. Soon after the vigil, more customary job descriptions and job classifications were developed for Duke's nonacademic employees and, under Huestis's leadership, the payroll system was administered in a more professional manner. As plans for an employee council were worked out with Duke's nonacademic employees, communication between workers and the university improved along with working conditions for the employees. "Some of this [improvement in worker conditions] would have happened anyway," Cell commented.[111] Still, the vigil caused the changes to occur sooner than anyone would otherwise have expected.

Although the positive changes that ensued were one reason why the Silent Vigil is regarded with such favor, another is the self-discipline and order many saw in the protest. Semans had not approved of the occupation of Knight's house. "It was a violation of his rights," she explained, "showing bad manners." Yet her view of the Silent Vigil was much more positive. For her, it was "purposeful and amazingly impressive, non-violent and constructive." Huestis saw the vigil in a similar light. "I think [the vigil on the quad] was a very responsible approach on the part of students," he commented, "who wanted to be heard, who were genuinely concerned and who did it in a style and in a tone that I think reflected credit on the Duke student body." Sociology professor Alan Kerckhoff joined the chorus of praise. "These were all well-mannered, middle-class young ladies and gentlemen who were brought up properly and did things properly. More importantly," he commented, those organizing knew that the "only way to accomplish anything was to do it in a proper manner. . . . It isn't bloodletting, it isn't climbing walls, it isn't destroying property."[112]

Some who admired the self-restraint and orderly nature of the vigil even viewed those attributes of the protest as the reason for its "effectiveness." Huestis observed, for example, that the peaceful, controlled vigil "was really a far more effective demonstration than a violent demonstration." Kerckhoff agreed, explaining, "We are dealing with people for whom any overt attack would be defined as not only unacceptable from a legalistic point of view, but would completely erode the bargaining position of the people involved." "We appealed to the better aspects of the white southern church-going population," Kinney explained. "In order to build popular support for [the vigil], . . . we had to do things that were not the same as they did" at Columbia University, where the student protests turned violent. "It was just a totally different environment."[113]

The white students and faculty who participated in the Silent Vigil did so, in part, to demonstrate to Black students and workers at Duke and in Durham that nonviolent protest could still work. They wanted to show that by working within the system, a white institution such as Duke could be forced to make dramatic, meaningful changes to advance the cause of racial justice. Knight appears to have concluded that the Silent Vigil accomplished this goal. He described the protest in his memoir as "highly effective."[114] Yet how effective was it actually? Answering this question requires more than simply determining whether the vigil resulted in positive developments for the university and its students, which it certainly did. One still must ask whether the vigil was successful in accomplishing the specific objectives it set out to achieve. Did the remarkably self-regulated, highly organized protest that occurred at Duke in April 1968 achieve the four demands it presented? If not, did it otherwise summon the university to respond to the racial crisis in America by taking a dramatic step to advance racial justice? Did Duke students show that a protest that operates squarely inside the "system" can force meaningful change?

The disposition of the four demands begins to provide an answer. The first demand, that Knight sign the *Durham Morning Herald* ad, was not accepted. Knight refused to lend his name to the ad. Regarding the second demand, that Knight resign from Hope Valley Country Club, the Duke president appeared to be more receptive. He agreed that at some point in the future he would resign from the club, although he would not commit to a specific time frame. It would be another ten months before he took this step, and only due to escalating pressure from Duke's Black students. The third demand—to increase the minimum wage for Duke employees to $1.60 per hour—received a more positive response. The university in fact did agree to a significant increase in the minimum wage for Duke workers, a step taken at no small cost. Still, while many observers viewed this wage adjustment as a response to the vigil, other factors were also certainly at work. At the same time as the Silent Vigil, Duke service workers staged a highly effective strike that lasted for almost two weeks. It is at least possible that this strike was a contributing factor in the university's decision to raise the minimum wage. The compensation study presented to the Special Committee at the same time also certainly played a critical role. How much and how quickly the board would have raised wages in the absence of the worker strike or compensation report cannot be known.

The fourth issue—collective bargaining—is the most problematic and most central. Because it involved a change in the power dynamic between Duke and its workers, acceptance of collective bargaining represented the most dramatic step the university was asked to make in order to distance itself from its traditional "plantation system." As events demonstrated, the demand for collective bargaining was a nonstarter for the Duke board. Not only did the board refuse to grant this right in any form, but it delayed disclosing its inflexible position until the end of the spring semester. Ultimately, Duke would cede no authority or leverage to the workers in negotiating wages and working conditions at the university.

Every observer is entitled to their own opinion as to whether Duke University rose to the moral challenge posed by the King assassination and the Silent Vigil. Samuel DuBois Cook, King's longtime friend and the man whose speech to the vigil captured the spirit of the protest, answered the question in the negative. While not "for a moment [questioning] the good will, motives, honor, or decency of the administration," Cook assessed the university's overall response to the vigil critically. "Honestly, painfully, unfortunately, and regretfully," he wrote thirty years after the event, "the response of the administration was . . . weak, myopic, institutionally unimaginative, ethically insensitive, humanistically blind, extremely disappointing, and quite unworthy not only of Duke, but also its own great potential." Cook could not "escape or hide the feeling that the administration was terribly on the wrong side of a great moral issue and missed, so sadly, a great and unique opportunity." "Thankfully," Cook added, "Duke's remarkable sense of community stayed intact."[115]

With the vigil over, Black campus activism would regain center stage. Attention would turn to the Black students' demands that the university finally take steps to address their cultural, social, and academic needs. How would these students approach protest and how would the university react? Would Duke's "remarkable sense of community" survive the encounter? Events occurring at Duke in the fall semester of 1968 would begin to provide these answers.

(*above*) Segregated seating at Duke University Stadium, Notre Dame versus Duke football game, December 2, 1961 (Duke University Archives). A report prepared in 1962 explained that "the Negro section at the outdoor Stadium is predicated on the assumption that Negroes prefer to sit together and that such separation avoids 'incidents.'"

(*right*) First three African American Duke graduates, 1967 (Duke University Archives). Among the "first five" in 1963, Wilhelmina Reuben, Nathaniel White Jr., and Mary Mitchell Harris were the first African American undergraduates to receive their degrees from Duke in 1967.

(*left*) Douglas M. Knight speaking at his inauguration, December 11, 1963 (Duke University Archives). Offered the presidencies of Duke and Cornell at the same time, the forty-two-year-old Knight was among the youngest university presidents in the nation.

(*below*) Martin Luther King Jr. speaking to an overflow crowd in Page Auditorium at Duke on November 13, 1964 (Duke University Archives).

(*opposite*) Samuel DuBois Cook, 1966 (Duke University Archives). Political science professor Samuel DuBois Cook became the first African American faculty member at Duke in 1966.

(*opposite*) A Black student band member remains seated, refusing to participate in the playing of "Dixie" at a Duke athletic event, circa 1968 (photo by Larry Funk; *Chanticleer*, 1969, p. 34). Among the initial AAS "concerns" presented to the administration, the playing of "Dixie" and the display of the Confederate flag at university events were discontinued in 1968.

(*right*) Wilhelmina Reuben, May Queen, 1967 (Duke University Archives). In 1967 Wilhelmina Reuben was elected by the Woman's College as the first Black May Queen in Duke history. Trustee C. B. Houck wrote to President Knight that Reuben's election was in "bad taste," and trustee George M. Ivey Jr. found it "nauseating to contemplate" that Duke would attract students who would make such a choice.

(*below*) Stokely Carmichael speaks to a full house in Page Auditorium, March 17, 1967 (Duke University Archives). The appearance of the chair of SNCC at Duke catalyzed Black students to meet as a group for the first time.

Approximately 250 nonacademic employees, students, and other supporters protest outside the Allen Building on April 19, 1967, seeking impartial third-party arbitration of employee grievances (Durham Civil Rights Heritage Project; photo by Bill Boyarsky).

Labor leader Oliver Harvey (*center*) and an unnamed student distribute Local 77 literature on the Duke campus, April 1967 (Durham Civil Rights Heritage Project; photo by Bill Boyarsky).

Black students hold a "study-in" in the anteroom outside President Knight's office on November 13, 1967, to protest the continued use of off-campus segregated facilities by Duke student organizations (Duke University Archives). Although Knight maintained he was not responding to Black student pressure, the university prohibited the use of segregated facilities by student groups less than four days later.

On April 5, 1968, approximately 250 students, the vast majority of them white, occupy the home of Duke president Douglas Knight following a memorial march for Martin Luther King Jr. (*Duke Chronicle*, April 4, 1988). Knight gave the students permission to remain overnight, and they stayed in the house for thirty-six hours.

(*left*) The Silent Vigil, April 1968 (Duke University Archives). The Silent Vigil on the main quadrangle was highly organized. Protesters sat in rows. Rules included "No talking. . . . No eating except at group snack and meal breaks. . . . No sunbathing" and "No singing except at specified periods under the direction of the song leader."

(*below*) The Silent Vigil, April 1968 (Duke University Archives). The first protest for most participants, the Silent Vigil had a powerful impact on the individuals involved. One protester said it was "as close as I ever came to a religious feeling."

The Silent Vigil, April 10, 1968 (Duke University Archives). Silent Vigil participants demanded that Duke's nonacademic employees be granted the right to bargain collectively. Dining hall workers and students organized picket lines outside the campus dining halls.

The Silent Vigil, April 10, 1968 (Duke University Archives). Silent Vigil protesters remained on the Duke quadrangle even after it started to rain.

The Silent Vigil, April 10, 1968 (Duke University Archives). *Left to right*: Charles Huestis, Frank Ashmore, Wright Tisdale, student Reed Kramer, and student Jonathan Kinney. Tisdale, the board chair, and administrators joined in singing "We Shall Overcome" after Tisdale addressed the vigil. "If you saw the picture" of me singing, Tisdale told an alumni group a few months later, "you'd know I wasn't happy about it."

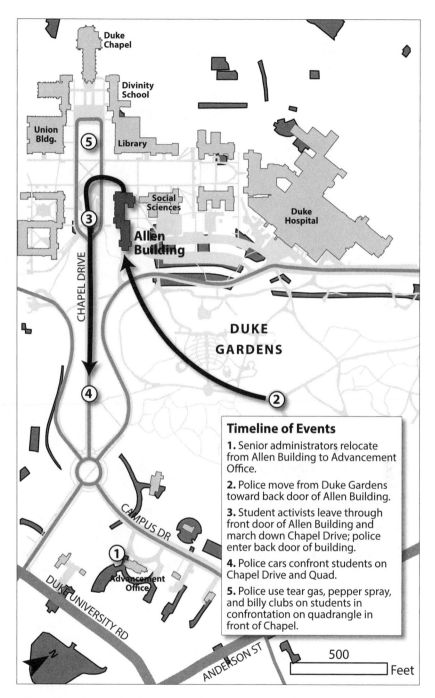

Timeline of Events

1. Senior administrators relocate from Allen Building to Advancement Office.

2. Police move from Duke Gardens toward back door of Allen Building.

3. Student activists leave through front door of Allen Building and march down Chapel Drive; police enter back door of building.

4. Police cars confront students on Chapel Drive and Quad.

5. Police use tear gas, pepper spray, and billy clubs on students in confrontation on quadrangle in front of Chapel.

500 Feet

Map of West Campus of Duke University showing movements of administrators, students, and police during the afternoon of the Allen Building takeover on February 13, 1969. Map by Tim Stallmann.

Activist and comedian Dick Gregory speaks to a crowd of 3,000 people at the Duke indoor stadium on February 10, 1969 (Duke University Archives). Knight believed that Gregory's speech, titled "Nigger," was "the explosive one" that triggered the Allen Building takeover.

Students inside the Allen Building during the takeover, February 13, 1969 (photo by Lynette Lewis). *Left to right*: Carolyn Day, Josie Knowlin, C. B. Claiborne, and Leonard Brown. Duke decision-makers made only one attempt to engage in discussions with the protesters during the takeover and declined to send a faculty member into the building to speak to them, citing "hostage dangers."

Students inside the Allen Building during the takeover, February 13, 1969 (photo by Lynette Lewis). *Left to right*: Chuck Hopkins (*on phone at desk*), C. B. Claiborne (*at desk*), Bertie Howard (*seated on chair*), Cheri Riley, unidentified student (*seated on desk*), Charles Becton, and Clarence Morgan. Students took turns answering the many calls that came in from media, friends, faculty, members of the local Black community, and parents, among others.

The Allen Building takeover, February 13, 1969 (Duke University Archives). The administration immediately adopted a "no negotiations" stance toward the protest, and Durham police and the state highway patrol were called to campus soon after administrators learned of the takeover. Police in full riot gear assembled in Duke Gardens, awaiting instructions, which came hours later.

The Allen Building takeover, February 13, 1969 (Duke University Archives). A large crowd of white student activists, Black students, sympathetic faculty, and members of the Durham Black community, among others, assembled outside the Allen Building to protect the protesters from the police. Once mobilized, police encircled this group.

Police standing outside the Allen Building (photo by Larry Funk; *Chanticleer*, 1969, p. 54). One member of the police contingent told a protester years later that having been on standby in Duke Gardens for hours, the officers arrived on the quad "pumped up and primed" and ready to "whip some heads and get this thing in order."

Students on the quad after the Allen Building takeover, February 13, 1969 (Duke University Archives). Although Black students had left the Allen Building, police determined that it was necessary to clear the quad. "Tear gas was flying everywhere," one eyewitness said, and "police started hitting people with billy clubs."

Policeman approaching unidentified student, February 13, 1969 (Duke University Archives). One student reported seeing police "striking anything in their path." "Kent State could very well have happened at Duke," one protester thought later.

Police approach students on the quad after the Allen Building takeover, February 13, 1969 (Duke University Archives). In addition to tear gas, police deployed a pepper gas machine that one observer described as looking like "a combination-vacuum-cleaner-ray-gun." Police efforts to clear the quad lasted for over an hour.

The central records office after the Allen Building takeover, February 13, 1969 (Duke University Archives). Because they exited in haste, students left behind the supplies they had taken into the Allen Building. A sweep of the occupied area showed that no records had been destroyed and little damage had occurred.

"Weapons" brought into the Allen Building (Douglas Knight Records, Duke University Archives). The university presented this picture at the disciplinary hearing as evidence that students had brought "weapons" into the Allen Building. Students maintained that these items were used only to secure the occupied area.

University House, February 15, 1969 (Duke University Archives). Students confronted Knight (*circled*) outside his house the day following the takeover. After the chaotic, combative session, students, faculty, and administrators agreed to meet in the evening to discuss Black student concerns.

CHAPTER 6

———

Humiliating to Plead for Our Humanity

Negotiations

———

Just as the Silent Vigil was ending, the *Duke Chronicle* wrote on April 12, 1968, about the "new Duke University" that had emerged from the protest.[1] Thanks to the vigil, the paper noted, Duke faculty members had become more engaged, and more students were socially conscious and politically active. Even the university's board of trustees showed signs of listening to students and workers, exhibiting at least some concern for the social impact of the university's labor policies. Many students returning for the fall semester of 1968 experienced the "new intensity" on campus that John Cell observed after the vigil.

Duke was indeed changing. A new chemistry building and Perkins Library addition were almost ready for occupancy. The East Campus science building was being transformed into an arts center. New rules allowed women on East Campus to sign out of their dorms overnight, no longer requiring permission from a house counselor. On West Campus, returning men encountered what the *Duke Chronicle* called, only half-jokingly, "a drastic change in their lives." "Starting this September," the newspaper reported, "maids will no longer make beds for West Campus students."[2] In many areas, Duke appeared to have become less regional, less isolated, more in the mainstream of American universities that entertained national ambitions.

If some sensed the emergence of a new Duke University in the fall of 1968, however, one group did not—the school's Black students. Arriving back on campus, these students faced essentially the same challenges that had made their lives so difficult in the years since desegregation. Cell wrote in late 1968 that desegregation at Duke had meant permitting Black students to "enroll as members of the student body" but without any of their distinctive needs and concerns acknowledged. Through what Cell characterized as a policy of "passive acceptance," the university had "thoughtlessly" adopted an "assimilation-ist model" of desegregation—Black students would be admitted to Duke, but the university would not change. Cell was correct. Duke had done nothing to address the needs of its Black students, who, he noted, were called on "to do all the adjusting."[3]

Compounding matters, administrators seemed almost totally unaware of the problems that Black students were facing. According to Cell, the reason was straightforward. "From the fall of 1963 to the fall of 1968," he wrote, "there was no effective communication between the black students and the University at large." Administrators and faculty made little effort to get to know these students or to develop relationships with them. In his classroom interactions, Cell encountered a "formidable barrier of distrust and suspicion" in the Black students he taught. Without communication, white administrators had no chance to learn about, or try to understand, the reality Black students at Duke were experiencing every day.[4]

Because Duke administrators remained so passive, racial matters at Duke were static, even as the university was undergoing rapid change in other areas. "In effect," Cell wrote to provost Marcus Hobbs in February 1969, "there is enough of the old climate left to lend substance to the students' impressions [that Duke is racist]. 'Dixie' and Hope Valley memberships are but the tip of the iceberg," he added. The school's Black students still remained isolated; as of the fall of 1968, Duke only had one Black administrator and two Black professors. Black students comprised just over 1 percent of those attending Duke's undergraduate, graduate, and professional schools. In the employment area, Duke's director of employee relations described the school as having "a white top and a black bottom." Fully 70 percent of the 1,500 unskilled laborers and service workers at the university were Black. Yet outside campus, the university had no business contracts with Black-owned companies in Durham. This created a deteriorating situation. "As the tone of the Black movement has turned from legal rights to economic and social equality," Cell warned in December 1968, "it has grown more militant. . . . Black awareness has increased, [and,] as the crisis in American society has deepened, the situation in the microcosmic community of Duke University [has] worsened." With the increase in Black militancy nationally, Bertie Howard saw the atmosphere on campus begin to change. "People no longer thought they needed to be solicitous of Black students," she remembered. There was "more open hostility," more "mistrust."[5]

On October 4, 1968, representatives of the Afro-American Society (AAS) met members of the administration for the first time to discuss the issues Duke's Black students were facing. This meeting—along with several follow-up sessions—provided a singular opportunity for the university to address the concerns of its Black students prior to confrontation. Yet with little prior communication and few, if any, relationships between students and university administrators, this already difficult task proved nearly impossible. As events would soon show, race not only created the problems Black students were facing but undermined the efforts of students and administrators to find a path forward together.

....

President Douglas Knight met for the first time with Duke's Black students to ask for a list of their concerns on January 9, 1968, just as the spring 1968 semester was getting underway. The Orangeburg Massacre had followed in February, then the assassination of Martin Luther King Jr. in April. After the King assassination, historian Ibram X. Kendi wrote, "higher education shuddered in a paroxysm of . . . black student power." Black campus activism was present in almost every state—Iowa, California, Michigan, Connecticut, Wisconsin, Illinois, Massachusetts, Oregon, Alabama, and New York, among many others.[6]

Although the massacre and assassination were watershed events for Black students at Duke, it was the Silent Vigil—an event Charles Becton described as "mostly a white vigil"—that was the focal point for protest in the immediate aftermath of King's death. As these events were unfolding, assistant dean of Arts and Sciences William Griffith followed up on Knight's request that Black students provide him with a list of their concerns. Initially, Griffith contacted Lee Hatcher and Joyce Hobson. He was, according to a chronology prepared by vice president for institutional advancement Frank Ashmore, "assured that the list would be forthcoming." Yet by May, the list had still not materialized. Hence Griffith had lunch with a group of Black students, repeating his request for a "written report." Again, nothing was sent, leading Griffith later in May to suggest to Chuck Hopkins that a group of Black students meet with "faculty and administration over the summer for an in-depth discussion of problems related to black students on campus." Griffith told Hopkins that the university would underwrite the travel costs of the Black students. Although Hopkins agreed to the meeting, no further contact occurred over the summer.[7]

Duke administrators and faculty assumed that Black students would readily produce their list of concerns and were baffled when they failed to do so. Since they had no effective lines of communication with the students, faculty members and administrators could only speculate on the cause. Ashmore reasoned that the students simply did not consider preparing the list a priority. "The students intended to prepare the report, but simply never got around to it," he observed. Griffith attributed the delay to tactics. "I couldn't help but [feel]," he recalled, "that they didn't . . . want to identify everything. . . . They were reluctant to put [the specifics] down . . . because then [in two weeks] there might be another problem that they'd see."[8]

Given the lack of contact between university administrators and Black students, it is not surprising that these were erroneous observations. It was not that the students lacked focus. Rather, generating a list of specific concerns was not easy given their own internal political conflicts. By January 1968, the group faced real divisions. "Black students were far from monolithic," Kendi explained. Like any other group of students, "black student communities comprised collections of minigroups ordered by charismatic students, fraternal connections, artistic talents, hometowns, and mutual interests and friendships, to name a few distinguishing factors."[9]

Internal political conflicts came to a head with the AAS leadership elections in February 1968. With Brenda Armstrong's election as chair of the AAS, the group had a leader who could unite varied factions and move the group forward. Yet even with her leadership, significant ideological and political challenges remained. The Black students—none "professional educators"—were operating in a rapidly changing political and social environment, fraught with tension. Neither the Black campus movement nor academia had developed a template of concerns that set forth the institutional changes a white southern university should make to eliminate decades of racial exclusion. "Just as white universities [had] failed to anticipate the impact of the Black influx onto their campuses," historian Allen B. Ballard wrote perceptively in 1974, "so had Black intellectuals and Black students failed to conceptualize exactly what was wanted from the white universities into which they were entering."[10]

Students held widely differing views about what to include in their list of concerns. Some issues, such as the need for a Black barber on campus or a ban on the playing of "Dixie" at university functions, were noncontroversial. But others, like Black studies and the high attrition rate among Black students, were ideologically more complicated. They generated significant internal debate. To avoid splintering further, the AAS would need to reach consensus on which concerns to focus on. William Turner described one aspect of the challenge the students faced. "As students we could not articulate [the issues] as perhaps we can now," he recalled. "The things that are closest to you and that are most a part of your life—they're the most difficult to talk about and rationalize."[11]

Although for the most part the list of concerns was finalized by late spring, Armstrong and other leaders decided not to give it to the administration until the fall. "One of the things we were very careful about," Armstrong explained, "was what we said to the administration . . . and when we said it. [Even] the silences were planned."[12]

"A lot of the concerns we had were crystal clear by the end of the [school] year," Armstrong remembered. "But we felt that there was no reason to meet with the administration in May, when summer would come, [and] everyone was going home. Giving them a set of grievances [and] the summer . . . to answer them," she explained, "would be one way to defuse the issues."[13]

....

By September 1968, Knight had recovered from his relapse of hepatitis. As he prepared to resume a full-time schedule, he reached out to Griffith for an update on how things were going. "Sometime before the fall," he wrote Griffith in August, "I hope we can get together and talk about what's been planned, during the summer, concerning our black student groups." Knight recalled "how they came to see me last winter, and I think I need to catch up on where we stand at the moment."[14] By his own admission, Knight had been out of the loop. Indeed, he was unprepared for what he was about to confront.

Yet this was only one of the problems Knight faced upon his return. Perhaps most challenging was his relationship with the board of trustees. They had become increasingly concerned with maintaining order on campus. The Silent Vigil intensified these concerns. Early in 1968, the university had announced a new policy that sought to ban "illegitimate" protests that disrupted the "orderly operation of the institution."[15] As subsequent events showed, board chair Wright Tisdale, along with other trustees, worried that existing policies were not sufficient to maintain order. They also wondered whether university administrators could be trusted to respond effectively to disruptive activity.

Just after the vigil, in May 1968, university counsel Edwin Bryson informed his administrative colleagues about a recent conference call with Tisdale. According to Bryson, Tisdale "stated that he had polled the members of the executive committee by telephone. [They] were unanimous in their decision" that the existing rules regarding picketing and demonstrations should be rescinded and new ones adopted and made immediately effective. Under the new rules, "disruptive practice[s]," including sit-ins, violence, injury to person or property, or specific threats to person or property, would "not be tolerated." Any person (including faculty, students, or nonacademic employees) engaged in such practices would be notified that "he is in violation of University regulations . . . and that unless he should forthwith discontinue such practice he will be arrested and summarily dismissed from the University."[16] Instead of using the time since the Silent Vigil to encourage greater administrative recognition of student concerns, the trustees had instead sought to make certain that these concerns were stifled.

Before Tisdale's new rules were implemented, a special committee of university administrators was formed to consider ways to strengthen the school's existing "pickets and protests" policy. When the special committee presented its proposed changes to the Executive Committee, they were rejected as *not strong enough*. The special committee was instructed to "give the report further study . . . and to present revised recommendations . . . as soon as possible."[17] Clearly, a wide gap existed between university administrators and the executive committee on how to respond to campus protests.

Once the revised pickets and protests policy had been finalized, Tisdale directed that it be sent to every Duke student at home over the summer. In his transmittal letter, Knight described the policy as a "framework" through which various members of the university community could "resolve, as reasonable people, the differences which may from time to time arise among us." Tisdale was much less accommodating. "I hope these [policies] are studied by others as well as the trustees," Tisdale wrote to Knight in late August. Tisdale explained, "In my view, there is [a] clear . . . need to take a firm hand and not let a few create another situation like we had [during the vigil]. Many students have gotten the impression from the acts of a few, and our reaction, that we are weak and they can have what they want."[18]

Undoubtedly, part of this more aggressive response to student protesters reflected the university's increasingly difficult relationship with its alumni and donors. In December 1967, Ashmore had provided the Duke president with a list of "Criticisms of Specific Actions of University by Conservatives." Seeking to make Knight aware of how changes at Duke were affecting the school's development program, Ashmore set forth what he characterized as the "Extreme Interpretations" of recent developments at the school. "Admission of students without regard to race, color, or national origin" was seen by some, according to Ashmore, as a "liberal sell-out to attract Federal money." Election of Knight as president, "a non-Methodist, non-Southerner, Ivy League product," was seen as "Duke becoming another Harvard, Yale, or equally liberal and dangerous institution." Faculty and student participation in demonstrations meant that these groups were "not restrained properly from radical and un-American causes." Those holding an "extreme interpretation" perceived the election of a Black May Queen as a "deliberate insult of all white people, especially women, and [an] example of student defiance of all authority." Finally, such people saw the administration's response to the AAS study-in over segregated facilities as "giving in to student demands [and] failure to exercise control and create examples."[19]

Ashmore concluded by providing Knight with "Generalizations Being Made about Duke's Administration and Policies." According to Ashmore, those raising questions believed that "Duke is being run by a group of liberal, fuzzy-minded intellectuals; . . . the University is changing in character from Southern to national, from religious to pagan, from moral to amoral, from controlled environment to complete lack of control, and the students are running the University." "I think a number of our people," Ashmore told Knight in a cover letter, "likely feel as I have described their thoughts here."[20]

The reactionary attitudes described by Ashmore had certainly been inflamed by the Silent Vigil. To these "conservatives," the vigil provided further evidence that Duke students were out of control, with an administration unable—or unwilling—to impose order. For them, the vigil meant that cherished "traditional" values were being cast aside, as Duke moved ever further into the mainstream of liberal, secular, national universities.

Starting early in Knight's tenure, Duke also began experiencing significant physical and cultural changes. In 1965, the university had announced its Fifth Decade Plan, Knight's strategy for transforming Duke. The plan promoted significant investment in new buildings and other resources as well as the largest fundraising initiative in the history of the university.[21] New buildings were appearing on campus, the quality of the student body was increasing, campus social policies were relaxed, and changes to the curriculum were made. Knight never missed an opportunity to point out Duke's rapid transformation, or the connection it had to his national ambitions for the school. But as Duke changed, many trustees and alumni, particularly those from North Carolina, became concerned. According to director of alumni affairs Roger Marshall, they worried that "the university was not going to serve its *region* in its efforts to serve the nation." Many donors, he explained, "became uncertain, somewhat bewildered, [and] weren't real sure just what their contribution was going towards, what kind of institution it was supporting."[22]

Compounding all these issues, the university faced a significant budget shortfall in 1968–69. In May, dean of Arts and Sciences Harold W. Lewis wrote to department chairs, deans, and directors, alerting them that the salary increases promised to nonacademic employees at the time of the Silent Vigil required that "every possible economy must be made in all areas of the University" for 1968–69. Lewis announced a hiring freeze, asked that "small enrollment" and "non-essential courses" be considered for elimination, and drastically limited budget increases for nonsalary items. Even with savings from these measures, vice president of business and finance Charles Huestis told his colleagues in late August that his "latest calculations set the proposed 1968–69 deficit at $2,009,000." In September, Huestis urged that the need for permanent replacements for vacant positions be "critically reassessed" and asked that word be "passed along" that future facility renovations would be "attractive but Spartan."[23]

As the 1968–69 school year began, Knight's days as Duke president seemed numbered. The timing of his leave of absence for health reasons—just as the Silent Vigil was starting—could not have been worse. "If you're taken out of the picture at the critical time of the university's" life, Griffith explained, "it would be self-evident that [Knight] would have lost the chance to get back in as a viable president." Many trustees, including those on the Duke Endowment board, no longer supported the Duke president. William Anlyan, dean of the School of Medicine, remembered times he was with Duke Endowment trustees "when some of them . . . would take Barnes Woodhall and me aside to try to persuade us to help them get rid of Doug Knight." Knight recalled "constant veiled threats of the withdrawal of Endowment support." Finally, there was a meeting in the late 1960s, Knight recounted, where Endowment trustee Amos R. Kearns "finally came out from under his rock" and confronted him. Unhappy that Knight had failed to carry out the wishes of the Endowment on university matters, Kearns told Knight angrily that "you haven't done what we told you to do." Soon thereafter, Knight was eliminated from monthly Endowment board meetings, and direct encounters with Endowment board members stopped. "They're going to get him," a member of the Executive Committee told board chair Charles Wade after this confrontation with Kearns. "They're after [Knight], and they're gonna get him."[24]

Knight recalled 1968 and 1969 as an "embattled time." Yet he believed that he was "moving and getting things done" upon returning in the fall, despite "the fact that the Endowment members of the Executive Committee literally no longer spoke to me. They acted," Knight remembered painfully, "as though I wasn't there." Still, the stress was taking a huge toll on his family. Years later, Knight recalled an evening during the fall of 1968 "when I said to my wife . . . 'I'm feeling a lot better and there's still so much to do and I think I can stick it out for a while.'" But as he looked over at her, he saw "tears were running down her face." "You can't do this to these people who are your family," he said to himself. "I knew at that moment that I had to find a decent way out."[25]

The summer of 1968 was a turbulent one across the globe. In June, presidential candidate Robert F. Kennedy was assassinated just after winning the important California primary. Prague Spring continued in Czechoslovakia as protests against communist rule intensified. In August the Soviet Union invaded Czechoslovakia with 200,000 Warsaw Pact troops. Ralph Abernathy, Martin Luther King Jr.'s designated successor, spearheaded the establishment of Resurrection City on the National Mall as an antipoverty protest. Approximately 2,500 people occupied Resurrection City for almost six weeks, until the encampment was raided and demolished by police. Thousands of protesters gathered in Chicago in August for the Democratic National Convention. "In response," one historian has written, "Mayor Richard Daley had turned the city into a virtual fortress, mobilizing almost 12,000 police, preparing to call out 7,500 national guardsmen, and denying demonstrators the right to hold protest rallies." After the demonstrators convened one protest, the police responded violently. "The cops had one thing on their minds," one journalist reported: "club and then gas, club and then gas, club and then gas." At least 100 protesters went to emergency rooms after the melee and more than 150 were arrested.[26]

With these tumultuous events as a backdrop, 104 Black students enrolled in degree programs at Duke for the fall semester of 1968. Of these, 82 were undergraduates, 12 attended graduate school, and 10 were in professional schools; 43 Black students matriculated as freshmen. While the number of Black students at Duke had increased steadily since 1963, their number remained miniscule—just over 1 percent—at a school with a total of more than 8,000 students.[27]

Still, the increased size of the Black student body was significant. "I remember [in the fall of 1968] there were a lot more Black students on campus," Brenda Brown recalled. With more students, perceptions changed. "We felt," she explained, there were "enough of us here, they have to deal with us. . . . There were enough [of us] that our demands could not be shut off to the side."[28]

Griffith remained intent on establishing a dialogue with the Black students. His persistence, Cell commented, came because he "sensed unrest among the Black students before anyone else did." Few others in the administration shared Griffith's urgency. Assistant dean of instruction Annie Leigh Broughton, for example, wrote administrators in July 1968 suggesting that more consideration be given to the needs of Duke's Black students. But for Broughton, any such discussion could wait until well into the fall semester.[29]

Griffith, by contrast, wanted to move quickly. Just after classes started, he again approached Hopkins, asking him to assemble a group of Black students to discuss their concerns. At the meeting, Griffith suggested that an ad hoc committee of Black students, faculty, and administrators be assembled for "in-depth discussions of problems related to black students." The students agreed and members of the ad hoc committee were jointly selected—Cell, Robert F. Durden, and Richard L. Watson Jr., all professors from the history department; dean of Trinity College James Price, acting dean of the Woman's College Jane Philpott, and assistant dean and vice provost Frederick Joerg; students Tony Axam, Becton, Vaughn Glapion, Hopkins, Bertie Howard, Stef McLeod, and Katherine Watson. Griffith chaired the committee.[30]

Two factors loomed large for Black students as they considered a meeting. The first was recruiting incoming freshmen into the AAS. "We felt . . . that the problems we thought were pivotal [in the spring] would get magnified," Armstrong explained. She believed October was the "ideal time" for an initial meeting because, by then, freshmen had been on campus for "six or eight weeks" and would have had the chance to be exposed to the AAS.[31]

A second factor had to do with planning for Black Week, the student-organized festival of Black arts, drama, culture, and politics, to be held during the first week of February 1969. A much smaller version of the event had occurred in early 1968. "All of us recognized from the year before," Armstrong remembered, "how you could draw even the quietest students out by allowing them to express themselves in their own ways during Black Week." A meeting with the administration in October, therefore, seemed well timed. Armstrong explained that the AAS could "make a statement of the issues in October, and then have our students work for two months on Black Week—knowing that the issues were out there." The first meeting of the ad hoc committee was scheduled for October 4, 1968, at 5:00 p.m.[32]

....

Hopkins opened the meeting of the committee. "The problem," he said, "is how can we together solve the problems of black students on a white campus?" Hopkins explained that the assimilationist approach of the university was deeply flawed. "Integration," he explained, "is not [just] taking a person into a society which is almost totally different from his own and asking him . . . to forget who or what he is and assume the appearance of something else." "Sociologists, anthropologists, and educators . . . tell us," Hopkins noted, "one of the foremost goals of education is the passing of culture from one generation to the next." This made the process of finding one's identity central to the educational process. For white students, this was "easy," Hopkins explained, "because their elements of identification are interwoven throughout the educational structure." For Black students, however, "the situation . . . is quite different." A Black student faces three choices: "accepting the educational structure [at a white institution] as it is and seeking his real self outside of it; . . . rebel[ling] at the lack of himself in the [existing] educational structure with extreme expressions of militancy; . . . or . . . attempt[ing] to have some of his own ideas and culture [be] incorporated into the overall structure of the educational institution. . . . We are here this evening," Hopkins explained, "to discuss the [last] alternative."[33]

Hopkins then outlined twelve areas that he urged the committee to address "as quickly as possible." He presented these as "concerns" and not "demands." The first group of concerns involved the Black educational experience. First, the Black students asked for the establishment of a Black studies program, preferably taught by Black faculty members, as well as additions to the library's book and magazine holdings on topics relevant to the Black experience. When it was pointed out that a course, The Negro in America, was already offered in the sociology department, Black students highlighted "problems inherent in" the course, including, in their view, the fact that the professor "is not up to date in the material presented."[34]

The size and composition of the Black student population at Duke represented a second area of focus within this first group of concerns. The students asked that the number of Black students on campus be increased, with a focus on recruiting Black athletes and those from urban areas.

Finally, regarding the Black educational experience, the students sought the establishment of a summer program for incoming Black students and the appointment of a Black adviser with an administrative connection to senior university leadership. The summer program would focus on English, math, and foreign languages and would also ease the transition to college by giving Black students "a feel for the Campus before the beginning of the academic year."

A second group of concerns focused on the need for social arrangements to be developed on campus for Black students. In this area, the students requested official university endorsement for Black Week, a Black barber in the campus barbershop, office space for the AAS, and the opportunity—if they wanted—for Black students to live in an all-Black dormitory. The minutes of the meeting noted that the Black students "strongly felt that . . . local fraternity chapters are racist." As to independent dorms, the students objected to the significant cost of participating in a social program that "does not speak to the black student."

A third group of concerns called for the elimination of racist symbols at the university. The students asked for a complete ban on the playing of "Dixie" and a regulation against any display of the Confederate flag at university functions. The Black students also made clear that the president's country club membership remained an area of "great concern," signifying "support of segregated institutions and thus an abdication [to] those racial inequalities which Duke is attempting to overcome." They again demanded that Knight resign from the club.

The October session lasted about ninety-five minutes and included what Griffith described as "a fair bit of discussion" about the concerns raised. Cell characterized the tone of the meeting as "friendly." When submitting the minutes to Knight, Griffith reported that a group of senior administrators—the Provost Group—had already met to discuss the issues. That group "felt that a number of the items were valid and did have solutions" but that "others were of a more difficult and perhaps questionable nature." The administrative group recommended that the ad hoc committee be reconvened "to identify ways in which to [immediately] deal with a number of these questions." Griffith also invited Knight to make any suggestions he might have.[35]

Knight soon responded. On most issues, he showed a continued adherence to assimilation as the appropriate model for integration. Regarding university support for Black Week, Knight commented that there was "obviously some dynamite" in the prospect. Knight also stated that he was "disturbed about the [potential reverse segregation] aspect" of having a Black barber and a Black adviser and emphasized that he was "very opposed" to the idea of a separate dormitory. "This is an integrated" university, he declared. Perhaps most revealing, Knight was dismissive toward the request that symbols of racism, like the playing of "Dixie" and the display of the Confederate flag at public university events, be eliminated. Characterizing the issue as a "mixture of [the] truly important and truly unimportant," he observed "how touchy this is, but the very touchiness is worrisome." Apparently Knight believed that "Dixie" was not a "segregation song" but "originally a black man's song." Hence, he was unable to grasp the significance of the issue. Knight was apparently unaware that "Dixie"—the anthem of the Confederacy—had originated as a "plantation song and dance" in the racist blackface minstrel shows of the mid-nineteenth century.[36]

Knight's strongest reaction, though, came in response to the demand that he resign from Hope Valley Country Club. The statement that his membership "signified support of segregated institutions" and represented "an abdication [to] those racial inequalities which Duke is trying to overcome," Knight commented, was "False, Untrue, Unfair." If they forced him to resign, Knight explained, they "nullify any opportunity I have to accomplish anything constructive in that area." In Knight's view, resigning would only strengthen those in the community who opposed racial progress. "This is rough language (and you will have to tone it down)," he told Griffith, "but if they want to work for those very people they think they are resisting, there isn't a better way to do it than to push me in this way."[37] Knight knew he would pay a political price if he resigned from Hope Valley. Given how little political capital he still had, the Duke president hoped to delay any decision on his Hope Valley membership for as long as possible. In doing so, he failed to recognize the import of his response to Black students at Duke.

Knight's final comments reflected how limited his insight was into the world of Black students at Duke. Knight commented that the Black students "have to realize we are working on the good will and the truth." If they didn't share this perspective, "nothing can be done."[38] Here, Knight was reflecting a view shared by many white administrators that Black student demands constituted "reverse discrimination." The Black students, he wrote, "must not think they can solve problems by [discriminating against] others." The Black students will "make me useless," Knight concluded dismissively, "if they push some of these useless things."[39] With these words, Knight seemed to equate Black hostility to segregation with reverse racism.

Still, in his desire to advance the dialogue on the issues Black students had raised, Griffith convened a second ad hoc committee meeting on October 15. In his opening remarks on October 4, Hopkins had asked that the twelve issues he raised be addressed "as soon as possible." Yet if Black students had hoped that they would quickly receive positive feedback from the university, they were disappointed. Instead, following the suggestion of Dean Price, the committee chose to designate subgroups to address each issue. The subgroups would then meet "with the appropriate persons to pursue further the individual questions raised."[40]

On the key issue of Black studies, administrators described a "general feeling . . . that at least a number of departments would be receptive to . . . courses dealing in subject matter more germane to the Black history and culture." Yet funding and "the ability to secure competent teachers," they said, were problems. Given the budget issues, the group reached a consensus that "the first approach should be made through the departments, with a possible secondary approach through the sub-committee on curriculum of the Undergraduate Faculty Council." The subgroups working on other issues were referred to the appropriate university administrative channels.[41]

During this time, Knight seemed completely out of the loop on the issues raised by Black students. In late October, Provost Cole had seen a note from Knight suggesting the "appointment of a committee to look into the development and experiences of the Negro undergraduate at Duke." In his reply, Cole reminded Knight of the informal ad hoc committee chaired by Griffith that "has [already] been functioning in this area" and suggested waiting for a report from that group before appointing another committee. Knight responded that Cole "was absolutely right about the informal committee. All I want," he added, "is to make sure that we are ahead of our own black students in working with the puzzles of their position here."[42] Why and how Knight saw these issues as "puzzles" says much about his grasp of the concerns that Black students had presented to the university.

On the same day that Griffith's ad hoc committee would meet for a third time, a separate committee of faculty members chaired by political science professor J. Harris Proctor (Proctor Committee) met for the first time to "consider the desirability of developing a proposal for . . . African and Afro-American Studies at the graduate level at Duke University." Although the initial focus of the Proctor Committee was a graduate program, the group would also eventually begin to explore a secondary priority—an undergraduate program in African and Afro-American studies. No students served on the Proctor Committee, nor were they consulted about what a graduate or undergraduate program in Black studies might look like. Indeed, since the university made no announcement about the formation of the Proctor Committee, students were unaware of its very existence.[43]

The ad hoc committee reconvened on November 4 to receive reports from a number of subgroups. Progress was reported on at least some issues. Cell told participants that in a meeting with Robert H. Ballantyne, the director of admissions had explained the challenges Duke had faced in recruiting Black students and asked for a list "*at once*" of people willing to devote time to the project. From that list, one or two students would be selected to accompany Ballantyne on future recruiting trips, where appropriate. Likewise, Watson and Axam reported a productive meeting with the university's assistant librarian, who pointed out that the library already subscribed to some of the newspapers and periodicals requested and agreed to order others.[44]

McLeod and Cell also offered an encouraging report on their meeting with Knight. The president, according to Cell, was "genuine in his concern" about the issues raised by Black students. Knight made clear, however, that outside funding would be required for initiatives like Black studies to be implemented. His ability to make concessions, he told them, was severely limited by internal budgetary and political pressures. "Knight . . . was a good man," Cell believed. "He wanted to do the right thing." But others, like Harold Lewis, vice provost and dean of Arts and Sciences, was one of the "very hard-nosed administrators" Knight had to deal with. "Lewis . . . was reluctant to do anything," Cell recounted. "He didn't think Black studies was going anywhere." In addition to colleagues like Lewis, Knight felt that he had to deal with "silent, perhaps unspoken opposition, but opposition you knew would be there." Still, he failed to acknowledge his own accountability for the slow progress. Samuel DuBois Cook saw this as a failure of presidential leadership. "It goes back to the president," he said. Cook saw Knight as "ambivalent" on the issues raised by the students and thought that "had he been more committed to" them, progress could have been made more quickly.[45]

On other issues, little headway was made. McLeod and Hopkins were unable to persuade the Duke bands to voluntarily stop playing "Dixie" or displaying the Confederate flag. After much back and forth, the band voted "not to decide" on the issues, effectively retaining the ability to continue existing practices. "People couldn't understand the request," Hopkins commented. As for a Black adviser, Lewis reported that the university "could not create an official position at this time," although several interim alternatives were discussed.[46]

The greatest amount of time was spent discussing the most difficult and important issue—development of a Black studies program. As at many other campuses, this proved to be an extraordinarily difficult issue to navigate. Black studies, according to historian Martha Biondi, "arrived like an explosion on the American scene." In the fall of 1968, focus on the idea was still new. The first Black studies program had only been established at San Francisco State College in the fall of 1966. Harvard's announcement that it would move to create a Black studies department—seen by Ballard as conferring the "imprimatur of academic respectability" on the new discipline—did not occur until January 1969. Moreover, there was little ideological consensus on what a Black studies program would entail. "Some colleges choose to emphasize Pan-Africanism," Ballard described, "others the Black experience in America, still others concentrated on contemporary Black life in urban areas, while some programs were deep into 'Third Worldism.'" Whatever the focus, "Black students, faculty, and administrators worked to infuse Black studies with the Black Power ideology," education professor Joy Ann Williamson explained. Civil rights activist and scholar Vincent Harding has said that these programs were "proudly, openly pro-Black, and recognized predominantly white universities as part of [a problematic] American political structure."[47]

As they considered demands for a Black studies program, Ballard observed, faculty and administrators at white universities encountered what he described as "a complex set of problems." According to Ballard, they had to address "serious doubt . . . that any such body of knowledge as 'Black studies' existed," concerns that "the program would be highly politicized and doctrinaire, . . . fear . . . that the quality of the programs would be inferior since there was a severe shortage of scholars . . . trained in the discipline," and "concern over dangers to academic freedom implicit in the student demands for complete autonomy of the program." "Black studies was seen by many," Biondi summarized, "as an academically suspect, antiwhite, emotional intrusion into a landscape of rigor and reason."[48]

These dynamics complicated the conversations between Duke professors and subgroup members on Black studies. Although Cell found his meeting with Becton and economics professor John Blackburn "encouraging and productive," clear differences soon emerged. Blackburn suggested an economics course with a "theoretical" approach, looking at how economic systems ought to work and what happens when racial prejudice and discrimination are added to the mix. Becton wanted a curriculum that covered specific conditions in the "ghetto" (such as loan sharking, price fixing, and job discrimination) along with practical responses. Blackburn "strongly oppose[d]" offering any course without a prerequisite of three hours of introductory economics. Without such background, he said, any course would be "second-rate" and "have little interest" in the department. Because economics, like other departments, operated by committee, Blackburn indicated that the next step would be for Cell and Becton to talk with the "departmental committee on undergraduate curriculum."[49]

Other differences arose in a meeting between subgroup members Axam and Watson and political science professors John Hallowell and Samuel Cook. Axam advocated for a political science course dealing with Black people in American politics and taught by a Black professor. While supportive of a course in which Black politics would be studied in the context of American politics, the two professors thought the topic could be addressed in the introductory political science course or in the existing course Groups in American Politics. Hallowell strongly resisted the idea that only a Black professor could teach the course. According to Watson, "Hallowell stated that it was important to recognize the requirements of political science as a discipline . . . and that it should not be necessary to be black in order to teach black politics." For Hallowell, the principal criteria for selection "should be the academic qualifications for a particular position." That said, Hallowell indicated that the department would welcome suggestions of available teaching candidates "contingent upon the availability of funds and an appraisal by the Department of the academic qualifications of the candidate."[50]

Differences of opinion on Black studies also arose at the November 4 meeting of the ad hoc committee. In discussing a proposed Black history course, Hopkins stressed the importance of a Black professor, arguing that a Black person would be better able to speak "from the reality of the situation." One faculty member on the committee responded sharply that "it is not the purpose of the historian to solve identity crises." A report to the board of trustees accurately summarized the uncertain status of discussions on Black studies. "The department chairmen were receptive to the curriculum requests," it commented, "but their response was restricted by the lack of precise clarity in stating what was desired, [as well as] by the lack of funds, the lack of expertise, the lack of time . . . required to develop the courses, and the lack of authority to make an outright commitment." An administration report called the Black students' response to these developments "somewhat negative"—an understatement.[51]

Still, the November 4 meeting was civil. Administrators and faculty were encouraged, believing that the members of the AAS saw progress, however incremental, on the twelve concerns that they had presented weeks earlier. Black students, on the other hand, had a very different take on the sessions. Hoping for resolution of their concerns "as quickly as possible," they found themselves navigating an increasingly complicated bureaucratic maze with no end in sight. Capturing the frustration and growing alienation felt in the process, Hopkins told the ad hoc committee that Black students found it "humiliating to plead for our humanity."[52]

To be sure, some issues did end up being resolved before Christmas break. Huestis committed to the university hiring a barber able to cut the hair of the Black students. Griffith found dedicated office space for the Afro-American Society. The university agreed to provide financial support for Black Week.[53]

The controversy over "Dixie" and the Confederate flag was also resolved. Facing pushback from students, band members, and alumni, Griffith stepped in. "I met with the officers of the marching band" and told them not to play "Dixie," Griffith remembered. Later, when the band again balked, he was even more direct. "I finally said, 'Look—we can talk about this all day,'" Griffith recounted. "As long as you are the Duke Marching Band, you aren't going to play 'Dixie.'" Although no formal university ban on the playing of "Dixie" was ever adopted, the band "voluntarily" agreed not to play the song.[54]

By contrast, the university stalled on the students' request for a Black adviser. Dean Price had said that hiring such an adviser would involve three steps. "First, the administration must be receptive and sympathetic towards the idea," he explained. "Second, there must be sufficient funds to pay the salary. Third, the right man must be found." "The administration is hopeful that a black advisor can be found," the *Duke Chronicle* summarized, "but it is still too concerned with the problems of finding the money and the man to express much optimism."[55]

In early December, Cell completed a draft proposal to fund Black studies and implement other changes at the university requested by the Black students. The proposal was ambitious. Cell wrote,

If Duke is to meet the challenges posed by these students, it must do so on a massive scale and within a special, enlarged framework. The students are asking for something big, exciting, and expensive, something far larger than they themselves imagined at the outset. Duke cannot solve these problems by means of the adjustment of this or that social regulation, by the appointment of a part-time counselor, or by a couple of additions to our list of courses. The problems demand a comprehensive, well-financed program.

Cell proposed that the university seek $600,000 in outside funding to be spent over a three-year period on a summer program, new faculty, scholarships, a Black adviser, library support, and cultural events organized by the Afro-American Society. As he had promised, Cell circulated the draft to Hopkins and other Black students on the ad hoc committee.[56]

In fact, Cell received no comments on the draft proposal. "The students and I were supposed to get back together and discuss [the] document," Cell recounted. "They were to criticize it, react to it, and then we would draw up one that represented what we all thought. That never happened. It wasn't that I didn't ask them. They just didn't do it."[57] In late December, Cell decided that he could not wait for student comments any longer. "We are just not going to be able to count on" the students, he told Griffith. "We are just going to have to go ahead." On December 30, 1968, Griffith sent Cell's draft proposal to Knight, the other members of the ad hoc committee, and the Provost Group. "The Afro-American Society has some further suggestions regarding this proposal," Griffith informed Knight, "but they will not be forthcoming until after examinations due to the press of academic work at this time."[58]

From mid-December to early February, little contact occurred between the AAS and the administration on *any* of the issues.[59] When students returned in mid-January from Christmas break, exams and planning for Black Week occupied most of their time. As a result, there was no progress on critical concerns like Black studies, the Black adviser, the summer program, and dedicated housing on campus for Black students. Knight had also not announced any decision on his Hope Valley membership and remained a member of the club.

During the period from October 1968 to early February 1969, fundamentally different perceptions of the negotiating process began to emerge. For administrators, the view was positive. "I thought it was very clear in these meetings," Griffith observed, "that communication was occurring." Cell described the meetings as "extremely informative and educational," commenting that "both groups have learned something." Knight had the same sense. "We were going along steadily settling" the issues, he recounted. Many in the administration believed that the university was making a serious effort to address the Black students' concerns. "The administration has repeatedly taken the initiative in attempting to define the concerns of our black students," Ashmore reported to the board of trustees, and "diligent efforts have been made to understand and meet these needs within the framework of the established policies and procedures of the University."[60]

The view of the AAS was starkly different. "We were getting nothing done in the meetings," Hopkins described. "We were missing each other. It's almost like they didn't realize what we were saying, although we were sitting there saying stuff to them." Although the university might have believed that it was taking the initiative in addressing Black students' concerns, the students saw it differently. "I don't think the university had really come to terms with what it meant, practically speaking, to have a significant Black student population on the campus," Turner observed. "Their lack of . . . responsiveness," C. G. Newsome explained, "signaled to us that they did not see us, they did not hear us," and "that they considered us non-persons."[61]

These profoundly different perceptions arose because the negotiations—the first substantive discussions between the university and its Black students since desegregation—had primarily served to highlight the *differences* between the parties, not narrow them. "We were talking about institutional change," Hopkins explained. "We were talking about new courses, changing courses. And that's where Watson and Durden sat back and said, 'We are a top school in the nation. What are you talking about—we are here to teach you. You have critiqued us and said that we are lacking in something.'"[62]

To Janice Williams, the university's attitude was "'This is a plantation and it runs real smoothly and nobody makes waves. . . . By you making waves, you bring attention to this university, to this administration. You're actually making people question us.'" Turner saw the university's attitude as patronizing and dismissive. "We have brought you from your impoverished, underprivileged, deprived conditions," he imagined university officials thinking. "What else do you want? Why keep being a nuisance? Just be nice and appreciate what's been done for you." "We were saying we wanted Black courses," Hopkins recounted, "and Durden and somebody else was sitting there saying 'we already have this.'" For some in the history department, according to Hopkins, a course was a Black history course even if it only "mentioned Black people" and then only "the proper Black people." The university's position, Hopkins recalled, was "that basically there was really nothing much wrong with Duke, so it wasn't a real open dialogue." Looking back, Hopkins realized, "*we* weren't talking about the kind of stuff *they* were talking about."[63]

Friction arose even when the university responded favorably on an issue. "The [discussion] that sticks in my mind was the . . . hiring of a Black adviser," Kerckhoff recalled. "Marcus Hobbs had said two or three times that 'the university is committed to this.'" For Hobbs, these words meant that the hiring of a Black adviser was "going to happen, in due time." Despite these assurances, however, the students kept returning to the issue. Finally, Kerckhoff remembered, "one gal . . . just exploded. . . . 'We don't care about that, we want to know is it going to happen?' Hobbs felt he had said that. He just sort of looked startled at her because it never occurred to him that anyone could have interpreted his words in any other way than 'Yes, it's going to happen.'" "Clearly the difference between the soft, academic, bureaucratic, cloudy way of saying things," Kerckhoff explained, "and the hard-nosed-demand kind of language was a part of the whole difficulty of communication." University assistant registrar Clark R. Cahow characterized interactions between the university and the AAS even more succinctly. "If ever there was a gap in communication," he commented, "there was one here that was as broad as the Grand Canyon."[64]

Most fundamentally, differences arose because faculty and administrators did not share the fierce urgency the students were feeling. "Insensitivity was a basic part of it," Cook explained. "I'm sure that [administrators and faculty] just thought . . . the situation would go away, that the students would get tired of it [and] forget about pushing their demands." "The amazing thing is how we were actually missing each other," Hopkins remembered.

> They never realized how intense we felt about things we were talking about. . . . With us, it was an everyday thing. . . . But they were . . . like they were off somewhere and comfortable. It was like they were dealing with another university to have some kind of a collective curriculum. They were just easy, in a very gentlemanly fashion, scholars taking their time. They were on a totally different kind of time frame than we were. And when I look back on it, they didn't realize that. I don't see how they escaped it, but they couldn't pick up the intense feelings we had about this stuff.[65]

In retrospect, members of the administration had clearly failed to see the missed signals. "Around me the attitude was 'what's the hurry?'" Knight remembered. "None of us understood their urgencies." "Circumstances were beyond the insight of any of us right at that point," he concluded. "And our efforts, as a result, went awry." "I don't know what the barrier was," Watson recalled. "In one way or another we weren't able to convince [the Black students] that we were seriously interested [in solving their problems]." "We were living entirely different times, different rhythms, different cycles," Cell observed wistfully. "I was trying to work to use a power structure that I know a little about. . . . I don't think they were ever in that game at all."[66]

Without a common view of events and issues, differences hardened. Griffith's "perception" was that they were not meeting in good faith, he explained. "I certainly felt [that they didn't want an agreement] after a time." Even when the university would make concessions, "they would never recognize that we had done that," Griffith recounted. "That was one of the frustrations." Cell questioned the failure of the AAS to comment on his draft funding proposal for a Black studies program. "I still don't know how much of that was sloppiness . . . and how much of it was just tactics," Cell recalled. "By tactics, I mean . . . the effect of that was to paralyze the administration . . . in the three or four months before the Black consciousness reached its crescendo. I don't know if [Knight and others] would have done anything. But the effect of this was to paralyze efforts in November, December, [and] early January." It was "not possible . . . to make any progress" from mid-December through early February, Ashmore told the board, "because black students were not available for the kind of direct involvement they had consistently requested."[67]

For members of the AAS, it seemed clear that the university could not—or would not—take their concerns seriously. Despite movement in a number of areas, the most significant issues the students had raised were bogged down in university committees that seemed unable to cut through bureaucratic red tape, let alone respond to the existential crisis the students were now experiencing. Even where issues like the Black adviser or summer transition program were agreed to in concept, the students could not trust that the university would implement them in a way that met their needs.

"Soon it got around," Hopkins recalled, "to the thing where we said, 'Hey, we got to do something about this to get them to respond.'"[68]

CHAPTER 7

——

Now They Know, and They Ain't Gonna Do

Planning

——

On February 12, 1969, members of Duke's Afro-American Society (AAS) final-ized plans for the takeover of key areas of the Allen Building—the administra-tive hub of Duke University. Although unaware of these specific plans, some administrators and faculty close to the situation had begun to view such a confrontation as unavoidable. History professor John Cell, as close to Duke's Black students as any faculty member, saw a "sudden, swift, astonishing trans-formation . . . among the [Black] students" in January and February 1969. Black student participation in committee meetings had ceased. Instead, "there was a lot of talk of revolution, [and] a lot of anger." "I honestly do not think," Cell remarked, "that . . . there was any way that the takeover of Allen Build-ing could have been prevented." Assistant dean of Arts and Sciences William Griffith also saw the Black students carried along by historical forces they could not—or would not—resist. "I think they were living out an inevitability across the country," he commented, "that you didn't gain your . . . 'mantle of Blackness,' until you've taken over a building. I sort of felt this was their com-ing of age."[1]

It was clear by early 1969 that support among Black students for direct action was growing. They believed that a targeted protest would trigger an immediate, definitive response to their demands from the university. However, to characterize the confrontation that occurred as *inevitable* indicates how out of touch even sympathetic Duke administrators and faculty members were with the Black students who were finalizing protest plans. In fact, for these students, the decision to occupy the Allen Building was an agonizing one. Brenda Armstrong remembered the first meeting when a takeover was discussed. "It was more like a sensitivity session," she recalled. "Everybody talked about their fears. . . . The fact that although we needed to do it, [we] weren't sure [we] were doing the right thing." "A lot of people were frightened," Armstrong recounted. "Me included."[2]

Some students consulted their parents, though these conversations often only deepened their anxiety and inner conflict. "I was scared, and I had talked with my mother," Brenda Brown said. "She was very upset. In fact, she packed up and went to California. She decided she just wasn't going to bother about me and my militant ways. . . . She felt like that wasn't why she and my father sent me to Duke. . . . She just didn't feel like that was the way to do it. She felt like we had been watching too many takeovers on TV." "It might not be the way to do it," Brown told her mother, "but this is the way the majority wants to do it, and I feel like I'm part of the group." Brown's mother asked: "Why couldn't you just go get your education and get out of there? Why do you have to cause all this ruckus?"[3]

For parents, their children's physical safety was a paramount concern. "A lot of [parents]—most of them—were afraid of the fact that the campus was ripe for us to be attacked or assaulted," Armstrong explained, "not just in verbal ways but physically. My mother, although she herself was an activist . . . did not want her children to have to grow up that way." William Turner recalled that his father "wanted the best for his sons and daughters." Like other parents, he had seen firsthand the consequences that activism could have. "There were many parents who marched in the '50s and early '60s that had the same fear for their children," Turner explained. "It wasn't that they didn't want what their children wanted. It's that [they knew] their children . . . could be severely threatened by lethal contacts with the law. . . . And they were right. We had folks [in the civil rights movement] who were beaten, battered, killed, bludgeoned, or who had their futures tarnished."[4]

Why then did this group of Duke students decide to put aside their doubts and fears and occupy Duke's main administration building? How were they able to overcome the grave concerns of parents who feared that such an action could derail their children's future plans and expose them to physical harm?

How did Duke administrators understand the unfolding events and what role did race play in shaping their perceptions? Events of late 1968 and early 1969 begin to reveal the answers.

....

All students who participated in the Allen Building takeover came to the decision to act in their own way, operating in an environment fraught with tension, where national, local, and personal factors were powerfully converging. "The thing you have to understand," Black student leader Chuck Hopkins noted, "is that the times were such that the things that were happening in and around campus, in the local community, the stuff that was happening nationally, the militant sixties—all of that stuff was bearing in [on us]. . . . It was all of those things that kind of set the general consciousness level."[5]

National events provided one context for the rapidly escalating Black student activism on Duke's campus in early 1969. Indeed, it was during this period that the Black campus movement was reaching its zenith across the country. "With the onset of Black Power, the urban uprisings in such cities as Detroit and Los Angeles, and the increasing enrollment of Black students at white institutions," wrote education professor Joy Ann Williamson, "Black student activism turned toward their own institutions, and Black student activism grew." "Dozens of white colleges were . . . disturbed by blacks demanding a more relevant education in November and December of 1968," Ibram X. Kendi observed. Schools as varied as University of Massachusetts–Amherst, Bluefield State, Fordham University, Brown University, University of Wisconsin, Case Western Reserve, and the University of San Francisco saw significant protests. Moreover, "Black students on white campuses became the vanguard of the student protest movement," Williamson explained. She reported that Black students were involved in 57 percent of campus protests at predominantly white institutions during the 1968–69 academic year.[6]

Administrators and faculty at Duke looked at Black student protests roiling campuses across the nation and saw an ominous pattern. "Our students sought out movement leaders," Knight wrote, "and Duke in turn was sought out. In this way we became a target university—in many ways *the* target university—for the Southeast." Cell agreed. "I knew there was . . . a national Black students' conspiracy," Cell noted. "That's clear, isn't it?" For support, Cell pointed to comments made to him by AAS member Michael McBride after returning from the November 1968 Towards a Black University conference held at Howard University and attended by two thousand students. "I know there was a meeting to which our people sent representatives and delegates," Cell recalled. McBride "came back and I remember . . . he said: 'Well, things are going to be shaking this year.'"[7]

"Allen Building was there in all of our minds," Hopkins explained, "because it was happening all over the country." Moreover, escalating events at other campuses created a "pressure to act." But there was no organized Black student conspiracy, according to Armstrong. Rather, it was like a "contagion," she explained. "The media had helped to put the . . . grievances of various Black [student] groups in the fore . . . and that whole aura of student activism was on the scene. There was not a unified effort among any of the schools to pull this off at the same time." Instead, Armstrong recounted, this was "the simultaneous expression of the dissatisfaction that Black students were feeling." Williamson agreed, noting that no "umbrella organization coordinating protest on several individual campuses" existed.[8]

Still, the absence of a "conspiracy" did not mean Duke's Black students acted in isolation. "Students on various campuses," Williamson explained, "talked to one another about strategy, published their demands in one another's newspapers, and even travelled to one another's campuses for support." These interactions led to similar events occurring on different campuses, even if they did not reflect conscious collaboration. "No matter where they were located," Williamson wrote, "Black students demanded similar concessions from administrators and used a common ideology to understand their role in the Black liberation struggle." This was true for the Black students at Duke. "We had made connections at Cornell, at Princeton, and at Berkeley," Armstrong recalled. "Once we had a chance to figure out we had the same issues, we felt empowered that we weren't stupid and that we weren't isolated." Not only did Duke students learn from events at other schools, but, because the university was a "southern, very traditional school," the impact of developments at Duke was all the more significant. People said, according to Armstrong, "if it works [at Duke], maybe it will work at Cornell."[9]

Given this context, Cell was mistaken in concluding that the Howard University conference in November 1968 was part of a national conspiracy among Black students. According to Kendi, the Towards a Black University conference attended by Duke representatives in November 1968 was "quite possibly the most activism-inducing" program held during the period. Yet even with Stokely Carmichael imploring the two thousand student attendees "to quit talking and start acting," the conference was only one piece of a much larger picture. "I'm sure [the meeting in Washington] . . . did have an impact," Hopkins stated. "But Duke's Black students didn't have to go to Washington [because] there was stuff happening in Durham. Howard Fuller was here. Neighborhood organizations were protesting. . . . So the Washington [conference] was . . . not a turning point. . . . It was just one . . . part of a whole activist era."[10]

Events in the local Durham community were important for Duke students. Since desegregation, Duke's Black students had found purpose and acceptance through their work with Durham community organizations and local political activities. Some were active in the local YMCA or the Durham Big Sister program, while others participated in voter registration. A number of Duke's Black students, including Hopkins, participated in a community-based summer internship program sponsored by the Foundation for Community Development under the direction of Fuller. "This involvement" in the community, Hopkins explained, "created a new atmosphere of cooperation between Black college students and neighborhood people. During this time, Black students at Duke underwent some important ideological changes," he noted. "The students began to think and talk about [the] relevance of the entire educational process to the needs of the Black community. They concluded that the process as it exists is, in fact, irrelevant."[11]

Fuller's role in all this was important as well as misunderstood by many. By 1967, with his organizing efforts in Durham, Fuller had become the most visible Black activist in North Carolina. Adopting the ideology, terminology, and tactics of Black Power, he became identified as a leader of the local movement. Duke's Black students were among those who felt a strong connection to Fuller, who was not only a bridge to Durham's Black community but also an experienced sounding board and adviser.

The white community, however, viewed Fuller differently. In his memoir, Fuller wrote that by late 1967, he was "one of the most hated Black men in North Carolina in certain circles of white people with power." "To them," Fuller described, "I was an 'outside agitator' stirring up discontent wherever I went." For their part, Durham's newspapers referred to Fuller as a "Negro activist," "militant," "Black Power Advocate," "revolutionary," and an "Advocate of the destruction of the Capitalist system."[12]

Most Duke faculty and administrators embraced this negative view of Fuller. They also believed that he played a critical role in shaping the tactics that Duke's Black students employed in dealing with the university. "Clearly, they turned to [Fuller] as one who knew how to do things," Alan

Kerckhoff commented. Fuller "clearly was attempting to foment something," he cynically observed. "When one thing failed, he seemed to turn to another." In the view of law school dean Kenneth Pye, it was inconceivable that Duke's Black students arrived at the decision to occupy the Allen Building on their own. Pye felt that "only someone who wanted to exacerbate the [Duke] situation for broader political purposes . . . would have recommended" a takeover. Pye saw Fuller particularly as giving the students "bad advice." The Black students, in Pye's analysis, were "susceptible to people [like Fuller] who had a quite different agenda than reforming the university."[13]

Duke's Black students acknowledge that Fuller was important to them. Still, he did not, as administrators imagined, play a key role in directing events. Fuller "did nothing to suggest a course of action," Charles Becton reported. "The decision to sit-in at the president's office, to picket Hope Valley Country Club, to march to the president's house, and to take over the Allen Building were made in meetings . . . without Howard being present," he explained. Fuller "did not instigate any of this." Indeed, Hopkins said that Fuller was "totally out of" the decision to occupy the Allen Building. Duke students informed Fuller "*after* we had made the decision." The Black leader "had absolutely no part."[14]

Why then were Duke faculty and administrators so ready to believe that outsiders were responsible for Black student activism at Duke? One explanation is provided by historian Jason Sokol, who saw a similar readiness on the part of white southerners to blame Black activism in the civil rights movement on a communist conspiracy. "White southerners continued to equate attacks on remnants of segregation with communist conspiracies," Sokol observed, "because red cries fit snugly into their traditional racial views. Anticommunism occupied the place it did because of its unique ability to explain changes in African-Americans, and to do so in ways that reinforced rather than disrupted stereotypes. Black southerners were happy, docile, and susceptible to manipulation, many whites believed. When they suddenly looked organized, discontented, and autonomous in the 1960s, whites attributed it to a communist plan."[15]

Similarly, at Duke, by attributing Black campus activism to external forces, administrators and faculty were able to maintain their view that Black students lacked the agency, intelligence, and skill to plan a sophisticated protest. "They never gave us credit," Armstrong observed, for "the brilliance in the planning for Allen Building."[16] By adopting such a perspective, university officials were also able to blame Black activism on external forces rather than the failure of the school to exercise responsible leadership on racial matters.

Against the backdrop of national and local events, the focus on Black Power ideology grew more intense among Black campus activists. "No generation of students," Kendi wrote, "read more political literature than these black campus activists." "I read everything I could find by Black authors," Becton recalled. His racial consciousness evolved as he read books like *The Wretched of the Earth* by Frantz Fanon as well as works by James Baldwin and Dick Gregory. "For a while I didn't go to class," Turner remembered. "I just sat around and read. . . . I almost flunked out." "I'm willing to . . . say," Becton recounted, "that every junior and senior [who participated in the Allen Building takeover] had read fifteen books on Black awareness and had a good idea about what it takes to get what you want."[17]

Issues raised in these books were dissected and debated for hours. "We would always stay up at night talking," Hopkins recalled. "I was saying stuff about our situation at Duke and our situation in this country." "I still see that house on Cornwallis," Turner commented wistfully fifty years later. "We were laying up in that house, reading and rapping and talking, discussing."[18]

In these interactions, Biondi explained, "students began using a new language: embracing 'revolution' and 'revolt,' questioning 'working within the system' and openly challenging the 'white power structure.'" The strategy of nonviolent protest also came under intense scrutiny. A study of Black high school students conducted in 1970, Biondi reported, determined that "nearly half of the activists agreed with the statement [that] 'violence is cleansing,' as did more than a third of the nonactivists." Just as significant, the study found that "only 7 percent of all the Black students thought that whites could be 'persuaded' to change." Still, despite the new terminology of "revolution," Biondi insisted that at most campuses, "even as students embraced many aspects of Black nationalism, they remained nonviolent in both theory and practice." Kendi agreed. "Most activists seem to have been moderates," he observed, "juggling (and separating) the politico-cultural struggle with their academic and social lives, while also ideologically juggling radical and liberal thoughts, socialist and capitalist ideas, the desire to work in and outside of the 'system,' protest tactics with negotiations, . . . and optimism and pessimism for American institutions."[19]

The cumulative impact of national, local, and ideological factors remained transformative. "The attempt was [made] to put us in our place," Armstrong recalled, to tell us "that we were not good enough to come to Duke. . . . Most

[of] us came from schools and families that were so strong and came from such traditions of surviving," she explained, "that we thought they were crazy. We did not feel the least bit intimidated by them. . . . It was empowering," she recounted. "I wasn't the same person by 1969," Turner remembered. "I wasn't the same person as when I came. I wasn't reading the same things. I wasn't having the same conversations." For Turner, the transformation had a powerful religious dimension. He explained:

> You have a generation of young [people] that are involved in some serious, serious existential conflicts. What does it feel like to wake up one morning and realize everybody you trust has been lying to you or speaking out of both sides of their mouth? You teach all of this wonderful stuff in Bible school and church and you come and arrange your society in an antithetical way. . . . You got to live out what you know is a lie. You know it's a lie. You feel it inside. The tension is palpable. You're talking about good Sunday school children who took seriously what the . . . preacher said.[20]

Triggered by events on campus, soon these "good Sunday school children" would be discussing strategies on how to force the university to respond conclusively to their concerns.

....

Returning to campus in January 1969, members of the AAS received shocking news—approximately fifteen of eighty-two Black undergraduates had either been dismissed from school for academic reasons or voluntarily dropped out of school following the fall semester. This equaled an 18 percent attrition rate for Black undergraduates after one semester, twice the university's overall annual attrition rate of 9 percent. Later in January, Griffith advised the Administrative Council that "11 of the 22 freshman black students in Trinity College had failed academically the first semester, and others are barely holding on."[21]

This accelerating attrition rate among Black students escalated tensions within the university dramatically. For one thing, as Bertie Howard described, "there were a lot of people we liked" in the group that was forced to leave. More broadly, the timing was problematic. "While we're in there talking to them about some of the things that were happening," Armstrong recalled incredulously, "they're out there putting somebody out." Hopkins remembered "Black students having to leave for academic reasons" as a "new [issue] that was inserted. There were strong feelings about it," he recounted. "I had [Black] students . . . who had never participated in [the AAS], who had never spoken to me, [come to me and say], 'Chuck, we need to do something.'"[22]

Throughout January, the tempo of internal discussions accelerated among Black students. "Many of us weren't going to classes," Hopkins recalled. "It happened rapidly in terms of our consciousness." Events on campus "began to move in rapid succession," he wrote later. "We met more frequently," Brown said, and "it just generally escalated." "The only reports [of negotiations] that we got were of stalemate," Turner remembered. "It seemed like every time it was the same thing over and over." "We had presented demands and hadn't gotten any answer," Brown recounted. "People were tired of [the] committees . . . we were sitting on."[23]

In tandem with these developments, plans for Black Week in early February were being finalized. Since "Negro History Week" was first celebrated in 1926, early February had been important in the Black community as a time to focus on the study of African American history. Arriving at Duke, the school's Black students found that the university's all-white students, faculty, and administrators did nothing to mark the special time. "Black History [Week] has always been . . . part of our culture," Janice Williams remembered. "They weren't going to do anything," she recalled bitterly.[24] This omission became even more glaring in the late 1960s when Black student organizations across the country began to organize annual Black Cultural Weeks on campus.

Duke's Black students had organized their own small Black Cultural Week program in early 1968. In 1969 they undertook planning for a far more ambitious celebration of Black history and culture. Scheduled for February 4 through February 11, Black Week had two stated purposes. First, it provided an opportunity for Duke's Black students to celebrate their history, culture, and identity. Second, the week was to "educate the whites at Duke," the *Duke Chronicle* reported, "attempting to dispel their ignorance and myths about black culture and the demands of the black movement." While the university paid the out-of-pocket costs for Black Week, all programming, scheduling, and logistics were handled by Duke's Black students.[25]

As Black Week approached, the AAS was finalizing a "Ten-Point Program" laying out "What We Want and Why We Want It." A combination of specific demands and more sweeping pronouncements, the program showed how much the thinking of those in the AAS had evolved since October 1968 when the group first met with university administrators to present their "concerns." The AAS now demanded "the power to determine the basis for our educational environment," calling any academic program not developed in tandem with

Black students "indoctrination." Recognizing the "necessity for revolutionary change," the AAS wanted "an education which will sustain the culture of black people" while providing skills that would address "the needs of our people in this racist society." Asking for "an equitable representation of Black students at Duke," the program called for the student body to be 29 percent Black by the fall of 1973. The ten-point program also included a call that the university "disemploy grading" in evaluating the academic achievement of Black students and support the struggle of its nonacademic employees for "unionization and liberation." It demanded an end to "racist living conditions" on campus, "police harassment of Black students," and "tokenism of Black representation in university power structures."[26]

Reproduced in *Harambee*, a Black student–sponsored newspaper published at the beginning of Black Week, the ten-point program of the AAS addressed issues Black students had been facing at Duke for many years. In addition, the program set forth a number of new issues and demanded changes to the racial status quo that went well beyond prior discussions with the university. Historian Allen B. Ballard viewed Black student demands in this period from a historical perspective. "The Black students' demands," he wrote, "often from fewer than 50 people on a campus of 10,000—carried with them the weight of every slight and injury suffered by Africans from the time they were stolen from their ancestral villages." "Behind the . . . demands," he explained, "some clearly logical, some apparently absurd—lay a deeper unarticulated demand: to be taken seriously as human beings and to be treated as any respected human being would be treated." In retrospect, Knight appeared to grasp the message the demands communicated. "The nonnegotiable demands often meant," the Duke president wrote later, "'Hey, look at me. I want to talk as an equal, and I want to keep all of my differences intact. I want to be visible to you *as myself*.'"[27]

Griffith was growing frustrated. "It seemed like the demands were . . . always in a state of flux," he recalled. "This was . . . one of the problems we had in trying to deal with them. We would talk about one [demand] and then another one would surface. And it was very hard to tie down what they wanted."[28]

More broadly, as events were unfolding, university administrators were unable to comprehend—let alone respond to—the anguish and frustration the school's Black students were expressing. At a meeting of the Administrative Council held on January 30, the group of senior administrators received a report from Griffith on "requests from the Afro-American Student Group." Griffith told the council that the ad hoc committee formed in October 1968 had "resolved several requests" and that "other problems are under close consideration." He acknowledged, however, that the committee was "without prerogative" to deal with the Black students' more significant requests, including those seeking additional Black faculty members, more Black students, a Black student adviser, and summer and tutorial programs. Referring to the 50 percent attrition rate experienced by Black freshmen following the fall 1968 semester, Griffith warned that "frustrations are mounting."[29]

Presiding over the Administrative Council, Knight remained unwilling to think outside the box in responding to Griffith's report. Knight asked Duke provost Marcus Hobbs to "pursue the establishment of an advisory committee composed of Academic Council members to sit with Mr. Griffith in meetings with students, including disadvantaged students, on non-academic affairs." Resisting demands that the university address the distinctive needs of Duke's Black students, the committee agreed that the problems presented by the AAS "involve all disadvantaged students, not just a special few, and will be approached from this viewpoint." Vice provost and dean of Arts and Sciences Harold W. Lewis appeared focused on optics. "We must show at least that some program is coming," he told the group. Lewis suggested that "the most graceful way is that we have a committee . . . to look at the academic situation of all students who have failed to make it this semester and why, and further, at what can we do to [get] them up to standard."[30]

Rather than move toward decisive action, Knight requested additional information. He asked the group to look into "(1) the academic problem and (2) the black student situation from the viewpoint of (a) what response to their situation have we already developed (b) the visible committees for the continuation of our efforts (c) what have we done over the past several months and whether this is the direction we want to move." The administrators should come back to him, Knight said, in "all due haste."[31]

On January 31, the AAS held a forum on the quad to discuss the high attrition rate among Black students. According to the *Duke Chronicle*, nearly all of Duke's Black students attended the forum, along with three hundred white students and professors. In "speech after speech," the Black students discussed the causes of the high attrition rate. Among the factors cited, the *Duke Chronicle* reported, were "academic weakness, racism, cultural shock, hostility, difficulty in adjusting to dorm life, frustration and bigoted professors."[32]

At the conclusion of the forum, a "progress report" on the AAS demands was provided by Black student leaders along with a discussion of each. Listening to the report, Griffith heard no mention of progress the university had made on issues like a Black barber, library holdings, dedicated office space for the AAS, financial support for Black Week, and the playing of "Dixie" at school events. Griffith felt he had no choice but to correct the record. "At a forum on the quad," he said later, "I just went down item by item, because I was really so upset that they were putting out material that was just untrue." However, Griffith had no progress to report on key issues such as Black studies, recruitment of Black faculty, and the president's Hope Valley membership.[33]

Many Duke administrators and faculty now perceived the school's Black students as more interested in confrontation than in effectuating change. "It was more for disruption than wanting any particular thing," Hobbs commented. "If you agreed in one area, it was immediately upgraded—you needed to acquiesce in another two or three." Some of the protesters, Hobbs believed, "wanted to run the university." "I was convinced that [the takeover] was just an inevitability," Griffith recollected. "I do believe that if we had opened up and said, 'We'll do anything you want us to do' [a confrontation still] would have happened." "I don't think the Black students were interested in . . . an agreement," Cell commented. "They were presenting demands for the purpose of creating a confrontation. The end was not the Black studies program or this or that concession. These were means; the end was a confrontation with a university that very much needed to be confronted. I'm not quarrelling with that. Except that this was very difficult to deal with. In fact, impossible to deal with."[34]

As for the Black students, after the January 31 forum, their internal discussions began to increasingly focus on a takeover of the Allen Building. No action, however, was imminent. "We decided," Armstrong explained, "to see if Black Week would loosen things up."[35]

....

When Knight had learned of the Black students' request that the university support Black Week in October 1968, he responded that there was "obviously some dynamite" in such a prospect.[36] With Black Week now only days away, Knight tried to mitigate the destructive force he feared the event would generate.

First, Knight wrote the trustees, alerting them to the upcoming Beauty of Black symposium. He described the weeklong program and warned that the student publication *Harambee* would include student essays, "some of which are expected to be critical of Duke" and "use language which will be offensive." Knight reassured the trustees that no university funds had been used to produce *Harambee*. "A careful reading [of *Harambee*] will tell us a good deal about what these students feel," he explained, "and we need to know."[37]

At the same time, on February 4, Knight published a statement in the *Duke Chronicle* endorsing Black Week. Hoping to defuse growing anger, he used his comments to respond to a number of the Black students' demands. Knight commended the AAS for "providing opportunities to consider aspects of black American culture of which they are justifiably proud" and encouraged the entire university community to take full advantage of them. Acknowledging both "genuine successes" and "undoubted failures" in the university's dealings with its "minority group students," Knight noted that some of the recommendations made by the AAS in October 1968 had been approved "without delay" while others "will require careful study." The Duke president announced steps designed to deal with the "disproportionate attrition of our black students," including implementation of a summer transition program, appointment of an adviser to all minority groups, and identification of "those students whom we have already lost" who might qualify for readmission following participation in the new summer program.[38]

Knight's final announcement was by far the most difficult for him. Because "there must be a clear commitment on the part of us all to the proposition that this University is *one* place and *one* community," Knight said, "as President of the University, I can no longer be a part of organizations which practice racial discrimination." On the same day, he advised the president of Hope Valley Country Club of his resignation, telling him that "I regret that this is made necessary by Club policy, and I retain genuine good will for my many friends who have reached conclusions which differ from my own." His withdrawal was an "insult" to club members, Knight said later. "If you want to take something that called for real fortitude, that was a real winner."[39]

While Knight later characterized his Hope Valley resignation as "a matter of conviction," his decision-making process was more complicated. Approached initially about his club membership in 1966, Knight had resisted repeated calls to resign because he feared doing so would weaken his position at Duke. "This was a very sharply defined issue," he explained, "because it involved what were regarded as the social rights of every member of the club. . . . It was a devastating thing that I had to do. . . . It called into question the judgment of all of the people around me. It would have been a small fraction of 1 percent of the people around me who would have taken . . . that position," he concluded. "And yet it was the right one—so there you are."[40]

In public, Knight had defended his continued membership as necessary to allow him to work from within the club to effectuate a change in its membership policy. "I think [Knight] had really mixed emotions about that country club situation," Griffith recounted. "He was caught pretty much between a rock and a hard place. . . . He was not happy about the [Caucasian-only] clause being in there [but] felt that if he left, he'd be doing more harm to the situation. He was the liberal Duke president who would basically cut off his connections with the segment of Durham that was important to Duke." Griffith reported about Knight, "He felt that from within the club he could" change the policy.[41]

Knight eventually saw that getting Hope Valley to reverse its segregationist membership policy was impossible. "I think I knew what a forlorn hope it was when I started off," he recounted, "but I thought I had to play it out. . . . I discovered that there wouldn't be a bit of movement on the part of the Hope Valley folk, so that all the movement had to be mine. . . . They weren't about to show even a slight degree of change in their membership policy," Knight recalled painfully. "Not a flicker."[42]

Even after this became apparent, Knight agonized. In January 1969, with pressure on him reaching a crescendo, the Duke president asked for Griffith's advice on what to do. "I must confess from where I sit," Griffith responded, "my recommendation would be to resign your membership in light of the fact that there can be no anticipated change in the club membership [policy] in the foreseeable future."[43]

Knight's response to Griffith showed how conflicted he was. "The public problem remains as vexed as ever," he told Griffith, "in the sense that if I take the step we have discussed, I think I may pretty effectively neutralize whatever remains of my usefulness down town. On the other hand," he wrote, "my own conscience bothers me so seriously that I think I may have to resolve the question on that ground alone (hardly the weakest ground, after all)."[44]

Knight looked back bitterly on how little credit he got for making such a politically costly choice. "The irony of it," he commented, was that resigning "was a very difficult thing to do. And in the temper of the student mind, this was something that they had forced and it really didn't cost them anything. And the thought that this was just one more step in the destruction of my position," Knight reflected, "just didn't really cross their minds."[45]

Knight was correct that he garnered little credit from Duke's Black students for his Hope Valley resignation. "We would appreciate more him doing nothing," McBride, AAS president at the time, told the *Duke Chronicle*, "than coming out and telling [us] how liberal he is. . . . They either think that we are joking or that we'll give up and forget about it." McBride called on every Duke student to reinforce how "dead serious" they were about the changes Blacks were demanding. Hopkins dismissed Knight's announcement as a "pacification effort." "When he feels that something is imminent as far as unrest among the black students," Hopkins commented, "he comes up with a few concessions." Griffith, not surprisingly, was more positive. "I interpret [Knight's] statement," he said, "as a commitment to make considerable effort to resolve some of the remaining questions that exist."[46]

The tense racial climate on campus became clear when, on the same day that the *Duke Chronicle* reported on Knight's endorsement of Black Week, it published a column by Chuck Hopkins titled "Why Duke Is Racist." White people seeking to understand the Black student experience at Duke, Hopkins wrote, must first ask what institutional changes "were undertaken when blacks were brought to this campus." Calling Duke before 1963 "a bulwark of institutionalized human degradation," he argued that "since its integration Duke has done nothing institutionally to deal with its own racism." As proof, Hopkins pointed out that "the same racist structures and personalities which ran this University in its pre-integrated state are still running it today." The problem of Black student unrest could be solved, Hopkins explained, only when the people who run the university "decide that it is necessary for them to sit down with Black people and deal effectively with the racism which prevails here. . . . But if they continue to believe they can buy time with their pacification efforts," he warned, "they are dealing with a myth that they clearly can no longer afford."[47]

Rumors that a building takeover was imminent now actively spread around campus. Knight increasingly worried about a confrontation. "This is no easy road," he reminded a group of white students who wrote to him after his February 4 announcement to ask that he "give immediate attention" to the remaining AAS demands. "We could find it impossible to accomplish the very things you believe in most," he warned, "if by some grave error" Black students tried to use force to achieve their demands. An even clearer statement came at an off-campus dinner discussion at the start of Black Week when the Duke president was asked what would be done if a group of students seized a university building. Such an action "would be a great error," a red-faced Knight responded. "It had damn better not be taken."[48]

The road signs to disaster had become even clearer.

....

Black Week at Duke in February 1969 was a remarkable event. It featured twenty-one scheduled speeches, seminars, plays, and other programs as well as soul food, a boutique of African fashion, Black music (on the campus radio station), and an exhibit of works by Black artists.[49]

Harambee set the tone with essays, poems, free verse, interviews, and photographs. The newspaper expressed the insight, frustration, bitterness, and pride Duke's Black students were experiencing. In its "Statement of Purpose," the paper spoke directly to white readers. "The motive" behind *Harambee*, the editorial board wrote, "is to dispel your ignorance and myths. Please, realize Blacks did not enter this institution on a premise of becoming hopelessly bitter. . . . Blacks believe that blatant racism, subtle bigotry, dehumanizing effects of shallow liberalism and the belief that a white 'superior' culture is liberating the minds of Black people generated our present mentality. . . . The essays [in *Harambee*] show the epiphany of Blacks who were once negroes." "To be Black," the Statement of Purpose concluded, "is to emerge from the shackles of lies and deceit that make people niggers."[50]

Hopkins published an essay in *Harambee* called "Black Rap," discussing the educational system in America. "It is crystal clear," Hopkins wrote, "that the intellectual bullshit which is taught on campuses today is directed towards maintaining the established ruling class in this country. The Black student," he explained, "must cleanse himself of all value teachings from the reactionary American educational system." Hopkins argued that a new ideology would emerge "from the bosoms of the loving, hating, destructive, creative, and beautifully passionate masses of Black people."[51]

Other essays and poems conveyed direct or implied threats of violence. "We now see a new Black man," freshman Larry Weston wrote, "who is willing to utilize any means necessary to ensure that his voice is not only heard, but respected. . . . It must be increasingly recognized," he wrote, "that the Black man . . . must wield the awesome power which he controls if he is to survive. . . . Like it or not world, your time has arrived. . . . Move over, baby, or we shall move over you."[52] In his poem "A New Language," McBride was equally direct:

There is one language
      that even pigs understand
It's spoken with lead teeth,
A mouth of steel,
And a tongue of hot, burning powder. . . .
Now all you people who
      don't know this language
You'd better learn it fast
'Cause we all are going to need it
To talk to our "pig chowder."[53]

Trustees, alumni, and administrators who saw a copy of *Harambee* were deeply offended. One trustee who had seen excerpts from the newspaper called them "vile, filthy, and obscene. . . . No Duke student," he wrote Knight, "should be permitted to remain in school who would write . . . any of these thoughts" for publication. The contents of the newspaper triggered alumnus William Werber's worst fears. *Harambee*, he said, "advocated teaching young blacks to murder white people" and contained threats to "burn white homes and white businesses." Another alumnus, Sim A. DeLapp, asked what defense the university had to "the depraved minds who give utterance to these filthy, dangerous comments? An administration that will allow this to pass unnoticed," he charged, "is not worthy of the respect of decent, free men."[54]

Black Week began when Howard Fuller spoke on Thursday, February 6, at a seminar called No More Orangeburgs. Fuller told the group he saw "no distinction between the physical violence which took place in Orangeburg, and the killing of minds that is taking place in our school systems." "Black people cannot allow people to be slaughtered," he argued, and "must stop turning the other cheek." Fuller dismissed a system of education that is "brutally destroying black minds" and called for the creation of a Black studies program at Duke that would "meet black needs and goals."[55]

President Knight attended a number of Black Week events, including a performance of *God's Trombones* by James Weldon Johnson. First published in 1927, the work's subtitle is *Seven Negro Sermons in Verse*. Its penultimate message, "Let my People Go," is based on the book of Exodus and tells the story of the liberation of the Hebrews from Egypt. Performed by William Turner, the sermon carried a special message for the Duke president. Knight "was there in Branson that night in the audience," Turner recalled. "The words 'Let my

People Go' [in the sermon] were directed explicitly and clearly right to him in his face. '*Let my people go!*'"[56]

Cell also attended the plays. Afterward, he offered some unsolicited tactical advice to Black student Tony Axam. "Don't go into Allen Building," he told the Black student leader. "Once you do, [the administration] will know exactly what to do. . . . It's your trump card," Cell cautioned, "but it's the last one you've got. Don't play it." The suggestion, Cell thought, "got nowhere."[57]

The most anticipated event of the week was the appearance of comedian and activist Dick Gregory. During the late 1960s, Gregory spoke at hundreds of academic institutions. "I spend about 98 percent of my time today on college campuses," Gregory commented, "and for a reason. I feel that you young folks in America today are probably the most morally committed, ethical group of dedicated young people that have ever lived in the history of this country." Gregory's speech—titled "Nigger"—was scheduled for 8:00 p.m. on February 10.[58]

Knight did not attend Gregory's speech. However, aware of Gregory's importance, the Duke president invited the Black leader, along with sixteen Black students, to dinner at University House before the speech. Knight looked forward to hosting what he hoped would be "a good and proper dinner." The evening did not turn out as planned. "Armored in our white liberal innocence," Knight recounted later, "we were a bit bewildered when . . . no one [came] for dinner—just a terse message saying that if all could not come, none would come. Our black servants (good friends by now) were far more outraged than we," Knight recounted, "and said so with considerable vigor." "You are doing the thing that's right," Knight said later. "Then you find out that the request [for a dinner] was nothing but a ploy . . . on the part of all black students [to object] that they couldn't all be there." "One gets caught," Knight concluded. "There is almost nothing you can do that's right. Almost nothing."[59]

Unfortunately for Knight, the dinner snub did not end his evening. The Black students "got together in a meeting," Hopkins reported, "and said, 'Hey, these are grievances we all are going to raise. Let's all go out there.'" Joined by Gregory, "all of us walked into Knight's house. He took it well," Hopkins recalled. "It was kind of tense at first, but then we got to talking."[60]

Knight and the seventy-five Black students discussed a list of nine demands the AAS was now presenting to the university. The wording of the nine demands was more urgent than in the past, focusing on the issue of control. The Black students wanted a Black studies program "right away." They insisted on a Black dorm, promising to be "just as selective as to who stays there as the fraternities on campus already are." On academic matters, they wanted reinstatement of all Black students who "failed to make a successful academic adjustment to the University," and an academic adviser selected by them—not "an administration appointee who identifies with the white power structure rather than us." The language in the demands showed how wide the gulf between the administration and its students had become. "We will not be appeased by the tidbits the administration has handed out," the first demand said. "We will not compromise our humanity. . . . We want a say in everything that involves us. . . . We want to be in on . . . any plans or decisions that have anything to do with us."[61]

Gregory remained quiet through much of the discussion with Knight. "We were trying to figure out what Gregory was going to say," Hopkins recounted, "which way he was going." Finally, Gregory "just came out and told Knight," Hopkins recounted, "'Give the students what they are asking. They're not asking that much.'" Before departing, the students turned up the heat further. They warned the Duke president of "an unspecified action" in the "near future" if he did not comply satisfactorily with the demands.[62]

Gregory's speech later at the indoor stadium was attended by three thousand people. "This is the most morally polluted, degenerate, insane nation on the face of the Earth," Gregory told the crowd. "We're saying we're tired of this institutionalized racism. We're saying we want Black studies because we all at once want to find out who we are. Since we decided we ain't your nigger," Gregory said to cheers and clenched fists from Duke's Black students, "we wanna know who we are."[63]

The next day, Knight issued a statement. His concern was not the substance of the Black students' grievances but the process, especially their use of the word *demands*. "I didn't have a group of students at University House making 'demands' on Monday evening," he told the Duke community in a statement that appeared in the *Duke Chronicle*. "The way the university works, we don't make demands of one another. I don't accept demands from the trustees," he went on, and "I don't make demands of any of my faculty colleagues." Desperate to characterize his interactions with the Black students as part of the university's more customary decision-making process, he explained that the students on Monday had simply "described . . . matters which are of deep and genuine concern to them." Knight said the issues raised would be considered "without any of the delays of which people are so suspicious these days."[64] Yet by framing his remarks as a rebuke to the notion of "making demands," Knight had further polarized the situation.

The day after he released his statement, Knight told a joint meeting of the Administrative Council and the Executive Committee of the Academic

Council that he had talked to the Black students at University House on Monday night "with what he felt was good rapport." In fact, he was mistaken: the students viewed the evening as a turning point. "During Black Week we went to visit Dr. Knight with Dick Gregory," Brown recounted. "That was the point everyone went back and said we've got to talk about something that's gonna do something."[65]

Knight thought Gregory's visit and speech were a direct precursor to the Allen Building takeover. "Dick Gregory was the trigger," he said later. "I would say the speech he gave that night was undoubtedly the explosive one. It was designed to be, [and] in that sense it was a very well worked out enterprise." Like others who blamed campus unrest on "outside forces," once again, Knight was wrong. Gregory "might have said a lot of things that . . . firmed it up in some people's minds," Becton recalled, but "nothing that he said was the spark for 'Let's take over Allen Building.' The idea came from within."[66]

The programming on Tuesday, the final day of Black Week, further accelerated matters. At 10:00 a.m., Fannie Lou Hamer, leader of the Mississippi Freedom Party, spoke on the "politics of liberation." "I don't want to hear any more talk about 'equal rights,'" she told the audience. "I don't want to be equal to people who raped my ancestors, sold my ancestors and treated the Indians like they did. I don't want to be equal to that. I want 'human rights.'" The events of the day ended at 10:00 p.m. with *six* concurrent student-led seminars, titled "Where Do We Go from Here?—Community or Chaos?"[67]

Members of the AAS hoped that the events of Black Week would sensitize Duke administrators and students to the issues Duke's Black students were facing, but this did not occur. Attendance by whites at Black Week events was largely confined to the plays that were presented. "The purpose of Black Week was to educate, not to entertain," Hopkins commented. "I feel that we failed . . . in this respect as the only events well attended by whites were the entertaining ones." Black Week "probably didn't change their minds," Bill Werner observed. "We saw the same white faces at all the seminars, the same radical few."[68]

Beyond apathy, Black students sensed a generally negative reaction to Black Week among many administrators. "They were so angry with us," Janice Williams recalled. "They just got really upset with us pulling that off and pretty much let us know that they didn't appreciate it," she said. "The response to Black Week was very negative." According to Armstrong, "Duke's Black students came away from Black Week wondering, 'Who's listening to us?' . . . Nobody cared that we were there. Nobody cared to find out anything about us."[69]

If Black Week had little impact on Duke's white community, it had a profound effect on the school's Black students. As leaders of the AAS had anticipated, Black Week brought Duke's Black students closer together as they began to coalesce around the demands of the AAS. "Black Week was very pivotal for people allowing their collective ethnicity to come out," Armstrong noted. "It was nice to congeal the interests of a lot of the 'conservative' factions with the political 'issue oriented' interests of the 'militant faction.' You could do that in the context of Black Week."[70]

Speakers like Dick Gregory, Howard Fuller, and Fannie Lou Hamer, Turner said, created "a revolutionizing experience" for many Black students. Black Week is what really "radicalized me," Turner explained. "I'll never forget the people." One question Gregory asked made a particularly strong impression on Armstrong. "Dick Gregory talked to us about what we were doing at Duke," she recalled. "He said, 'They don't want you here in the first place, and they've made it so hard for you to live here and study here that you're not going to get an education. What are you doing here besides satisfying a quota?'" For Turner, Hamer, who passionately described her suffering in the racist South and a career in civil rights activism, was "probably the one with the greatest impact of all." Hamer also moved Bertie Howard. "For a lot of us," Howard recalled, she "caused us to stop and pause and think about what we were going to do."[71]

Planning for a building takeover was by now underway. Hamer's presence on campus solidified the resolve of a number of the participants. "To think that a woman could tolerate all the stuff that she had and go on," Howard remarked. "And here you are in a real luxurious situation. . . . In the face of that, taking a building was a very tame thing."[72]

....

Duke's Black students met at Becton's off-campus house during Black Week to consider their next steps. Despite discussions with school administrators that had started months earlier, Black students felt they had made few advances. "The people who were talking to the administration," Armstrong remembered, "proved that they had gone the 100 percent route and that they had nothing to show for it." When the option of occupying the Allen Building was brought up, it was not a new idea. "It was a time that these things were happening on other campuses," Brown explained, "and it was in the minds of many students." Until Black Week, however, occupation of a building as a way of focusing attention on university racial issues had garnered little internal support. "It was viewed on a continuum . . . as . . . the most radical" thing to do, Hopkins said. "It had come up in previous discussions, but . . . somebody would always get up and say, 'We're not ready to do that.' So it was held in abeyance."[73]

Although a substantial number in the group were now open to the strategy, there was still no consensus. At least one group of students felt that the right approach was to continue discussions with the administration. "Let's try talking to the faculty some more," Armstrong remembered these students saying. "I don't think we've exhausted all the channels." A second option—a mass withdrawal of Black students from the university—had more support. Brown favored this approach. She explained:

> I just felt like the only thing that would really shock these people was for every Black student there to go see their dean and tell them that they were withdrawing, pack their bags, and leave the place all white. And the next time they . . . go out and recruit some Black students [they would have] to explain why all these Black folks left [and] maybe they would sit down and try to figure out what they needed to do to make life livable for us on campus. We sat arguing for three hours [about] alternatives.

There was "a lot of yelling," Armstrong remembered. "There were sixty of us. Maybe thirty or forty were sure they wanted to [occupy the Allen Building]. There were five or six guys on the athletic teams who could not participate actively [because they could lose their scholarships]. Fifteen people weren't really sure."[74]

No final decision was made that night at Becton's house. "We talked about it and everybody went home," Armstrong recounted. "We didn't make a decision, we didn't say, 'Yes, we're going to do this.'"[75]

Still, the meeting was critical. "We decided it was the only option we had—either that or just forget about it," Armstrong recalled. Mass withdrawal was off the table. "I don't think 75 or 80 percent of us thought that there were any other options available to us that were reasonable," she explained. "For the vast majority of the people in the AAS, leaving school was not an option because we knew that if we left, they would just get another group of students."[76]

When the group reconvened several days later, those supporting the occupation prevailed. "The vote was 90 percent to go in and occupy," Becton reported. Most of those voting against a takeover, he recalled, felt it was "too drastic a measure to take." Despite strongly differing opinions, however, Brown saw no "sense of divisiveness" in the group. "Once the group decided 'this is what we're going to do,'" Brown remembered, "it was up to those with indecision to make up their minds on their own. . . . Most of us understood the reasons why [students] decided not to participate." This "inclusiveness" reflected the maturation of the AAS and its leadership. "By the time we got to Allen Building," Hopkins explained, we were committed to "letting everybody contribute what they want[ed] to rather than making everybody be the 'militant.' A lot of people felt as strongly about the issues as we did but parents were calling in to students asking what was happening, saying, 'I didn't send you to Duke to get involved with that.' People wanted to keep their scholarships, the athletes didn't want to jeopardize playing on the team. We didn't alienate anybody," Hopkins recounted. "We let people contribute what they were ready to contribute." According to Brown, the vast majority of those Black students who decided they could not join the occupation of the Allen Building nevertheless "did something to help." People acted "with one mind," Turner remembered. "We felt like we were part of each other. We had everything at stake together."[77]

Attention now turned to planning and logistics. The group decided to occupy the central records office and the bursar's office in the Allen Building because "that was the hub of Allen Building and we didn't need anything else," Armstrong recalled. The takeover would be planned for precisely 8:00 a.m., the time that the safe containing Duke's central records opened automatically each day. "I'd go [into the Allen Building] every day and commit the floor plans to memory," Armstrong explained. Another student, Clarence Moore, also had classes in the building. "Between the two of us, we figured out how many doors, what they were like, how they were locked. From that we could figure out how to take over the building in the most expedient way . . . and how long it would take us to do it."[78]

Other jobs were also assigned. "There were . . . people who were to find out how easy it would be to . . . get on the roofs and . . . be able to see what . . . was going on," Armstrong explained. "There were people who had to get us walkie-talkies; there were people who were to get rations, blankets, medical supplies; there was one person who was to get the truck. There was one person who was to figure out how to establish communications once we got inside the building. There were one or two people who were to find out how to defend ourselves, or what to do if we got into a confrontation."[79]

Hopkins recalled that a transfer student from North Carolina College arranged for the truck to transport students to campus the morning of the takeover. "He had come from NCC to Duke," Hopkins recalled, "which was a big step up. He was doing well in his courses and he wasn't about to jeopardize all of that. So he was the one who volunteered to get the truck. That was his thing."[80]

Even as planning proceeded, differences emerged on the tactics to be used in the takeover. The biggest problem came when a small faction proposed taking guns into the Allen Building. "I said, 'You all are crazy,'" Hopkins recalled. "What are we going to look like trying to outshoot cops and stuff holed up in Allen Building," he said. "It was Chuck's position and mine," McBride recalled, "that we not do anything to give anyone an excuse to not address our demands. My concern was that I thought . . . we might die, and . . . if we had guns, I was *certain* we would die."[81]

Even so, the suggestion was more than empty talk. "Some of the Black people on campus were more violence-oriented," SDS member Hutch Traver recalled. "I was once asked by a Black student if I knew where I could get some guns." This represented "a splinter group," Traver noted, and the talk of guns was just "radical euphoria." "They had no idea of what would have happened if someone had shot a gun in the air at Duke University," he recounted. "It would have been a whole different ball game."[82]

The diversity of opinions in the discussions reinforced Becton's decision to participate in the takeover. "One of my concerns was that there was a wide range of opinions about what ought to be done and how it ought to be done," he explained. "There were . . . some freshmen who had been reading and breathing Watts and all these other places who were just basically hot heads. I was concerned that there be a balance of power [in the building] and that there be level heads. Because if the thing got out of hand, I wanted to be sure that there were enough people to be thinking clearly and rationally, as opposed to emotional sorts of things that had been present at some of our meetings. Some people went in," he explained, "to make sure that we don't just blow things by being totally destructive [and] lose sight of what we really want." Michael LeBlanc recognized this dynamic. "There was a radical faction," he acknowledged, "and there was a faction that, thank God, was a whole lot more sensible."[83]

One idea that initially gained acceptance was a proposal to bring kerosene into the Allen Building. Knowing that they would have control of central records, the students' rationale was defensive. The kerosene "was an ace in the hole . . . that was protection," Howard explained. In effect, the students were saying to anyone who tried to end the takeover by force, "If you come in here and take the building, you've got to remember that . . . there's all this kerosene laying around [and all these records], so you better be careful what you do." "We never really thought of destroying property," Armstrong recounted. "Even if it was raised, it was objectionable. *Extremely objectionable*."[84]

Since the moderate, nonviolent Black students controlled the planning and execution of the Allen Building takeover, the decision was made, according to Brown, to avoid a "violent confrontation." "We wanted [to get people to] negotiate with us on a serious level. . . . I don't think we had any intentions of hurting anyone, or physically damaging the building."[85]

Despite their talk of revolution, leaders of the AAS still clung to the liberal notion that people of good will could be moved to action. "Although we were militant and outspoken," Hopkins explained, "all of us came out of a consciousness [that said], if you show the oppressor his wrongs, he'll change them." "I think all of us held on in the back of our minds," Armstrong remembered, "to that last vestige of hope for reason among those in the administration."[86]

The takeover was set for February 13. All planning had been completed and supplies and transportation arrangements were in place. On February 12, the Black students gathered for a final meeting at Becton's house to confirm the decision to move ahead with the takeover. "It could have been called off as late as the night before," Hopkins recalled. But "when we broke up that night, . . . the decision had been made. It was just a matter of everybody meeting at the right time and the individuals who were supposed to do certain things doing them."[87]

Duke administrators also gathered on February 12 at a joint meeting of the Administrative Council and the Executive Committee of the Academic Council. The minutes of the meeting indicate that Griffith "observed with concern that just prior to and during [Black Week], notable deterioration had taken place in University relationships with its black students." Griffith saw "an impatience and apparent unwillingness to cooperate" among the Black students, "making it hard for him and others working with him to do anything about their petitions for changes." McBride, the new president of the AAS, Griffith told the group, had "expressed little interest in meeting with committees" and "become demanding in talks with [Griffith] about what is to be done. . . . A demonstration was possible at any time," Griffith warned.[88]

Aware of a looming crisis, the administrators decided to form yet *another* committee. Hobbs expressed displeasure with the ad hoc committee that had been working on the Black students' demands. "Hobbs's foremost objective," Cell described, "was to try to get things back into channels. It had gone all haywire. . . . Provosts and deans running around like chickens with their heads cut off."[89] He preferred "one committee somewhat akin to a steering or a grievance committee composed of faculty and, perhaps, students having knowledge of, rapport with, and access to all campus groups." Such a committee would serve as a clearinghouse for all student suggestions and demands. "It would be understood," the minutes reported, "that if one wanted to be heard, he was expected to go through this committee."[90]

Thus, at the very moment that Black students were preparing a takeover to focus attention on their demands, administrators were urgently seeking to reestablish order. All demands would go to the new committee. The minutes of the joint meeting showed that administrators had determined that, going forward, "channels must be followed." "No other procedure is acceptable to Duke University," Hobbs wrote at the time, "and individuals who advocate or practice violent or massive confrontation . . . will be declared *personas non grata* and procedures will be instituted to deny [them] access to the property of Duke University."[91]

The two meetings, the same day, dramatically illustrated the chasm that had developed between Duke and its Black students. Six years into desegregation, Black students looked at the university and saw indifference, intransigence, and bad faith. "I guess initially we thought all you had to do was say, 'Look, you overlooked something,'" Brown explained. "Well, now they *knew* they had overlooked a whole lot of things and they *still* weren't doing anything. . . . It wasn't just a matter of letting people know. Now they *know*, and they ain't gonna do." For their part, administrators saw the Black students' demands as without substance and simply designed to provoke confrontation. "Everybody ought to have a voice," Hobbs acknowledged, but matters had gone too far. The Black students "wanted everyone else to do what *they* wanted them to do," he commented. "That's . . . real anarchy as far as I was concerned. . . . You can't have an institution and have anarchy at the same time."[92]

By morning, these two groups would face each other in a confrontation that carried enormous risk and potentially dire consequences for the university and the individuals involved. As it had from the moment Black students stepped onto Duke's campus, race would shape how events unfolded.

CHAPTER 8

———

No Option to Negotiate

Confrontation

———

The Black students who spent the night at Charles Becton's house on February 12 stepped inside the back of the U-Haul truck to travel to campus to take over the Allen Building just after 7:30 a.m. "There was a giddiness at first," Brenda Armstrong recounted, "but when they closed the door and it was dark . . . it jolted everyone into [a] reality of how important and . . . potentially dangerous what we were doing really was."[1]

For Armstrong, the short trip to campus brought to mind thoughts of her ancestors. "I remember talking to my best friend . . . about knowing what it was like in the 'Middle Passage,'" the brutal sea journey that took slaves from West Africa to the West Indies. "It was dark," she recalled. "My hands were just full of sweat. . . . It was the most frightening thing I've ever been through in my entire life." Bertie Howard had more immediate concerns. "The gas fumes were terrible," she vividly remembered. "It was early in the morning. I hadn't eaten. I hadn't slept. . . . I remember thinking to myself, 'I'm going to throw up.'" For everyone, the stakes were momentous. Students realized, as Armstrong said, that if the takeover failed, "we had put [our lives] and careers on the line."[2]

The takeover was planned for 8:00 a.m. That time was selected because the safe in the registrar's office containing the only copies of the permanent academic records of Trinity and Duke students going back to 1854 opened without fail at that hour each day. At precisely the designated time, Becton recounted, "the truck stopped, the back came up, the kids jumped out, [and] ran into the back of Allen Building. At the same time, kids were coming from all four points on the quad, running toward Allen Building." Even with this precision, not everything went exactly as planned. The last one off the truck, Stef McLeod, had brought a box of chocolate bars to use as energy food during the takeover. Chuck Hopkins described how McLeod,

> as he was coming off the truck, dropped the box and had chocolate bars all over the place. . . . We were going into Allen Building, trying to get everyone in there quick, and there was Stef out there trying to gather up chocolate bars. And [the driver] Jim was trying to get the truck out of there. I yelled to Stef, "Man, leave those chocolate bars alone." . . . So the scene was Stef holding on to the back of the truck trying to hold on to the chocolate bars. [Finally he] jumped off and ran in.[3]

As the students entered the building, "the adrenaline was flowing," Janice Williams remembered. "We wanted to do things just right so that they would know we meant business." The first step was to usher employees already at work out of the building. In the registrar's office, Mary Seabolt tried unsuccessfully to close the vault containing the university's irreplaceable academic records. Clark Cahow, university assistant registrar, later described the students as having been "very polite." Upon entering the registrar's office, he said, the students informed Seabolt and others "that they were taking over the building. [They] asked them please [to] get their personal belongings . . . so they could be escorted out of the building."[4]

In a letter to the editor of a North Carolina newspaper, employee Joyce Siler described her experience in the bursar's office very differently. "A Negro male entered the Bursar's Office and firmly commanded that we 'get out,'" she wrote. "Baseball bats, lengths of pipe, and chains . . . were being banged against the walls and floors of the office and shouts of 'get out' could be heard from all sides. I took my coat from the rack and headed toward the door when a Negro male carrying a baseball bat . . . grabbed my dress sleeve and shouted obscenities, demanding that 'I get out now.'"

Siler felt "man-handled, pushed, [and] terrorized." Other secretaries testified that they were "frightened to death," "very afraid," or "shocked."[5]

However different these perceptions, no employees said they were physically harmed when the offices were vacated. Although deeply unsettling to some of the Duke employees in the Allen Building, the takeover had been completed without violence.

The Black students then proceeded to secure the space. A metal bar and chains were inserted through the handles of the glass doors that opened to the Allen Building lobby, and furniture was piled in front of the doors. A pair of wooden doors at the opposite end of the first-floor corridor was nailed shut. Other access points were chained. Windows from the lobby into the offices on the first floor of the Allen Building were covered with a hand-lettered sign announcing that the area had been renamed the "Malcolm X Liberation School." The entire operation was completed in just two minutes.[6]

William Griffith "heard some pounding on [the] back double doors" of the Allen Building as he headed up the stairs to his office on the second floor. "I went to see what was going on and I couldn't get in," he explained. "I looked through the crack and . . . knew it was being barricaded. I said, 'Look, let me talk to you.' . . . They came to the door and [said] that they couldn't talk to me. . . . I went around the other side of the building and saw it was also barricaded." With Douglas Knight out of town, Griffith called university provost Marcus Hobbs, telling him, "We've got a situation here."[7]

Duke was far from the only school to experience Black activism on February 13, 1969. On the same day, historian Ibram X. Kendi wrote, "black students disrupted higher education in almost every area of the nation." Indeed, Kendi described February 13, 1969, as "a day, or *the* day, that black campus activists forced the racial reconstitution of higher education." "It was a day," he wrote, "that emitted the anger, determination, and agency of a generation that stood on the cutting edge of educational progression."[8]

Each school experienced Black protest in its own way, with events playing out against the backdrop of Black activism and the impact of different personalities, entrenched power dynamics, and aspirations unique to each institution. At Duke, one key part of that context was the Silent Vigil that had occurred in April 1968—only ten months earlier. Although they were very different events, the Silent Vigil and the Allen Building takeover presented those in power at Duke with many of the same agonizing decisions. Would the university negotiate or make concessions in the face of student protest? What strategies, relationships, and resources would Duke deploy to persuade the students to end the crisis peacefully? How quickly would decision makers give serious consideration to the use of force to end the occupation, and on what basis? Answers to these questions on

February 13, 1969, show how powerfully race shaped the university's response to protest.

....

Although planning for the Allen Building takeover had been done in secret, advance notice of an "unspecified action" the next day was provided to a small group on Wednesday night, February 12. One recipient of the news was Benjamin Ruffin, a Black community leader and close associate of Black activist Howard Fuller. Takeover planners told Ruffin, Hopkins explained, "because we wanted support from the Black community." Black student leaders also alerted several staff members of the *Duke Chronicle*, all of whom were sworn to secrecy. The Black students "wanted to be sure that outside media were notified as soon as possible," executive editor Tom Campbell recalled. "They felt that might help to protect them from a brutal response from the police and administration." The student leaders also wanted to be certain that the national media were made aware of the protest. Hopkins commented: "We were smart enough to know back then that we didn't want [the takeover] to be an isolated event down here in Durham. We wanted the nation and the world to know what was going on."[9]

As requested, the *Duke Chronicle* staff members convened at approximately 7:30 a.m. on February 13 and awaited word from the students. That word arrived just after 8:00 a.m. The students released a statement to the *Duke Chronicle*, drafted the prior evening, that set forth eleven demands, along with the rationale for the takeover. The statement issued from the Malcolm X Liberation School inside the Allen Building announced in capital letters:

> WE SEIZED THE BUILDING BECAUSE WE HAVE BEEN NEGOTIATING WITH DUKE ADMINISTRATION AND FACULTY CONCERNING DIFFERENT ISSUES THAT AFFECT BLACK STUDENTS FOR 2 1/2 YEARS AND WE HAVE NO MEANINGFUL RESULTS. *WE HAVE EXHAUSTED THE SO-CALLED "PROPER CHANNELS."*

After contacting the *Duke Chronicle*, Hopkins called Griffith and said, "We've just taken over the administration building, and these are the demands." Hopkins recalled that after hearing the demands, "Bill Griffith sort of stuttered a little bit and he finally said, 'OK, Chuck, I'll get back to you.'"[10]

Chronicle editor Alan Ray also received a call from a student inside the Allen Building. "He said for me to call the security cops," Ray recounted, "and tell them the blacks would burn the records if the police were sent in."

Chronicle managing editor Bob Ashley received an even stronger warning. If the demands were not met immediately, the student journalist said, and the telephone line into the Allen Building did not remain open, the records would be burned.[11]

Despite these warnings, the threat to burn the records did not reflect the views of the vast majority of takeover participants or of Black student leaders. Destroying university property was contrary to the wishes of the majority of the group. Although kerosene was brought into the Allen Building, Armstrong recounted how, within an hour, the group "put it in the toilet. We decided," she explained, "that even as a final act of desperation, [burning records] would not serve any purpose." Shortly thereafter, the *Duke Chronicle* reported that any threat to burn the university's records had been withdrawn. "No property has been destroyed," Hopkins commented through a window in the Allen Building, "nor is there any intention to do so." He warned, however, that "if attacked, the black students will defend the black women in the building."[12]

The students had planned for a prolonged occupation. Hopkins told the *Duke Chronicle* that they had enough food to last for a week. "We have lots of food," Josie Knowlin wrote her parents from inside the Allen Building: "peanut butter, jelly, gum, life savers, candy, bread, coffee, sugar, coffee mate, and water, all of the essentials to or for surviving." Supplies also included cups, pots, toilet paper, mouthwash, deodorant, bulbs, batteries, towels, a crowbar, and hammers. Walkie-talkies for communication with spotters outside the building were available. So was a police radio scanner. At least one item included in the planning proved unnecessary. "We had portable commodes," Hopkins recalled. "And we get inside and somebody said, 'Hey, there are bathrooms in this area we have taken.'" Everybody cheered this news, Hopkins remembered.[13]

Howard Fuller received word of the takeover as he was speaking at a convocation at Bennett College in Greensboro. Hearing the news, he was "immediately concerned for [the students'] safety" and canceled plans to travel to Atlanta later in the day. Instead Fuller "headed back to Durham and straight to Duke."[14]

As the students settled in that Thursday morning, their mood was generally positive. Armstrong remembered "a lot of rejoicing," because "all of a sudden [the takeover] was beginning to become successful." Initially, "there wasn't an atmosphere of much tenseness," Brenda Brown recalled. Knowlin wrote her parents that the students were "playing cards, listening to the news, carrying on semi-intellectual conversations, sleeping, [and] playing ball." "Some people would tell jokes," Armstrong recounted, "[and] there would be a silly tense laugh [from] everyone else." These lighter moments, however, simply masked more intense focus. "The whole atmosphere was that we had a goal to accomplish," Williams explained, "and by God we were going to do it."[15]

···························

Initial reactions to the takeover among administrators and faculty varied. Some were sympathetic. "I was not shocked at all," political science professor Samuel DuBois Cook commented. "I'm sure they felt that [this] was their only way out." Cahow, whose Allen Building office was occupied, shared Cook's perspective. "They felt they were getting the 'cold shoulder,'" he commented. "They were absolutely convinced that they weren't being heard and that no action would ever be taken. . . . You just live with that kind of frustration for so long and then something has to give." Some expressed surprise. "Many of us were startled," Knight said. "We had come eight miles out of nine" on the Black student demands. "All of us were quite astonished," history professor Richard Watson remarked. "We thought we were making headway." Most others were deeply critical. "My gut reaction was 'Jesus Christ, they've made another blunder,'" law school dean Kenneth Pye recalled. Before the takeover, he reasoned, "they were . . . in the best possible position to negotiate almost whatever they wanted from the president. He would have given away the Chapel!" Pye thought that by occupying the Allen Building, the Black students "had played their trump card." History professor John Cell was more succinct. Told of the takeover by a colleague, he responded, "Shit." Most telling was the initial reaction of dean Harold Lewis. After talking about the takeover with Cahow, his first response was "Well, we better call the police."[16]

A group that eventually included as many as twenty-five senior administrators, faculty, and two student representatives began to gather in the board room on the second floor of the Allen Building around 8:20 a.m. Until midafternoon, this served as the "situation room" for the university in dealing with the takeover. University secretary Rufus Powell took detailed contemporaneous minutes of the meeting. Knight was not present but in New York for meetings with the Ford Foundation seeking funding, ironically, for a Black studies program. A plane was chartered to bring Knight back to Durham and he arrived on campus in the afternoon.[17]

The first minutes of the meeting were spent exchanging the sketchy information attendees possessed about the events that were unfolding. Hobbs shared what he knew about the occupation. Perhaps believing that all of Duke's Black students had participated in the takeover, he said that there were "approximately 70–80 inside." In fact, only around forty Black students occupied the Allen Building. Despite only incidental physical contact between the protesters and vacating Allen Building employees, Hobbs passed along reports that the Black students "had somewhat maltreated some of the people that they put . . . out of the building. . . . Some of the girls who were in the building were pushed around a little bit," he said. More significant, the provost told the group that the students were reported to "have kerosene" and said they were insisting upon their demands as set forth in the *Chronicle*. Griffith reported on the message Ashley had received from the Black students moments earlier. "They told Bob they have the records," Griffith recounted, and "if their demands . . . were not met immediately, . . . there will be fire." Griffith also reported that the Liberal Action Committee had called for a forum on the quad at 11:30 a.m. as a show of support for the Black students. Cahow almost certainly shocked the group when he reported on the contents of the open safe in his office. "Our records from the beginning of time are open to them, from the beginning of the University," he explained, "and there are no copies." "We realized they had everyone by the short hairs," Griffith recalled.[18]

By 8:40 a.m., Hobbs had spoken to Knight. Immediately adopting the "no negotiations" stance that prevailed throughout the day, Knight advised Hobbs that the administration "was not in a position to accede to demands." Hobbs reported that Knight did not "intend at the present time to take police action" but also relayed instructions from the president that began to frame the rationale for the use of force against the students later in the day. If they did not vacate the offices "within an hour of notification," Knight instructed, "they are to be suspended, . . . are guilty of trespass, and their action goes beyond the Pickets and Protests policy." Hobbs went further. If the protesters did not leave the Allen Building, they "will have to get off the campus" until "a hearing under due process." Less than one hour into the takeover, the university's two top administrators had characterized the Allen Building protesters as "trespassers," and as such, they were subject to removal from campus—by force if necessary. A deadline for resolution of the takeover had also been established. It was "apparent that Knight had made the decision," Griffith commented, "that the building would be cleared *that* day."[19] The patience and restraint white protesters had been accorded during the University House occupation and Silent Vigil ten months earlier clearly would not extend to the Black students in the Allen Building.

The news of Knight's hard line deepened concern at the meeting. While the safety of the students was a worry, preserving the university's irreplaceable academic records was also a focus. Cahow saw the threat to burn the records as the students' "hole card" and recalled that the group "stewed and stewed over what to do." University counsel Edwin Bryson and vice provost Frank de Vyver commented that they hoped no police action would be taken because of "jeopardy of the records." Education professor and Academic Council chair William Cartwright, vice provost Barnes Woodhall, vice president of business and finance Charles Huestis, and vice president for institutional advancement Frank Ashmore suggested that an offer of amnesty be made to the students "to protect the records."[20]

Others were less worried. "The gasoline thing never impressed me as being a serious threat," Hobbs later explained, "because if they did [burn the records], it would endanger them as well." University registrar Richard L. Tuthill also discounted the possibility that the students had kerosene and pressed a plan for security forces to storm the registrar's office through its plate glass windows. "I just felt we could get through and get them out before any records were burned," he commented. Moreover, since the records were "very durable, high quality, rag content paper," Tuthill considered it a "seriously open question . . . how many [records] could have been burned [and] and how rapidly."[21]

Any thought of amnesty for the students—to preserve the university's records—or attempts at substantive discussions with protest leaders soon evaporated. Ashmore reported that in a call with Charles Wade, the chairman of the board had directed the administration to "give them one hour to vacate." There would be "no promises, no amnesty," Wade said. Only "after they leave or are removed," Ashmore relayed, would "a decision . . . be made as to what to do." Less than thirty minutes later, at 11:00 a.m., Hobbs confirmed that Knight agreed with Wade. Although the president saw no reason Duke decision makers "should not stay in touch with the students," amnesty was "not under discussion." Like Wade, the president was prepared to accept the risk of a fire in an office packed with Duke students rather than deviate from his uncompromising position. Before using force to clear the building, however, Knight wanted a statement presented to the students setting forth "all that we have done toward [addressing their] stated goals."[22]

Cartwright later described the hours-long meeting of administrators, faculty, and student representatives as a "full, open, long, and difficult session." Although a range of topics were discussed, minutes of the meeting indicate that only once did any participant suggest that the university consider substantive discussions with the Black students. Sociology professor Alan C. Kerckhoff asked whether there was "anything in the proposals [that was] feasible." Seeing the use of force approaching rapidly, Kerckhoff thought it "a shame to take this action when [action on] some goals [was] possible."[23]

Kerckhoff's suggestion gained no traction. In fact, the minutes say he was met with a "chorus of voices." "Action has been going on [on] a great many" of the issues, Kerckhoff was told. "We cannot act under demands," Hobbs commented. "I think the answer is no negotiations while [the] records are in their possession." Seeking to portray the university as blameless for the confrontation, dean of Trinity College Robert L. Price reviewed what the administration had done to date on the demands, the "promptness of the university [and] the failure of the students themselves to follow-up on meetings—even today."[24]

Although, as Cartwright described later, "all of us in [the] meeting were in agreement that we could not act on these demands under threat of violence," the university did remain willing to consider the Black students' "requests and proposals for the university" after the takeover ended. Accordingly, with students barricaded in the Allen Building and police action under active discussion, Hobbs announced the formation of the "special committee on student concerns," chaired by Kerckhoff (Kerckhoff Committee). This committee would be the university's central point of contact for future discussion of Black student issues. At around the same time, a general faculty meeting was called for 4:00 p.m. on East Campus, in part to announce the creation of the Kerckhoff Committee.[25]

Griffith, the Duke administrator with the most prior contact with the Black students, also spoke up during the discussion. Having played a central role in peacefully resolving the University House occupation and Silent Vigil, he questioned the growing consensus to use force to end the occupation. "I felt that they could be talked out," he recalled. "I just said it was counterproductive to try to drag them out of the building. I thought [the Black students] would realize that it was counterproductive on their part to stay" and that "they would leave." During the morning, Griffith also relayed a warning from Cell, who asked that the administration refrain from taking precipitous action. He advised the group of a mobilization taking place in the Black community and among the faculty in support of the students. "I told Griffith," Cell recounted, "that if they brought in the cops, it would be over my dead body."[26]

Griffith also heard from Cook, who considered the use of force "a very serious mistake." Cook conceded that force was used by the students in the takeover. "But the police are a great symbol of *naked* force," he argued. "When you invite them into your campus, . . . you're really asking for a lot of trouble. . . . Because [calling in the police] means . . . that you've abandoned completely the rule of reason and commitment to the rule of reason. . . . You've surrendered to *naked* force. . . . That's when things really, really take off." Like Griffith, Cook urged patience. He favored isolating the protest "for a while. . . . Wear them down. . . . Wait it out." "I was hoping that someone would get to . . . the president to make the decision that they would not call in force," he said.[27]

Yet, in contrast to the University House occupation and Silent Vigil, Griffith found little support for a more measured approach among other administrators. "I think there were some who agreed with me," the dean recalled, "who were more reluctant to speak out . . . because there was a feeling of being [seen as] soft." "The university was getting entrenched in a pretty hard line," Griffith observed. "There was a strong feeling that something had to be done." He sensed others thinking, "Well, Bill, you've said your piece, let's get on with it."[28]

Momentum toward a confrontation continued to build. Just after 11:00 a.m., Hobbs reported that the police could have fifty officers on campus within an hour.[29]

....

At the 11:30 a.m. forum on the quad convened by the Liberal Action Committee, a crowd of more than 350 could hear in the speakers' remarks that an escalation of the confrontation was now looming. Mark Pinsky, a student leader, told the crowd that they would "have to choose sides within the next couple of hours." The Black students' "struggle is your struggle," he declared.[30]

An AAS spokesman described efforts to get their demands met through the "proper channels" and insisted on the need for Black students to control the implementation of university commitments made to date. "History has shown," the speaker said, "that when we do not have control, . . . we cannot rely . . . that anything such as a Black course or a Black adviser appointed by the administration . . . will be beneficial to us."[31]

Cartwright agreed that "not nearly enough [progress] has been made" on the issues presented, but he urged patience. "Although each demand has at least some kernel of justice in it," he said, "progress on any major social issue will not be made overnight, and will not be brought about . . . as a result of violence."[32]

The Student Liberation Front followed Cartwright, stating that it "fully supports the demands and actions of the Afro-American Society." The group announced the establishment of a "freedom school" on the third floor of the Allen Building to demonstrate solidarity with the Black students "and consider the larger issue of racism in our society." Eventually as many as two hundred students participated in these discussions.[33]

History professor Thomas Rainey also spoke, lauding "the patience shown heretofore by the Afro-American Society" and urging the faculty to support their demands. Rainey outlined three "levels of commitment" for faculty members to consider. He asked his colleagues to "call for reason on the part of the administration, and urge them not to use force on Blacks in the building." He requested that his colleagues sign a petition in support of the students, and then raised the stakes even further. Rainey urged faculty "to join with a few of us that intend . . . to put our bodies on the line to keep the administration from using force at this time on the Afro-American Society."[34]

Finally, Griffith summarized the status of each of the twelve issues raised by the Black students at the initial meeting of his ad hoc committee on October 4. "I think you can see," Griffith concluded his review, "that those [issues where] there has been an ability to work [in] an immediate context have been resolved." Other questions, like the implementation of a Black studies program, he explained, "need time and . . . input of considerable numbers of the university community."[35]

Back on the second floor of the Allen Building, Griffith, Price, and Ashmore met to prepare the statement and ultimatum Knight had requested. Others, remaining in the board room, began discussing the best way to communicate with the Black students in the Allen Building. The questions they raised dramatized how little these administrators and faculty knew these Duke students. Hobbs asked whether there was "any group through which they can be reached, with whom they relate." In contrast to the vigil, where Griffith, political science professor John Strange, and Huestis, among others, were able to call on long-standing relationships with moderate white student leaders to defuse the protest, the university could think of no "trusted advisor" who could be sent to talk to the Black students. Even Griffith demurred. Recommending that any intermediary be someone higher than himself in the university hierarchy, Griffith said that he had "arrived at a plateau in my discussions" with the Black students. "I've gone as far as I can," he confessed. "I'm talked out." Griffith also believed that, because of his history of advocating for the students, he had lost the confidence of some in the administration. "I'm not sure [hard-liners] would have even trusted me," he thought.[36]

Hobbs also asked who from the university should be the point of contact with the students. The suggestion that a faculty member attempt to deliver the university's message in person was rejected because of "hostage dangers."[37] That some university leaders seemed to think that the protesters occupying the Allen Building might take Cook, Cell, or another faculty member hostage shows that the students were perceived as completely out of control.

Even as events accelerated, however, Hobbs decided to propose a face-to-face meeting with Black student representatives. He wanted to do so before the university's one-hour ultimatum was delivered. Hobbs proposed suggesting that the Black students send five representatives to the board room to speak to "five of us." The purpose of the meeting would be to "discuss the situation for 30 minutes or so." No substantive discussion of the Black student demands was contemplated. At approximately 12:15 p.m., Hobbs, professor and chair of the electrical engineering department Thomas G. Wilson, and professor and chair of the physics department Henry A. Fairbank left the second floor of the Allen Building to deliver the proposal for a meeting to the students.[38]

Speaking to McLeod and Hopkins through a window, Hobbs introduced himself and said that he would like to talk. According to an account of the meeting prepared by Fairbank and Wilson, the students did not recognize Hobbs—the university provost—by "face, name, or office." Tuthill recounted hearing a student shout, "Go get somebody important," not aware that Hobbs was, in Knight's absence, the acting senior administrator of the university. Hobbs proposed a five-on-five meeting between university representatives and Black student protesters. "We've chatted for two or three years already, man," one of the student leaders responded to Hobbs. When Fairbank stated that the university believed that there was "a great deal of interest in your problems," the student responded sharply, "We want something concrete. Do you have the power to deal with this matter? We want to speak to those who have the power." The students also conveyed to Hobbs that two new demands had been added to the original list of eleven—"amnesty" for the protesters and an end to grading for all Black students. Hobbs assured his counterpart that the student representatives would have "free access" to return to the Allen Building and urged that representatives for the two sides meet for "30 or 40 minutes to see if we can reach agreement." While the students were open to a discussion, the format proposed by Hobbs was unacceptable. "We'll deal with you as a group, not as individuals," the student responded. When Hobbs answered that a group meeting was "not a very reasonable alternative," the Black student asked the provost to call back in a half hour.[39] The student protesters had bought time to consult with each other.

In retrospect, it is not at all surprising that the initial window conversation was so unproductive. The brief interaction with Hobbs, Wilson, and Fairbank was the first communication the students in the Allen Building had received from any official university representative. The students did not know, as Cahow later said, "who the provost was or what a provost was." A former chemistry professor, Hobbs had assumed the provost position only in January, one month prior to the takeover. During his brief tenure, Hobbs had participated only "indirectly" in discussions with the Black students. Thus, the brief conversation among Hobbs, McLeod, and Hopkins was a first meeting for the three of them. Tuthill almost certainly spoke for other administrators. "They didn't know anybody," he commented. "I didn't know any of them." This was hardly a good foundation for further discussions.[40]

The morning and early afternoon were a heady time for the occupying students. Community leaders who had been role models for the students came by and spoke to them through a window. Media inquiries, including from the national press, started to arrive. Others in the community reached out by phone, including a call from the Ku Klux Klan (KKK). A Black student interviewed by WDBS from inside the Allen Building sounded a positive note. "We felt that it was a good strategic move today, that the timing was right, right after Black Week," he said. "Everything's coming off smoothly now. . . . We plan to stay until the university concedes to our demands. . . . We have nothing offered to us but a white man's education, which has no relevance to us."[41]

When the Black students met to discuss Hobbs's proposal for a meeting, the group was unimpressed. "We decided it was a diversionary move," Armstrong explained. "If they got five people out, all five people would not be able to talk for all the people who were in there. . . . It seemed to us to be a compromise of sorts. It wasn't what we were after."[42]

Significantly, although the Black students considered Hobbs's proposal unappealing, they were not unwilling to negotiate with the administration under *any* circumstances. "We didn't go in there with the stance of not negotiating," Hopkins recounted. "That's why we went in there—to force a negotiation." What the students were demanding, however, was the chance to negotiate with someone in the university hierarchy who had the power to act definitively on their demands. "We looked at it as an operation," Hopkins explained.

"No more of these long meetings, no more of these long periods between meetings. We want[ed] to get people's attention and get them to address these issues."[43] Without knowing that Hobbs was second-in-command, they viewed him as yet another functionary without authority to commit the university to specific actions. Hence, the students found the prospect of meeting with him unacceptable.

Around this time, Cell had a call with Hopkins, urging the Black students to vacate the Allen Building. Hopkins refused, telling Cell, "We're staying until our demands are met." "They wanted to negotiate with Knight," Cell recounted. He considered this a miscalculation resulting from a misunderstanding of how the Duke bureaucracy operated. "Hobbs sent word to them that he was the provost," Cell explained. "They don't even know who the goddamn provost is. They don't understand that the provost is more important than the president—especially then. Hobbs is a strong and effective administrator who had the confidence of the university, the faculty—which Knight certainly did not. And they don't even know that." Cell was exasperated that Hopkins and his fellow protesters did not "know a damn thing about how a university worked."[44] Left unsaid, of course, was that neither Hobbs nor Knight had the authority to respond unilaterally to Black student demands.

Hobbs called the registrar's office at 12:50 p.m. as instructed by the Black students. McLeod and Hopkins told Hobbs that "they had been talking for two and one-half years without action." When Hobbs asked specifically if they were refusing his proposal for direct talks, "the response was clearly negative." When Hobbs asked a second time "if they were in fact refusing to send out representatives who would be guaranteed re-access," Hopkins and McLeod "seemed to have hung up." The entire interaction had lasted less than ten minutes.[45]

Hobbs returned to the board room at 1:13 p.m. to report on the call. "The university has heard the demands," he quoted the students as saying, "and these are the things that determine whether the Afro-Americans will start talking or not." Hobbs also told the group that the students had hung up when he specifically asked if they absolutely refused the proposal for a meeting.[46]

The conversation from the Allen Building window and the subsequent brief follow-up call with Hopkins and McLeod were the *only* attempts by university decision makers to interact with the students during the takeover. Despite the high stakes involved, Hobbs believed that he had discharged any responsibility the university had to reach out to the protesters. "I think I've made a reasonable, honest try," he told the group. Based on this interaction,

Hobbs and the other administrators concluded that the students were unwilling to engage in discussions of any sort. "They were not in much of a mood to talk," Hobbs commented later.[47]

Not long after this, at approximately 1:45 p.m., Hobbs reported to his colleagues on a telephone conversation with Knight. The Duke president was back in Durham and Hobbs had raised the possibility of a call by Knight to the students in the Allen Building. "He had considered every alternative . . . without any conviction it would do any good," Hobbs quoted Knight as saying. Hence, no call would be made.[48] In spite of the dire situation, Knight did not even attempt to speak directly to the students inside the Allen Building.

The statement and ultimatum drafted by Griffith, Lewis, and Price was nearing completion. Since the document called on the students to arrive at a decision to leave the Allen Building within one hour, the administrative group decided that delivery would be delayed until word was received that the "police are ready for action." At 1:50 p.m., Huestis called to say that the police had been summoned to campus and were mobilizing.[49]

<hr />

Events now moved forward rapidly. The group of about two hundred students and faculty participating in the Student Liberation Front's "freedom school" in the Allen Building moved their discussions to Duke Chapel. By midafternoon, the group had increased to five hundred. Student Mark Pinsky reported that a student renewing his driver's license at the highway patrol station "had seen patrolmen with gas masks loading into cars at the station." Word reached the Allen Building board room that the students in the freedom school were discussing "what other buildings they might take over."[50]

Members of the Durham Black community also started to mobilize. "Howard [Fuller] and Ben [Ruffin] and Reverend Cousin had gotten to the community," Armstrong recounted. "They said, 'You must come [to campus]. You must come and protect these children. . . . We should be afraid for them but we should all be proud of them.'" Students at NCC heard about the takeover on the radio, and many came to the Duke campus. Asked by a WDBS reporter if the NCC students supported the Black students' demands "completely, or half, or what?" the NCC representative was direct. "There is no half-Blackness. . . . We support all of the demands they have submitted." Fuller was back in Durham and climbed through a window into the registrar's office in the Allen Building. He found the students "calm, pretty well organized, and determined."[51]

Not everyone on campus supported the takeover. "Right wing students," the *Duke Chronicle* reported, "including members of the Young Americans for Freedom, were said to be considering 'direct action' against the blacks, possibly including an invasion of the occupied building." Other students who opposed the takeover, including members of the Kappa Alpha fraternity, were beginning to congregate on the quad.[52]

Around 2:00 p.m., Knight's fifteen-year-old son told his father that he would "go out and just look around" campus. "He came back," Knight recalled, and said "things were relatively quiet [on campus], but [that] he did notice a certain amount of activity around the edge of the campus." "By midafternoon," the Duke president wrote later, "I was getting reports of men in pickup trucks, shotguns in the window racks, driving slowly around the outer perimeter of West Campus, watching, waiting for dark." For Knight, this information was pivotal. "I had an acute distrust of anybody with a gun rack in his truck," Knight said. "The threat to our black students during their day of occupation was only too clear," he wrote later. "If there had been any easy way to get at them, several would have been injured or killed." The report from his son "was about all I needed," he commented. "It was evident we couldn't temporize."[53]

For many, Knight's fear of men with gun racks in their trucks was exaggerated. "I don't believe that [a] thought [of vigilantes] ever crossed my mind," Hobbs said. "It really wasn't a consideration." "My feeling in Allen Building," Howard commented, was that members of the Kappa Alpha fraternity "were a bigger threat than the KKK. . . . Those were some crazy people." Armstrong called the notion that Knight summoned the police to protect the protesters from attacks by whites "a bunch of crap." "The people we were most afraid of," she said, "were the Durham police."[54]

Police cars were now gathered at a staging area in Duke Gardens, just off the quad on West Campus. Seventy-four armed police officers had arrived with tear gas at the ready. Lookouts carrying walkie-talkies relayed this ominous news to the protesters in the Allen Building. Around 3:00 p.m., Griffith reported to the administrative group that students were aware that police had gathered in Duke Gardens.[55]

Inside the Allen Building, the mood was changing. The excitement of earlier in the day had given way to what Armstrong described as a "sense of tenseness [and] frustration." "I thought about my folks a whole lot," she recalled, "because my father was very against me being involved." This time was "very tense—very, very tense," Josie Knowlin recalled, "because we didn't know what to expect."[56]

Not optimistic that the students would comply with the university's ultimatum, Hobbs drafted a brief second notice that would be delivered if they refused to vacate the building. Around 3:20 p.m., Huestis called to report that the police had completed all final preparations. With this news, Hobbs, Fairbank, and Wilson approached a window outside the registrar's area of the Allen Building. Hobbs requested permission to pass copies of the statement and ultimatum to the students, and a window was opened to receive the documents. Hobbs read the statement through the window as the students followed along. "President Knight has acknowledged our genuine concern that your legitimate needs in the University be met," he said. "At his request numerous meetings have been held since early October with the Afro-American Society. At that time your major concerns were identified, and an honest effort was made to understand them." After reviewing the university's commitments on issues such as a Black dorm, summer program, recruitment, and a Black adviser, Hobbs reported the formation of the Kerckhoff Committee. The new committee, he said, would meet with "you and with other groups of students who feel the University is not adequately meeting their needs." Pursuit of the issues raised by the Black students, the provost told the students, "can and will take place when you depart voluntarily from this building."[57]

The ultimatum Hobbs then issued was cryptic. "We realize that you must discuss this among yourselves and arrive at your own decision," he said. "In order to permit you the opportunity to do this you are advised that you may take the next hour to arrive at your decision. It is imperative, however, that your decision be reached within one hour." As Hobbs completed reading the statement, a student demanded to know the significance of the one-hour time limit. Without being specific, Hobbs responded only that the orderly process in the university had been disrupted. "You've given us one hour and we've given you two-and-one-half years to solve the problems of this racist institution," Hopkins shouted back. Despite student requests for further explanation, the provost and his colleagues concluded that "further discussion at this point would be useless." "One was attempting to communicate through a slit window . . . across a concrete moat," Hobbs wrote later. "The occupants in the Registrar's area had full telephone service, directories, etc. and could pursue the matter by telephone if there was real interest in discourse." With the sixty-minute clock now ticking, Hobbs and other senior administrative colleagues left the Allen Building. All "adjourned to the advancement office on Campus Drive," out of harm's way. Griffith was one of the very few administrators who remained on the quad. "I didn't want force to come to campus," Griffith explained, "so I wanted to mobilize all the resources against force that I could."[58]

When word of the ultimatum reached the five hundred students meeting in the chapel, leaders reached out to the Black students to find out what course they wanted the group of sympathizers to follow. The Black students asked for wet towels "because the man is coming with gas" and requested that a human shield be formed outside the Allen Building by supporters. A little later, Ashmore reported that meetings of ASDU legislators and dorm house counselors resulted in requests to the administration that no police action occur.[59]

At 3:45 p.m., Griffith called the advancement office to report that there were now one thousand students outside the Allen Building, many encouraging the Black students to hold out. Hearing this, Bryson said it would be "foolish" to send seventy-four police officers into a crowd of this size without backup. It was decided that delivery of the second notice that would trigger police action would be deferred until the National Guard could be mobilized.[60]

A general faculty meeting in Baldwin Auditorium convened just after 4:00 p.m. Knight attended. At the request of a faculty member, Cartwright read the statement that had just been delivered to the Black students by the provost. A member of the faculty commented that he was "disturbed by the use of force implied in the statement." He asked the president to suspend the use of force "until the deliberations of this Faculty meeting have been completed." "At certain times it [is] impossible to suspend an action," Knight replied cryptically. "The context is not one of our devising," he continued. "A threat of force has been brought to bear on us. The students have refused to proceed with discussion and conference."[61]

"At this moment," the minutes of the meeting record, Professor Blackburn reported on a telephone conversation he just had in which an ASDU representative said that the students in the Allen Building were "very eager to discuss matters with the Provost." Knight was encouraged. "If indeed this report is accurate," he said, "we may have a real chance for renewal of conference."[62]

Knight was now pressed again to answer directly whether the police had, in fact, been called. He finally confirmed that police had been summoned to campus. "You cannot exist without recognizing the pressure of force," the president commented. "We would have been irresponsible had we not called the police." About thirty faculty members sympathetic to the students bolted from the meeting, many heading to West Campus. As they left, one faculty member recounted to WDBS, they heard "jeering, hisses, and derisory applause [from] a large number of our colleagues."[63]

Even those faculty members who remained at the meeting were concerned. Knight "was very vague . . . in defense of what was taking place," Richard Watson recalled. "He found it very difficult to admit that the step [to call in force] had been taken. . . . It didn't appear to us at that point," Watson described, "that the president was giving the kind of leadership that . . . really had been thought through."[64]

Around 4:30 p.m., Knight left the meeting to join the administrative group in the advancement office. Before the faculty meeting adjourned about an hour later, they voted overwhelmingly to support the actions of the president and administration.[65]

Griffith called the advancement office at approximately 4:30 p.m. to report that the crowd in front of the Allen Building now numbered about 1,500. The situation was dynamic and increasingly unpredictable. Since he had no walkie-talkie or other means of direct communication, Griffith had to leave the quad to find a phone to report updated information to decision makers. "By the time you would get to the phone and back to the crowd," Griffith said, "the scene would have changed."[66]

....

With pressure building rapidly, the Black students in the Allen Building were outraged that police action was looming. They had no guns, knives, axes, or weapons of any kind. They had no kerosene. Their threat to burn the university's records had been withdrawn, even if the administration seemed unaware of that fact. No one had been hurt or manhandled as the building was vacated. Rumors to the contrary, they said, were "lies." From their perspective, the protest was nonviolent. They blamed the administration for risking a physical confrontation. "You can't kick people around and treat 'em like dogs and expect them to say, 'Thank you, white man,'" one student told WDBS from inside the Allen Building. "We're saying, 'white man, give us what is ours!' He brought us here. He said he would give us what we needed. He ain't given us a goddamn thing! He put us here like a bunch of dogs. He called the pigs in," the student said. "He called the pigs in because he thinks that's the thing to do."[67]

Many of the Black students were surprised at the university's readiness to use force. "I didn't think any of us thought it would be violent," Armstrong recounted. "The last thing that ever came to our mind was that they would . . . call the state [police] or National Guard," Williams recounted. "We thought they would give a lot of threats. We didn't really feel that they would actually endanger our lives."[68]

Cook sensed a potential disaster looming. He had talked to Hopkins several times during the takeover. "I said, 'If the police should come, don't let [them] catch you and the other Blacks in this building behind closed doors. They will bludgeon you. They will crack your head.' I'd seen it in Georgia and Alabama. . . . I knew from experience."[69] Cook joined the human shield that had formed around the Allen Building.

Hobbs did not share Cook's concern about law enforcement. "Nobody anticipated violence," Hobbs said later. Told of Cook's comment that the students would be "bludgeoned" if caught by police in the Allen Building, Hobbs called it "a misdirected statement" and "unnecessary." "There was no reason to feel that the police would do more than say, 'You're going to be arrested if you don't get out,'" Hobbs recounted. "That's [what we] thought would be done." Belying this confidence, however, Hobbs was in touch with Duke hospital personnel to ask that they prepare to treat anyone injured in the approaching police action.[70]

Meanwhile, efforts by ASDU leaders, dean of freshmen Hugh M. Hall, and others to head off conflict intensified. In the late afternoon, Ben Ruffin approached Joe Martin, head of student activities at Duke, asking if Martin "could possibly get Dr. Knight to talk with the students who were now willing to come out and talk." The proposal was that three students would meet three university representatives in the Social Sciences Building right next to the Allen Building. The other protesters would remain in the Allen Building. Martin called Ashmore and communicated the proposal. Ashmore relayed the offer to the administrative group at 4:55 p.m. He also reiterated Wade's view that "vacating is a *sine qua non*."[71]

At 5:05 p.m., Bryson reported a call from the mayor, who advised him that 240 guardsmen were mobilized. The mayor was clear, however, that he would not "hold the men for action at night." He was distressed, Bryson said, over the delay that had already occurred.[72]

Knight entered the advancement office at this highly charged moment. Hobbs relayed the students' proposal for negotiations. Bryson told him the National Guard was mobilized. The classics-professor-turned-university-president, exhausted from months of illness and conflict, now faced the fateful choice he had hoped "moderation" would allow him to avoid.

"We have no option to negotiate," Knight told his colleagues. Later, the Duke president justified this decision as based on principle. He had no choice, he advised the *Duke Chronicle* the next day, but to put "the freedom of the University above the force used by the black students." "If this group can win by this means," he asked, "what about the far right? Look at the Nazis in Germany." "You can't use the wrong means to accomplish the right ends," he argued. "If we do, then evil men are going to use the same means for wrong ends." Knight was also concerned about precedent. He mentioned a call he received during the takeover from Ben Roney, an assistant to Governor Robert W. Scott. "If one University gives in to a set of demands," Roney warned the Duke president, "within 24 hours demands [will] appear on other campuses."[73]

Knight was also influenced by internal political considerations. "There was no way to consider the demands until they were out of there," he explained. "That would have been the immediate kiss of death. . . . If I had sat down with five of them during the day and said, 'OK, we'll negotiate these [demands] and then you will come out if we agree,' . . . I'm certain the board of trustees would have repudiated me. We would have had a real donnybrook on our hands," Knight thought. "It wasn't an available option."[74]

Knight's decision-making latitude was limited from the start by his waning power among his colleagues and the board of trustees. In effect, his impotence simply exacerbated the likelihood of a confrontation.

Whatever the mix of reasons, the decision triggered complex emotions for Knight, including what he described later as "a terrible, terrible pleasure. . . . You say, 'now something is going to be settled,'" he explained. "Compared to all the attempts to hold force back and to protect people from the results of their actions, . . . it was an unambiguous act. . . . It was psychological relief. . . . I'm not happy with that [emotion] looking back on it," Knight reflected, "but that's how it was."[75] Knight's capacity to seek the "middle ground" had clearly disappeared.

Only when he learned of the administration's late afternoon refusal to negotiate did Hopkins realize how unbridgeable the gap had become between the Black students and the university. "We want to get people's attention, to get them to address these issues," he explained. "The administration [view] was, 'What have these crazies done?' So they brought the police down on us. We still saw ourselves as Duke students trying to get the attention of the administration. They saw us as subversives who were going to tear down their campus. Allen [Building] was a confirmation of something they had in the back of their heads already," Hopkins now understood. "That we were destructive-oriented, that we weren't talking about anything serious."[76]

By now, the scene on the quad had become surreal. "I remember standing there thinking this really isn't happening," student eyewitness Harry DeMik described. He explained,

> If you walked between the Allen Building and Social Sciences Building, you could see the police assembling down in the gardens. You could see the Black students inside [the Allen Building]. It was starting to get a little dark. . . . You could see the real radical white kids up against the doors of Allen Building with Vaseline and towels. . . . There was a Black student with a megaphone . . . reading off the demands. . . . The KAS were on the other side of the quadrangle . . . waving the Confederate flag and singing "Dixie." A lot of white students were just milling around . . . just to see what was going to happen.[77]

Around this time, Cell spoke to Knight. "I knew the cops were coming," he described, "and I'm afraid somebody is going to get killed." "It's out of my hands," Knight responded. Cell warned the Duke president that police action on campus was going to "blow the university up." According to Cell, Knight responded, "Yes, I know."[78]

At approximately 5:15 p.m., Fairbank and Wilson left to deliver the second message to the students. Knight called the mayor. H. Franklin Bowers, Duke's manager of operations and point of contact with police during the takeover, left to talk to T. B. Seagroves, captain in charge of the Durham police detail now on the Duke campus. The administrators acknowledged that from this point forward, they would have little say about how events unfolded. They agreed that "the question of action at this hour [was] up to the Durham Police," meeting minutes record. "We knew in advance that once the police came on campus," Griffith recounted, "they were in control and we had no control."[79]

Fairbank and Wilson handed copies of the second statement to the students through the same Allen Building window they had used before. "We request that you leave this building peacefully," the brief statement said, "and to do so immediately. . . . You are now suspended pending due process, and if you do not vacate the building immediately, all who are present will be deemed to be trespassers and will be subject to criminal charges for trespassing and other violations of law which may occur." After reading the statement, a student inside the Allen Building said in a loud voice, "Let it be known for the record that we have offered to meet and talk with the Administration, and now they refuse to do this." Without any further discussion, Fairbank and Wilson left, entering a nearby building to phone the group in the development office to "let them know that the documents had been received by the students and read by them."[80]

At 5:40 p.m. Hobbs told his colleagues, "It is on." The police were on the move. A WDBS reporter described a "mass [of] troopers starting to march through the gardens. They are all armed with clubs, three tear gas guns. A couple of riot guns. Each man of course has his pistol, and they're all equipped with a gas mask." The Black students learned of the police activity from spotters on the outside of the building and a police scanner they had brought with them. Ashmore reported that Chief William Pleasants had offered assurances "that there were enough men to handle the task."[81]

Inside the Allen Building, an intense debate was taking place over whether to stay or leave. Some were daring and unafraid. "Come on baby," one student commented to WDBS at this dangerous moment, "because we're ready for you." Asked if he thought the student demands would be met, another student said, "We can't say we are going to get 'em. But I can say this much—we're going to fight it all the way to the end." When the reporter wanted to know what the students would use to fight the police, he responded: "Whatever we can get our hands on. . . . There's plenty in the records office that you can use to beat people with when you're being struck." Aware that the university's one-hour ultimatum had passed, the student had a message for police. "Do me a favor," he told the reporter. "Tell the pigs if they're gonna attack, we'd appreciate if they'd be on time. Because they're already fifteen or twenty minutes overdue."[82]

William Turner explained the genesis of provocative statements such as these years later. "You are part of the vanguard of a revolution," he recalled. "Fear and risk take on different proportions. . . . It's a whole different mental state. Your cause is noble. . . . You don't have a choice. . . . People were aware of the fact that they could have been hurt, or injured, or killed. But it wasn't something that stood out in your mind." That students were being killed on other campuses, Turner explained, "served to *intensify* your zeal." Michael McBride had a simpler explanation. "We were young and so naive," he said. "We were too young to be afraid."[83]

Not everyone, however, was feeling defiant. "The resolve of some of the students appeared to be weakening," Fuller wrote. "A few of them grew quiet and somber. . . . 'My parents did not send me to Duke to go to jail,'" one student told the Black Power leader.[84]

At this point, Fuller assumed a critical role. "He's the one who said we need to take a vote about whether or not we were going to go or stay," Becton recalled. "He put the options on the table of what could happen," Hopkins remembered. The "stay" option, as Fuller described it, was grim. According to Williams, Fuller said, "Look—these walls—nobody can see through them. The guard's going to come in here, they've got weapons. . . . You are going to be a bunch of dead people. Because their adrenaline is pumping and they are armed for combat. They are going to come in here to fight. They don't care what you do. It's going to be your word against theirs as to what happened inside this building."[85]

"We gathered together in one of the rooms in Allen Building and took a vote," Hopkins remembered. "The first vote was whether to send the female students out so they wouldn't get hurt." "The men took over," Williams remembered. The men said, "The women have to leave. Get out." "If we're gonna die, or we're gonna be hurt, or we gotta fight," Williams recalled the men saying, "Y'all gotta go." This sparked what Howard described as "a really big battle." "I was a stay person," she remembered. Howard told the men, "I can probably do more than half of you-all." Despite this intense disagreement, all but three of the women left the Allen Building through a window. "We were real chauvinists at that time," Hopkins acknowledged years later. "We were being Duke gentlemen in spite of ourselves."[86]

"When I went out the window" of the Allen Building, Williams remembered, "you are going across a moat. . . . The men helped us . . . out from the inside [of the building], and the community . . . grabbed [us] and helped [us] come . . . out. I was terrified." All of us "are kind of frightened, kind of scared, kind of upset," Armstrong told a reporter from outside the Allen Building. "We've been going through all kinds of mental pressure all day long."[87]

The group remaining in the Allen Building now voted on what they should do. "Everybody voted to stay," Hopkins related. "People started bracing themselves to fight the cops." To help deal with tear gas, "we started to put [cigarette filters] in our noses," Catherine LeBlanc recalled. "We had been told that if we put lemon juice in our eyes it would [also] help us . . . with the tear gas." Some students also placed ashtray lids on their heads for protection. "We had filters coming out of our noses, lemon in our eyes, crying, and a silver ash tray on top," Michael LeBlanc described. "We were ready to fight the man . . . and thinking that that was going to work."[88]

The women who had left the building were frantic. "We were all outside crying," Williams recounted, "saying, 'You all have to come out.'" Asked by a reporter if they were going to "stick around," several of the women responded with disbelief. "I wanna see those men come out of there," Armstrong said. "They're our brothers. . . . Whatever happens to them happens to us."[89]

With the police drawing closer, Fuller again intervened. "I wanted to help them leave the building with a feeling of triumph," he wrote later, "even though their demands had not been met." The group was unanimous that exiting the Allen Building through a window would send the wrong message. Instead, the students discussed leaving the building through the front door with "our fists raised high." "If you leave as a group protected by the community," Armstrong recounted Fuller arguing, "it will [show] that the community has a vested interest in you and that you left with your heads up. You will have accomplished what you came here to do," he said, and that was to "bring the university to its knees."[90]

"Shortly before the cops got there," Hopkins recalled, "somebody shouted, 'Let's take another vote.'" Becton counted the tally. This time the vote was close and difficult to count. "People would raise their hands, take them down, raise them back up," he recalled. Although the group had decided—by a single vote—to remain in the Allen Building, Becton was determined to avoid a bloodbath. The group turned to him for the final count. "I said 'thirteen to twelve to go,'" Becton recounted. "Becton lied to save us from dying," Michael LeBlanc said five decades later. "I am so glad he lied."[91]

"We had just decided we had done all we could," Turner recalled. "I don't think we really expected to accomplish that much by staying and getting our heads whipped." "We were not interested in any violent confrontation," Brown explained. "We saw that we weren't going to get what we wanted right then, and if we wanted to avoid people getting physically hurt and beat up, . . . it would be better to leave." "None of us wanted to be martyrs," Howard commented. Fuller was central to the group's decision to avoid a battle with police. He said, according to Armstrong, "there is just no reason to [stay], it will turn into a melee and people will get hurt." People who favored staying "decided to leave" after Fuller spoke. "Howard Fuller came in and actually saved our lives," Williams recounted later.[92]

Even with their decision to leave, however, the students were not out of danger. Griffith heard from the Black students that they had decided to exit the Allen Building. He also learned, likely from the students, that the police were moving toward the Allen Building. "I didn't know the police had been called initially," he recalled. "I ran to the telephone [and] called Knight and said, 'Stop the police because they are coming out! They are coming out, stop the police!'" Griffith learned that his call had come too late. "Once [the police] had been put in motion," Griffith was told, "our people had no control over them. They were subject to the control of their officers."[93]

The students now moved to the front door of the Allen Building. "They had chained us in the building for some reason," Hopkins recalled. "They had this chain around the front door of Allen Building and this lock on it. We told the campus cop [standing just outside] that we were coming out," Hopkins remembered. "The campus cop said, 'I don't have a key.'"[94]

A good-sized crowd had assembled in a tightly packed group at the two basement entrances of the Allen Building. Campus police "quietly moved into position near the crowd," and people "pressed more closely together and locked arms singing 'We Shall Overcome.'"[95]

Meanwhile, the police had reached the back door of the Allen Building. "It was real tense because we were all crowded at the front door," Hopkins described. "We had voted to come out. And the cops were coming in the back way." At the very last moment, a key was found. "He finally got the door open," Hopkins recalled with relief. "We almost got caught in there in spite of ourselves." Although reports on the precise timing of the arrival of the police differ slightly, Becton also recalled that "we went out the front door [as] police were . . . breaking down the back door." As they left, some students held coats over their heads to prevent being photographed. They raised clenched fists. They walked out between groups of white students and faculty who had assembled to protect them. This was critical. "If they had not linked arms to protect us," Michael LeBlanc described later, "we might be here, but I don't know if all of our limbs would be working the same way."[96]

Turner had what he described as "an interesting conversation" years later with a member of the Durham police force who had been called to campus during the takeover. The officer described to Turner "how pumped up and primed the police were" when they reached the Allen Building. "They had been waiting down [in Duke Gardens] all day. They were going to whip some heads and get this thing in order. They were pounding their billy clubs in their hands. . . . By the time they came to flush us out, we were gone. But they were ready to crack some heads."[97]

At this point, the occupation was over. The Black students had departed and were marching down Chapel Drive, away from the Allen Building, joined by about 250 supporters. They carried the Malcolm X Liberation School banner that had hung from the Allen Building throughout the day. The group shouted, "Hell no, it ain't over." Campus security entered the Allen Building offices just vacated by the students. Without further intervention, students and other onlookers on campus, including those surrounding the Allen Building, planned to disperse. But then, tragically, police action began. Once underway, the police would not turn back without a confrontation.[98]

On Chapel Drive, "police cars . . . started driving through the crowd" of marchers, Williams recounted. "They were not stopping for anybody. White students as well as Black students were having to be pulled out from in front of the cars. . . . You could see even the white students getting mad, saying, 'What have we done to make you treat us like that?'" she recalled, saying, "'We are just out here looking.'"[99]

A similar scene played out on the quad. Students and other onlookers were milling around the Allen Building when "approximately five or six patrol cars" arrived, joining those police who had come on foot from Duke Gardens. "There's a bunch of cops all over the place," a WDBS reporter commented. The arrival of the police cars drew more students toward the Allen Building, including some who had left with the Black students. "With helmets, tear gas, and what some people refer to as cattle prods," WDBS reported, police "are now standing at the doorway of Allen Building, completely surrounding it." Police had also encircled students at the two back doors, Griffith told administrators, holding them in place with billy clubs. Students started shouting "Sieg Heil," "fascist," and "Nazi" at the police, some throwing their arms upward in the Nazi salute. Observing the scene, Martin called the advancement office around 6:00 p.m., suggesting to Ashmore that "if we could get the police moved, we could avert a confrontation." Ashmore responded, "All right, I have Frank Bowers right here." But although Bowers had been designated university liaison with the police, no effective line of communication had been established. The senior administrators in the advancement office were unable to control the police who were now on campus.[100]

The exact precipitating event for what came next is still in dispute. Many reports cite rocks or other projectiles thrown by students at the police. What is clear, however, is that the police now determined it was necessary to disperse the crowd. "Oh boy," a WDBS reporter said, gasping for breath, "cops started throwing tear gas grenades into the students." Students were "running away, . . . throwing anything they can get their hands on" at the police. Police were "running around tear gassing everything in sight," one student was overheard commenting on WDBS. "One demonstrator picked up a [tear gas] grenade," another reporter described, and "threw it at the police still smoking. That evoked a great cheer from the crowd and the spectators surrounding them."[101]

"It was like a war broke out on the quad," DeMik recounted. "Tear gas was flying everywhere. . . . The police ran out of tear gas and they were beaten back towards [the Allen] Building. . . . When the police came out, . . . they started hitting people with billy clubs and tear gas started going through the air. [It] lit a fuse among [the] students . . . and a lot of them fought back." A number were catching tear gas canisters in towels and throwing them back at police. Football players, who had been on the quad to taunt white supporters of the Black students, got caught up in events. They "ended up involved in the riot," Campbell recalled. "All of a sudden [they] were getting tear gassed and clubbed." Each time the police ran out of tear gas, DeMik reported, "they started to retreat back towards Allen Building." As "the police retreated toward Allen Building," the *Duke Chronicle* reported, "the crowds of students followed at a distance. The police charged again, and the crowd retreated again. The police retreated again and the crowd moved in again." This continued for more than an hour. Many students sought refuge in the chapel. Police chased them into the chapel, spraying tear gas in the building. "Go Home, Go Home," students were shouting at the police. "It was all pretty ludicrous," Griffith commented later.[102]

Soon, police brought out a pepper gas machine, which Martin described as looking like "a combination-vacuum-cleaner-ray-gun." "Clouds of . . . pepper gas would just billow out," DeMik recounted. Martin at one point saw "two policemen, one carrying the smoke-spewing machine, chasing one lone person across the lawn." Another student reported seeing police "striking anything in their path, including a dog that later died and several students and at least one adult." "One policeman tripped a student with his club," he wrote, "and then struck him after he had fallen." Students started "taking out their frustrations," DeMik commented. "They were breaking the windows [of a police car]; they were breaking the headlights."[103] Soon the police car went up in flames.

During the chaos, Fairbank and Wilson saw fires erupting in the woods between the chapel and the physics building. Soon, "ten or more fires [were burning], each of which were confined to an area of about 100 square feet or less."[104]

Cook witnessed the scene on the quad from the front of the Allen Building. The police "were just brutal," he described, "knocking folks down and . . . screaming . . . 'Move, move, move, move! Get out of here!' . . . Those policemen were rough. . . . One guy, they hit him on the head and [he] had to go to the hospital. . . . Someone said to me, 'This is like Nazi Germany.' Well, you know, the harsh brutality." Marjorie Becker, a student, was standing near Cook watching the melee. She grabbed him and said, "Oh, Dr. Cook!" the professor recalled. "I was her protector." Trying to break the tension with humor, Cook told the student he was "protecting," "You're going to have me lynched out here!"[105]

Cell recalled feeling "absolutely helpless" watching events unfold. Campbell was "very frightened. . . . Here were a hundred or so police in full riot gear," he recounted, "with tear gas cannons and all that." "I remember thinking at the time that I wouldn't be surprised if the police actually started shooting people. They were so angry." "A Durham police officer drew his gun and pointed it at me and some of the [other] students," Wib Gulley recalled, "and I was very concerned about what was going to happen." "Kent State could very well have happened at Duke," Howard thought later. "I think the potential was there."[106]

Throughout much of this time, Cahow reported, Duke administrators in the development office "didn't know what was going on. . . . They were isolated down there. It was amazing," the assistant registrar thought. "Absolutely amazing." "We should have had complete control and communication between the police and the persons who were serving as communication links," Hobbs acknowledged. "That was the crazy part of it," he explained. "The Black students got out of the building before all of this other mess developed. . . . Had there been proper communication between the people who were serving as a communication link and the police, the police [could] have stopped at a totally different location."[107] In effect, the melee on the quad would have been avoided altogether.

One administrator who was not isolated from the crisis was Griffith. He remained in the middle of events, urgently attempting to get the police off campus. The officers had retreated into the Allen Building. "It seemed to me," Griffith reasoned, "that if we got rid of the police, there would be no problem." At 6:45 p.m., Powell's minutes indicate, Griffith called the advancement office "suggesting police be called off campus without attracting attention." The feeling of senior administrators, Griffith recalled, "was that if the police left the building, it would be re-occupied by Blacks." After he was able to show senior administrators and the police that no reoccupation would occur, the order came for the police to leave. They withdrew in stages, the first group departing campus at around 7:45. "Within twenty minutes," Griffith remembered, "the campus was quiet." "A great deal of credit . . . needs to go to Bill Griffith," Cahow thought. "He stayed in the middle, and he's the only one that did."[108]

An initial sweep through the registrar's office showed that no records had been destroyed and little damage had occurred. "There was no real damage to the office," Cahow commented. "They didn't disturb anything from what I could tell that belonged to the university." "We were relieved that nobody had been killed in the building," Cell recounted. He also recalled feeling "very very depressed, very numb, defeated. . . . It felt like hell," he said. "It was a bad day."[109]

Nineteen people were admitted to the Duke hospital emergency room on the evening of February 13 with injuries "related to the disturbance on campus." Injuries included hematoma to the temporal scalp, a mild concussion, laceration to the scalp, a sprained ankle, and third-degree burns on a hand. Two police were treated, including one listed as a "25 year old male struck on [the] back of [a] helmet with [an] unknown object" with "brief loss of consciousness." Five students were arrested.[110]

The Black students who participated in the takeover went in various directions. Some walked to a Black church to discuss what to do next. Another group went to the AAS office to confirm that they could account for every Black student who had participated. McBride called his parents: "I knew they would see this on the news," he recalled, "and I wanted them to know I was OK." Others returned to their dorms. "I remember it was 6:30 and Walter Cronkite was on," Armstrong recounted, "and all of a sudden we hear all this noise and people were screaming. Chuck said, 'What is going on?' And that is when the tear gas got started. . . . It was so ironic because all of us were inside and safe."[111]

Howard thought the fact that few, if any, Blacks remained on the quad when the confrontation between the police and students erupted was illustrative of different attitudes toward law enforcement. White students, she believed, "had this feeling 'the police would not do this to us,'" and thought, "'They're bluffing.'" Black students "had just the opposite" reaction, she explained. Many in the Allen Building believed the police would "shoot us down, [and] burn the building down with us in it." "I voted that we should stay" in the Allen Building, Hopkins acknowledged. "But after I got out there and saw what the police had done, I was glad we voted again."[112]

A forum attended by more than one thousand students, faculty, and members of the administration was held at Page Auditorium that evening. Hopkins described the takeover as "one battle . . . in [our] struggle to gain our humanity at this university. . . . Our main aim," he told the cheering crowd, "is to intensify the struggle we have begun." "So I say that this university should be stopped and the *people* should decide how it's going to be run," Hopkins implored. "We've got to get them pigs out of Allen Building . . . 'cause . . . they've lost their place in humanity."[113]

Hobbs and Cartwright also appeared at the forum. They announced the formation of the Kerckhoff Committee and said the president would address the university community on Saturday at 1:00 p.m. in the indoor stadium. To angry shouts, Cartwright insisted, "We cannot operate a university unless we can operate it with rational discourse."[114]

At the end of the forum, the group voted overwhelmingly to declare a three-day boycott of classes and to establish a "free university" to operate during the boycott. It also called for amnesty for the Black student protesters and reinstatement for Blacks forced to leave the university in the fall because of their academic standing.[115]

Students returned to their dorms. Hobbs made it home around 10:30 p.m. The events of February 13, 1969, at Duke were now over. But the university's efforts to grapple with the fallout from the Allen Building takeover were only just beginning.

·······························

The events of February 13, 1969, at Duke University represented the culmination of racial and interpersonal dynamics that had existed from the moment of desegregation. The university failed completely to anticipate the needs of Black undergraduates or to plan for their adjustment to a previously all-white campus. No effort was made to get to know the students or to learn about the communities and families from which they had come.

As a result, it was left to the students to "assimilate." Most officials at Duke believed that the new students were fortunate simply to have the chance to attend the school. They felt that no changes were necessary to create an academic environment where Black students could learn and grow. In the absence of any initiative by the university, relationships between Black and white students—and with faculty and administrators—were left to chance. In almost all instances, Duke's response to its Black students was shaped by Jim Crow racial views still held by many trustees and alumni. Put simply, Black students were not viewed as part of the Duke University "family." Rather, as President Knight explained later, they were regarded as "intruders."[116]

Black students thus encountered a hostile environment when they arrived at Duke. Their feelings of isolation and alienation grew. As they became more organized, the Black students demanded changes. They sought a university able to provide a meaningful academic, social, and cultural experience for both white *and* Black students. Change came very slowly, and only in response to government directives or escalating pressure from the students. Frustration and anger increased. Notwithstanding enormous risks, members of the AAS finally decided to occupy the Allen Building. Their goal was to force change at the university.

This was the context for Duke's response to the Allen Building takeover. When University House was occupied on April 5, 1968, by a group consisting primarily of white students, the protesters were called "guests" and allowed to remain for more than thirty-six hours. Women were given permission by the president himself to stay overnight and thus escape punishment for violating dorm rules. Griffith explained that administrators believed that the university should refrain from using force to clear University House. Despite repeated shouts of "hell no, we won't go," protesters, according to Griffith, were "our students, they weren't our enemies. They were part of our university family." Asked afterward by a faculty member why the Silent Vigil protesters who occupied the quad for four days were not arrested, Huestis was direct. "Well, you know, I don't think I could quite bring myself to do that," he told his faculty colleague. "I had too many friends out there."[117]

Black student protesters enjoyed no such deference. The university's response to them was dismissive, condescending, and arbitrary. While the takeover differed from the occupation of University House and the Silent Vigil in important respects, all three protests resulted in only minimal destruction of property and no injury to persons. Both the Allen Building takeover and the Silent Vigil disrupted university operations. Unlike the takeover, however, the Silent Vigil—with its concurrent boycott and strike—effectively shut down the university. Because university decision makers had few, if any, personal relationships with the Allen Building protesters, they could only view them as outsiders. Race made it almost impossible for those in power at Duke to establish close connections with these students. In stark contrast to the occupation and Silent Vigil, just over one hour from the time they learned of the takeover, university officials drew a "line in the sand." Black students would receive an ultimatum from the university, then face whatever force was necessary to eject them.[118]

The university could envision only two possible responses to the Allen Building takeover. The first was conducting substantive negotiations on Black student demands while protesters occupied the building. This was politically untenable. The second was the deployment of overwhelming force to clear the building by nightfall. No serious consideration was ever given to maintaining the status quo long enough for a peaceful way out of the standoff to emerge.

Knight would explain later that speed in deploying force was necessary to protect the Black students from white vigilantes who were waiting for nightfall to attack. Few, including the Black students, shared this concern. Silent Vigil participants on the quad received bomb and other threats of physical violence from those who opposed their protest. In that instance, Durham police were also summoned to campus. Their job, however, was to protect the protesters from threats, not clear the quadrangle. There is no indication that Knight or his colleagues ever considered using the police to protect the Allen Building protesters from threats they might face.

Unlike the ongoing contacts between administrators, faculty, and protest leaders that occurred throughout the University House occupation and the Silent Vigil, no such interactions occurred during the Allen Building takeover. Hobbs, who had never previously met with the Black students, tried only once to engage directly with the protesters. When he issued the university's ultimatum to the Black students, he refused to answer questions. Once back in Durham, Knight was offered the chance to call the protesters. Only ten months earlier, the Duke president had invited a group of predominantly white students into his home for what became a thirty-six-hour occupation because, he explained, "he wanted as little distance as possible between [students and himself] when the important questions turned up." Given the chance to call the Black students in the Allen Building, however, he declined, concluding that such a call would be pointless. No one ever asked Cook or Cell—the professors closest to the Black students—to reach out to them on behalf of the university. That Hobbs considered one effort at communication a sufficient precursor to invoking force is telling. He did not know these students, and they did not know him. How could Hobbs even imagine that further outreach might defuse an escalating situation? In the end, Hobbs seemed more interested in creating a record that he had made an attempt to contact the protesters than in actually engaging with them. Even after the Black students expressed a willingness to negotiate a resolution, confrontation by force remained the university's preferred option. Duke "was willing to go to the brink of disaster by bringing police on the campus," Becton summarized correctly, "but unwilling, after Blacks had occupied Allen Building for six hours, to talk to those students who occupied the building."[119]

Because university officials focused almost entirely on regaining control, they failed to fully consider the risks associated with bringing police onto campus. Hobbs, among others, appears to have been unconcerned about the possibility that police might use excessive force against the Black student protesters. Even with 1,500 students, faculty, and members of the community gathered on the quad, university leaders hesitated in using force only long enough to mobilize the National Guard. Without effective communication among administrators, or the ability of university officials to direct police activity, it is not surprising that the introduction of police to an already volatile campus situation led to chaos and violence. Black protesters were lucky enough to escape physical harm because trusted advisers and historical experience made them aware of the peril they faced. Many others at Duke that day were not so fortunate.

If the Black students had vacated the Allen Building when first asked to do so, the day of the takeover would have ended differently. Yet the more challenging question is whether the use of force by the university against its students had to happen once the takeover occurred. Knight, for one, saw race playing a role in the crucial decisions made that day. Asked if it was "easier" for the university to use force against Black students than white students, the Duke president was candid. "Of course. . . . That isn't a difficult question to answer, that's just how it is," Knight said. "That's just the nature of things."[120]

CHAPTER 9

We Shall Have Cocktails in the Gloaming

Aftermath

The Allen Building takeover and the ensuing melee on the quad triggered intense reactions among all segments of the Duke community. Letters poured in to Knight and other members of his administration. Differences of opinion were stark. "Everybody had an idea about what to do," Knight wrote to one alumnus, "but naturally the ideas were in violent conflict with one another." As a result, the takeover and the events that followed were, according to the Duke president, "as strenuous an experience as I can remember."[1]

Trustees were pleased that the police had been called in. "I have heard nothing but praise from those I have talked with for this prompt and firm action," trustee and Executive Committee member Henry Rauch wrote to provost Marcus Hobbs. Tom Finch, president of Thomasville Furniture Industries, commended Knight for his "firmness." He likened the takeover to "sitdown strikes" in an industrial plant. "If management does not act promptly . . . and with extreme firmness," he told Knight, "management loses control of the situation," warning that "it may be as many as 10 years before any semblance of proper order can be restored."[2]

Faculty were also mainly supportive of the administration. In response to a questionnaire circulated by sociologists Allan Kornberg and Kurt Black,

87 percent called the occupation "unjustified" and fewer than 25 percent called the administration's handling of the occupation "bad." "A considerable number [of faculty] felt that the black students had a more than ordinary duty to conform," Knight explained, "to be good 'white' students." He saw a "lively sense of outrage" among faculty over the takeover. "There can be no compromise whatever with violence and destruction," faculty member and nuclear physicist Lawrence Biedenharn wrote. "When students perform criminal acts, they must be treated as criminals," biochemistry professor Irwin Fridovich commented. He called for the expulsion *and* criminal prosecution of the protesters and opposed any form of amnesty for students he called "outlaws." Faculty who opposed the administration's handling of the takeover felt strongly as well. "I am ashamed of what you have done today," assistant professor Robert Jackson wrote to Knight in a telegram. "This should be a community of reason, not of force."[3]

Student opinion was divided. As many as 56 percent of undergraduates and 68 percent of graduate and professional students called the takeover "unjustified." But 51 percent in each group described the administration's handling of the event "bad." In an editorial, the *Duke Chronicle* called the administration's decision to call in the police "reprehensible and immoral" and "stupid in the extreme." Graduate student James Huntley Grayson wrote to Knight just after he was released from the hospital following the melee on the quad. Grayson protested the "completely irresponsible action of the police," saying he "was beaten for no other reason . . . than the fact that I did not move fast enough." Student Ray Winton objected to the takeover. "As a fellow student of [those] students who took over the offices in Allen Building," he wrote, "I am in favor of nothing less than their expulsion from Duke University."[4]

Not surprisingly, the Kornberg and Black questionnaire found that the intervention of police on campus made students more sympathetic to the occupation and increasingly likely to consider the administration's handling of the protest "bad." Cook observed the unfolding of this dynamic, going so far as to call the police "the great evangelicals." The police, Cook believed, "did more to help the blacks' cause at Duke than almost all the liberals who had ever been there." "For that brief moment," Brenda Armstrong explained, "everybody [on the quad] understood the desperation, the feeling of not having any options. . . . They felt what it was like to not be heard."[5]

Alumni reactions were the most negative. With few exceptions, Duke graduates were profoundly disturbed by the takeover and angry that Duke administrators had allowed matters to reach this point. "We are waiting to see who is in control of Duke University," one wrote. "Duke is too great a school to be dragged down by a bunch of punks." William J. Massey, a 1962 graduate, urged "maintenance of administrative control by whatever means necessary." "Trespass and destruction of private property are as wrong in 1969," an alumnus from Florida wrote, "as they were when the Goths overran Rome, and when Nazi legions pillaged Poland and France." "If there must be a war on the Duke University campus," another said, "let it be said that Duke fought for the aims for which it was created."[6]

A number of alumni used racially charged language to express their concern. "Expel the Black Bastards," one alumnus wrote. "Expel 'em all and admit no more of them," a double-degree graduate from Asheville urged. "Otherwise, they will expel you." "Your first mistake was to enroll them," a class of '49 graduate wrote to Knight. "Organize Duke grads all over the world if need be not only to drive the animals out but keep them out." One alumnus from Gastonia, North Carolina, drew on his sense of Duke history to make his point. James Duke's sole purpose in setting up the Duke Indenture, he said, "was to provide for the education of the young people of the South. I do not believe that he intended the school to be established for the purpose of integration. It is a shame to permit a handful of burr-heads to disrupt . . . Duke University," he concluded.[7]

Such comments, according to Knight, "weren't just reflecting the feeling of the moment. They were reflecting feelings that were years long." "The assumption was that once a commitment had been made to accept black students, that was all we needed to do," Knight recounted. "The fact that Ralph Ellison's 'invisible men' were still invisible was of no concern." In this context, demands by the Black students for changes to university policy, curriculum, and culture seemed unfathomable. "It was only [after the Allen Building takeover] that I found out how deep the racist convictions went," Knight reflected. "Then the requirement to bow to racial equality would evaporate."[8] Challenged from all sides, Knight would struggle to find a path forward for the university—and himself.

In the days following the takeover, tensions on campus remained high. Following up on a request from Knight, Durham mayor Robert Wensell "Wense" Grabarek sent a telegram to Governor Scott on February 14. "Due to uncertainty of existing conditions and possible attendant repercussions," the mayor requested that "National Guard troops remain available for immediate call through the weekend of February 15 and 16." Acting at the request of the state adjutant general, Knight's previously announced speech on February 15 in the indoor stadium was canceled. A statement by the university said that the action was taken "in order to avoid a large gathering during a time of tension on the campus." The Duke president "feared that with a number of polarized groups there might be disruption."[9]

The administration's attempts to avoid a "large gathering" on campus were unsuccessful. On Saturday at 12:30 p.m., the time of Knight's scheduled speech, a crowd of two thousand packed Page Auditorium for a community "convocation" to discuss events since the takeover and the student response. When Black students arrived minutes later, led by Howard Fuller, they were greeted with a standing ovation.[10]

Michael McBride, president of the AAS, spoke first. He emphasized the importance of Black student control over matters that involved them. On Black studies, for example, McBride argued that "white people cannot objectively set up a program about Black people." Accordingly, he said, "Black people will set up the program; Black people will control the program; Black people will teach the courses." McBride also made clear that any Black student adviser must be selected "in direct consultation" with the Black students. "How in the hell," he said, "are them white people over in Allen Building going to select a Black adviser for me? They don't know what Black people are. They don't know who can relate to us."[11]

After other speakers, including Fuller and William Griffith, addressed the gathering, someone suggested that a group march to Knight's house to ask the Duke president "for a just redress of our grievances." After Fuller "seconded the motion," the march began. Just after a crowd of about one thousand arrived at University House, what the *Duke Chronicle* described as "a tired, frightened Douglas Knight" met them outside.[12] A chaotic, combative exchange followed.

"You've never really shown good faith," one student charged. Claiming that steps taken by the university thus far were only those necessary to "placate a few people," the student demanded that Knight "do a lot of things right now." "We have met several of those demands . . . and you know it," Knight responded. "And we will work with the others as fast as we can if we have that chance." "We want some action!" a student shouted. "I'm sorry that the things that have been done . . . fit your idea of nothing at all," Knight said, "because they have been considerable."[13]

Knight thought he could demonstrate the university's good faith by discussing progress on a Black studies program. Presumably referring to the work of the Proctor Committee appointed in early November, he told the group about a department of Afro-American studies that "respected members of the faculty" had "recommended . . . to us." The department would "take some time to put . . . together," he explained, and "has to be approved by the entire faculty." Continuing, Knight described how "a great many of the courses that made the best sense in that department are already being taught in the university. . . . There will be others," he said, "that I'm sure we'll want to work out together." These facts, Knight said, showed that the university had "honestly, in good faith . . . worked toward this department. Is that an unfair statement?" Knight asked.[14]

"Yes," Chuck Hopkins responded, "it's unfair." In fact, the university had never announced the formation of the Proctor Committee and students were unaware that specific planning for a Black studies program for undergraduates had started. Far from confirming that the university was working "honestly" and in "good faith," Knight's reference to a faculty recommendation on Black studies only confirmed the Black students' fear that they would have little, if any, input into the program. "Who developed this program?" Hopkins asked. "We had no part in developing it." As to Knight's assertion that many courses in Duke's Black studies program were already being taught at the university, Hopkins was incredulous. "The people who run these departments are old and are not qualified to deal with what we are talking about," he told Knight. "They are not qualified to relate to Black people. They're not qualified to relate to a Black studies program. We will not accept such a program being forced down our throats. You can name it a Black studies program, but it's not a Black studies program. It's something you've thrown together to appease people."[15]

For Fuller, student involvement—from the outset—was the key issue. "Are you prepared," he asked Knight, "to give Black students the voice and control of various aspects of the Afro studies program? Who's going to write up the whole Afro studies program to start with?" he asked. "We're saying Black students are the ones who've got to be involved with it." Knight was willing to concede some student participation but only to a point. Students would be "involved" but not "controlling all by themselves," he clarified. "I'm not saying that any one group controls it."[16] Black students took Knight's response to mean that since "control" of Black studies was shared among groups, they would have the power to block any proposal they did not endorse. In truth, the university had no intention of ceding this level of control over the development of a university academic program. The stage was thus set for further conflict in the coming days.

After more back-and-forth, Knight and the students agreed to hold a follow-up meeting to discuss the Black students' demands. Attended by AAS representatives, faculty, and administrators, the meeting would convene at University House at 8:00 p.m. that evening.[17]

Early Saturday evening, Knight's first public comments on the takeover were broadcast over WDBS. After providing reassurance of his "longstanding and deep concern for the position of black students on the Duke campus," the Duke president said that police were called to campus only as a last option. "I regret more than I can ever tell any one of you, that it was necessary to bring police onto the campus," he said. "But no honest choice was made evident to us during the ten hours . . . in which we proposed a great variety of possible solutions to those occupying the building."[18] The fact that the university had made only one attempt to speak directly with the Black students and that it had refused a late afternoon offer by students to negotiate seemed to directly contradict the "great variety of possible solutions" that Knight mentioned.

Following his remarks on WDBS, the 8:00 p.m. meeting at Knight's house was productive. Board chair Charles "Wade was there, Knight was there. Howard Fuller was there and a half a dozen Black students, all dressed in black," Richard Watson recalled. Joining them were three members of the Kerckhoff Committee and Hobbs. "Howard Fuller was very eloquent in outlining the so-called demands," Watson noted. "In almost every instance, Knight seemed to give assurance that there was no real problem in working them out." After three hours, an agreement "in concept" was reached on all but one of the issues—amnesty for the Black student protesters. The group agreed that the Kerckhoff Committee and the AAS would work on a "joint statement" setting forth the points addressed at that evening's meeting. The statement would be presented to the Duke community in Page Auditorium at 2:30 p.m. on Sunday. The *Duke Chronicle* reported that before the Black students left, Knight counseled them "not to act victorious" and "not to boast that they gained concessions from him and others attending the meeting." The students agreed. "It was a very congenial affair," Watson said later of the meeting.[19]

Hopkins was the first to speak at the Sunday afternoon meeting in Page Auditorium, confirming that the Black students had agreed to the statement Kerckhoff would be reading. The students hoped, Hopkins said, "that the constructive results obtained [at the Saturday night meeting] will make Duke University more relevant to the needs and aspirations of black people."[20]

The "statement of understandings" Kerckhoff read was promising. At the Saturday night meeting, the discussion was "at a level of specificity and depth of meaning that was most impressive," he noted. "A great deal of information was exchanged" and "some real understanding was achieved." Kerckhoff reviewed the issues in three categories. The first were actions that had been taken by the university "about which the Afro-American students had not been fully informed." As an example, Kerckhoff pointed to the "felt need for an advisor for black students." Here he reiterated the university's commitment to hire such a person but added that the individual selected "will be (must be) mutually acceptable to the students and the administration." Applause greeted this clarification.[21]

The second category involved issues on which "tangible progress has been made and on which future plans have been made." By far, the most important item in this category was Black studies. Referring to the funding proposal prepared by Professor Cell in late 1968 and the more recent work of the Proctor Committee, Kerckhoff characterized both as merely a "rough outline" for a Black studies program. He announced that an intensive multiday retreat would be scheduled in the near future "to move forward [on a Black studies program] at a rapid pace." Black student representatives would attend the retreat, along with Duke faculty, members of the Kerckhoff Committee, and one or two outside consultants. A deadline of April 15 was established for completion of a Black studies proposal with at least some parts to be implemented by the start of the fall semester.[22]

This sounded positive. Not only would Black students participate in a retreat to plan the Black studies program at Duke, but the university had agreed to consult outsiders with deep experience in the area. Moreover, the deadlines Kerckhoff announced showed a sense of urgency. The crowd once again applauded.[23]

This positive response, however, turned out to be premature. The issue of how much control Black students would have over the development and implementation of the Black studies program remained unresolved. Asked if Black students would have "some sort of voting power in the hiring or firing of professors in the program," Kerckhoff was ambiguous. He pointed to the upcoming retreat. "Where it goes from there depends on the outcome of that meeting," Kerckhoff explained.[24] Whatever his intention, Black students heard this statement as confirmation that no framework for a Black studies program would emerge from the retreat without their agreement.

The final category involved issues about which "the expression of need by the [Black] students was not clearly understood." These items included grading, the formation of a committee on Black activities within the student union, a reconsideration of admissions criteria, an increase in the number of Black students on campus, and problems of police harassment. Without being specific, Kerckhoff had acknowledged that each issue required attention and agreed, in most instances, that his committee would help facilitate further discussions.[25]

Those in attendance felt that some progress had been made. After a brief question-and-answer session, the group voted to suspend the class boycott originally scheduled to run through Monday. The university later made clear that, notwithstanding their suspension "pending due process," takeover participants could continue to attend classes, at least until a disciplinary hearing was held.

On Sunday evening, Knight again broadcast remarks over WDBS. The items covered in the "statement of understandings" read at Page in the afternoon were not "major new decisions," Knight told the Duke community. Rather, they were "matters which actually have been concerns of the University for months or even years." The results achieved "were not brought about by confrontation," the Duke president insisted. Rather, "they were brought about . . . by human beings who met in mutual faith and true desire for the understanding of one another's points of view." In comments to the press, Frank Ashmore was even more direct. "The only thing [the protesters] accomplished," he said, "was a recapitulation of what is being done or previously has been announced."[26]

The university's claim that no concessions had been made to the Black students was lost in the press coverage of the meeting. "University to Meet Most Afro Demands," the *Duke Chronicle* announced in a large front-page headline. "We got more done in that three hours" at Knight's house, McBride commented to the paper, "than we ever have before. . . . It's amazing what they can do when they realize they have to do it." As to Knight's protestation that the items announced were already in the works, McBride was skeptical. "No matter what they want to say," he commented, "we now have some specific answers we didn't have before."[27]

Newspapers throughout the South described the statement of understandings as capitulation by the university. "Stripped of its camouflage of misleading academic language," the *Charleston Evening Post* editorialized, the "'peace settlement' arrived at by Duke University administrators and dissident Negro students boils down to one thing: abject surrender by the administration." "The concessions which Duke University granted this weekend to a handful of black militant students are a sell-out to violence," the *Richmond News Leader* wrote. "When confronted by campus revolutionaries, Duke president Douglas M. Knight demonstrated weak-kneed ambivalence."[28]

Letters and telegrams, most of them furious, again flooded in from alumni. Some blamed events on broader changes they had seen at Duke during the 1960s. "I have not approved of the growing liberal policy at Duke," one wrote, "and feel sure that the present ultra-liberal policy is the reason students felt they could get by with revolution." Another alumnus claimed that "Duke has let the character of the student body deteriorate" and argued that it was "in the name of liberalization" that the university "did not take a strong stand against the rebels."[29]

Many alumni responded to news reports by withdrawing their financial support from the university. "Your capitulation in the face of most unreasonable demands by Duke's Negro students has assured the University a future of mediocrity," a member of the class of 1962 wrote. "In the past, I have regretted that I was unable to contribute more to Duke's future. Now, I regret that I have contributed at all." Another was "ashamed" at the university's response to the "black militants." "In the future," he said, "do not send me any further requests from the Alumni Association for loyalty fund pledges. You can get money from the NAACP or others."[30]

By far, the greatest anger was directed personally toward Knight. He was seen as weak for failing to control events on campus and giving in to Black student demands. "If the Board of Trustees had hired you for the sole purpose of wrecking Duke University," one wrote to Knight, "you couldn't have done a better job." Citing Knight's "complete lack of courage in every crisis you have faced," this alumnus said the Duke president had "destroyed our reputation among those who love this university." "So you finally gave in to the bastards, eh?" an alumnus asked rhetorically. "Brother, are you really chicken." An alumnus from Raleigh, North Carolina, communicated his concerns directly to the chairman of the board. "It is the consensus of those to whom I have talked that Dr. Knight has finally brought complete chaos, embarrassment, and total failure of the University." The Duke president had "recruited, coddled and cajoled a group of neurotic mal-contents," this alumnus wrote, "whose only interests are disruption, contempt and ridicule." He implored the chairman to "remove the blight which has smitten an outstanding [university] and to restore some degree of leadership and behavior."[31]

Inevitably, these concerns became a primary topic of discussion at the March 7, 1969, meeting of the board of trustees. At that meeting, Wade provided copies of an alumni petition to board members. The document "expressed profound dissatisfaction with the administration of the University." It also "expressed . . . the hope that the Board would take action to prevent wrongful, unwarranted and unlawful acts on the part of students and others." The minutes of the meeting do not document what response, if any, the Duke president had to the petition.[32]

Knight left most letters from alumni unanswered but did respond to Alexander T. Davison, who wrote that he had "come to the reluctant conclusion that [Knight had] abdicated the office of the President, and become a conciliator." Knight was angered by this characterization. "Why do you think I have become a conciliator," he asked, "when I am the only man who, within a radius of 500 miles, has called in the police to stop student interference with the ordinary and free operation of the University?"[33]

In response to the avalanche of comments, Knight decided to issue a public statement "to correct the rather widespread impression that Duke University capitulated on most, if not all, of the 13 demands made . . . by a group of our black students." Knight again declared that the university "already was working very hard to overcome problems which were included among the demands of the black students, and those demands which had no merit were rejected." The Kerckhoff Committee issued a separate statement repudiating "the view that the use of force is an effective means of accomplishing goals in a university community."[34]

It is not known whether the clarifying statements by Knight and the Kerckhoff Committee satisfied unhappy alumni, but it was clear that Duke's Black students considered them "irresponsible." "I don't care what Knight called the school's action," McBride told the *Duke Chronicle*. "He is trying to save face for the school and he is doing it in a manner which provokes bad feeling [among] black students."[35]

Just as Knight was being attacked as a "conciliator," he was forced to respond to criticism from the city of Durham. Watching the national news on Friday, February 14, Durham city manager I. Harding Hughes was upset to hear university spokesperson Clarence Whitfield comment that "we were horrified at the use of tear gas." Hughes reminded Knight in a letter that it had been the university's decision to summon the police to campus and that it did so "*with the express understanding* that the police would come prepared with such equipment necessary to discharge their duties." Tear gas was used, Hughes wrote, "*only after the police had been assaulted* with objects capable of causing serious injury or death." Under these circumstances, Whitfield's comments were, according to Hughes, "a hard thing for the policemen to take." Warning that the "morale" of police personnel would be important in any "future incident," Hughes told Knight that a "forthright, unequivocal statement now by Duke University would clear the air and contribute to the good morale of the police personnel." Going further, he said a "commendation of the good work of the police under trying circumstances would seem to be in order."[36]

Knight responded to Harding on the same day he received his letter. Whitfield's comments, he said, were not a criticism of the police. What the university regretted, he explained, was "the *necessity* for the use of tear gas, harmless as it is." Knight expressed "the gratitude of the University for the prompt and full cooperation which [it] received from the civil authorities." Knight went much further in a letter to the chief of the Durham Police Department. He offered the Durham police and State Highway Patrol the university's "most sincere commendation. Because of the proficiency of these two groups," he wrote, "order was quickly restored" and "National Guard troops which were on standby were never needed." Members of the Duke community, Knight told Chief Pleasants, are "indebted to your men and the State Police for your assistance last Thursday."[37]

Knight's letters satisfied Harding and Pleasants. When they became public, however, many in the Duke community reacted with disbelief that Knight would "commend" police who only days earlier had clubbed and gassed Duke students on the main quadrangle. In an editorial, the *Duke Chronicle* called Knight's commendation "an aggravation of the offense he committed" when he called police to campus and "a foolish provocation to those who are already disgusted by his recent behavior." In a joint letter, the ASDU and WSGA presidents, the executive editor of the *Duke Chronicle*, the chair of the University Christian Movement, and the president of the junior class of the divinity school were equally critical. The student leaders protested Knight's praise for "what was felt by those present to be [an] unwarranted and brutal overreaction to a situation that need not have occurred at all." They warned the president that his statements "served only to antagonize increasingly large segments of the student body." Black students were among those most upset. "There would have been no trouble had it not been for the cops," McBride told the *Duke Chronicle*. "This is the sort of statement which makes us distrust the University's motives." Even the Kerckhoff Committee wrote to Knight to say that it considered his statements about the police "unfortunate from the point of view of the campus situation which the Committee is attempting to confront and deal with. . . . We are concerned," the committee told the Duke president, "with the erosion of faculty support for and student body confidence in the University."[38]

Knight must have felt the walls closing in on him as he struggled to defend his position and retain his job. In a response to an alumnus who wrote to congratulate him on his actions following the takeover, Knight wrote, "We have moved, I think, as best we can, as far as we can, as fast as we can." Fearing backlash, he commented that "there are men like myself who will be caught right in the middle of it, and there is absolutely nothing we can do to protect ourselves." In his report to the board at its March 7, 1969, meeting, Knight described his situation. "The president of Duke has been a college and university president for nearly sixteen years," he said.

> At some point, . . . I think I ought to say to you that I've done my job as president of the University because I don't think any one man . . . is the right man . . . for the long history of a place these days. . . . People get worn out and worn down. . . . I wouldn't be honest with you . . . if I didn't say that the point has to come where this kind of job must change for me.[39]

Almost a prediction of his demise as Duke president, the statement was full of foreboding. Events would further unravel for Knight as the semester continued.

··

For the remainder of the spring semester, negotiations over who would control any Black studies program at Duke became a flash point. "We want an education which will sustain the culture of Black people," the AAS demanded during Black Week, "while . . . allowing us to develop skills which will satisfy the needs of our people in this racist society." Lacking evidence that the Duke faculty was capable of developing a program that met their needs, Black students demanded a central role in shaping Black studies at Duke. "We want the power to determine . . . our educational environment," the students insisted. Such power would enable them to "engage in a meaningful educational process" that was "relevant." Failing this purpose, any course of study, Black students believed, "is not education, but indoctrination."[40]

In stark contrast, the university "wasn't enthusiastic about Black studies at all," according to Cook. Harold Lewis, vice provost and dean of faculty, was to have a central role in developing any program, but English professor

Louis Budd, who would soon head a Black studies committee, did not believe that Lewis "himself had any commitment to Black studies." Budd described this as a "difficulty." Cell was more direct, saying that Lewis "was reluctant to do anything." Kerckhoff was also skeptical. Some had the perception that the Black studies curriculum might include "how to make a Molotov cocktail." Acknowledging that the premise sounds "absolutely outrageous," Kerckhoff believed that such a prospect was "not too far from what some people would define as the outer fringe of what . . . a [Black studies] program would do." Kerckhoff thought that the goal of a Black studies program "as some people saw it . . . was to teach Blacks how to bring about social change in society." It was "a way of mobilizing educated Blacks to take part in the revolution."[41]

These profoundly different perspectives played out at the planning retreat held during the first weekend in March. The goal of the meeting, as Kerckhoff described it, was to "attempt to establish a framework for a specific [Black studies] program which will be developed in the next few months." Attendees at the weekend retreat included the eleven members of the Proctor Committee, four representatives of the Kerckhoff Committee, and five representatives of the AAS. Four consultants also participated. Selected by the university were Martin Kilson, head of Harvard's African American studies program, and Roy Bryce-Laporte, who would lead Yale's program the following year. At the Black students' suggestion, William Couch Jr. and Andres Taylor from historically Black Federal City College in Washington, DC, were also included.[42]

Although discussions at the meeting lasted a total of eighteen hours, the retreat was a "fiasco," according to Cell. The issue, not surprisingly, was control. "We got hung up all day," Cell recalled, on whether "students [should] be on [the committee] and how many." What the students wanted, according to student Adrenée Glover, one of the AAS representatives, "was a . . . mutual consensus," to avoid "decisions that would be totally unacceptable to either group." Those speaking on behalf of the university saw matters differently. Martin Kilson's comments to the AAS representatives were particularly rigid. "He told them," Cell recounted, "that students are at a university to learn, teachers to teach, and administrators to administer." Kilson "was so conservative," Cook remembered, "he didn't want to see students on committees." For Cook, Kilson's view was that "students don't know anything. That's why they come to college." Cook disagreed. "You couldn't be serious," he told Kilson. "One thing they do know is how they feel, what's inside them. What's bugging them." Unmoved, Kilson "thought everything the students said was supercilious," according to Cook.[43]

Discussions of content were equally problematic. For example, Charles Becton reported that when asked what materials the library had that would be useful in a Black studies program, a faculty member responded, "The Library has many collections on the Plantation System."[44]

Inflaming matters further, it soon became apparent that the Proctor Committee was already well along in finalizing its proposal on Black studies. Black students believed they had been promised the opportunity to participate in a "meaningful dialogue [on Black studies] among various [retreat] participants." They also believed that their consent would be obtained before any proposal on Black studies was released following the retreat. Now they saw themselves "relegated to . . . 'advising' the Proctor Committee," which would "go off among themselves and decide what would be recommended." "They listened politely," Hopkins said of the Proctor Committee, "but they had already made up their minds."[45]

The Kerckhoff Committee published a statement about the results of the retreat in the *Duke Chronicle* on March 4, 1969—the day after the weekend meeting. Highlighting areas of consensus, the statement reported that all retreat participants agreed that there would be a program in African and Afro-American (A&AA) studies at Duke starting in the fall and that a major in the area would be established. The statement was also clear, however, that Black students would not control the program. The statement outlined that a Supervisory Committee, consisting entirely of faculty, would be established. Students would have input into the selection of faculty to serve on the committee but would not be included among its members. It would be "the first order of business" of the Supervisory Committee, the Kerckhoff Committee wrote, "to consider the role and function of the black students in decision-making concerned with the program."[46]

As if to leave no doubt that the university was prepared to proceed without the consent of Black students, the Proctor Committee also issued *its* report on the day after the retreat. Consisting of ten "recommendations," the report said that Duke should establish an interdepartmental major in A&AA studies. New courses and other "learning experiences" in the discipline should be developed by various academic departments. Departments should be "encouraged to make vigorous efforts to recruit additional faculty members competent to teach courses in the Program." A committee consisting "exclusively of faculty members" should initially supervise the program. The role of Black students would be limited to providing input on the membership of the Supervisory Committee and serving on subcommittees regarding matters such as curriculum, to be established in the future.[47]

Black students viewed these developments as a complete breach of faith. In a separate statement, also published in the *Duke Chronicle* on March 4, they charged that the report produced by the Proctor Committee was not based on "give-and-take-discussion" at the retreat. Rather, "basic decisions concerning the [proposed] program had been made by the Proctor Committee during the week *preceding* the retreat." Rather than provide input into the appointment of the faculty Supervisory Committee as recommended by the Proctor Committee, the Black students proposed that a ten-member committee composed of an equal number of students and faculty be established. Because such a group would be "more representative of the various groups and interests concerned," the AAS said, it would be "more effective in implementing a program acceptable to all concerned." The relationship between the university and "the students who have unwittingly served in the present master-slave relationship has terminated as of now," the students announced. "Public discourse between the Afro-American Society and the University" could resume, they said, only "when Black students are given equitable representation in the events that affect them."[48]

Kerckhoff saw the statement from the AAS in the *Duke Chronicle*. There is no record that he reached out to Black student representatives. Instead, Kerckhoff wrote Hobbs, urging the provost to act on the Proctor Committee's recommendation that he invite the AAS to appoint a committee of students to meet with him to discuss faculty membership of the Supervisory Committee. "Today's statement in the *Chronicle*," Kerckhoff acknowledged, "would suggest that this request for their participation would be rejected. However, we are not certain that this would, in fact, occur. Even more important," Kerckhoff told the provost, "we think it is essential that the University move in good faith in the direction of establishing a Program and of doing so with student participation. Should that prove impossible," he said, "it should be perfectly clear that it resulted from the student rejection of the offer of joint action."[49]

Kerckhoff appeared to have largely abandoned hope of finding a shared path forward with Black students. His concern now was assigning blame if they refused to accept the limited role the Proctor Committee had assigned them.

Hobbs followed Kerckhoff's recommendation. On March 5 he wrote the AAS, asking stiffly that "three *bona fide* student members" be selected to meet with three administrators to "effect the suggested consultation and discuss specifically the possible membership of the Supervisory Committee." Hobbs wanted there to be no doubt about where control of the nascent A&AA studies program resided. "It should be clearly understood," he told the AAS, that "implementation of the adopted program is in the area of responsibility of the Undergraduate Faculty Council."[50] University faculty would control all decisions.

The AAS responded to Hobbs immediately. Writing on behalf of the AAS, McBride demanded "that the Proctor Committee be abolished." Instead, a Supervisory Committee "composed of five black students and five faculty members" would be appointed to "work out the specific details relating to the departmental structure of the African–Afro-American Studies program." "We would like to see positive action taken on fulfilling these requests," McBride wrote ominously, "by Monday, March 10, 1969."[51]

That evening, a rally attended by seven hundred students was held at Baldwin Auditorium. "If the administration does not respond by Monday night," Mc-Bride told the rally, "further action will be taken." In his remarks, Howard Fuller implied that Black students were considering withdrawing from the university. "Duke University has to decide," he said, "if it wants to have black students or not." "Knight says, 'have faith,'" Fuller declared, "and I say, 'In who?' You are asking for us to have faith in people who have already betrayed us." Black student Vaughn Glapion dismissed the university's proposed A&AA studies program as just a shell game. "There is more interest in shifting existing courses at Duke, North Carolina College and the University of North Carolina," he said, "than in creating meaningful courses for black students at Duke."[52]

On the following evening, three hundred students marched in a torchlight parade to East Campus. Those leading the march carried a banner that read, "Power to the Blacks, Power to the Students, Power to the People." One of the signs held above the crowd asked, "Do we beg for the right to live—or do we take it?" McBride and Tony Axam reported no progress on the development of a Black studies program or the inclusion of students on the Supervisory Committee. The *Duke Chronicle* commented correctly that "Duke University is once again rapidly approaching a crisis situation."[53]

By this point, the composition of the Supervisory Committee had become the sole focus of discussions and the cause of the standoff. Having demanded equal representation on the Supervisory Committee, the AAS did not respond to the provost's invitation to consult on the composition of an all-faculty committee. Axam called it "a delaying tactic." Eager to finalize the membership of the Supervisory Committee and move forward, Lewis commented to the *Duke Chronicle* that "it will be a question of how long we wait" before appointing the committee.[54]

The answer was "not long." On March 10, Lewis appointed five faculty members to serve on the Supervisory Committee, asking Professor Louis Budd to serve as chairman (Budd Committee). Lewis asked that the committee meet first "to determine the extent of any student participation."[55]

The Budd Committee convened almost immediately. Deliberations on student committee participation did not take long. "We first agreed that we would have students on the committee," Cell recalled, "and second that we would have three. . . . The feeling" was, Cell explained, "that between five and none, three might be an acceptable compromise." One reason the members of the committee were able to decide quickly was that they viewed the issue of student representation as having little practical consequence. "It didn't make a damn bit of difference how many students we had on the committee," Cell believed. "It was a symbol. . . . Once you have any students on there, it doesn't matter" how many there are. In Cell's experience, committees do not resolve differences by voting—"you talk them out. . . . I knew very well that once we got to substance, we wouldn't be voting. . . . That's the way committees work."[56] Students, however, did not view it this way.

Nine AAS members joined the Budd Committee meeting after about an hour. Kerckhoff described the encounter as a "thing of wonder." He was shocked by the physical transformation the students had undergone. "They all came in with black leather jackets and shades, [and] caps with afros," he described. These students "who had been wandering around looking like ordinary students," Kerckhoff recalled, "looked like something out of the East Side of New York." The students had undergone "some degree of radicalization," he realized. "The students . . . weren't there to become friends with 'whitey,'" Budd recounted. The students resisted attempts to hold the discussion "on a friendly basis." Budd did not "think it was rudeness" but rather "very studied mock aggression."[57]

The students presented a compromise proposal—a Supervisory Committee composed of five faculty, four students, and one member of the Duke community acceptable to both parties. This proposal was rejected. The Budd Committee "simply told the students, 'This is the way it's going to be,'" Kerckhoff described. "That was not a smart thing to do." "In retrospect," Cell thought, "we should have said, 'We cannot decide this now. We will make a decision later.'" "The meeting was very brief," Kerckhoff recounted, "and broke up with a real split." Describing the meeting as a "final disastrous encounter," Kerckhoff saw a lot of "hard work [go] down the drain in a very short period of time." "I guess I felt that we had failed about as badly as we could have under the circumstances," he said sadly.[58]

"We cannot participate under the inhuman conditions we have been subjected to," Hopkins told a rally of three hundred students on the chapel steps just after leaving the Budd Committee meeting. He then stunned the crowd by announcing that Black students would be withdrawing en masse from the university. Withdrawal, Hopkins told the rally, "will put an end to the constant destruction of our minds and humanity." Later, the AAS reported that twenty-three undergraduates would be withdrawing from Duke immediately, with another seventeen leaving Duke at the end of the semester. The *Duke Chronicle* calculated that when added to the fourteen Black students who had been dismissed for academic reasons at the end of the fall semester, "59 percent of Duke's 91 black undergraduates will have left the University by the end of the school year."[59]

Following Hopkins's announcement, Black students, along with supportive white students and faculty, led a torchlight procession to downtown Durham. At the same time, Fuller led hundreds of community members in a separate march, meeting the Black students at Five Points. From there, the two groups marched together to St. Joseph's AME Church for a rally. "The procession was intended to be symbolic," Fuller wrote. "The black students were in essence returning home to their community with the support of their white peers from Duke." A crowd of two thousand packed into the church, with Duke Black students "occupying honorary positions on the altar." Hopkins announced the formation of a new Malcolm X Liberation School, asking the crowd for "support and solidarity." A *Chronicle* reporter noted that a "strong feeling of brotherhood could be felt throughout the hall."[60]

The decision to withdraw was the subject of intense debate within the AAS. "We had a real struggle amongst ourselves," Hopkins recalled. "My position was that we had lost the battle but not the war. And that it was just a matter of getting together, regrouping, and coming up with some new strategies. . . . I argued down to the last breath," Hopkins remembered, "but I lost out." Cook thought the idea of withdrawing was "insane." "I said, 'You don't want to withdraw from the university,'" Cook remembered. "'Look at what it would mean. You want to see this university become lily-white again?'"[61]

A majority of AAS members saw it differently. By withdrawing, Becton explained in a statement published in the *Duke Chronicle*, "many Black students are . . . saying, 'Duke University, at this stage of the battle, you can keep your white system . . . for it is morbidly masochistic at best for us to fight when you have all the power and are unwilling to give it up.'" Why give up on Duke? "Duke has been de-segregated for the last seven years," Becton answered. "It has never been integrated." Becton wrote that he was "not aware of any program Duke has implemented at its own initiative in regards to Black students save those programs under which Duke received monies for having black bodies here." Even Duke's "talk-and-do-nothing committees," he argued, were formed only when "Black students had . . . created such a crisis that Duke could no longer be insulated or unaware of distressing conditions." Duke's Black students had "petitioned; marched to the President's house; held 'sit-ins' and 'study-ins'; liberated the first floor of Allen Building; and . . . followed the ill-spun web of proper channels," Becton recounted. Duke had shown itself unwilling to give the Black students even limited control over the Black studies program that had become central to their identities and needs as Duke students. Black students, Becton explained, now faced only two choices— "destruction and withdrawal."[62]

The *Duke Chronicle* supported the move. "Some of Duke's most moral and courageous students walked out of the University Monday," the paper editorialized. "They did it, because, after so much indifference, they were too alienated from the white community to trust whites."[63]

When students approached their deans about withdrawing, some encountered resistance. "We all went to Dean Bryant," Howard recalled. "We wanted it to be a real simple process. . . . She said, 'I'll have to see each one of you individually.' . . . And [when] I went in . . . she just cried. And she cried. She knew me. She . . . went on about how she didn't understand and how it was such a serious mistake." Howard remembered Dean Bryant asking, "'What are you going to do?' . . . It doesn't matter," Howard responded, "I just don't want to be here." Finally, the dean "very reluctantly" gave Howard the withdrawal form.[64]

Among senior administrators, public opinion was the primary focus. Knight and newly designated interim chancellor Barnes Woodhall published a three-page statement to the Duke community commenting on the planned withdrawals. Noting that the Black students had accused "the University of bad faith and of an unwillingness to work with them in a meaningful way" in planning a Black studies program, Knight and Woodhall declared, "There is simply no basis for this charge." Knight and Woodhall then outlined, in great detail, the university's efforts toward implementation of a Black studies program at Duke. "Despite the reported plan of some black students to withdraw from Duke," the statement said, the Supervisory Committee "will continue to work—with students—to develop a program of academic integrity which will be both respected and respectable."[65] Within a couple of days, the Undergraduate Faculty Council voted to approve the Budd Committee's recommendation that three students be added to the committee.

Meanwhile, Kerckhoff reached out to the AAS. In a letter to McBride, Kerckhoff expressed "regret" that Black students had announced plans to withdraw. "Although we understand the sources of strain," Kerckhoff wrote, "much more of value can be gained by working together within the University than by leaving. We thus urge all of you to continue to work within the University."[66]

McBride's response was brief. "Although the Afro-American Society will continue as an organization until the end of the semester," he wrote to Kerckhoff, "it will in no way communicate with the University. In view of this," McBride concluded, "your committee need not concern itself with the Afro-American Society."[67]

Learning of McBride's response, Hobbs wrote to Kerckhoff. "I was sorry to learn of the rejection of the Afro-American group," the provost said parenthetically, "though I guess this has been [the] case all along."[68] Hobbs appeared to have blamed the Black students alone for the impasse.

The next week was eventful, to say the least. Discussions within the AAS and between the AAS and the university continued. A rally attended by eight hundred Duke, NCC, and Durham Business College students was held in downtown Durham. Although alluding to the possibility that the Black students might revisit their decision to withdraw, McBride remained defiant. "We live what we believe," he told the crowd. "We won't be messed over no more. I'd rather be a poor black than a rich nigger," he declared. After the rally, violence erupted. Durham police were called in after twenty-five downtown store windows were smashed. The mayor imposed a 7:00 p.m. to 5:00 a.m. nightly curfew in Durham. National Guard troops were called in to help enforce the curfew. Several days later, on March 17, the Malcolm X Liberation University opened with about forty students.[69]

During this week, no Black students completed the paperwork necessary to withdraw from the university, and only a handful notified Duke of their intent to leave the school. With support for the withdrawal strategy eroding, members of the AAS released a statement reversing the decision announced only a week earlier. "As revolutionary forces within one of the most conservative and oppressive institutions in America," the statement read, "we deem it necessary to remain here and continue the struggle." Black students would be entering Duke in the future, the statement explained, "making it imperative that the [AAS] continue to exist to meet the needs and aspirations of black people." Malcolm X Liberation University would meet the Black students' immediate needs. The statement concluded: "Power to the people; student power to students; BLACK POWER TO BLACK PEOPLE!"[70]

Reading in the *Duke Chronicle* that Black students would be staying, Budd wrote to McBride. "I hope that you will feel inclined to get in touch with me," he said. The Budd Committee "would like to have student members," he reminded McBride, "and I am sure that the Committee would welcome your advice as to whom [Dean Lewis] should appoint as its student members."[71]

The university's position had prevailed. Students would serve on the Supervisory Committee but would have no power to direct, or block, any action. Full control over the A&AA studies program would remain with the faculty. Not surprisingly, Hobbs commented later, "we got things under reasonable control."[72]

In early May, the Proctor Committee met with a member of the Budd Committee for a progress report on the proposed interdepartmental Black studies major. After the meeting, Proctor wrote to Hobbs that the Proctor Committee was "distressed to learn that [the Budd Committee] has experienced considerable difficulty in securing cooperation from the various Departments in development of a curriculum" to support the major. "There has clearly been a loss of the sense of urgency which prevailed in March," Proctor wrote, "to say the least." The Proctor Committee considered this state of affairs "to be most unfortunate" and had agreed unanimously to tell Hobbs of its "grave concern."[73]

It took Hobbs almost a month to respond, having met in the interim with Proctor and Cook. "It is next to impossible for us to deal with these matters rapidly," he wrote, "but we can deal with them consistently." In their meeting, Cook had suggested that the university add "five or six" individuals with expertise in Black studies over a short time frame. Citing budget constraints, Hobbs said the university could afford to add "occasional new people," but not the number suggested by Cook. As to finding a director for the Black studies program, Hobbs said he had been "totally immersed in budgetary problems" and had not gotten around to working specifically on the matter. Calling it a "first priority," Hobbs said that he "should get to it sometime within the next several weeks." "We can, I hope, solve this problem at least," he concluded, "and hopefully show good evidence of continued interest and high priority consideration to making a viable Afro-American Studies Program."[74]

Clearly, Hobbs was in no rush to move Black studies forward, notwithstanding his statement that the matter would be treated as a high priority.

Knight commented later that the provost felt "things were moving too fast for his comfort." This gradualist approach, of course, meant that the needs of the university's Black students continued to be unaddressed.[75]

Ultimately, it was the Budd Committee that directed the university's nascent Afro-American studies program during the 1969–70 school year. A search committee for a permanent director of the program was not appointed until December 1969. As 1969 ended, a faculty committee found "few signs to indicate that the employment of black academics is a matter [of] priority" at the university and highlighted "the critical need for more incisive commitments and statements from [the university] on priorities in the area of black students and black studies."[76]

As had been the case since desegregation, these changes would occur very slowly.

....

In the midst of the turmoil, the university's disciplinary hearing to consider punishment for participants in the Allen Building takeover was held on March 20, 1969. The outcome of the hearing carried enormous consequences for both the students and the university.

Knight was under intense pressure to deal swiftly and decisively with the protesters. Calls and letters flooded in. "Smash student anarchy immediately and decisively," an alumnus implored, "and expel the anarchist." "There is nothing like expulsion for what ails you," Russell Price, a member of the class of 1952, wrote. "Stand fast." An alumnus from Newport News, Virginia, was most succinct. He wrote simply, "EXPEL THEM!"[77]

Knight saw how racial attitudes informed many of the demands for strong action. "It was clear," the Duke president observed, "that people had been waiting for a moment where you could really move in on the black situation." "You have a God given chance," one alumnus told Knight, "to rid the school of a number of people who should not have been admitted." Knight heard this type of refrain from board members, alumni, and many others: "We haven't had a clear cut case, but now you've got it." "Wonderful—Now you have them where you want them; you must throw them all out." These comments, Knight said, were repeated "just that nakedly." "All the unspoken fears and resentments came into the open," Knight wrote later. "These black students were intruders; they should be intruders in the dust, cast down, cast out."[78]

The students were also under tremendous stress. "I think it was clear to all of us that there were a lot of people asking for extreme measures to be taken to make an example" of us, Becton recounted. This prospect "was something that was thought about before we went into the building." Even so, calls for the students' suspension or expulsion were frightening. Beyond academic and professional considerations, male students who fell out of good standing at the university faced the draft. So grave was this concern, Kerckhoff told Knight, that at other campuses "the popular characterization of suspension has been the 'death penalty.'"[79]

Students also faced anguished parents. Among the "best and the brightest" of their generation, the Allen Building protesters arrived at Duke bearing the hopes and expectations of their families, communities, and race. Now, everything they hoped to accomplish was in jeopardy. Howard remembered all the calls that flooded in from "moms, grand moms, and aunties." "All of us had turmoil within our families," Armstrong remembered. The anguish many parents felt was expressed in a letter Tom and Ruth D. McBride wrote to Knight asking that their son, Michael, be allowed to complete his Duke education. "We know these young people have disrupted the normal operation of the university," they told Knight, "but . . . we beg of you to ask that these bright young black Americans be given both justice and mercy." Promising to "do everything that we can to prevent Michael from becoming involved in future demonstrations," they concluded by telling Knight that their son "is a good and kind boy who is active in the movement only because he feels that America must accept blacks and whites on an equal basis." Knight acknowledged receipt of the letter but told the McBrides that "the deeply saddening events of the last days make it difficult for me to answer you wisely at the moment. I . . . would do everything I could for Mike," he told the young man's parents, "if he'd give me half a chance."[80]

As the disciplinary process moved forward, the university was unable to identify all the students who had occupied the Allen Building. Contact between Duke administrators and protesters during the takeover had been extremely limited. The protesters emerged from the Allen Building to a chaotic scene and asked that no photographs be taken. Many covered their faces to avoid being recognized. Complicating matters further, according to C. G. Newsome, a significant number of Black students from NCC had come to the Duke campus to support the Allen Building protesters. Because "you couldn't tell whether they were from Central or Duke," the university could positively identify only twenty-five of the approximately fifty Allen Building protesters.

Duke decided to proceed against those students, who received papers charging them with violating the university's regulations on pickets, protests, and demonstrations.[81]

Aware of the university's problem identifying protesters, members of the AAS took a profoundly dramatic and risky step. Writing in the *Duke Chronicle* on February 27 that "our struggle is a group struggle," the AAS petitioned the university that "any so-called charges [it] wishes to bring against us . . . be brought against the group as a whole or not at all." The petition listed the names of more than sixty AAS members who demanded to stand trial for the takeover. "All of the work that had been done to make Black students into a cohesive force," Armstrong explained, "came to fruition . . . when we all decided to surrender." For the Black students who had not come into the Allen Building, she recounted, "this was their way of expressing their anger." Moreover, the "surrender" by all sixty members of the AAS put the university in what Armstrong called "a very precarious position." "They really couldn't put us all out," Brenda Brown remembered thinking. Acting as a group, Brown believed, provided "protection" for those students the university could positively identify as takeover participants.[82]

The disciplinary hearing began at 9:00 a.m. and lasted nine hours. Law school dean Kenneth Pye, two professors, and two students made up the hearing committee. Although only twenty-five Black students had been formally charged, forty-seven appeared at the hearing asking to be tried by the university. The parents of many of the Black students attended the hearing. Both the university and students were represented by outside counsel.[83]

The hearing began with the student defendants entering a plea of "nolo contendere" to the charge of violating the university's regulations regarding pickets, protests, and demonstrations. Although not an admission of guilt, this meant that each defendant accepted conviction for violating the regulations as though a guilty plea had been entered. In effect, the defendants would not dispute that the Allen Building takeover occurred or that each of the forty-seven defendants participated in the protest. With the plea, the hearing dealt exclusively with the appropriate sanction for the defendants. If the hearing committee determined that a sanction was called for, it could choose among only four options: reprimand, probation, suspension, or expulsion.[84]

The university's case, presented by attorney Marshall Spears Jr., focused only on how disruptive the takeover had been for the university and its employees.[85] Frances Baker, an employee in the bursar's office, testified that one Black student held a raised pipe in his hand when he told employees to "move out." "I was scared to death," she told the committee. Bobbie Jean Day recalled being told, "Move it move, it. If you don't get out, some one's going to get hurt." As she exited, Day passed a student with a pipe in his hand "who used profane language" as he demanded that she leave. Day testified that she was "very much afraid and very much shocked." Day was among three employees who, it was alleged, quit their jobs at Duke because of the takeover. University registrar Richard Tuthill described the condition of the registrar's office after the takeover and testified that the office was closed for two days as a result of the protest. Clark Cahow, assistant registrar, testified about the various pipes, crowbars, chains, hammers, and other materials left in the Allen Building by the protesters after the takeover. Although the students testified that these items were carried in only to secure the building, witnesses for the university characterized them as "weapons." Griffith described the progress that had been made on the list of concerns presented to the ad hoc committee by the Black students in October 1968. He denied any "foot-dragging on the university's part." Under questioning, Griffith acknowledged that the ad hoc committee had no jurisdiction to implement a Black studies program—the most important issue for the Black students.

In their case, presented by J. W. Ferguson, the defendants focused entirely on the harsh conditions at Duke that had given rise to Black student activism at the university. They testified about the frustration they felt over the school's inability to address their needs. Stef McLeod testified that "nothing major" had come from the extensive discussions with the university and described his feelings of deep alienation. Asked if any further recourse was available to Black students as of February 13, 1969, McLeod responded no. Bertie Howard testified to the hostile racial climate Black students endured at Duke, including the long struggle to force Duke to ban the use of segregated off-campus facilities by university groups. McLeod and Howard both refused to state unequivocally that Black students would never again violate the regulations regarding pickets, protests, and demonstrations. Asked if she felt the AAS had "a right to take over control of an area of Duke University," Howard answered, "I think in this situation it was justified."

In his closing statement, Spears argued for the university that the defendants had presented "testimony of motivation—but not justification." He dismissed the students' assertions that the history of their treatment by the university legitimized the takeover. "If we have any degree of maturity," he said patronizingly, "we must realize that we can't have what we want when we want it." The Black students "should not be excused or patted on the head." The takeover, Spears concluded, "demands a serious punishment."

In his closing statement on behalf of the defendants, Ferguson spoke of the history of race relations at Duke and the events leading up to the protest. The occupation "did not begin when a group of students met and decided to do this," he said. Rather, it originated one hundred years ago when all-white Trinity College was established. It began when Duke's first Black undergraduates arrived in 1963 and realized that Duke was not equipped to deal with them. It moved closer when the university sponsored events at segregated facilities Black students could not attend and when fraternities said they "would like to have black members but can't." It advanced each time a Black student "realized [his] education was not relevant to his needs" and that requested changes were "deferred to one committee or another." Their protest was "a symbolic act to say listen to us and minister to our needs—give us a relevant experience at Duke." "The way to deter further actions," Ferguson told the hearing committee, "would not be to take serious action against these students, but to take serious action on the *needs* of these students." He urged the members of the hearing committee to "open their hearts." "Fifty black students went into Allen Building and said 'somebody listen to us,'" Ferguson concluded. "Today we ask the same." Ferguson's closing statement "had everyone in tears," Armstrong recalled.[86]

Before concluding the hearing, Pye asked if anyone had further comments for the committee to consider. Armstrong described what happened. "Most of us had one parent who was there," she recalled. "Parents got up [and spoke]. They were just beautiful. All of that anger that our parents had lived with and had no way of expressing came out through their children. I remember [parents] saying, 'This is my child, and you are not going to put my child out without me having something to say.' It's not that they understood or even condoned what we did. [But] parents were going to back their children," Armstrong remembered. "There was absolutely no way they were going to leave that place with their children being put out of school."[87]

The disciplinary hearing was important for many of the parents who attended. "They had no idea of the pressure we were under; they certainly had no idea of how difficult it was socially to live at Duke," Armstrong described. As a result of the hearing, attitudes were transformed. "My mother changed sitting there," Armstrong observed. "I could never talk to her about the take-over; someone else had to tell her." But after the hearing, Armstrong's mother said, "If you had to do it over again, I would support you."[88]

In its decision, the hearing committee made clear that "a sentence of suspension would be clearly appropriate for individuals who planned and led the take-over of the building regardless of their motivations." The committee was unable, however, "to determine relative degree of culpability among the [forty-seven] defendants. . . . We are particularly concerned," it stated, "that over one-half of the defendants before us appeared voluntarily to be tried in the absence of any charges brought against them by the University." Treating these individuals severely, the committee said, "might constitute a substantial miscarriage of justice." Accordingly, the committee placed "all persons charged on probation for the period of one year from this date." Hopkins called this punishment "a tap on the back of our hands."[89]

The Black students' solidarity had protected them. "I was convinced," Armstrong explained, "and no one will convince me otherwise, that we were going to be put out of school. It was the intention to make an example so it would not happen again." By standing as one, Black students had made this impossible. In Armstrong's words, they had become "an undeniable force."[90]

If parents were relieved that their children would be allowed to remain in school, many students were unhappy with the outcome of the hearing. "If they think that in 1969 five whites can sit in judgment on 47 blacks," Hopkins commented, "they're crazy." Hopkins also made clear that probation would not deter the students from further protests if the university did not follow through on its commitments. "To get our demands," he said, "we won't hesitate to take another building."[91]

The roiling conflicts Knight faced with trustees and alumni only intensified after the hearing committee failed to suspend or expel the Allen Building takeover participants. "I don't know as a fact," Pye recollected, "but it was my clear impression that when I notified the president of [the sanction] that he was shocked."[92] Knight likely sensed that any hope of remaining the president of Duke was disappearing.

....

In the aftermath of the Allen Building takeover, Douglas Knight feared for his physical safety and that of his family. During the takeover, the Duke president had been concerned about reports he received of vigilante forces circling campus and preparing to attack Black students in the Allen Building once night fell. Witnessing what he described later as the "savage reaction of the regional community" to the takeover, Knight believed that these same forces were now targeting him and his family. The location of University House—bordered in the rear by woods with easy access to a public road—

added to his alarm. "It was obvious," he wrote, "that the threats against us could easily be carried out."[93]

The Knight family took steps to protect themselves. A security guard was posted at University House and the family decided that their youngest son—twelve at the time—would sleep at a friend's house for a while. Most dramatic was a nightly routine the Duke president adopted. At 1:00 a.m. each evening, Knight would slip a loaded pistol into the pocket of his dressing gown and take "a little tour" of the University House grounds with the security guard.[94]

Fewer than six years had elapsed since the summer of 1963, when Knight had arrived at Duke to universal excitement and acclaim. Inaugurated president at age forty-two, Knight's future seemed boundless. Now, in March 1969, he was wandering the grounds of his home each evening, carrying a loaded gun. Peering into the woods and looking for signs of danger, Knight saw himself as a hunted—and haunted—man.

Opinions differ on how much actual physical danger the Knight family was exposed to during this traumatic time. Professionally, though, Knight was clearly in a situation of high risk. "There was substantial agreement among Trustees, the Duke Endowment, the regional community, and a disturbing number of alumni," Knight wrote, "that the situation was out of control and that I had failed to control it." "There was no support left in the situation," Knight realized. "It was a dramatic example of watching the support cut away from you on every possible side. The metaphor I've used" to describe the situation, Knight commented poignantly, "is that of a man with a begging bowl, standing where the five roads intersect. Down the five roads," the president related, "come not the people he wants who will put goodies into his bowl, but come the thundering herds. All opposed to one another and all intent on demolishing him."[95]

With his Duke Endowment critics playing a central role, trustees began to press for a special meeting of the board where a formal demand for Knight's resignation could be made. "This was vicious business," Knight commented later. The trustees conspiring to remove him were "jungle fighters," he said. "These were guys with knives in the dark. That was their basic nature. That's how they got their other business done."[96]

Board chair Charles Wade took on what historian Robert Durden described as "the painful task of persuading Knight to resign before he could be formally asked to do so." "A vote would have been forced on whether to fire me," Knight explained. There were "many trustees who had been whipped up to that." Wade encouraged Knight to take the initiative. His resignation was necessary "for the good of the university," Knight recalled Wade saying. "It had to take place."[97]

"I have conveyed to Chairman Wade my desire to be relieved of the office of president of Duke University," Knight wrote to the board on March 27, 1969. "It is not easy for me to leave Duke University," he explained, "but after more than fifteen years as a college and university president, I have an obligation to protect my family from the severe and sometimes savage demands of such a career." Knight asked to stay on until June 30, 1969. The board accepted Knight's resignation "with regret." "Basically, Doug Knight has been a most generous man in allowing us to work this thing out so that it does not reflect [badly] on him or the University," Wade told Marshall Pickens, "and to him is due most of the credit for the way I was able to handle it."[98]

Many trustees and alumni were relieved at the news that Knight had resigned. The *Duke Chronicle*, despite many conflicts with Knight over his tenure, wrote that it was "deeply grieved" that the Duke president was stepping down. A number of trustees were also dismayed. "Some trustees said to me the day I resigned," Knight recounted, "'You know, we want to apologize to you, we weren't there when you needed us.' And there was nothing I could say except, 'Yes, that's true.'"[99]

For Knight, his resignation marked a professional and personal inflection point that permanently altered the course of his life. The academic world was what he knew and loved, and until his time at Duke, he had encountered only approval and success. After his Duke experience, however, Knight felt himself an outcast from the only professional world he had ever known. "The sequence of those years [at Duke] just finished my academic career," he reflected. "I could never go back into the university world again." "It was quite an experience to find that I'd been exiled from the [university] community where I'd made my whole life," he wrote almost two decades later. "I found the trauma so deep," he commented, "that for several years I could not spend time on a university campus at all—even for the graduation of our third son." He added: "Mine was certainly the wrong temperament to go through that without some major destruction taking place. I can see that . . . from a distance."[100]

Knight deserves credit for the role he played in the transformation of Duke from the accomplished regional university it was when he took office into the preeminent international powerhouse it later became. "Doug Knight was a consummate gentleman and scholar," Duke's ninth president, Richard H. Brodhead, said after Knight passed away in 2005. "Duke emerged from the tumultuous years during which he served as president as a stronger institution, and the foundation Doug Knight laid enabled the university to rise in the ranks of the nation's leading universities today." Duke's eighth president, Nannerl O. Keohane, described Knight in 2003 as a "poet and scholar." "The breadth and sensitivity of his thinking," she said, "informed not only his public pronouncements as the CEO of a rollicking, feisty, ambitious Southern institution of higher education, but also the work he undertook behind the scenes as a collaborative leader and administrator."[101] To honor him, Duke renamed University House—the setting for so much of Knight's anguish—the Douglas M. and Grace Knight House.

Without diminishing this legacy, Samuel DuBois Cook saw Knight's tenure as more complicated. "In many ways, Dr. Knight was a tragic figure," Cook commented. "I think he was caught up in forces over which he had no control." Still, Cook saw Knight as at least partially responsible for the problems he encountered at Duke. "He had great liberal credentials and tradition and commitment," Cook explained. "But . . . when he got here—it often happens—he [got] in an environment that's conservative and he [was] inclined to forget the liberal issues. . . . Perhaps, had he been more outspoken, more courageous, more determined, he would have gotten much more done. . . . But he would have encountered opposition and he would have had to fight for what he wanted. He wasn't willing to fight for it," Cook concluded. "I don't think he was willing to pay the price for doing it."[102]

In his remaining months as Duke's president, Knight acted as a caretaker. He spent most of his time answering correspondence and dealing with routine administrative matters. Mindful of the toll his time at the university had taken on Knight, his colleagues took steps to celebrate the end of his tenure as Duke president. A group who worked with Knight on the second floor of the Allen Building presented him with a set of "Absolutely Non-Negotiable Demands." Referring to themselves as the Continuing Sit-in—Second Floor Allen, they demanded that Knight "remember your many warm friends here," "sail often," "create poems now and then," and "keep in touch and come back to see us."[103]

In early June, Frances and Barnes Woodhall, and a group they described as "your faithful staff and friends all," held a farewell dinner in Knight's honor. Most of Duke's highest-ranking administrators and their wives were invited— William Anlyan, Frank Ashmore, Edwin Bryson, William Cartwright, Frank de Vyver, William Griffith, Marcus Hobbs, Charles Huestis, Harold Lewis, and Rufus Powell. "We shall have cocktails in the gloaming and dinner when we are relaxed," the Woodhalls wrote to the Knights. As going-away gifts, the Knights were presented with what the Duke president described in thank you notes as "books and silver." So where did this impressive group of senior Duke leaders gather at 6:30 p.m. on June 4, 1969, to honor Douglas Knight? The French Room at the segregated Hope Valley Country Club.[104] Whatever changes in racial attitudes and practices had occurred at Duke during Knight's tumultuous six years as president, senior leadership held fast to the prerogatives white privilege afforded them.

....

Until the fall of 1963, educational opportunities at Duke University were only available to young white men and women. Students would graduate having benefited from rigorous classroom instruction. In addition, attending events at Hope Valley Country Club and on campus, they would learn to move comfortably at the country clubs, office parties, neighborhood gatherings, and other social settings they would encounter later in life. In this sense, Duke also operated as a finishing school for the attitudes and behaviors that defined white privilege.

When Black undergraduates arrived on campus, Duke faced a historic challenge. Could a university that had previously catered only to the needs of white students extend the full benefits of a Duke education to Black students as well? The university's bylaws set forth the values Duke sought to embody. Duke aimed "to assert a faith in the eternal union of knowledge and religion; . . . promote a sincere spirit of tolerance; . . . and to render the largest permanent service to the individual, the state, the nation, and the church."[105] Would the university embrace its responsibility to make these values real in the college experience of the Black undergraduates who joined the Duke community?

Duke University fell far short of meeting this moral imperative. In critical respects, Duke was unable to manifest the values it held out as central to its mission. On matters of racial progress, Duke was at best reactive and at worst highly resistant. It refused to devote finite university resources to creating an inclusive environment where both Black and white students could thrive. Only when pressure was brought to bear did racial change occur. Progress was at best sporadic. "The University must not continue to be in a defensive position," the Faculty Committee on Student Concerns warned the provost in its final report in June 1969. "It must propose courses of action, actively seek student (and other) support for its actions, and take the initiative in the implementation of those principles which all of us profess." Concerned that the university had previously acted only when compelled to do so, the committee cautioned that "it is all too easy to relax during a 'quiet period' and wait for the next explosion."[106]

Black student activism was by far the key driver of racial change during this period. Yet even with their best efforts, Black students could only accomplish so much. White supremacist attitudes persisted among some university trustees, administrators, and faculty, and the prerogatives of white privilege proved to be unshakable for many. This is no surprise. What is revealing, however, is the number of racial myths and justifications embraced by those at Duke who found change in race relations abhorrent, impolitic, inconvenient, or just uncomfortable. Few, if any, would identify as white supremacists. But racial progress stalled because so many found a way to avoid meeting the challenge of desegregation.

Central to the university's failure was ignorance of the background, goals, challenges, and strengths of the new Black students. The university did almost nothing to prepare for the arrival of these students or to understand their distinctive needs. Having chosen to remain oblivious to the lived experiences and strengths of its Black students, racial myths determined how they were received. Professors assumed that even the most intellectually gifted among them were deficient academically. Deans communicated that certain professions—such as medicine—were beyond their reach. Most fundamental, however, was the belief that Duke's Black students should want to simply fit in to the Duke experience that had been crafted over generations to meet the needs of white students. Griffith, along with his colleagues, simply expected the Black students to take their place as members of the Duke community through a "natural kind of amalgamation."[107]

The controversy over the use of segregated off-campus facilities by campus groups and Knight's membership in one such facility illuminated other attitudes. Knight had initially assumed that there was no substance to the dispute and that the controversy was being "fabricated" by internal factions.[108] Once it became clear that the problem could not be wished away, various justifications for the continued use of segregated facilities arose. Many believed that prohibiting campus groups from using off-campus segregated facilities infringed on their freedom of choice. "Pragmatism" was another reason some resisted a ban, with university finances always a concern.

When pressed to resign his personal membership in Hope Valley, Knight added "gradualism" to the arsenal. Only by remaining a member, Knight argued, could he use his influence as an insider to effect a change in the club's exclusionary racial policy. Any such change would take time.

Escalating Black campus activism in 1968 and 1969 exposed still other attitudes. The university insisted that any change to university policies should come only through "proper channels," and committees were the decision-making forum of choice. Indeed, starting in late 1968, a dizzying array of committees were formed to consider Black student demands and advance Black studies: an ad hoc committee of administrators, students, and faculty; subgroups of the ad hoc committee assigned to investigate specific issues; the Proctor Committee; the Kerckhoff Committee; and the Budd Committee. During this period, administrators and faculty remained convinced that they were acting in "good faith" in responding to Black student demands. For administrators and faculty, formation of these various committees and attendance at meetings were proof of their good faith. But for students, such actions only signified delay. With rare exceptions, administrators and faculty were unable or unwilling to respond to the profound urgency Black students were communicating.

Furthermore, during meetings in late 1967 and early 1968, university officials developed a pattern of blaming the *students* for the slow pace of progress on their demands. As activism reached a crescendo in late 1968 and 1969, this thinking morphed into the belief that the demands students presented were not real issues of legitimate concern but convenient means to provoke a confrontation. Black student activism was not considered to be a reaction to racial conditions at Duke but instead part of a national Black student conspiracy or a rite of passage. In this view, Duke students did not organize and plan the Allen Building takeover. Rather, Howard Fuller pulled their strings or Dick Gregory lit the fuse. As ignorance interacted with misperception, the view of Black students as "intruders" solidified. Once the occupation of the Allen Building was underway, it became far too easy for university officials to use force against students they readily saw as trespassers operating outside the bounds of the Duke University family.

The arrival of Black students at Duke was a first encounter between young people who had grown up in segregated communities and white trustees, administrators, faculty, and students who had rarely, if ever, interacted with a Black person other than across the "veil" created by Jim Crow. One can, perhaps, imagine a parallel universe where this encounter could have occurred unburdened by the racial dynamics that distorted how whites at Duke perceived, and responded to, the school's new Black students. In that universe, desegregation would have played out very differently. Faithful to the university's values—the union of knowledge and religion, a spirit of tolerance, and a dedication to service—whites would have embraced the new students without the ignorance, racial myths, and self-serving justifications that shaped desegregation. Such a world, however, required self-reflection, empathy, and a moral commitment to racial justice that those who ran Duke could not entertain. Creating this world of racial inclusion and diversity at Duke University would remain an ongoing project for decades to come.

Epilogue

Something Has to Change—2019, Fifty Years Later

―――――

More than fifty years have passed since the Allen Building takeover. Race remains a flash point for conflict in our national politics, at Duke, and throughout higher education.

The Black students who participated in the takeover—now around seventy years old—went on to lead lives of remarkable accomplishment and service. Janice Williams became a social worker, spending forty years focusing on children in foster care. Charles Becton was a judge on the North Carolina Court of Appeals, became a law professor, and was the first African American to serve as president of the North Carolina Bar Association. William Turner served as dean of Black affairs at Duke, directed the Black studies program, was a professor in the divinity school for decades, and served for many years as the pastor of Mt. Level Missionary Baptist Church in Durham. Joyce Hobson was a university professor and research director, serves as co-executive director of the Beloved Community Center in Greensboro, North Carolina, and is the director of the Jubilee Institute, a nonprofit focused on leadership development and training. Brenda Armstrong, the second Black woman in the United States to become a board-certified pediatric cardiologist, was a professor in the Department of Pediatrics at Duke until her death in 2018. As dean of admissions at the Duke University School of Medicine for more than twenty years, she recruited the most diverse classes in the school's history. Armstrong was a respected and beloved figure at Duke, and the Chapel was filled to overflowing for her 2018 memorial service, and flags across campus were lowered to half-staff.

Many former students see a cause-and-effect relationship between participation in the Allen Building takeover and the lives that unfolded for them. "Those Blacks who went [into the Allen Building] have almost twice as many advanced degrees as the white student body," Becton commented. Catherine LeBlanc recalled the day of the Allen Building takeover as one in which she was "bathed in the commitment [of] wanting to make a difference in my community." The takeover, she said, gave her "a very strong sense of purpose about my life and what I do." "It made a difference," Armstrong said. "Allen Building represented the turning point in all of our lives, I know it did in mine. . . . Allen Building showed us there was nothing we couldn't do. There was nothing that has matched it, and I'm sure there never will [be]."[1]

Although participation in campus activism caused conflict in the families of many of Duke's Black students, the passage of time puts these events in context. Far from representing a sudden break from the past, the bold actions these students took were a continuation of the struggle for Black education that had been ongoing since before emancipation. "It was almost like a mission," Armstrong reflected, "and we were the ones at the time—the right time—to carry it out." Often, it was parents who inspired protest. "We saw the world through our parents' eyes," she explained, and "the pain that they experienced . . . being segregated, but we also saw the hope. . . . Because they were willing to tell me their stories, I understood who I was supposed to be." Even as events were unfolding, Armstrong saw herself as part of a continuum of change. One older adviser told Armstrong and her fellow students, "There will be a time when people will . . . talk about you-all like you-all talked about us." She responded, "Well, I certainly hope so."[2]

The takeover also changed Duke. "The occupation of Allen Building was one of the most pivotal moments in our university's history," Duke president Vincent E. Price told participants on the fiftieth anniversary of the protest. "In your actions on our campus and the lives of purpose you have lived since, you have forever changed this place for the better and improved the lives of many who followed." "It was . . . a dramatic, cataclysmic . . . intervention," Armstrong reflected. "We helped Duke become the school it is today."[3]

After the resignation of Douglas Knight, Duke made an inspired choice for his replacement. Looking beyond the academy, it hired Terry Sanford, the progressive former governor of North Carolina, to be its sixth president. Sanford brought to campus stature, creativity, a willingness to take risks, and a deep commitment to the cause of racial justice. The head of the search committee accurately described Sanford's record as one of "integrity, honesty, vitality and verve." In Samuel DuBois Cook's words, Sanford was "a moral force" on racial matters. He set a new tone and direction almost instantly. In his first public appearance after being chosen president, Sanford commented that he was "certainly not against collective bargaining" and, in January 1972, Local 77 was recognized as the union representative for Duke's service employees. "He had his creds" as a graduate of UNC, Turner explained, "he had his creds from the governor's office, and he had his creds from his work with John Kennedy." In Turner's view, Sanford's background allowed him to give "permission slips" to the many at Duke who wanted the institution to move beyond the toxic conflicts over race and student activism that had ensnared his predecessor.[4] In Sanford, Duke finally found a leader able to unleash and harness the school's great potential.

Under Sanford's leadership, and that of the presidents who followed him, Duke has achieved a stature that even James B. Duke may never have dreamed of. For 2020, *U.S. News and World Report* ranked Duke tenth among national universities overall and eighth for providing the best value. The *Wall Street Journal* also ranked Duke tenth among national universities and tied for third in a measure of how much value a school adds to its students' future financial lives. *U.S. News and World Report* ranked Duke the best hospital in North Carolina, and ten adult specialties and nine children's specialties were nationally ranked. It also ranked the Duke School of Law tenth in the country, the School of Nursing second, and the School of Medicine thirteenth. And then, of course, there is the Duke men's basketball team, a source of great pride for the university, winning the coveted national championship five times between 1991 and 2019.[5]

Over time, one constant has been the university's deep financial resources. Initially entitled to a share of the $40 million Endowment James B. Duke created in 1924, Duke University now has an endowment valued in 2019 at $8.6 billion. On June 30, 2017, the university completed its most ambitious fundraising campaign ever, having raised $3.85 billion over the previous seven years. More than 315,000 donors participated. Admission to Duke is highly competitive. More than 41,000 applications were received for the Duke class of 2023, and 7.8 percent of applicants were accepted.[6]

Over the years, Duke has made significant investments in becoming more diverse and inclusive.[7] The school has an internationally recognized Department of African and African American Studies. In 1983, fourteen years following the Allen Building takeover, the Mary Lou Williams Center for Black Culture was opened.[8] The Black Student Alliance, one of a number of affinity groups for students of color, provides a cultural base for Black students at the university and a platform for continuing the struggle for solutions to the problems faced by Black students on campus. The Center for Multicultural Affairs supports community engagement, multicultural education, leadership development, and social justice education. Through a partnership between the Center for Documentary Studies at Duke and the SNCC Legacy Project, Duke has become a center for civil rights scholarship. The Samuel DuBois Cook Society recognizes, celebrates, and affirms the presence of African American students, faculty, and staff at Duke University. The society held its 2019 awards ceremony at Hope Valley Country Club.

The composition of Duke's student body reflects an institutional commitment to diversity. In the class of 2023, 55 percent of students are nonwhite, 12 percent are Black/African American, and 8 percent are first-generation college students. Admission is "need-blind." Applicants are accepted based on their merits, regardless of their ability to pay for college.[9] In part to foster communication and relationships among students of diverse backgrounds, all Duke freshmen live on East Campus.

The university has also taken important symbolic actions. Its main quad has been renamed Abele Quad, to recognize the contributions of Julian Abele, the African American architect of Duke University's original campus. The Sociology-Psychology Building on West Campus has been renamed the Wilhelmina Reuben-Cooke Building in honor of her many contributions to the university, including her role as one of the first five Black undergraduates. A statue of Confederate general Robert E. Lee was removed from the entrance to Duke University Chapel, a step taken to express the "abiding values" of the school. Most recently, the university announced that the Carr Building on East Campus will be renamed. Despite Julian Carr's philanthropic contributions to Trinity College, a committee determined that his "white supremacist actions . . . , even when considered in light of the time in which they were held, are inconsistent with the fundamental aspirations of this university."[10] Other steps are under consideration.

Still, even with these initiatives and investments, Duke has yet to create a campus culture of inclusion and racial justice. Indeed, parallels to the issues and conflicts of the 1960s abound.

The absence of interaction among students of diverse backgrounds is one issue. "I think if you did a dot map of color or socioeconomic status . . . and you looked at East Campus," 2019 graduate Trey Walk commented, "it would be super spread out in diversity." But after freshman year, students move to West Campus, where fraternities, sororities, and other selective living groups dominate. At that point, Walk—a Black student elected a "young" Duke trustee in 2019—observed, "enclaves of different groups" emerge. The amount of intergroup interaction drops significantly.[11] One professor who leads a DukeEngage project in South Africa continues to be surprised that Black and white student participants had never engaged in discussions of race until attending a program located thousands of miles from campus.

Student activists continue to press many of the same issues that were the focus of 1960s protest. The university's treatment of its nonacademic employees and contract workers remains a central concern. In 2016 Duke executive vice president Tallman Trask hit a contract parking worker with his car and allegedly used a racial slur as he drove off.[12] Workers were furious. Then Duke president Brodhead received a report from a former special events manager at Parking and Transportation Services describing a culture of "racism, harassment, retaliation and bullying" in the department. The same person reported "innumerable" incidents in which members of the special events department were called "n*****, coon, porch monkey, bull dagger and dyke while working Duke special events."[13]

On April 1, 2016, nine Duke students occupied the second floor of the Allen Building, demanding better treatment for Duke workers. Among the demands were that Duke commit to paying all its employees the current Durham living wage of $12.53 per hour and offer basic health care to these employees. On April 6, the university announced that it refused to negotiate with the protesters until they left the building. The sit-in ended after seven days. "Though we have disagreed about . . . their demands and their choice of means," President Brodhead said, "I respect their underlying passion for making Duke and the world a better place." In 2017, Duke raised the minimum wage for all employees to $13 per hour, with further increases to $14 in 2018 and then to $15 per hour by July 1, 2019—a 37 percent increase in Duke's minimum wage over four years.[14]

Student activists are convinced that the 2016 Allen Building takeover and other campus protests have forced the university to act on various issues, even if Duke administrators refuse to acknowledge that fact. "People always tell me, 'You'd get stuff done if you just went through the right channels,'" activist

Sydney Roberts commented. They say, "'That's not how you talk to people. You're just gonna make them angry.'" It is clear to Roberts, however, that only direct action gets the administration's full attention and prompts action. "It has always been calculated, collective disruption that has made the university realize, 'Oh, we have to actually pay attention to this,'" Roberts observed.[15]

Current activists see themselves as continuing work started during the 1960s. "At some point we came together," Roberts commented, "and we looked back and realized that a lot of concerns, grievances we had, were actually the demands from 1969 that have not been fulfilled."[16]

The hate and other racially charged incidents that occur at Duke are perhaps the most troubling echo of the 1960s. Such incidents are on the upswing on college campuses throughout the nation, and Duke has experienced numerous examples. In 2015 a noose was found hanging near the student center. Also in 2015, a death threat was made against gay freshman Jack Donahue when "Death to all fags @Jack" was scrawled on a wall in his dorm. In October 2015, a Black Lives Matter flyer posted in a Duke lecture hall was defaced with racial slurs.[17]

In November 2015, Duke convened a "community conversation" to discuss the racist and homophobic incidents. "I do not feel safe as a black female at Duke," Katrina Miller told President Brodhead and other administrators in attendance. "I shouldn't have to feel obligated to call my mother every night to tell her that I survived another day at Duke." "If everything had gone according to plan," a female Asian American student said through tears, "I would have been another suicide because I don't feel safe here. I don't feel that I belong here." "You have created a space for us to fear for our lives," one hundred students said in unison. "Duke, you are guilty."[18]

In 2017 NPR reported that African American students matriculating at Duke's divinity school felt that they have "entered a racial nightmare seemingly from another era." "One of my classmates . . . texted me and asked me to come to her class," Amber Burgin, president of the Black Seminarians Union, told NPR, "because a student was in her class saying, 'N***** like you come here and think that you can just change everything.'" Burgin told of white students using slurs like "jigaboo" and calling a Black classmate "ghetto." "I've had classmates who have left the program because they were tired of being treated in such a way," Burgin said.[19]

In 2018 the incidents continued. In January a Black student said she was passed by two men who said, "F*** you, n*****" to her. During the last week of the spring semester, two Snapchats made by a Duke student using a racial epithet were posted on the memes page and the racial epithet "n***** lover" was written on sophomore Cara Kim's door. Just after the Snapchat incident, Larry Moneta, vice president of student affairs, generated controversy when he tweeted that "freedom of expression protects the oppressed far more than the oppressors," urging that those who want to ban hate speech read "Free Speech on Campus," a book he found illuminating. "I think telling students who are asking you to do something about being targets of hate speech to 'go read a book' is intellectually dishonest and ethically irresponsible," Henry Washington, a former president of the Black Student Alliance, responded. After the racial epithet was posted on a student's door, Moneta commented, "I don't have a plan for a major initiative." Saying, "You want to be careful," he observed, "I think we need to just sit back and think about what is going on that a few people would feel like that was a good way to behave." Students were outraged. Junior Mumbi Kanyogo commented that the Duke administration is "more concerned with the mental gymnastics of avoiding responsibility for policy failure" than ensuring that Black students at the university are safe.[20]

In April students circulated a petition demanding that the university "create and enforce a standardized set of consequences for acts of hate and bias on campus." They collected almost seven hundred signatures before presenting the petition to the university administration. The hate speech "is just a reminder," Kim commented, "of the deep-rooted racism that still exists on this campus and through its students." "I just want to see my university be the leaders they are hoping to produce," Kim said. "A leader . . . doesn't just put out the fire, but stops it from even happening." A couple of weeks later, provost Sally Kornbluth and Richard Riddell, senior vice president and secretary to the board of trustees, told students that "when the fall semester begins, we will re-engage with interested students with the goal of further clarifying our hate and bias policies." "We fully understand the urgency of these issues," they said, "but also feel that careful consultation is imperative so that we, as a community, can understand the ramifications of any such policies."[21]

Before the spring semester was over, Moneta was again in the middle of controversy. A regular at the campus coffee shop Joe Van Gogh, Moneta visited the store on May 4, 2018. While inside, he heard the song "Get Paid," by Young Dolph, playing over the store's sound system. Hearing lyrics that included "n*****" and "f***," Moneta said he was "offended." He told the *Duke Chronicle* he found the lyrics "quite inappropriate for a working environment that serves children, among others." Moneta asked barista Britni Brown, who is Black, to turn off the music. She did so immediately. Apologizing profusely, Brown explained that the song had been streaming from a radio playlist on her phone. Because she kept the volume low so she could hear customers' orders, Brown did not know what song had been playing.[22]

The episode did not end there. After leaving the store, Moneta immediately called Robert Coffey, head of Duke dining services, to complain about the song he had heard in the coffee shop. Several days later, on May 8, Brown, and Kevin Simmons, a second barista working during Moneta's visit, were summoned to Joe Van Gogh corporate offices and were told that they could no longer work for the chain. "We had gotten a call from Robert Coffey of Duke saying that the VP of the university had come into the shop and that there was vulgar music playing," Joe Van Gogh's head of human resources, Amanda Wiley, explained. "Duke University has instructed us to terminate the employees that were working that day."[23]

Although Moneta told the *Duke Chronicle* that the decision to fire Brown and Simmons had been made by Joe Van Gogh, not Duke, protests soon followed. The incident, many believed, reflected callous indifference to the employment security of two Duke workers. Protesters also pointed to Moneta's earlier statements defending "free speech," even in the face of hate incidents. After protesters went to Moneta's office to express their concerns to him directly, he issued a statement that "if my actions in any way led to [the workers'] dismissal, I apologize and hope that the JVG management consider ways to reinstate their employment." Joe Van Gogh also apologized for its handling of the situation and offered to reinstate Brown and Simmons. Both declined the offer. On May 11, the owner of Joe Van Gogh announced that the company was severing ties with Duke "to preserve Joe Van Gogh's brand independence. . . . Joe Van Gogh has always been about bringing people together, not driving them apart," he said.[24]

In the fall, incidents of hate speech resumed. On August 25, 2018, the word *Nigger* was found scrawled over the word *Black* on a wall in the Mary Lou Williams Center for Black Culture. A mural celebrating Latinx Heritage Month was found defaced in September. In mid-October, a swastika was found carved into a stall in the bathroom of the Languages Building and, the day after Halloween, a pumpkin with a swastika carved into it was found on campus. In November 2018, a mural honoring the victims of the Tree of Life synagogue massacre in Pittsburgh was painted over by a swastika.[25]

Disturbing events continued in 2019. Duke garnered unfavorable worldwide attention after Megan Neely, the director of graduate studies in the Department of Biostatistics, sent an email warning Asian graduate students in the program not to speak Chinese in social settings with other students. The email was prompted by a report from two faculty members that they had heard two Chinese students speaking to each other in Chinese "VERY LOUDLY" in a student lounge. They criticized the students for "being so impolite as to have a conversation that not everyone on the floor could understand."[26]

Racial incidents now occur at Duke so frequently that some students have become numb to them. "It's in the water," Trey Walk said with resignation. "When they happen at this point, we're not surprised."[27]

Neely stepped down as the biostatistics chair not long after the incident. Duke leaders also issued a statement acknowledging the "exhausting and hurtful" events that had taken place at the university. "These events are not restricted to one school or group," they stated, but "they are widespread on our campus." As they had in the past, Duke leaders reiterated the university's commitment to inclusion. "We emphatically affirm our promise to value the identities, heritage, cultures, and languages of every individual at Duke," they said.[28]

After the incident, Nayoung Aimee Kwon, the director of Duke's Asian American studies program, issued a statement. Acknowledging that there is a "national and global uptick" in discriminatory incidents, she observed that Duke had experienced "more than our share." Four task forces had been formed in the wake of prior incidents, Kwon said, but their recommendations "are still to be circulated widely or implemented in visible ways, sometimes years after . . . the submission of their reports." "The ongoing problem of racism in our campus community has reached a boiling point," she warned. Kwon urged the university to "lead with a zero tolerance policy toward any forms of bias and discrimination." "Our students are watching us," she said, "and now the world is watching us, to step up and take action now."[29]

This returns us to the central question of this book: Is "inclusion" a core value of Duke University? Although Vincent Price, Duke's current president, has identified "inclusion" as one of five core values at Duke, fifty years after the Allen Building takeover, many think not. Even as a freshman, Walk witnessed hate incidents on campus that were not dealt with effectively—if at all. He saw how poorly laborers on campus—still primarily Black Durham residents— were treated. Walk also noted how few Black professors he had had while a Duke undergraduate. He concluded that "there was a commitment on paper and in words to [the idea of] inclusion," but that "Duke's money [and reputational] interests were at the forefront, beyond those things." Creating a culture of inclusion on campus was viewed by administrators, according to Walk, as "something that would be good to do" but was not "essential for Duke's identity." "Everybody has a gift," Armstrong observed, "and nobody's gift is better than anyone else's. But that culture of sharing and appreciating each other's gifts has not been achieved on the Duke campus." "Duke is not what it once was," Mark Anthony Neal, chair of the Department of African and African American Studies at Duke, commented, "but it certainly is not where it needs to be." "The truth is," Chandra Guinn commented in 2019, "the experience of black students at Duke is one that continues to need care."[30]

In May 2018, after the Joe Van Gogh incident, Price addressed the university's attempts to create a culture in which all members of the community felt safe and respected.

> When we learn a racial slur has been scrawled on a dorm door, a social media posting has used abhorrent language, anti-Semitic posters have been distributed in Durham, or workers on our campus have been treated unfairly, we feel angry, discouraged, and disappointed. Duke should be a place where these things don't happen. They are a painful reminder that we have more work to do to make our Duke community the dynamic, diverse and welcoming community of students, faculty, and staff we aspire it to be. . . .
> Something has to change.
> I will simply say that I am deeply sorry that we are not where we want to be as a university. . . . We must do better.[31]

Still, Price urged patience: "We cannot and will not succumb to a rush to judgment that demands instant retribution absent context and deliberation." Duke's problems of "basic decency, and our legacies of racism, intolerance and xenophobia, that continue to follow us, and indeed all of society . . . do not lend themselves to easy answers or quick fixes," the Duke president wrote. "But they will continue to plague us," he concluded, "unless we address them directly, honestly, in good faith, and with a healthy dose of courage."[32]

So the problem remains. Race is, and has always been, the core issue for Duke. Only after Duke's Black students forced the university to consider the implications of desegregation and the aftermath of Jim Crow could the institution achieve the national and international prominence to which it aspired. But true greatness will only become possible if the university is able to create the diverse and inclusive culture it seeks. To complete this project, Duke leaders will require self-reflection, empathy, and a moral commitment to racial justice that so many of their predecessors lacked. For now, whether Duke can become an institution that achieves its lofty aims remains an open question.

In June 2020, not long before this book was published, Duke's Black students, faculty, and staff spoke out about racism at the university during an all-day event, "Living while Black." Soon thereafter, Duke president Vincent Price committed the university to taking "transformative action now toward eliminating the systems of racism and inequality that have shaped the lived experiences of too many members of the Duke community." He acknowledged that members of the Duke community had "often not fully embraced" their mission of serving as "agents of progress in advancing racial equity and justice." Price outlined a series of bold and specific actions that would "resolutely turn [the university's] attention toward the mission of anti-racism."[33] Though these issues had confronted the university since the 1960s, both the tone and the substance of Price's words conveyed new urgency.

The work of antiracism, Price recognized, would depend on sustained effort and deep engagement by those not subject to racism "with humility, with humanity, and with honesty."[34] It would also require significant resources during a very challenging time for higher education. Is change really coming? Only time will tell.

NOTES

ABBREVIATIONS

AARC · Alumni Affairs Reference Collection, Duke University Archives, David M. Rubenstein Rare Book and Manuscript Library, Duke University, Durham, NC

ABTC · Allen Building Takeover Collection, Duke University Archives, David M. Rubenstein Rare Book and Manuscript Library, Duke University, Durham, NC

ABTOHC · Allen Building Takeover Oral History Collection, Duke University Archives, David M. Rubenstein Rare Book and Manuscript Library, Duke University, Durham, NC

ACK · Alan C. Kerckhoff

AHE · A. Hollis Edens

AHE Papers · A. Hollis Edens Papers, Duke University Archives, David M. Rubenstein Rare Book and Manuscript Library, Duke University, Durham, NC

BCB · Brenda C. Becton (Brenda C. Brown)

BEA · Brenda E. Armstrong

BoT Records · Board of Trustees Records, Duke University Archives, David M. Rubenstein Rare Book and Manuscript Library, Duke University, Durham, NC

BRH · Bertie R. Howard

CBH · Charles B. Huestis

CLB · Charles L. Becton

CWH · Charles W. "Chuck" Hopkins

DC · *Duke Chronicle*

DMH · David M. Henderson

DMK · Douglas M. Knight

DMK Records · Douglas M. Knight Records, Duke University Archives, David M. Rubenstein Rare Book and Manuscript Library, Duke University, Durham, NC

DUA · Duke University Archives, David M. Rubenstein Rare Book and Manuscript Library, Duke University, Durham, NC

DVC · Duke Vigil Collection, Duke University Archives, David M. Rubenstein Rare Book and Manuscript Library, Duke University, Durham, NC

JDH Records · J. Deryl Hart Records, Duke University Archives, David M. Rubenstein Rare Book and Manuscript Library, Duke University, Durham, NC

JW · Janice Williams

JWC · John W. Cell

MEH · Marcus E. Hobbs

OP Records · Office of the Provost Records, Duke University Archives, David M. Rubenstein Rare Book and Manuscript Library, Duke University, Durham, NC

RHP · Rufus H. Powell

RTC · R. Taylor Cole

SDC · Samuel DuBois Cook

SOHP Collection · Southern Oral History Program Collection, Southern Historical Collection, Wilson Library, University of North Carolina at Chapel Hill

VPSA Records · Vice President for Student Affairs Records, Duke University Archives, David M. Rubenstein Rare Book and Manuscript Library, Duke University, Durham, NC

WCT · William C. Turner Jr.

WJG · William J. Griffith

INTRODUCTION

1 Duke University, "50 Years of Black Students at Duke."

2 BEA, interview, December 17, 1978.

3 CWH, interview, January 19, 1979.

4 Although some sources quoted in this book use the words *desegregation* and *integration* interchangeably, they have very different meanings. Desegregation is a legal or political process eliminating laws, policies, and practices separating different racial and ethnic groups. Desegregation meant that HWCUs admitted Black students but simply tolerated their presence at these schools. By contrast, integration is a social process by which members of different racial and ethnic groups receive fair and equal treatment following desegregation. Establishing an inclusive environment is essential for integration.

5 The Black students at Duke were far from monolithic in their approach to protest. Generational differences existed between the desegregation "firsts" who matriculated in 1963 and those Black students who arrived in 1968, when the Black student movement at Duke and nationally was reaching its peak. Most Black students at Duke after 1967 became members of the Afro-American Society (AAS). But even within the AAS, sharp differences emerged around ideology and tactics. This book tells the story of those Black students who were politically active while at Duke and engaged in protest. Notwithstanding individual

differences, the narrative presents a composite picture drawn from numerous interviews and other sources.

6 *Bulletin of Duke University*, 8.

7 William Preston Few, "Trinity Becomes a University: Dr. Few Issues Statement to Students Urging Them to Be Worthy of Great Benefaction," *Trinity Chronicle*, January 7, 1925; *Annual Catalogue of Duke University: Constitution and By-Laws*, 47.

CHAPTER 1. A PLANTATION SYSTEM

1 James B. Duke, "Indenture and Deed of Trust of Personalty Establishing the Duke Endowment," December 11, 1924, in Durden, *Lasting Legacy to the Carolinas*, appendix 2; Kean, *Desegregating Private Higher Education in the South*, 36–37; Durden, *Launching of Duke University*, 496–501; Durden, *Lasting Legacy to the Carolinas*, 142–43.

2 Galen Griffin, "'Potentially Best' Freshmen to Face Academic Emphasis," DC, September 11, 1959; Knight, *Street of Dreams*, 100, 97.

3 Tindall, *Emergence of the New South*; Duke, "Indenture," article 7. Duke was sixty-seven when he executed the indenture.

4 Durden, *Launching of Duke University*, x. Including an additional $65 million transferred upon his death, Duke's gifts to the Endowment would, adjusted to present value, aggregate to more than $1 billion.

5 Porter, *Trinity and Duke*, 234.

6 Egerton, *Speak Now against the Day*, 26; Durden, *Bold Entrepreneur*, xiii; Duke, "Indenture," article 7; J. W. Cash quoted in the *American Mercury*, cited in Egerton, *Speak Now against the Day*, 234.

7 Duke, "Indenture," article 5; Porter, *Trinity and Duke*, 235–36; Durden, *Lasting Legacy to the Carolinas*, appendix 1; Knight, *Dancer and the Dance*, 128. The initial Endowment trustees included men who held or would hold one or more of the following positions with Duke Power Company: chairman, vice chairman, honorary chairman, director, president, vice president, secretary, treasurer, assistant secretary, executive committee, and chair of the finance committee. For the remaining initial trustees, Duke selected men with deep business experience outside the power industry. A speech at Duke in December 1930 by Norman Thomas, six-time presidential candidate for the Socialist Party of America, showed the potential for conflict between the Endowment and the university. Learning of the speech by Thomas, William R. Perkins, Endowment vice chair, asked William Preston Few, the Duke president, how the prominent socialist had been selected to speak on campus. Pointing out that a campus group—not the university—had invited Thomas to speak, Few wrote Perkins that "we must take a firm stand that it is the business of Duke University to hear both sides of

all questions that are fairly debatable." Perkins was not persuaded. Characterizing Thomas's socialist views as no more than a "germ" in the flow of ideas, Perkins asked Few, "Would not a proper pasteurization and filtration eliminate Norman Thomas and his ilk and their doctrines?" After a further exchange did not placate him, Perkins reminded Few that the Indenture gave the trustees of the Endowment the power to withhold funds from the university if not "operated in a manner calculated to achieve the results intended." For Perkins, it was the Endowment board that would have the final say on the most difficult issues of academic freedom on the Duke campus. Durden, *Launching of Duke University*, 50–52.

8 Maureen McCormick Harlow, "Duke University," Duke University Libraries, accessed August 15, 2017, https://library.duke.edu/rubenstein/collections/creators /corporations/dukeuniversity.

9 WJG, interview, January 16, 1979; Klopfer, interview, February 8, 1990.

10 "Report of the President to the Board of Trustees," June 6, 1959, Box 30, AHE Papers; Griffin, "'Potentially Best' Freshmen to Face Academic Emphasis"; RTC, "Annual Report of the Provost to the President," May 22, 1961, Box 3, R. Taylor Cole, JDH Records. During his Duke career, Jones also served as university chaplain and assistant professor in the Department of Religion.

11 "Report of the President to the Board of Trustees," June 6, 1959.

12 "Report of the President to the Board of Trustees," June 6, 1959.

13 *Brown v. Board of Education of Topeka*, 347 U.S. 483 (1954); "Board of Trustees Minutes," February 27, 1957, vol. 6, BoT Records.

14 Partner and Johnston, *Bull City Survivor*, 15; L. Brown, *Upbuilding Black Durham*, 11.

15 Litwack, *Trouble in Mind* (1975), 346; Rabinowitz, *Race Relations*, 187.

16 Litwack, *Trouble in Mind* (1999), 219; Smith, *In His Image*, 304; WCT, interview, April 17, 2017.

17 Litwack, *Trouble in Mind* (1999), 233; Flora Hatley Wadelington, "Assigned Places," NCpedia, January 1, 2004, http://www.ncpedia.org/history/20th -Century/segregation-1920s; Crow, Escott, and Hatley, *History of African Americans in North Carolina*, 177–83; Partner and Johnston, *Bull City Survivor*, 15–18, 20.

18 Crow, Escott, and Hatley, *History of African Americans in North Carolina*, 117–18; Kendi, *Stamped from the Beginning*, 273–74.

19 North Carolina Constitution, Article I, Section 27 (1868), Article IX, Section 2 (1868); Crow, Escott, and Hatley, *History of African Americans in North Carolina*, 123, 118. As an example, as late as 1938, a wage differential of 25 to 30 percent existed between Black and white teachers. Crow, Escott, and Hatley, *History of African Americans in North Carolina*, 136. Because the law required segregated schools, courts inevitably became involved in differentiating "white" students from "Black" students for purposes of making school assignments. In 1903 the

North Carolina legislature passed a law directing that "no child with negro blood . . . in its veins, *however remote the strain*, shall attend a school for the white race." Laws and Resolutions of North Carolina, N.C. Gen. Stat. C. 435, Section 22 (1903), emphasis added. According to Bruce Beezer, in one court case, a woman who was one-sixteenth Black had married a white man. Since their marriage did not violate North Carolina's miscegenation statute, the couple argued that their children—the "legitimate" product of a lawful union—should be permitted to attend a white school. The court rejected the couple's argument. "By no subtle alchemy known to the laboratory of logic," the court held, can a legal marriage "be claimed to have extracted the negro element from the blood in the veins of such offspring and made it pure." The court explained that "this construction clearly makes for the peace, harmony, and welfare of the two races." Otherwise, it concluded, "unpleasant antagonism would arise, which would prove fatal to school regulation and discipline." *Johnson v. Board of Education*, 166 N.C. 468 (1914), 471–72, cited in Batchelor, *Race and Education in North Carolina*, 14, citing Beezer, "North Carolina's Rationale."

20 Tumin, *Desegregation*, 34, 36, 37, 45; Kean, *Desegregating Private Higher Education in the South*, 144. In 1968 more than 75 percent of white residents in North Carolina agreed with the statement "whites work harder than Negroes." Sokol, *There Goes My Everything*, 98n70. Racist ideas have a long and deep history in the United States. See Kendi, *Stamped from the Beginning*.

21 Sokol, *There Goes My Everything*, 60, 61.

22 R. Irving Boone to AHE, September 21, 1951, AHE to R. Irving Boone, February 24, 1951, both in Box 33, Segregation Policy, AHE Papers. Since no Black students had ever attended or graduated from Duke, the school had no Black alumni.

23 John M. Dozier, "Employment Report by Race," unpublished data, April 8, 1964, Box 6, Civil Rights, DMK Records, 2; Leah Wise, "Stirring the Pot: Oliver Harvey's Narrative Account of the Struggle to Organize Duke University," 33–34, March 1980, Box 2, Student Papers Reference Collection, DUA. Duke's labor practices mirrored those at large industrial companies in North Carolina, including James B. Duke's American Tobacco Company. "Industrialists managed the labor market," historian Leslie Brown explained, "in ways that sorted whites and blacks hierarchically into skilled, semiskilled, and unskilled positions, creating an employment paradigm that favored whites over blacks and men over women." L. Brown, *Upbuilding Black Durham*, 44. A few Black workers in the dining hall and at the hospital held supervisory positions and had white subordinates. Jack J. Preiss, "Report on Racial Discrimination Policies on Campus," memorandum, May 1962, Box 11, Integration, JDH Records. One significant gap in the historical record of events at Duke in the 1960s relates to the university's nonacademic employees. These workers bore the brunt of Duke's Jim Crow

racial practices and were central actors in efforts to force Duke to confront its racial past. Oliver Harvey, a Duke janitor who became the leader of the movement to unionize Duke's nonacademic employees, is quoted extensively in this book thanks to the very good oral history of him prepared by graduate student Leah Wise. Other than Harvey, however, it has proven difficult to locate sources that capture the "voices" of rank-and-file nonacademic employees. This gap itself is evidence of the unchecked power the university had over the livelihoods of these men and women. Indeed, the authors of a 1959 article in the *Duke Chronicle* about the working conditions of Duke's maids found it "almost impossible to determine the maids' and janitors' opinions about their jobs [because] most of them were extremely reluctant to talk for fear of losing their jobs." John Strange and Scott Stevens, "Maids Sweep in Weekly Pay of $19.50," DC, March 6, 1959. Regrettably, oral histories conducted with key actors at Duke during the 1950s and 1960s focus on administrators, faculty, and students and not the nonacademic employees who worked tirelessly to support the efforts of these individuals.

24 Preiss, "Report on Racial Discrimination Policies."

25 Preiss, "Report on Racial Discrimination Policies"; Anlyan, *Metamorphoses*, 155–56.

26 Beach, interview, January 26, 1990. A very good discussion of the battle over desegregation in the Methodist Church is found in Murray, *Methodists and the Crucible of Race*; see also "Report of the Divinity School," n.d., Box 95, Integration 1965–1962, OP Records; James T. Cleland to Deryl Hart, November 25, 1960, Box 3, James T. Cleland, JDH Records; "Experts View Social Change, Religion," DC, April 10, 1964.

27 Preiss, "Report on Racial Discrimination Policies"; E. M. Cameron to RTC, "Golf Course Privileges," memorandum, September 8, 1964, Box 7, Integration, OP Records; Jacobs, *Across the Line*, 60. During the late 1950s, students in a designated section of the football stadium would hold up placards to form the Confederate flag. Duke University, "50 Years of Black Students at Duke."

28 Harry C. Boyte, "Suggestions from Duke CORE in Regard to Discrimination and Unfair Employment Practices at Duke University," n.d., Box 6, Civil Rights 1963–1967, DMK Records; William E. Forester to DMK, July 12, 1965, Mary Grace Wilson to Frank de Vyver, memorandum, October 18, 1967, both in Box 35, Fraternities and Sororities—Integration—1966, OP Records.

29 WJG, interview, January 16, 1979; Gay Weeks, "Administration Vetoes Plan to Integrate Play Audiences," DC, October 14, 1955.

30 Kean, *Desegregating Private Higher Education in the South*, 37, 38; "Honoring His Legacy."

31 W. B. to J. Deotis Roberts, March 31, 1960, Box 33, Segregation Policy, AHE Papers.

32 "Deed Duke University," n.d., Box 3, section 10a, James T. Cleland, JDH Records. In 1948 the Supreme Court declared such covenants unenforceable, ruling them a violation of the equal protection clause of the Fourteenth Amendment. Two years later, two white interns at Duke University Hospital asked the university to delete the restrictive covenant from their Duke Forest deed to satisfy lender nondiscrimination requirements. Edens refused. He insisted that Duke did not have "a legal or moral right to change the deeds on subsequent sales." AHE to E. C. Bryson, April 24, 1950, Box 7, Correspondence: Brown–Bs, AHE Papers.

33 "Statement—Duke University; Reimbursement for Membership Fee," n.d., Box 16, Hope Valley Country Club, DMK Records.

34 Quoted in Wise, "Stirring the Pot," 34, 36.

35 Wise, "Stirring the Pot," 37; "Maids Face Undesirable Conditions: All Work and No Pay," DC, April 12, 1963; Ludwig, "Closing In on the 'Plantation,'" 80.

36 "The Need for Impartial Arbitration of Labor Disputes at Duke University," September 1966, Box 1, Faculty and Student Groups, Labor Unions Reference Collection.

37 Pye, interview, March 2, 1985, ABTOHC; Wise, "Stirring the Pot," 34, 35; Strange and Stevens, "Maids Sweep in Weekly Pay"; Ludwig, "Closing In on the 'Plantation,'" 93n3; "Dozier Promises Wage Hike with Incentive Pay Scale," DC, May 19, 1965; "University Employees Get 5% Pay Increase," DC, January 7, 1966; McConville, "Oliver Harvey," 26; "Peonage at Duke," *Carolina Times*, March 21, 1959. At this time, colleges and universities were not legally required to meet the federal minimum wage standard.

38 Beach, interview, January 26, 1990; Klopfer, interview, February 8, 1990; Cushman, interview, February 28, 1990. Among the longest-serving trustees in 1957 were George Garland Allen (elected 1923), Donald Siler Elias (1929), Sidney Sherrill Alderman (1934), James Raymond Smith (1934), William Walter Peele (1921), Bunyan Snipes Womble (1915), and Robert Andrew Mayer (1897). *Bulletin of Duke University*, 19–20.

39 Chafe, *Civilities and Civil Rights*, 8, 7.

40 Bill Wells to AHE, February 17, 1953, AHE to Bill Wells, February 20, 1953, AHE to Helen Morrison, October 13, 1953, all in Box 33, Segregation Policy, AHE Papers; Chafe, *Civilities and Civil Rights*. A very good, detailed discussion of the process of desegregation at Duke is found in Kean, *Desegregating Private Higher Education in the South*.

41 "Divinity Student Body Petition," unpublished typescript, 1948, Box 33, Segregation Policy, AHE Papers; Cole, *Recollections*, 157.

42 Barney L. Jones to William E. King, September 29, 1975, Box 1, Reminiscences 1930–1960, Barney Lee Jones Papers; Cole, *Recollections*, 158.

43 Anne Corpening to Edwin L. Jones, December 6, 1956, Edwin L. Jones to Anne Corpening, December 20, 1956, both in Box 33, Segregation Policy, AHE Papers.

44 Roger Knapp, "Divinity Students Sign Admissions Petition," DC, February 22, 1957; James Cannon to AHE, February 7, 1957, "Board of Trustee Minutes," February 27, 1957, both in vol. 6, BoT Records.

45 "Board of Trustee Minutes," February 27, 1957, vol. 6, BoT Records; J. Bruce Eure to AHE, March 1, 1957, Edward J. Burns to AHE, March 4, 1957, both in Box 33, Segregation Policy, AHE Papers.

46 "Criticism Hits Student Group," newspaper clipping, n.d., P. H. Hanes to AHE, November 20, 1957, T. Conn Bryan to AHE, November 18, 1957, Sam B. Underwood to AHE, November 13, 1957, all in Box 58, Student Legislature, AHE Papers.

47 AHE to Board of Trustees of Duke University, "A Statement Concerning a Bill Introduced at the State Student Legislature Meeting Recently," memorandum, November 14, 1957, Box 58, Student Legislature, AHE Papers.

48 Cole, *Recollections*, 158; Barney L. Jones to William E. King, September 29, 1975, Box 1, Reminiscences 1930–1960, Barney Lee Jones Papers, DUA; Bob Windeler, "University to Continue Progress—Edens: President Gives Resignation, Committee to Nominate Successor," DC, February 2, 1960; Galen Griffin, "Board of Trustees Selects Hart as President Pro Tem," DC, April 22, 1960. Subsequently, Hart's "interim" status was removed.

49 "Barbaric Tradition," DC, December 13, 1955; Bob Windeler, "Senators Approve Integration Letter," DC, November 23, 1959; Scott Stevens, "Graduate, Divinity Petitions Gain No Admissions Change," DC, February 27, 1959; "Law School Bar Vote Urges Non-Racial Admissions Policies," DC, March 14, 1960; Annie Kohn, "Balance Trips Both Parties; Vote Favors No Racial Bias," DC, April 11, 1960; "Graduate Students Favor Integration of University," DC, May 11, 1960. Sixty-six percent of the graduate school's students and faculty supported the petition to eliminate Duke's racially restrictive admissions policy, and another 10 percent were found to have declined to sign for fear of reprisals. The vote by the law students was forty-nine in favor, thirteen opposed, and thirteen abstained. At least with respect to undergraduate men on West Campus, support for desegregation was far from unanimous. The *Duke Chronicle* reported that 56 percent of students on West Campus voted for admission of qualified students to the university regardless of race, either immediately or within three years. Statistics showed that almost all preregistered graduate students favored admittance of African Americans for graduate study (86.3 percent in favor; 9.6 percent opposed; 4.6 percent not responding).

50 Milligan, "Subsidizing Segregation"; RTC et al. to Board of Trustees, Duke University, "Some Considerations Regarding the Admission of Duly Qualified Negroes to the Graduate and Professional Schools of Duke University," memorandum, November 1960, Box 7, Desegregation, OP Records.

51 RTC et al. [Woodhall and MEH] to Board of Trustees, "Some Considerations." Woodhall ended by reassuring the trustees that "the Medical Center will never

admit unqualified students under any form of compulsion." The memo made clear that changing the graduate and professional school admissions policy "should not be considered an argument" for admitting Black students to the undergraduate school. "There are," the memo argued, "ample educational opportunities for Negro girls and boys in good undergraduate institutions in the state and area, as well as in many schools in other areas. For example, North Carolina College provides excellent undergraduate facilities, and there are a few Negro students enrolled as undergraduates at the three divisions of the University of North Carolina." Since Duke was not able to accommodate more than a fraction of qualified white undergraduates who already applied, the memo argued that "it would certainly appear unwise to accept responsibility for a new group of undergraduate students."

52 Knight, *Dancer and the Dance*, 127. Knight noted that "a strong minority of the Trustees had been opposed to [the] admission" of Black students.

53 Also in the fall of 1962, Reuben Lee Sparks became the first Black student to enroll in Duke Divinity School. He was classified as a "special student" because he had already received his divinity degree from another institution. "Black History at Duke."

54 The president of the Carnegie Foundation found the action "admirable" and representative of the "best of Southern leadership." John W. Gardner to Thomas L. Perkins, March 17, 1961, Box 11, Integration, JDH Records. The Rockefeller Foundation vice president was "truly impressed" and thought the action "clears the air a lot." Charles F. Cole to Thomas L. Perkins, March 15, 1961, Box 11, Integration, JDH Records. The president of the Ford Foundation was "glad to know" of the action. Henry T. Heald to Thomas L. Perkins, March 15, 1961, Box 11, Integration, JDH Records.

55 "Congratulations, Trustees," DC, March 10, 1961; A. T. Spaulding to J. Deryl Hart, June 4, 1962, Box 11, Integration, JDH Records.

56 Kean, *Desegregating Private Higher Education in the South*, 238; Bunyan S. Womble to C. B. Houck, March 8, 1961, Box 1, Board of Trustees 1960–64, Bunyan S. Womble Papers, DUA; Deryl Hart to Bunyan S. Womble, February 7, 1961, Box 33, Segregation Policy, AHE Papers; RTC, interview, March 1, 1990; Cushman, interview, February 28, 1990; Kotelanski, "Prolonged and Patient Efforts," 125. Kean rejected the view that private southern schools desegregated on their own accord, explaining that "the trustees of the private southern universities were committed to the belief that they had both the authority and the power to control their institutions. . . . Only when authority had been openly wrested from them could racial change come." Kean, *Desegregating Private Higher Education in the South*, 238.

57 RTC, interview, March 1, 1990; Barney L. Jones to William E. King, September 29, 1975, Box 1, Reminiscences 1930–1960, Barney Lee Jones Papers, DUA. Kean saw such a pragmatic decision-making process as typical of board

members at private southern universities more generally when considering a change in admissions policy. "The only arguments for desegregation [that trustees of southern private universities] would listen to," she wrote, "were those they saw as realistic or practical—that is, arguments that touched on the impact of segregation on *themselves*. Thus, moral arguments . . . fell on absolutely deaf ears." Kean, *Desegregating Private Higher Education in the South*, 236.

58 Bunyan S. Womble to Dean Boggs, June 13, 1961, Box 1, Board of Trustees 1960–64, Bunyan S. Womble Papers, DUA; "Chronicle Special Report," DC, April 12, 1963.

59 "Trustees Name President: Douglas Maitland Knight," DC, November 2, 1962.

60 Knight, *Dancer and the Dance*, iv.

61 Knight, *Dancer and the Dance*, v.

62 "President Douglas Knight Resigns from Lawrence: Ex-Yale Professor Accepts Duke University Presidency," *The Lawrentian*, November 2, 1962.

63 "President Douglas Knight Resigns from Lawrence."

64 DMK, interview, November 21, 1978; "President Douglas Knight Resigns from Lawrence"; Knight, *Dancer and the Dance*, 106.

65 "President Douglas Knight Resigns from Lawrence"; DMK, interview, November 21, 1978. In addition, the college student newspaper reported, Knight "doubled faculty salaries, created a substantial program of support for faculty research, and increased both the numbers and the scholarly preparation of the school's teaching staff." "President Douglas Knight Resigns from Lawrence."

66 Knight, *Dancer and the Dance*, 112; DMK, interview, November 21, 1978.

67 Knight, *Dancer and the Dance*, 120.

68 "Six Men Have Led University: From Minor to Major Stature," DC, November 2, 1962; Wright Tisdale, "To the Faculty of Duke University," memorandum, November 2, 1962, Box 16, Correspondence before Coming to Duke, DMK Records; "The Years Ahead," DC, November 2, 1962; RTC to J. Deryl Hart, memorandum, November 2, 1962, Box 3, R. Taylor Cole, JDH Records. Knight was the school's seventh president since the founding of Trinity College but only the fifth president since the creation of the Endowment and the transformation of Trinity College into Duke University.

69 Roger Marshall commented that Knight "would go to football games dressed the way he felt it appropriate to go to an Ivy League game." Marshall, interview, January 13, 1977.

70 Knight, *Dancer and the Dance*, 118; Knight, *Street of Dreams*, 97.

71 Marshall, interview, January 13, 1977; DMK, interview, November 21, 1978.

72 DMK, interview, April 16, 1979.

73 Knight, *Dancer and the Dance*, 121.

74 Marshall, interview, January 13, 1977.

75 Knight, *Street of Dreams*, 23, 18.

76 Knight, *Dancer and the Dance*, 107–8.

77 Knight, *Dancer and the Dance*, 109, 136, 119; wjg, interview, January 16, 1979. In his memoir, Knight repeated his observation that the presidencies of Lawrence and Duke were similar. "I had developed by the end of my Lawrence years a clear sense of duties and priorities," he explained. "Now I put them into play, as I discovered that—as Nathan Pusey said to me about the similarities between Lawrence and Harvard—the addition of a few zeroes in the financial statement had little to do with the essential jobs. Both places," Knight observed, "needed what I was within limits able to do; they had significant reputations which were not in fact borne out by their reality." Knight, *Dancer and the Dance*, 123.

78 Knight, *Dancer and the Dance*, 134–35.

79 Knight, *Dancer and the Dance*, 120.

80 Knight, *Street of Dreams*, 156.

81 jwc, interview, January 18, 1977; meh, interview, November 1979; Ashley, interview, August 29, 2018.

82 wjg, interview, January 16, 1979; Anlyan, *Metamorphoses*, 201.

83 dmk, "Founder's Day Address," dc, December 14, 1962; Frederick L. Schultz, "President Elect Knight: University Must Strive for Honor and Wisdom—Dr. Knight Stresses University's Role in Founder's Day Speech Last Night," dc, December 11, 1962.

CHAPTER 2. LIKE BARE SKIN AND PUTTING SALT ON IT

1 Jones, "How the 1968 Silent Vigil." Unless otherwise noted, students are referred to throughout with the name used during their Duke student tenure.

2 brh quoted in "Remembering the Vigil"; wct, interview, January 23, 1985, abtohc; clb, interview, April 19, 2017.

3 bea, interview, March 3, 2017.

4 jw and McBride in "Allen Building Takeover 50th"; wct quoted in Jones, "How the 1968 Silent Vigil."

5 J. D. Anderson, *Education of Blacks in the South*, 5 (incl. Washington quote); Litwack, *Been in the Storm So Long*, 474, 472. Black consciousness of, and commitment to, literate culture developed during slavery. See J. D. Anderson, *Education of Blacks in the South*, 16; see also Proctor, *Substance of Things Hoped For*, 1–12.

6 J. D. Anderson, *Education of Blacks in the South*, 9, 15.

7 Proctor, *Substance of Things Hoped For*, 11, 2, 17.

8 Armstrong, "Allen Building Takeover," 41–45; clb, interview, April 19, 2017; wct, interview, April 17, 2017. An excellent description and analysis of one such school, Caswell County Training School, Caswell County, North Carolina, is found in Walker, *Their Highest Potential*.

9   Forte, interview, February 10, 2005, SOHP Collection; Lucas, interview, April 15, 2005, SOHP Collection.

10 Forte, interview, February 10, 2005, SOHP Collection; Jacqueline Williams, interview, February 9, 2005, SOHP Collection.

11 Holt, interview, February 18, 2005, SOHP Collection; Lucas, interview, April 15, 2005, SOHP Collection.

12 Gaines, "Faces of Hope"; WCT, interview, April 17, 2017; JW, interview, February 13, 1985, ABTOHC.

13 Ernie Murray, "A Short History of Rocky Mount High School," Rocky Mount High School, accessed March 9, 2017, http://www.nrms.k12.nc.us/Page/982; Craig Kridel, "Secondary School Study: Booker T. Washington High School, Rocky Mount, NC," University of South Carolina Museum of Education, accessed March 10, 2017, http://www.museumofeducation.info/btw-rm.html; BEA, interview, March 3, 2017. According to Murray, Booker T. Washington High School was initially known as "the Negro School." By 1914 it had been officially named "Lincoln Graded School."

14 Kridel, "Secondary School Study"; Jamal Booker, "Dr. Tolokun Omokunde's Coca-Cola Moment with Dr. King," Coca-Cola Company, January 15, 2016, accessed March 10, 2017, http://www.coca-colacompany.com/stories/dr-tolokun-omokundes-coca-cola-moment-with-dr-king.

15 BEA, interview, March 3, 2017.

16 Kridel, "Secondary School Study"; Booker, "Dr. Tolokun Omokunde's Coca-Cola Moment."

17 Kridel, "Secondary School Study"; BEA, interview, March 3, 2017.

18 BEA, interview, March 3, 2017.

19 King, "'Facing the Challenge of a New Age,'" 7–8; BEA, interview, March 3, 2017.

20 Armstrong, "Allen Building Takeover," 41.

21 Armstrong, "Allen Building Takeover," 41; CLB, interview, April 19, 2017; RTC, "Report of the Provost to the President (For the Board of Trustees, June 1, 1963)," Box 36, Provost Annual Reports, DMK Records; Ainsworth and Williams, Legacy, 31, 33; BCB, interview, April 19, 2017; WCT, interview, April 17, 2017; BEA, interview, December 17, 1978.

22 WCT, interview, April 17, 2017; Hicks, "Talkin 'bout My Generation"; Cheraine Stanford, "Integrating Duke," DC, February 11, 2000; Armstrong, "Allen Building Takeover," 41–45. Duke's early Black students were celebrated in their communities. "Back home, we were celebrities," Turner recounted. "We were doing something new and revolutionary." Booher, "Duke Desegregates."

23 BEA, interview, December 17, 1978; WCT, interview, January 23, 1985, ABTOHC; April Dudash, "50 Years towards Equality," Durham Herald-Sun, October 5, 2013; Stanford, "Integrating Duke."

24 Ainsworth and Williams, *Legacy*, 32; Stanford, "Integrating Duke"; BCB, interview, April 19, 2017. William Griffith believed that Black students were given "special treatment" by students during the early years of desegregation. His impression is that they were "made to feel almost overly solicited, to feel welcome." WJG, interview, January 23, 1979. Interviews with the students indicate, however, that this "special treatment" was not present for every Black student in the first classes after desegregation and dissipated as the number of Black students increased.

25 WCT, interview, November 8, 1978; LeBlanc in "Allen Building Takeover 50th."

26 CWH, interview, January 19, 1979; BRH, interview, January 7, 1979; Newsome quoted in Saurav, "Allen Building Takeover"; BEA, interview, December 17, 1978.

27 BCB, interview, December 13, 1978; Jacobs, *Across the Line*, 67.

28 Gaines, "Faces of Hope"; WCT, interview, November 8, 1978; Dudash, "50 Years towards Equality."

29 CWH, interview, January 19, 1979; SDC, interview, March 1, 1985, ABTOHC.

30 BEA, interview, December 17, 1978; Ainsworth and Williams, *Legacy*, 36.

31 Armstrong, "Allen Building Takeover."

32 BRH, interview, January 7, 1979; BCB, interview, December 13, 1978, April 19, 2017; BEA, interview, December 17, 1978, March 3, 2017; Armstrong, "Allen Building Takeover," 42.

33 WCT, interview, November 8, 1978.

34 W. C. A. Bear to RTC, June 6, 1968, Box 3, Campus Security and Related Matters Sept. 1960–August 1968, OP Records.

35 CLB, interview, December 16, 1978, April 19, 2017; "Handwritten Notes of Disciplinary Hearing," working paper, March 19, 1969, Pickets and Protests Policy, ABTC.

36 Ainsworth and Williams, *Legacy*, 36; Gaines, "Faces of Hope"; WCT, interview, November 8, 1978.

37 BRH, interview, January 7, 1979; Jacobs, *Across the Line*, 67–68.

38 CWH, interview, January 19, 1979.

39 CWH, interview, January 19, 1979; WCT, interview, November 8, 1978.

40 WCT, interview, November 8, 1978.

41 WCT, interview, November 8, 1978; BEA, interview, December 17, 1978; BRH, interview, January 7, 1979. Chuck Hopkins also reported "a lot of fights" between Black students and the white fraternities that the football players were in. CWH, interview, January 19, 1979.

42 Armstrong, "Allen Building Takeover," 41; Ainsworth and Williams, *Legacy*, 35.

43 BEA, interview, December 17, 1978.

44 Armstrong, "Allen Building Takeover," 41; BEA, interview, December 17, 1978, March 3, 2017; DeMik, interview, February 12, 1985, ABTOHC; CWH, interview, January 19, 1979. Brenda Armstrong recalled "times when people would be

referring to something that had happened and they would refer to Black people as 'niggers' around us." BEA, interview, December 17, 1978. One white fraternity pledge remembered a fellow pledge insisting that he would sooner go thirsty than drink out of a cup after a "nigger." Statement by David Roberts in "Remembering the Vigil."

45 BEA, interview, December 17, 1978, March 3, 2017; CWH, interview, January 19, 1979.

46 BEA, interview, December 17, 1978.

47 Barney L. Jones to Bolon B. Turner, January 26, 1966, Mary Grace Wilson to Frank de Vyver, memorandum, October 18, 1967, both in Box 35, Fraternities and Sororities—Integration—1966, OP Records.

48 BEA, interview, December 17, 1978; BRH, interview, January 7, 1979.

49 WCT, interview, November 8, 1978, January 23, 1985, ABTOHC; MEH, interview, November 1979.

50 Alan Ray, "Class of '70 'Most Diverse' Ever," DC, September 17, 1966; CWH in "Allen Building Takeover 50th." These numbers overstate the number of Black undergraduates at Duke at any given point in time because a significant number of Black students at the university left before graduating due to academic, financial, or social considerations.

51 BCB, interview, December 13, 1978. Janice Williams remembered the small number of Black students in the context of social gatherings: "People who were interested in certain social functions could literally get together in one room. . . . You'd actually be surprised that a guy's [dorm] room . . . could actually accommodate all of us who wanted to party." JW, interview, February 13, 1985, ABTOHC; Gaines, "Faces of Hope"; WCT, interview, November 8, 1978.

52 JW, interview, February 13, 1985, ABTOHC; BEA, interview, December 17, 1978.

53 CWH, interview, January 19, 1979; WCT, interview, January 23, 1985, ABTOHC; BCB, interview, December 13, 1978.

54 BEA, interview, March 3, 2017.

55 WJG, interview, January 23, February 15, 1979.

56 Although Cole went on record in the spring of 1963 that Duke's decision to desegregate meant that Duke's new Black undergraduates could "expect to receive the same rights and privileges as all other students," he dismissed specific questions about university policies as "hypothetical." "An Integrated Duke," DC, April 30, 1963.

57 DMK, interview, November 21, 1978; WJG, interview, February 15, 1979. The arrival of Black students at Duke was treated without fanfare by the administration. The university archivist is unaware of any photos of the first five Black undergraduates moving into dorms or getting settled on campus.

58 Beach, interview, January 26, 1990; WJG, interview, January 23, February 15, 1979. Most Duke students were in the same position. "My guess," Becton com-

mented, "is 95 percent of [Duke students] had never seen a Black in any capacity other than working in their home or their parents' businesses." CLB, interview, February 20, 1994, SOHP Collection. North Carolina College was founded in 1910 as the National Religious and Training School and Chautauqua for the Colored Race. In 1925 the North Carolina legislature converted what was then the Durham State Normal School into the North Carolina College for Negroes, dedicating it to liberal arts education and the preparation of teachers and principals. Thus, NCC became the country's first state-supported liberal arts college for Black students. In 1947 the name was changed to North Carolina College at Durham. Finally, in 1969 North Carolina College at Durham was renamed North Carolina Central University. "History of the University," North Carolina Central University, accessed November 19, 2018, http://www.nccu.edu/discover/history.cfm.

59   W. L. Brinkley Jr. to RTC, memorandum, November 21, 1962, W. L. Brinkley Jr., memorandum, December 20, 1962, both in Box 3, W. L. Brinkley, JDH Records; WJG, interview, January 23, February 15, 1979; "First Report of the University Admissions Committee," June 12, 1962, Box 7, University Admissions Committee, JDH Records; BCB, interview, December 13, 1978. Tellingly, at the very same time university administrators were proceeding on the belief that Black students had no distinctive needs, consideration was being given to providing special support to another group that did not fit readily within Duke's prevailing culture—foreign students. In its first report in June 1962, the newly formed University Admissions Committee "strongly urge[d]" the appointment of a foreign student adviser who could "understand and sympathize with the problems of foreign students, who can treat [sic] with organizations that sponsor and support foreign student programs in this country, and who will have the moral and financial support necessary to work effectively with such students." "First Report of the University Admissions Committee."

60   WJG, interview, January 23, February 15, 1979; Cushman, interview, February 28, 1990.

61   Memo in provost's file; Richard L. Watson, interview, November 16, 1978.

62   WJG, interview, January 16, 1979; MEH, interview, November 1979.

63   WJG, interview, February 15, 1979; Knight, *Street of Dreams*, 134; DMK, interview, November 21, 1978.

64   Posting by Joyce Johnson to "A Tribute to Oliver Harvey: A Teacher of Public Work," DukeVigil68, March 16, 2018, https://groups.google.com/forum/#!topic /dukevigil68/NYth5xJS6oM; BEA, interview, March 3, 2017; WCT, April 17, 2017. "Many of our parents were maids and janitors," Becton described. "They had struggled hard to get us where we were." Sean Reilly, "Black Students during 1968," DC, April 4, 1988.

65   Greene, *Our Separate Ways*, 1. Booker T. Washington observed, "If blacks across the south would emulate blacks in Durham, they would be on their way to

prosperity and economic security." Quoted in Du Bois, "Upbuilding of Black Durham."

66 WCT, interview, January 23, 1985, ABTOHC.

67 Dudash, "50 Years towards Equality"; BRH, interview, January 7, 1979. Reverend Cousin also served on the faculty of the divinity school in 1967.

68 WCT, interview, January 23, 1985, ABTOHC; Eric Tullis, "C. B. Claiborne on Being Duke's First Black Basketball Player," *Indy Week*, February 13, 2013.

69 Robert R. Korstad and James L. Leloudis, *To Right These Wrongs*, 82.

70 Korstad and Leloudis, *To Right These Wrongs*, 115, 123. By the fall of 1965, Duke anticipated that as many as sixty of its students would be participating in the program either as summer interns or on a part-time basis during the academic year. Aline Mobley to DMK, June 15, 1965, Box 20, North Carolina Fund— Operation Breakthrough: 1963–1968, DMK Records.

71 Greene, *Our Separate Ways*, 119; Bermanzohn, *Through Survivors' Eyes*, 73. Born in Shreveport, Louisiana, Fuller moved to the Milwaukee housing projects at age six. He graduated from Carroll College in Waukesha, Wisconsin, in 1962, the only Black student at the college for three of his four years on campus. Fuller earned a master's degree in social work from Case Western Reserve University, where he joined the Congress of Racial Equality (CORE), working on voter registration drives, school boycotts, and other civil rights protests. Korstad and Leloudis, *To Right These Wrongs*, 179. In 1970, Fuller adopted the name *Owusu Sadaukai*. Although he has resumed use of the name *Howard Fuller*, he wrote in 2014 that "there are still people today who do not know me as Howard Fuller. To them, I remain Owusu, and the name continues to be meaningful and important to me." Fuller, *No Struggle, No Progress*, 112.

72 CWH in "Allen Building Takeover 50th."

73 Sokol, *There Goes My Everything*, 60–61; WCT, interview, April 17, 2017.

74 WCT, interview, April 17, 2017.

75 DMK, interview, November 21, 1978.

CHAPTER 3. RIGHTS, AS OPPOSED TO PRIVILEGES

1 "Remembering the Vigil"; LeBlanc in "Allen Building Takeover 50th."

2 BEA, interview, February 13, 1979; Newsome quoted in Saurav, "Allen Building Takeover"; WJG, interview, January 23, 1979.

3 CWH, interview, January 19, 1979.

4 CLB, interview, December 16, 1978.

5 Rogers [Kendi], *Black Campus Movement*, 92–101; BEA, interview, December 17, 1978.

6 E. Anderson, "White Space"; E. Anderson, "Black in White Space."

7 DMK, interview, April 16, 1979.

8 Marshall, interview, January 13, 1977.

9 "Our Story," Hope Valley Country Club, accessed December 7, 2019, http://www.hvcc.org/life; "Hope Valley," Preservation Durham, accessed October 17, 2019, http://preservationdurham.org/index.php/hope-valley/.

10 "Junior Celebration Is Postponed Again: Junior Social Planned for March 27 Fails to Materialize," DC, March 28, 1928; "Horseback Riding May Be Co-Eds Hobby Soon," DC, September 26, 1928; "Kappa Kappa Gamma Banquet," DC, October 28, 1934; "Delta Delta Delta Installation This Week," DC, November 4, 1931; "Strongest Duke Golf Squad Will Start Campaign," DC, March 16, 1932; "Schedule of Events at Commencement," DC, June 1962.

11 Constitution and By-Laws, article 7, Box 16, Hope Valley Country Club, DMK Records; BEA, interview, March 3, 2017.

12 DMK to T. S. White Jr., December 2, 1963, Box 16, Hope Valley Country Club, DMK Records; "Statement—Duke University," February 5, 1964, Box 16, Hope Valley Country Club, DMK Records.

13 A report concerning racial segregation at Duke prepared by sociology professor Jack Preiss in 1962 did not mention the issue. Jack J. Preiss, "Report on Racial Discrimination Policies on Campus," May 1962, Box 11, Integration, JDH Records.

14 Jacobs, Across the Line, 58, 55; "University Selects A. B. Duke Scholars," DC, April 9, 1965. At the time, athletic scholarships were not available to Black athletes. Eric Tullis, "C. B. Claiborne on Being Duke's First Black Basketball Player," Indy Week, February 13, 2013.

15 Hope Valley Country Club Yearbook, 3; Tullis, "C. B. Claiborne"; CLB, interview, April 19, 2017.

16 Bill Prindle, "Nurses Encounter Segregation at Club," DC, November 3, 1966; "Discrimination," DC, October 1, 1966.

17 "Administrative Appointments Head List of Staff Changes," DC, September 22, 1966; SDC, interview, March 1, 1985, ABTOHC.

18 Dick Shaffer, "Ku Klux Klan Storm Troops Bludgeon Student at Rally," DC, October 4, 1966.

19 Nelson Ford, "Frats Must Ban Bias Clauses," DC, October 1, 1966; Frank T. de Vyver to DMK, memorandum, June 7, 1966, Box 35, Fraternities and Sororities—Integration: 1964–1965, OP Records.

20 Prindle, "Nurses Encounter Segregation"; "Discrimination."

21 Prindle, "Nurses Encounter Segregation"; "NSGA Council's Referendum Set on Hanes Dance," DC, November 10, 1966; "Nurses Vote against Dance at Hope Valley," DC, November 12, 1966. The resolution that the 1966 dance should not be held at Hope Valley passed 162–32 and the resolution that the nurses would not schedule another social event at a segregated facility passed 179–17.

22 Stef McLeod, "The Half-Student," DC, November 15, 1966.

23 "Here We Go Again," DC, November 15, 1966.

24 DMK, interview, November 21, 1978.

25 Al Featherston, "Bill Werber: Duke's Oldest Living Sports Hero," *Blue Devil Weekly*, June 19, 2008; William M. Werber to Howard Snethen, January 18, 1966, Box 26, Werber: 1965–1967, DMK Records.

26 Roger L. Marshall to William M. Werber, January 27, 1966, Box 26, Werber: 1965–1967, DMK Records. After Duke trustee Merrimon Cuninggim read Marshall's response to Werber, he wrote Knight to express his unhappiness. "He sounds as if he secretly agrees with Werber," Cuninggim wrote, "and if that is in fact the case, then I *am* disturbed." Merrimon Cuninggim to DMK, March 25, 1965, Box 26, Werber: 1965–1967, DMK Records.

27 "University Caucus: Consideration and Reform in Four Areas of Concern," DC, October 18, 1966; Tupp Blackwell, "Students Picket Hope Valley CC," DC, December 1, 1966.

28 Janis Johnson, "WSGA Takes Anti-Segregation Stand," DC, December 1, 1966.

29 Roger Marshall, "Alumni Policy?," DC, December 1, 1966.

30 "Confrontation," DC, December 1, 1966.

31 "200 Picket Alumni at Segregated Meet," DC, December 3, 1966. The *Duke Chronicle* was likewise optimistic. "By . . . bringing the [use of a segregated facility by an alumni group] to the attention of the larger Duke community and the public, similar situations may be avoided here and in other places in the future." "Alumni Policy?," DC, December 3, 1966.

32 "308-A," DC, February 2, 1967; Bob Ashley, "Approved List Not Mandatory Dean Maintains," DC, January 12, 1967. Cox did add a notation to the list that the five segregated facilities were "disapproved by students."

33 DMK, interview, April 16, 1979.

34 DMK to RTC et al., November 17, 1966, Box 6, Civil Rights: 1968–1969, DMK Records.

35 W. G. Anlyan to DMK, November 18, 1966, DMK to W. G. Anlyan, November 23, 1966, Box 6, Civil Rights: 1968–1969, DMK Records. Restrictive policies at the two clubs, Anlyan explained, "related primarily to Negroes," and he noted that Hope Valley had "four non-Christian members."

36 RHP to DMK, "Segregation Practices, Private Clubs," November 17, 1966, Box 6, Civil Rights: 1968–1969, DMK Records.

37 "First Degree?," DC, February 4, 1967; Doug Adams, letter, November 16, 1966, Box 6, Civil Rights: 1968–1969, DMK Records.

38 University Caucus Resolution, n.d., Box 6, Civil Rights: 1968–1969, DMK Records.

39 DMK to Doug Adams, November 22, 1966, Box 6, Civil Rights: 1968–1969, DMK Records.

40 Christian W. Dame and Sandra N. Forrester to DMK, November 28, 1966, Box 6, Civil Rights: 1968–1969, DMK Records.

41 DMK, letter, n.d., Box 6, Civil Rights: 1968–1969, DMK Records.

42 Jordan Grant, "May Day: America's Traditional, Radical, Complicated Holiday, Part 1," Smithsonian Museum of American History, April 29, 2016, https://americanhistory.si.edu/blog/may-day-americas-traditional-radical-complicated-holiday-part-1; Farnham, *Education of the Southern Belle*, 169.

43 "Trinity College Co-Eds Remarkably Successful in Presenting Spring Carnival, May Day Revels, and Initial Home Talent Dramatic Performance: Martha Wiggins Crowned Queen of May in Beautiful Fairy Festivities," *Trinity Chronicle*, May 11, 1921.

44 "May Queen and Court Announced," DC, February 28, 1967; Mary Grace Wilson, memorandum, March 28, 1967, Box 23, May Queen, DMK Records; "Negro Named May Queen at Duke," Associated Press, 1967, newspaper clipping, Box 23, May Queen, DMK Records.

45 Randolph C. Harrison Jr. to DMK, March 4, 1967, Box 23, May Queen, DMK Records. Duke provost R. Taylor Cole reported to a trustee that "the members of the University Policy and Planning Committee (which includes the 7 members of the University Academic Council, the elected representative body of the faculty) had, with one exception, not received a single critical comment about the selection of Miss Reuben." RTC to C. B. Houck, March 31, 1967, Box 23, May Queen, DMK Records.

46 Jonathan C. Kinney, interview, September 12, 2017, Arlington, VA; "A Duke Alumnus," letter, n.d., "Lifelong Resident of Wilmington North Carolina," letter, March 21, 1967, both in Box 23, May Queen, DMK Records.

47 C. B. Houck to DMK, March 15, 1967, George M. Ivey to DMK, March 14, 1967, both in Box 23, May Queen, DMK Records.

48 Knight, *Street of Dreams*, 99–100; Knight, *Dancer and the Dance*, 127.

49 Knight, *Street of Dreams*, 99–100; Knight, interview, April 16, 1979.

50 WCT, interview, January 23, 1985, ABTOHC; JW, interview, February 13, 1985, ABTOHC; BEA, interview, December 17, 1978.

51 Alan Ray, "Class of '70 'Most Diverse' Ever," DC, September 17, 1966; Armstrong, "Allen Building Takeover," 42. The total number of Black students at Duke in the fall of 1966 was approximately eighty-five, including students in the graduate and professional schools and those enrolled in paramedical training. Richard Lovejoy Tuthill, "Enrollment Data—Race," unpublished typescript, October 15, 1967, Box 6, Civil Rights Compliance Reports: 1967–1968, DMK Records. The total number of Black students at Duke during the early years of desegregation, including students in the graduate and professional schools and those enrolled in paramedical training, were approximately nineteen (1963–64), thirty-one (1964–65), fifty-five (1965–66), and eighty-five (1966–67). Joseph B. Martin, "To Accompany Compli-

ance Reports for Duke University under Title VI of the Civil Rights Act of 1964," n.d., Box 6, Civil Rights Compliance Reports: 1967–1968, DMK Records. As a general matter, it is not possible to confirm precisely how many Black undergraduates were enrolled at Duke at any specific point in time. This is because, among other factors, admissions records that specify the number of Black undergraduates enrolled at the start of each year are not available, and attrition during the course of the academic year reduced the total number of Black students present at the start of the year. In any event, it is clear that the number of Black undergraduates at Duke, and Black students generally, began to accelerate beginning in the fall semester of 1966. This is consistent with national trends. Historian Joy Ann Williamson noted that "African American college student enrollment doubled between 1964 and 1970, with the greatest proportion of the increase noted at historically white institutions." Williamson, *Black Power on Campus*, 26.

52 Chafe, *Unfinished Journey*, 305.

53 Rogers [Kendi], *Black Campus Movement*, 78; Carmichael quoted in Van Deburg, *New Day in Babylon*, 32; Chafe, *Unfinished Journey*, 304. Carmichael changed his name to Kwame Ture in 1969 when he left the United States to take up permanent residence in Conakry, Guinea. He is referred to herein as "Stokely Carmichael" because that was the name he used at the time of his appearance on the Duke campus.

54 Ture and Hamilton, *Black Power*, 44; Chafe, *Unfinished Journey*, 306; Van Deburg, *New Day in Babylon*, 19.

55 CWH, interview, January 19, 1979.

56 Greg Perett, "Fuller Calls for 'Poor Power' Movement," DC, September 29, 1966; CWH, interview, January 19, 1979.

57 Rogers [Kendi], *Black Campus Movement*, 78; Hatcher quoted from "Audio Tape of Introduction of Stokely Carmichael and Stokely Carmichael Speech," April 1967, Box 8, Student Major Speaker: Mr. Stokely Carmichael, Radio TV Services Records, DUA.

58 Carmichael quoted from "Audio Tape of Introduction of Stokely Carmichael and Stokely Carmichael Speech." The text of Carmichael's address was an article, "Toward Black Liberation," that he had published in the *Massachusetts Quarterly*. Reprinted as Carmichael, "Toward Black Liberation." See also Marty Lloyd, "Stokely Defends Black Power," DC, March 18, 1967.

59 Carmichael quoted from "Audio Tape of Introduction of Stokely Carmichael and Stokely Carmichael Speech."

60 Carmichael quoted from "Audio Tape of Introduction of Stokely Carmichael and Stokely Carmichael Speech."

61 BEA, interview, December 17, 1978; Rogers [Kendi], *Black Campus Movement*, 79.

62 CLB, interview, December 16, 1978, April 19, 2017; CLB, interview, February 20, 1994, SOHP Collection; CWH, interview, January 19, 1979.

63 BEA, interview, December 17, 1978; CLB, interview, December 16, 1978.

64 CLB, interview, December 16, 1978; BCB, interview, December 13, 1978;
Exum, *Paradoxes of Protest*, 42; Williamson, *Black Power on Campus*, 28; BEA,
interview, December 17, 1978.

65 CLB, interview, December 16, 1978; CWH, interview, January 19, 1979.

66 BEA, interview, December 17, 1978; JW, interview, February 13, 1985, ABTOHC.

67 BEA, interview, December 17, 1978; CLB, interview, December 16, 1978.

68 BEA, interview, February 13, 1979; CWH, interview, January 19, 1979.

69 "Picket Planned at Hope Valley," DC, April 8, 1967; Grady Frank, "SAE Not Racist, Chose 'Nice' Site," DC, April 8, 1967; "Hope Valley Revisited," DC, April 6,
1967.

70 "Hope Valley Roster," DC, April 8, 1967.

71 BCB, interview, December 13, 1978; BEA, interview, December 17, 1978.

72 CWH, interview, January 19, 1979.

73 "Open Letter from Negro Students," DC, April 25, 1967.

74 "Open Letter from Negro Students."

75 BEA, interview, December 17, 1978.

76 DMK, interview, April 16, 1979.

77 Knight, *Dancer and the Dance*, 126; "Illness Strikes Knight, Cox," DC, September 15, 1967.

78 "Over 1200 Freshmen, Selected for Diversity, Arrive Today," DC, September 15,
1967; BCB, interview, December 13, 1978; BRH, interview, January 7, 1979. The
total number of Black students at Duke in the fall of 1967 was 177, including 8
students in the graduate and professional schools and 85 enrolled in paramedical training. Tuthill, "Enrollment Data—Race."

79 BEA, interview, December 17, 1978.

80 CWH, interview, January 19, 1979; BCB, interview, December 13, 1978; BEA, interview, December 17, 1978.

81 BCB, interview, December 13, 1978; BRH, interview, January 7, 1979.

82 BEA, interview, December 17, 1978. Armstrong also remembered the pride
Duke's Black students felt using a means of communication named for one
that their ancestors had developed. "In the homeland, drums were used for
communication between communities," she explained. "They had their own language and we had our own language as well—it was wonderful." BEA, interview,
March 3, 2017.

83 BEA, interview, December 17, 1978.

84 BEA, interview, December 17, 1978.

85 Goodwyn, *Populist Moment*, xviii. Goodwyn described "the sequential process
of democratic movement-building" as having four stages: "(1) the creation of
an autonomous institution where new interpretations can materialize that run
counter to those of prevailing authority . . . ; (2) the creation of a tactical means

to attract masses of people . . . ; (3) the achievement of a heretofore culturally unsanctioned level of social analysis . . . ; and (4) the creation of an institutional means whereby the new ideas, shared now by the rank-and-file of the mass movement, can be expressed in an autonomous political way."

86 Dee Dee Stokes, "Society to Boost Negro's Position," DC, September 29, 1967.

87 "Segregated Quarters Dropped from University's List for Students," DC, September 20, 1967. In the case of discrimination in off-campus housing, the policy change occurred just as the university was preparing to submit a "Compliance Report of Institutions of Higher Education" to the U.S. Department of Health, Education, and Welfare. The Compliance Report required the university to indicate, among other matters, whether "Negro and/or 'Other' students" are free to participate in "all campus housing, including dormitories," on a non-segregated basis. Under applicable regulations, without the policy change, the university would have been forced to answer 'no' to that question." Joe Martin to Gerhard C. Henricksen, "Compliance with the Civil Rights Act and 'Off-Campus Housing Listed by the University,'" September 19, 1967, Box 6, Civil Rights Compliance Reports: 1967–1968, DMK Records.

88 Bob Entman, "ASDU Prohibits the Use of Segregated Facilities," DC, October 18, 1967. ASDU had initially considered the segregated facilities issue in the spring of 1967. In May, Hopkins proposed a resolution condemning "the usage by University organizations" of segregated facilities and prohibiting such use by nonselective campus-wide organizations. As drafted, the resolution contained no enforcement mechanism. Although the ASDU legislature adopted the resolution overwhelmingly, Kinney, the ASDU president, objected. He asked the legislature to reconsider its action because the resolution failed to prohibit the use of segregated facilities by fraternities and sororities and other "private, selective, non-campus-wide organizations." Kinney wanted the legislature to prohibit the use of segregated facilities by these groups as well. Bob Ashley, "ASDU Votes Scholarship, Kinney Raps Racial Motion," DC, May 11, 1967.

89 Entman, "ASDU Prohibits the Use of Segregated Facilities."

90 David Pace, "MSGA Opposes ASDU Ban on Use of Segregated Facilities," DC, October 20, 1967; "WSGA Cabinet Supports ASDU in Segregated Facilities Statute," DC, October 25, 1967.

91 Jack Jackson, "IFC Votes against Banning Use of Segregated Facilities," DC, November 10, 1967; "Freshman Council against ASDU Bill," DC, October 25, 1967; "Sigma Nu Condemns ASDU Resolution, Passes Own Segregation Ban," DC, October 27, 1967. By November 10, six fraternities had voted individually to ban the use of segregated facilities for off-campus events. Jackson, "IFC Votes."

92 Cletis Pride, "Press Release on Study-In," November 13, 1967, Box 6, Civil Rights: 1968–1969, DMK Records; RHP to Frank Ashmore et al., "Memorandum on Administrative Council Meeting," October 31, 1967, Box 7, Administrative Council: 1967–1969, DMK Records; Robert Switzer, "Using Segregated Facilities Violates Civil Rights Bill," DC, October 25, 1967.

93 "Negroes Boycott Ban Referendum," DC, November 3, 1967; "Students Vote 60% against Segregation Statute," DC, November 8, 1967.

94 "Students Vote." The vote was 1,300 against the ASDU resolution and 884 in favor. "Students Vote."

95 CLB, interview, December 16, 1978.

96 CLB, interview, December 16, 1978.

97 BEA, interview, December 17, 1978; CLB, interview, December 16, 1978; BCB, interview, December 13, 1978. "Like African Americans in the larger community," Williamson noted, "Black students were not a monolithic group in any sense, including their ideas on the proper tactics and goals of Black liberation." Williamson, *Black Power on Campus*, 46.

98 BEA, interview, December 17, 1978.

99 CWH et al., "Black Students' Resolution," November 10, 1967, DMK Records; CWH, interview, January 19, 1979.

100 DMK to CWH et al., November 12, 1967, Box 6, Civil Rights: 1968–1969, DMK Records.

101 DMK, interview, April 16, 1979.

102 "Afro-Americans Hold Sit-In by Knight's Office: SFAC Acts on Segregated Facilities in Response to Protest," DC, November 13, 1967; BRH, interview, January 7, 1979; BCB, interview, December 13, 1978; study-in photographs, November 13, 1967, Box 54, Convocation 1964 to Demonstrations 1990s, University Archives Photographs Collection. The *Duke Chronicle* cited "reliable sources" that said that the Duke president spent the day at his nearby lake house. "Afro-Americans Hold Sit-In."

103 WJG, interview, January 23, 1979; Steve Johnston, "SFAC Calls on President to Extend Facilities Ban," DC, November 13, 1967.

104 CLB, interview, December 16, 1978; CWH, interview, January 19, 1979; Preiss, interview, February 5, 1977. Duke student Sally Avery recalled an off-campus meeting in late 1967 at which Howard Fuller "was talking black power, which he said meant 'No whites allowed.'" Moments later, Avery was expelled from the meeting. Bermanzohn, *Through Survivors' Eyes*, 73.

105 "Audio of Afro-American Study-In," November 13, 1967, Box 12, Radio TV Services Records, DUA.

106 "Audio of Afro-American Study-In."

107 "Afro-Americans Hold Sit-In."

108 "Audio of Afro-American Study-In."

109 "Audio of Afro-American Study-In"; Pride, "Press Release on Study-In."

110 "Afro-Americans Hold Sit-In"; "Student-Faculty-Administration Committee," November 13, 1967, Box 6, Civil Rights: 1968–1969, DMK Records.

111 Pride, "Press Release on Study-In"; "Defeat of Sit-In," *High Point Enterprise*, November 14, 1967; "Dr. Knight, Not Protesting Group, Still President of His University," *Daily Times-News*, November 18, 1967; Edwin L. Jones, letter, November 14, 1967, Box 20, Negro Sit-In, DMK Records.

112 Steve Johnston, "Knight Bans Use of Segregated Facilities by Student Groups," DC, November 17, 1967.

113 "Duke Resolves Its Conflict with Negro Students," November 17, 1967, DMK to Roger Marshall et al., November 21, 1967, both in Box 6, Civil Rights: 1968–1969, DMK Records.

114 Richard Smurthwaite, "Statement Satisfies Afro-Americans," DC, November 20, 1967; CLB, interview, December 16, 1978; BEA, interview, December 17, 1978.

115 Edwin L. Jones to DMK, November 20, 1967, George V. Allen to Edwin L. Jones, January 2, 1968, Eugene C. Few Jr. to DMK, November 15, 1967, Leonidas Hebrin Jr. to DMK, November 14, 1967, Theodore D. Pimper to DMK, November 19, 1967, all in Box 20, Negro Sit-In, DMK Records.

116 DMK to Mrs. James T. Hedrick, November 21, 1967, DMK to Leonidas Herbin Jr., December 1, 1967, DMK to Theodore D. Pimper, December 1, 1967, all in Box 20, Negro Sit-In, DMK Records.

117 DMK, interview, April 16, 1979.

118 DMK, interview, April 16, 1979.

119 DMK, interview, April 16, 1979; statement by DMK in "Remembering the Vigil."

120 Anlyan, *Metamorphoses*, 201; Ashley, interview, August 29, 2018.

121 DMK to George M. Ivey, February 23, 1966, Box 23, Student—Controversial Speakers: 1966–1969, DMK Records; Knight, *Street of Dreams*, 109.

122 Dan Berger, "Trapped by History: A Serene Knight Makes Peace with the Dark Days of '68," DC, April 4, 1988.

123 BCB, interview, December 13, 1978.

124 DMK, interview, April 16, 1979.

125 DMK to WJG, November 21, 1967, Box 6, Civil Rights: 1968–1969, DMK Records.

CHAPTER 4. WE WERE THEIR SONS AND DAUGHTERS

1 DMK to WJG, November 21, 1967, Box 6, Civil Rights 1968–1969, DMK Records; Frank L. Ashmore, "Draft History of Afro-American Relations Prior to February 13, 1969," March 7, 1969, Box 5, Campus Unrest: 1969, DMK Records; WJG, interview, January 16, 1979.

2 "Texts of New Regulations: Pickets and Protests," DC, January 8, 1968.

3 Carter, "Duke University," 514; William Johnson, "Timid Generation," 75; Dyke Stokely, "Friendly Protesters 'Sit-In' beside Army Recruiters Office on Tuesday," DC, January 10, 1968; "Student Blocks Door, Withdraws for Navy," DC, January 12, 1968; Bob Ashley, "Anti-Dow Demonstrations Today Spread to Allen Building Offices," DC, February 5, 1968; Jim McCullough, "Protest Time Limits Cut," DC, March 1, 1968. "Many students at Duke," William Johnson observed, "seem to be plodding patiently along, doggedly heading for some impenetrable post-college cubbyhole. . . . They seem to have put a low ceiling on their ideals, to have leaped into weary adulthood at a discouragingly early age. They seem unalterably sensible and strangely self-protective." William Johnson, "Timid Generation," 75.

4 BEA, interview, February 13, 1979.

5 CWH, interview, January 19, 1979; BEA, interview, February 13, 1979.

6 Rogers [Kendi], Black Campus Movement, 94. The nine police officers who were tried for the massacre were acquitted by an all-white jury. The only person ever convicted in connection with the Orangeburg Massacre was Cleveland Sellers, a civil rights activist who had been shot in the back. Biondi, Black Revolution on Campus, 32–33.

7 "If [the black campus movement] received a nudge from the Orangeburg Massacre," Kendi wrote, "then it received a shove from the murder of Dr. Martin Luther King." Rogers [Kendi], Black Campus Movement, 94. "King's death stirred a lot of people up," William Turner recalled. WCT, interview, November 8, 1978. Chuck Hopkins had a similar perspective. In his view, King's death was "one of the most significant politicizing [events]" for Duke's Black students. Sean Reilly, "Black Students during 1968," DC, April 4, 1988.

8 Chafe, Unfinished Journey, 351.

9 BEA, interview, December 17, 1978.

10 Bob Babcock, "The Duke Vigil: Some Student Views," 3, 1968, Box 1, Personal Narratives, DVC; BRH, interview, January 7, 1979. These comments were reported by a white student in the class.

11 BEA, interview, December 17, 1978, December 5, 2017; Reilly, "Black Students during 1968."

12 DMK quoted in "Remembering the Vigil"; Peter Applebome, "A Transformation? Well at Least a Change or Two!," DC, April 11, 1968; Knight, Street of Dreams, 121; WJG, interview, January 20, 1977. The university received reports, according to one account, "of the organization of vigilante groups among segments of the white community." Frank L. Ashmore, "A Crisis in Conscience," 4, April 24, 1968, Box 1, Official University Statements, DVC.

13 DMH and Boger quoted in "Remembering the Vigil"; Cheryl Fuller, "Letters to the Editor," Duke University Alumni Magazine, August 1998, https://alumni.duke

.edu/magazine/articles/duke-university-alumni-magazine-155; DMH, "A Journal of the Duke Vigil," 2, May 1960, Box 1, DVC. In 1977, as part of work at Duke on a history honor's thesis on the Silent Vigil, I distributed surveys to randomly selected alumni who had been at Duke during the Silent Vigil. Most respondents returned completed surveys anonymously. The surveys, each of which have been assigned a number, are in the author's possession and are referred to herein as Alumni Survey.

14 "Typewritten Chronology with Notes," n.d., Box 35, John H. Strange, DVC; DMH, interview, January 14, 1977.

15 DMH, "Journal of the Duke Vigil," 1; "Flyer for Memorial Vigil," Box 1, April 5, 1968, DVC.

16 DMH, "Journal of the Duke Vigil," 1–4.

17 DMH, interview, January 14, 1977; WJG, interview, January 20, 1977.

18 WJG, interview, January 20, 1977; DMH, "Journal of the Duke Vigil," 4.

19 DMH, "Journal of the Duke Vigil," 5; Harry Boyte, Cynthia Ganung, and David L. Singer, "Open Letter to the University Community," DC, October 1, 1966; "Students Rally for Arbitration," DC, April 20, 1967; DMH, interview, January 14, 1977.

20 The steps were (1) urge the president of the United States to push for congressional action to implement the recommendations of the President's Commission on Civil Disorder, (2) urge senators and congressmen to pass open housing legislation, and (3) call on city officials, insisting they show greater concern for grievances and problems of the Black community. "WDBS Tapes of the Duke Vigil, 1968 April 5–1968 April 10," tape 1, Box 5, Audio Tapes: 1956–1973, WDBS Collection, DUA.

21 DMH, "Journal of the Duke Vigil," 5.

22 Tupp Blackwell, "Pan-Hel President Resigns after Second Look at System," DC, September 22, 1967.

23 "Flyer for Memorial Procession for Dr. Martin Luther King," April 5, 1968, Box 1, Handouts, Flyers, etc.—Folder 1, DVC.

24 DMH, "Journal of the Duke Vigil," 5–9; DMH, interview, January 14, 1977; Bob Ashley, "400 Students Continue Sit-Ins, Pledge to Remain on Quad until Labor, Race Demands Met: Protest Leaves Knight's House as Tired President Isolated," DC, April 8, 1968; DMH quoted in "Remembering the Vigil."

25 "Typewritten Chronology with Notes."

26 DMH, interview, January 14, 1977; Small quoted in "Remembering the Vigil."

27 BRH, interview, January 7, 1979.

28 DMH, "Journal of the Duke Vigil," 6; WJG, interview, January 20, 1977; Knight, *Street of Dreams*, 122; Peter Neumann, "Letters to the Editor," *Duke University Alumni Magazine*, August 1998, https://alumni.duke.edu/magazine/articles

/duke-university-alumni-magazine-155; Bermanzohn, *Through Survivors'*
Eyes, 83. Bermanzohn wrote that 200 students were sitting in Knight's living
room, but the more accurate number is approximately 250. In addition, several
faculty members were present during some or all of the protest at University
House.

29 Knight, *Street of Dreams*, 122; DMK, interview, November 21, 1978.

30 Bermanzohn, *Through Survivors' Eyes*, 83; Boger quoted in "Remembering the
Vigil."

31 "Typewritten Chronology with Notes"; DMH, "Journal of the Duke Vigil," 6–7;
Knight, *Street of Dreams*, 123.

32 DMH, "Journal of the Duke Vigil," 6–7.

33 Burke, interview, February 6, 1977.

34 Boger quoted in "Remembering the Vigil"; Jeff Van Pelt, "Letter to Durham
Friends and Ad Hoc VROC," April 18, 1988, Box 13–16, A 91–96, Vigil, VPSA Records; DMH, "Journal of the Duke Vigil," 15.

35 BEA, interview, December 17, 1978.

36 Ashley, "400 Students"; "WDBS Tapes of the Duke Vigil," tape 6.

37 "Typewritten Chronology with Notes."

38 "Typewritten Chronology with Notes"; DMK quoted in "Remembering the
Vigil."

39 Doug Adams, letter, November 16, 1966, Box 6, Civil Rights 1968–1969, DMK
Records; "WDBS Tapes of the Duke Vigil," tape 8; "Typewritten Chronology with
Notes" (emphasis added).

40 "Typewritten Chronology with Notes."

41 "WDBS Tapes of the Duke Vigil," tape 8; Dan Berger, "Trapped by History: A
Serene Knight Makes Peace with the Dark Days of '68," DC, April 4, 1988.

42 DMH, "Journal of the Duke Vigil," appendix 3; Ashley, "400 Students."

43 DMH, "Journal of the Duke Vigil," appendix 3.

44 DMH, "Journal of the Duke Vigil," 15; "Typewritten Chronology with Notes";
DMK, interview, November 21, 1978.

45 "WDBS Tapes of the Duke Vigil," tape 18; Van Pelt, "Letter to Durham Friends";
"Typewritten Chronology with Notes."

46 "WDBS Tapes of the Duke Vigil," tape 6. Although Knight would later characterize the protesters as his "guests," R. Taylor Cole, university provost, observed in a
narrative written after the vigil that the president's invitation to stay "came only
after the students had refused to leave." RTC, "Pages on the Vigil," n.d., 134, Box
13–16, A 91–96, Vigil, VPSA Records.

47 "Typewritten Chronology with Notes." Henderson described the widespread
concern about violating dorm parietal hours as an example of "the political
inconsistencies that were rampant throughout the whole [protest]." DMH, interview, January 14, 1977.

48 DMH, "Journal of the Duke Vigil," 7; Knight, *Street of Dreams*, 125; Berman-zohn, *Through Survivors' Eyes*, 83; Ashley, interview, August 29, 2018. Strange did not participate directly in negotiations until the next morning.

49 Small, interview, April 12, 2018.

50 "The Vigil, 1968," tape 1, Box 2–3, Sound Recordings: 1968, DVC; Burke, interview, February 6, 1977; DMH, "Journal of the Duke Vigil," 19; Alumni Survey 23. An unidentified Duke student took a tape recorder to many of the events of the Silent Vigil and recorded what was said. He then rerecorded the tapes, adding his own comments to more fully describe the occupation of University House and the Silent Vigil.

51 BEA, interview, December 5, 2017; BRH, interview, January 7, 1979.

52 WJG, interview, January 20, 1977; Berger, "Trapped by History."

53 Kathleen Sullivan, "The Timid Generation: Administrators Faced Rebellion from Students," DC, April 4, 1988.

54 DMH, "Journal of the Duke Vigil," 11.

55 RTC, "Pages on the Vigil," 134–35.

56 RTC, "Pages on the Vigil," 135. The four options under consideration were, according to Ashmore: "(1) remove the Knight family to an undisclosed location, and bring in enough police to protect the property; (2) if the group was orderly, and the Knights were not uncomfortable, let them remain in the hope that an understanding could be reached on the issues being raised; (3) move police to all entryways to the house, permit those who wished to exit to do so, but allow no additional people to enter; and (4) remove first the Knights, and then everyone else in the house, using whatever force might be required." Ashmore, "Crisis in Conscience," 10.

57 Small quoted in "Remembering the Vigil"; Knight, *Street of Dreams*, 119.

58 Knight, *Street of Dreams*, 123; DMK, "Speech to Memorial Service—April 6, 1968," Box 1, Addresses and Speakers, DVC.

59 DMK, "Speech to Memorial Service—April 6, 1968," Box 1, Addresses and Speakers, DVC.

60 DMH, "Journal of the Duke Vigil," 14; Knight, *Street of Dreams*, 125.

61 DMK, interview, November 21, 1978; DMK quoted in "Remembering the Vigil"; RTC, "Pages on the Vigil," 135.

62 WJG, interview, January 20, February 5, 1977.

63 WJG, interview, February 5, 1977.

64 WJG, interview, January 20, 1977; RTC, "Pages on the Vigil," 140.

65 RTC, "Pages on the Vigil," 134–35.

66 WJG, interview, January 20, 1977; Ashmore, "Crisis in Conscience," 10; Kinney, interview, September 12, 2017.

67 DMH, "Journal of the Duke Vigil," 15.

68 DMH, "Journal of the Duke Vigil," 16; DMH, interview, January 14, 1977.

69 DMH, "Journal of the Duke Vigil," 13

70 WJG, interview, January 20, 1977; WJG quoted in "Remembering the Vigil"; DMH, "Journal of the Duke Vigil," 13.

71 DMH, "Journal of the Duke Vigil," 16; Babcock, "Duke Vigil," 1.

72 "WDBS Tapes of the Duke Vigil," tapes 2, 11.

73 "WDBS Tapes of the Duke Vigil," tapes 1, 2; Gillian Bruce, "Pressures of 1968 Hit Home in Durham: Curfew Failed to Quell Disturbances after King's Death," DC, April 4, 1988; Ashmore, "Crisis in Conscience," 17.

74 "WDBS Tapes of the Duke Vigil," tape 2.

75 "WDBS Tapes of the Duke Vigil," tape 10.

76 DMH, "Journal of the Duke Vigil," 19, 17; BRH, interview, January 7, 1979. On Saturday night, Henderson reported, Howard commented on the "party atmosphere" and "lack of discipline" in University House. DMH, "Journal of the Duke Vigil," 17.

77 BRH quoted in "Remembering the Vigil"; BRH, interview, January 7, 1979.

78 DMH, interview, January 14, 1977; DMH, "Journal of the Duke Vigil," 16.

79 Leah Wise, "Stirring the Pot: Oliver Harvey's Narrative Account of the Struggle to Organize Duke University," 104–5, March 1980, Box 2, Student Papers Reference Collection, DUA.

80 DMH, "Journal of the Duke Vigil," 18.

CHAPTER 5. HOPE TAKES ITS LAST STAND

1 "Interim Report to the Academic Council by the Committee on Non-Academic Employees," n.d., reprinted in DMH, "A Journal of the Duke Vigil," 169–85, May 1968, Box 1, DVC.

2 Flyers for April 7, 1968, rally, Box 1, Handouts—Flyers 1, DVC.

3 "WDBS Tapes of the Duke Vigil, 1968 April 5–1968 April 10," tape 12, Box 5, Audio Tapes: 1956–1973, WDBS Collection, DUA.

4 DMH, interview, January 14, 1977; Small quoted in "Remembering the Vigil." The inclusion of a "political rally" in the definition of a "demonstration" meant that the percentage of vigil participants engaging in a *protest* demonstration for the first time would be higher than 77 percent. "Statistics on Vigil Participants," n.d., Box 13–16, A 91–96, Vigil, VPSA Records.

5 "WDBS Tapes of the Duke Vigil," tape 2.

6 "WDBS Tapes of the Duke Vigil," tape 2.

7 "WDBS Tapes of the Duke Vigil," tape 11; Durden, *Lasting Legacy to the Carolinas*, 253; RTC, "Pages on the Vigil," n.d., 134; Ashmore, "Crisis in Conscience," 20.

8   "WDBS Tapes of the Duke Vigil," tape 3; DMH, "Journal of the Duke Vigil," 19; "Police Say Duke Vigil No Trouble," DC, April 10, 1968.

9   WJG, interview, January 20, 1977; CBH quoted in "Remembering the Vigil."

10 BRH quoted in "Remembering the Vigil."

11 "WDBS Tapes of the Duke Vigil," tape 3; "Ground Rules for Those Participating in the Vigil," April 8, 1968, Box 1, Monday, April 8, 1968, DVC.

12 "WDBS Tapes of the Duke Vigil," tape 8; "Police Say Duke Vigil No Trouble"; Traver, interview, December 7, 1978.

13 "The Vigil, 1968," tape 3, Box 2–3, Sound Recordings: 1968, DVC; BRH quoted in "Remembering the Vigil"; Kornberg and Smith, "It Ain't Over Yet."

14 "WDBS Tapes of the Duke Vigil," tape 9; Strange and Small quoted in "Remembering the Vigil"; WJG, interview, January 20, 1977.

15 "WDBS Tapes of the Duke Vigil," tape 9. Vigil leaders recalled the cleanup crew to the quad on Monday afternoon.

16 Bunny Small, Jon Kinney, and John Strange to DMK and Grace Knight, April 8, 1968, Box 1, Monday, April 8, 1968, DVC.

17 "WDBS Tapes of the Duke Vigil," tape 4.

18 Kinney, interview, September 12, 2017.

19 DMH, "Journal of the Duke Vigil," 19–20; Simons, interview, February 1, 1977.

20 "Statistics on Vigil Participants"; "WDBS Tapes of the Duke Vigil," tape 8; BEA, interview, December 5, 2017.

21 DMH, "Journal of the Duke Vigil," 22; Bob Ashley, "President Unavailable for Days Yet," DC, April 10, 1968.

22 "Operation Employees Demand Higher Wages," DC, April 10, 1968; flyer for strike meeting, April 8, 1968, Box 1, Monday, April 8, 1968, DVC; Small, interview, April 12, 2018. This decision took remarkable courage. Striking workers would have little money coming in during a strike. As "at will" employees, they could be terminated by the university at any time. Once fired, the employees might well be blacklisted from any future employment in Durham. By going out on strike, the workers put their already precarious financial circumstances in even greater peril.

23 Flyer for class boycott, April 8, 1968, Harold W. Lewis to Members of the Teaching Staff, memorandum, April 8, 1968, both in Box 1, Monday, April 8, 1968, DVC.

24 Mary Schuette, "Tapp Indispensable to Food Committee," DC, April 12, 1968; BRH quoted in "Remembering the Vigil."

25 Hans J. Hillerbrand, "Resolution of Divinity School Faculty," April 8, 1968, Box 1, Folder 5, DVC. Duke administrators rejected the suggestion as impractical.

26 DMH, "Journal of the Duke Vigil," 23; SDC quoted in "Remembering the Vigil."

27 Alumni Surveys 65, 101; Simons, interview, February 1, 1977.

28 Jeff Van Pelt, "Letter to Durham Friends and Ad Hoc VROC," 1, April 18, 1988, Box 13–16, A 91–96, Vigil, VPSA Records.

29 JWC, interview, January 18, 1977; SDC quoted in "Remembering the Vigil"; Huck Gutman, interview, April 13, 2018; Alumni Survey 3.

30 Student Letters to RTC, April 8, 1968, Box 1, Vigil, OP Records

31 Banks Arendell to DMK, April 12, 1968, Robert R. Fountain to DMK, April 10, 1968, W. Edwin Magee to DMK, April 17, 1968, Walter H. Schmitt and Gloria Flatemeyer Schmitt to DMK, April 9, 1968, all in Box 10, Vigil Letters, DMK Records; Marshall, interview, January 13, 1977.

32 Alumni Survey 100; Edgar quoted in "Remembering the Vigil."

33 CBH quoted in "Remembering the Vigil"; RTC, "Pages on the Vigil," 140, n.d., Box 13–16, A 91–96, Vigil, VPSA Records.

34 CBH quoted in "Remembering the Vigil"; CBH, interview, February 9, 1977.

35 WJG, interview, January 20, 1977; CBH, interview, February 9, 1977.

36 "WDBS Tapes of the Duke Vigil," tape 16.

37 "Operation Employees Demand Higher Wages"; "Class Boycott Is Effective," DC, April 11, 1968.

38 DMH, "Journal of the Duke Vigil," 27; "WDBS Tapes of the Duke Vigil," tape 16.

39 Robert F. Kennedy, telegram, April 9, 1968, "Compilation of Statements of Support for Vigil," April 9, 1968, both in Box 1, Statements of Support, DVC. Strange spoke about interviews he had taped with both the Associated Press and United Press International and of his recent contact with representatives of *Newsweek*. He also told them that radio station WPIX in New York was preparing a taped special on the protest, promising to "play it to the hilt." "Nationwide Coverage of Vigil Expands," DC, April 10, 1968.

40 "WDBS Tapes of the Duke Vigil," tape 4; Leah Wise, "Stirring the Pot: Oliver Harvey's Narrative Account of the Struggle to Organize Duke University," 103, March 1980, Box 2, Student Papers Reference Collection, DUA.

41 CLB, interview, December 16, 1978; Sean Reilly, "Black Students during 1968," DC, April 4, 1988; David Pace, "Vigil Ignites Hope for Blacks—Racial Cooperation May Occur: Some Doubt White Means, Commitment," DC, April 29, 1968.

42 Reilly, "Black Students during 1968"; Pace, "Vigil Ignites Hope for Blacks"; WJG, interview, January 23, 1979.

43 Reilly, "Black Students during 1968"; BCB, interview, December 13, 1978; Wise, "Stirring the Pot," 104–5.

44 Wise, "Stirring the Pot," 104–5; Bob Babcock, "The Duke Vigil: Some Student Views," 3, 1968, Box 1, Personal Narratives, DVC. These comments were reported by a white student in the class.

45 Pace, "Vigil Ignites Hope for Blacks"; DMH, "Journal of the Duke Vigil," 29.

46 BEA, interview, December 17, 1978.

47 RTC, "Pages on the Vigil," 140; WJG, interview, January 20, 1977.

48 "Operation Employees Demand Higher Wages."

49 "Typewritten Chronology with Notes," n.d., Box 35, John H. Strange, DVC; DMH, "Journal of the Duke Vigil," 27.

50 DMH, "Journal of the Duke Vigil," 28.

51 "WDBS Tapes of the Duke Vigil," tape 8.

52 "Operation Employees Demand Higher Wages."

53 WJG, interview, January 20, 1977.

54 DMH, "Journal of the Duke Vigil," 31; BRH quoted in "Remembering the Vigil."

55 SDC, "Speech to Vigil April 10, 1968," Box 1, Wednesday, April 10, 1968, DVC.

56 SDC, "Speech to Vigil April 10, 1968," Box 1, Wednesday, April 10, 1968, DVC.

57 DMH, "Journal of the Duke Vigil," 31.

58 CBH quoted in "Remembering the Vigil"; WJG, interview, February 5, 1977.

59 Wright Tisdale, "Speech to Vigil—April 10, 1968," Box 1, Wednesday, April 10, 1968, DVC.

60 CBH quoted in "Remembering the Vigil"; Wise, "Stirring the Pot," 104; Jeremy Hewes, "Chairman Tisdale Tells It Like It Is," DC, May 15, 1968.

61 DMH, "Journal of the Duke Vigil," 29.

62 "The Vigil, 1968," tape 4.

63 Semans quoted in "Remembering the Vigil"; WJG, interview, February 5, 1977; Hewes, "Chairman Tisdale."

64 DMH, "Journal of the Duke Vigil," 33; Kinney quoted in "Remembering the Vigil"; Richard Smurthwaite, "Vigil Needed Change in Tactics as Chaos Threatened Wednesday," DC, April 12, 1968.

65 George W. Williams, "Academic Council: Minutes of the Called Meeting April 10, 1968," Box 1, Wednesday, April 10, 1968, DVC; Richard Smurthwaite, "Four-Day Silent Vigil Ends; Tacit Accord Reached by Protestors," DC, April 11, 1968.

66 DMH, interview, February 9, 1977.

67 Smurthwaite, "Four-Day Silent Vigil Ends."

68 Smurthwaite, "Four-Day Silent Vigil Ends"; "Vigilance Now," DC, April 11, 1968.

69 Pace, "Vigil Ignites Hope for Blacks"; Carolyn Arnold, "Dining Hall Strike Goes into 3rd Day," DC, April 11, 1968.

70 WJG, interview, January 20, 1977; Roberts quoted in "Remembering the Vigil"; DMH, "Journal of the Duke Vigil," 34; Smurthwaite, "Four-Day Silent Vigil Ends."

71 Smurthwaite, "Four-Day Silent Vigil Ends."

72 Pat Black, "Knight in Hospital: Cole Takes Duties," DC, April 12, 1968.

73 "The New University," DC, April 12, 1968; John Buettner-Janusch, "Diary of Vigil Events," n.d., reprinted in DMH, "Journal of the Duke Vigil," 116; Smurthwaite, "Vigil Needed Change in Tactics."

74 DMH, "Journal of the Duke Vigil," 34; Carolyn Arnold and Gloria Guth, "Boycott Enters Second Week; 75% Effective," DC, April 15, 1968.

75 John Strange and DMH, "Statement," April 15, 1968, reprinted in DMH, "Journal of the Duke Vigil," 93–95. While the minutes of the April 15 board meeting are sparse, they indicate that Cole and other administrators recommended that "the Board not make an unequivocal statement at this time on collective bargaining." "Board of Trustees Minutes," April 15, 1968, vol. 12, BoT Records.

76 Cliff Feingold, "Students Call Board's Proposal 'Disappointing,'" DC, April 17, 1968. The statement acknowledged that the "concessions . . . reflect a change in attitude of most trustees." "Board of Trustees Minutes," April 15, 1968, vol. 12, BoT Records.

77 "Trustees' Study Unit to Meet Tomorrow," DC, April 19, 1968; Klopfer, "Duke."

78 Feingold, "Students Call Board's Proposal 'Disappointing.'"

79 Steven Evans, "Seeger Appears at Vigil Rally; Dr. Blackburn Reports on Faculty," DC, April 19, 1968; "WDBS Tapes of the Duke Vigil," tape 4.

80 Wise, "Stirring the Pot," 107.

81 Wise, "Stirring the Pot," 107–8.

82 Tom Dwiggins, "Sunday Vigil Receives Trustee's Statement," DC, April 22, 1968; DMH, interview, February 9, 1977; Gutman, interview, April 13, 2018.

83 Henry E. Rauch to Board of Trustees, memorandum, April 22, 1968, Box 16, Labor Relations 1967–1969, DMK Records

84 Henry E. Rauch to Board of Trustees, memorandum, April 22, 1968, Box 16, Labor Relations 1967–1969, DMK Records; Kathleen Sullivan, "The Timid Generation: Administrators Faced Rebellion from Students," DC, April 4, 1988.

85 RTC, "Pages on the Vigil," 138; Special Trustee-Administrative Committee, "Statement of Special Committee," April 20, 1968, Henry E. Rauch to Board of Trustees, memorandum, April 22, 1968, both in Box 16, Labor Relations 1967–1969, DMK Records.

86 DMH, "Journal of the Duke Vigil," 42; "The Vigil, 1968," tape 4; Strategy Committee, "April 20, 1968 Statement," reproduced in DMH, "Journal of the Duke Vigil," 106.

87 Dwiggins, "Sunday Vigil."

88 "WDBS Tapes of the Duke Vigil," tapes 5, 4.

89 DMH, "Journal of the Duke Vigil," 43.

90 Henry E. Rauch to Board of Trustees, memorandum, April 22, 1968, Box 16, Labor Relations 1967–1969, DMK Records.

91 Carolyn Arnold, "Workers Return to Work Today; Call 3 Weeks Moratorium on Strike," DC, April 22, 1968; Ann Colarusso, "Duke Strikers Decide to Work for 3 Weeks," Durham Herald, April 22, 1968.

92 Araminta Stone, "Trustee Action on Vigil Demands Still Awaited as Deadline Nears," DC, May 6, 1968.

93 "Statement of the Vigil Strategy Committee," April 11, 1968, Box 35, John H. Strange, DVC.

94 "Vigil Will Resume Tuesday on Main Quad: Duke Students Await Trustee State-ment on Validity of Union," DC, May 13, 1968.

95 "Vigil Will Resume Tuesday."

96 "Vigil Will Resume Tuesday."

97 "200 Students, Faculty Reconvene Despite Rain," DC, May 15, 1968.

98 Clay Steinman, "Vigilers Are Determined," DC, May 16, 1968.

99 Small, interview, April 12, 2018. These seven areas of focus were improved compensation administration, enhanced job security, maintenance of effective communication, more opportunities for personal development and advance-ment, better supervision, employee participation in matters pertaining to their collective interest, and reconstitution of the personnel policy commit-tee. Henry E. Rauch, "Report of the Special Committee as Distributed to the Blackburn Committee," May 10, 1968, Box 16, Labor Relations 1967–1969, DMK Records.

100 Pat Black and Alan Ray, "SDS Stages Brief Sit-In inside Allen Building," DC, May 16, 1968.

101 Henry E. Rauch to Board of Trustees of Duke University, memorandum, May 3, 1968, Box 16, Labor Relations 1967–1969, DMK Records.

102 Black and Ray, "SDS Stages Brief Sit-In"; Traver, interview, December 7, 1978.

103 Special Committee, "Trustee Statement," DC, May 16, 1968; "Students End Vigil Disgusted with Trustees: Trustees Promise to Spell Out Program for Employee Council, Representation," DC, May 16, 1968.

104 "Students End Vigil Disgusted"; "Closed Minds," DC, May 16, 1968.

105 "Workers to Meet with Trustees Wednesday," n.d., Box 1, Folder 18, Local 77, DVC.

106 "Students End Vigil Disgusted"; DMH, interview, January 14, 1977.

107 Cook, Semans, and Kinney quoted in "Remembering the Vigil"; ACK, interview, November 6, 1978.

108 Peter Applebome, "In the Twinkling . . . : A Transformation in Three Weeks?," DC, April 29, 1968; JWC, interview, January 18, 1977; Small, interview, April 12, 2018.

109 Van Pelt and Roberts quoted in "Remembering the Vigil"; Pace, "Vigil Ignites Hope for Blacks"; Applebome, "In the Twinkling."

110 Alumni Surveys 14, 37; Steinman and Clay quoted in Hendrick, "Silent Vigil 1968." Hundreds of participants returned to campus for the fiftieth anniversary of the Silent Vigil, and many credited it with fundamentally altering the direc-tion of their lives. As Small reflected during the anniversary, "All these people remained activists and were politically involved." Small, interview, April 12, 2018.

111 CBH, "Memo to Non-Academic Employees," September 3, 1968, Box 16, Labor Relations 1967–1969, DMK Records; JWC, interview, January 18, 1977.

112 Semans quoted in "Remembering the Vigil"; CBH, interview, February 9, 1977; ACK, interview, November 6, 1978. "The general reaction to Allen Building was one of a little disbelief that it happened here. That falls back to the vigil because that was a very peaceful demonstration, and I believe the Duke students felt in general that the [effective] way to do it was to apply peaceful pressure because the vigil did gain quite a few concessions from the university and there was no violence, no takeover of buildings." ACK, interview, November 6, 1978.

113 CBH, interview, February 9, 1977; ACK, interview, November 6, 1978; Kinney, interview, September 12, 2017.

114 Knight, *Dancer and the Dance*, 127.

115 SDC quoted in "Remembering the Vigil."

CHAPTER 6. HUMILIATING TO PLEAD FOR OUR HUMANITY

1 "The New University," DC, April 12, 1968.

2 "Fifth Decade Program First Phase Ending," DC, September 13, 1968; "East Judi Board Grants Overnight Area Leaves," DC, September 13, 1968; Richard Smurthwaite, "Men Must Learn to Make Beds," DC, September 19, 1968.

3 WJG to DMK, "Proposal for Afro-American Studies Program Drafted by John Cell," December 30, 1968, Box 71, Afro-American Studies: 1968–1969, VPSA Records.

4 Cell, "Proposal for Afro-American Studies Program."

5 JWC to MEH, February 6, 1969, Box 72, Afro-American Society Demonstration: 1969, VPSA Records; Joe Martin, "Statement to Board of Homeland Ministries, United Church of Christ," April 28, 1969, Box 72, Allen Building Takeover by Black Students: 1969, VPSA Records; WJG to DMK, "Proposal for Afro-American Studies Program"; BRH, interview, January 7, 1979.

6 Rogers [Kendi], *Black Campus Movement*, 95.

7 Frank L. Ashmore, "History of Afro-American Relations Prior to February 13, 1969," March 7, 1969, Box 5, Campus Unrest: 1969, DMK Records.

8 Ashmore, "History of Afro-American Relations"; WJG, interview, January 23, 1979.

9 Rogers [Kendi], *Black Campus Movement*, 85.

10 Ballard, *Education of Black Folk*, 75.

11 WCT, interview, January 23, 1985, ABTOHC.

12 BEA, interview, February 13, 1979.

13 BEA, interview, February 13, 1979.

14 DMK to WJG, August 13, 1968, Box 17, Afro-American Society: 1968–1969, Trinity College of Arts and Sciences, Office of the Dean Records, DUA.

15 Dave Shafer, "Protest Regulation Calls for Suspension, Arrest," DC, January 8, 1968.

16 E. C. Bryson, "Notice of Executive Committee Policy," May 9, 1968, Box 11, Special Problems, Pickets, and Protests: February 1967–August 1969, OP Records.

17 RHP, "Memorandum to Members of the Administrative Council," July 17, 1968, Box 7, Administrative Council: 1967–1969, DMK Records. "Suggestions [from the Executive Committee] included raising the maximum penalty to the level of dismissal, forbidding picketing and demonstrations inside any building, . . . and the elimination of the final step of appeal to the President."

18 DMK to men and women of Duke, August 15, 1968, Wright Tisdale to DMK and Frank Ashmore, handwritten note on memo to board, August 29, 1968, both in Box 21, Pickets and Protests, DMK Records.

19 Frank L. Ashmore, "Criticisms of Specific Actions of University by Conservatives," December 5, 1967, Frank L. Ashmore to DMK, December 5, 1967, both in Box 6, Civil Rights: 1968–1969, DMK Records.

20 Ashmore, "Criticisms of Specific Actions."

21 "Duke Announces Expansion: Ground Broken for Library," DC, September 23, 1965.

22 Marshall, interview, January 13, 1977.

23 Harold W. Lewis to chairmen, deans, and directors in Arts and Sciences and Engineering, "Budget for 1968–1969," May 6, 1968, Box 23, Trinity College: 1967–1968, OP Records; RHP to Administrative Council, memoranda on Administrative Council meetings, May 6 and September 11, 1968, both in Box 7, Administrative Council: 1967–1969, DMK Records.

24 WJG, interview, January 20, 1977; Anlyan, *Metamorphoses*, 202; Knight, *Dancer and the Dance*, 130; DMK, interview, April 16, 1979.

25 DMK, interview, April 16, 1979; DMK quoted in "Remembering the Vigil."

26 Chafe, *Unfinished Journey*, 358; Caitlin Gibson, "What Happened in Chicago in 1968, and Why Is Everyone Talking about It Now?," *Washington Post*, July 18, 2016.

27 Martin, "Statement to Board of Homeland Ministries"; Robert H. Ballantyne to WJG, August 29, 1969, Box 71, Afro-American Society: 1968–1969, VPSA Records. In addition, eighty-one Black students were in two-year or shorter paramedical training programs.

28 Brown, interview, December 13, 1978.

29 JWC, interview, January 9, 1979; Annie Leigh Broughton to Cliff Wing Jr., July 31, 1968, Box 17, Afro-American Society: 1968–1969, Trinity College of Arts and Sciences, Office of the Dean Records, DUA.

30 Ashmore, "History of Afro-American Relations."

31 BEA, interview, February 13, 1979. Using the early weeks of the fall semester for organizational activities was common throughout the Black campus movement. "The early fall had the lowest levels of activism," Kendi observed, "since the influxes of students compelled [Black student unions] and [student government associations] to reorganize, while leaders and their political ideologies jockeyed for control." Rogers [Kendi], *Black Campus Movement*, 96.

32 BEA, interview, February 13, 1979; WJG, "Minutes of Meeting Held with Representatives of the Duke Afro-American Society, Members of the Faculty, and Members of the Administration on October 4, 1968," October 11, 1968, Box 71, Afro-American Society: 1968–1969, VPSA Records.

33 WJG, "Minutes of Meeting Held with Representatives of the Duke Afro-American Society." All descriptions and quotations from the meeting are taken from the minutes unless otherwise indicated.

34 At this stage, although calling for prompt action by the university and requesting involvement in all substantive discussions, students at Duke, like their counterparts at other schools, were willing to work through "normal academic channels" to achieve their objectives. See Rogers [Kendi], *Black Campus Movement*, 111. "The purpose of Black studies was threefold," Williamson explained. "Corrective, to counter distortions, misperceptions, and fallacies surrounding Black people; descriptive, to accurately depict the past and present events constituting the Black experience; and prescriptive, to educate Black students who would eventually uplift the race." Williamson, *Black Power on Campus*, 30.

35 JWC, interview, January 9, 1979; WJG to DMK, October 11, 1968, Box 71, Afro-American Society: 1968–1969, VPSA Records.

36 Christian McWhirter, "The Birth of 'Dixie,'" *New York Times*, March 31, 2012; McWhirter, *Battle Hymns*.

37 DMK, response to AAS 12 demands, October 1968, Box 72, Afro-American Society Demonstration: 1969, VPSA Records.

38 This sentence was partially crossed out in the copy of DMK's typed draft found in the VPSA Records.

39 DMK, response to AAS 12 demands.

40 WJG, "Minutes of Second Meeting Held with Representatives of the Duke Afro-American Society, Members of the Faculty, and Members of the Administration on Thursday, October 15, 1968," Box 71, Afro-American Society: 1968–1969, VPSA Records.

41 WJG, "Minutes of Second Meeting."

42 RTC to DMK, memorandum, October 24, 1968, DMK to RTC, October 29, 1968, both in Box 71, Afro-American Studies: 1968–1969, VPSA Records.

43 Richard Smurthwaite, "Poor Communication Hurts Negotiations," DC, April 4, 1969.

44 JWC, "Interview with Dr. Robert Ballantyne, Director of Admissions," n.d., Tony Axam and Richard L. Watson to WJG, November 6, 1968, both in Box 71, Afro-American Studies: 1968–1969, VPSA Records.

45 JWC, interview, January 9, 1979; DMK, interview, April 16, 1979; SDC, interview, March 1, 1985, ABTOHC. Louis J. Budd, who chaired the committee charged with developing the African and Afro-American Studies Program at Duke, had a similar view of Lewis. "I don't think that [Lewis], really, himself, had any personal commitment to Afro-American Studies," Budd commented. "He would go as far as he thought he had to go." Budd, interview, March 1, 1985, ABTOHC.

46 No report was presented on some other issues, like financial support for Black Week and the requested support for the Black solidarity movement in Durham. WJG, "Handwritten Notes of November 4, 1968 Meeting," Box 71, Afro-American Studies: 1968–1969, VPSA Records.

47 Biondi, *Black Revolution on Campus*, 175; Ballard, *Education of Black Folk*, 110; Williamson, *Black Power on Campus*, 29–30.

48 Ballard, *Education of Black Folk*, 105–6; Biondi, *Black Revolution on Campus*, 174–75.

49 JWC, "Interview with Professor Blackburn, Economics," n.d., Box 71, Afro-American Studies: 1968–1969, VPSA Records.

50 Tony Axam and Richard L. Watson Jr. to WJG, November 5, 1968, Box 71, Afro-American Studies: 1968–1969, VPSA Records.

51 WJG, "Handwritten Notes"; Ashmore, "History of Afro-American Relations."

52 WJG, "Handwritten Notes."

53 Ashmore, "History of Afro-American Relations"; "Action Taken on Items Identified at Meeting of October 4, 1968," n.d., Box 72, Afro-American Society Demonstration: 1969, VPSA Records.

54 WJG, interview, January 16, 1979; "Action Taken on Items Identified at Meeting of October 4, 1968."

55 Diane Wheeler, "Black Students Request Advisor," DC, December 5, 1968.

56 JWC, interview, January 9, 1979; WJG to DMK, "Proposal for Afro-American Studies Program."

57 JWC, interview, January 9, 1979.

58 JWC, interview, January 9, 1979; WJG to DMK, "Proposal for Afro-American Studies Program."

59 Ashmore, "History of Afro-American Relations."

60 WJG, interview, January 23, 1979; WJG to DMK, "Proposal for Afro-American Studies Program"; DMK, interview, April 16, 1979; Ashmore, "History of Afro-American Relations."

61 CWH, interview, January 19, 1979; Newsome quoted in Saurav, "Allen Building Takeover."

62 CWH, interview, January 19, 1979

63 JW, interview, February 13, 1985, ABTOHC; WCT, interview, January 23, 1985, ABTOHC; CWH, interview, January 19, 1979.

64 ACK, interview, November 6, 1978; Cahow, interview, October 23, 1984, ABTOHC.

65 SDC, interview, March 1, 1985, ABTOHC; CWH, interview, January 19, 1979.

66 DMK, interview, April 16, 1979; Watson, interview, November 16, 1978; JWC, interview, January 9, 1979.

67 WJG, interview, January 16, 1979; JWC, interview, January 9, 1979; Frank L. Ashmore, "A Report to the Board of Trustees of Duke University," June 1, 1968, Board of Trustees Minutes, vol. 12, BoT Records.

68 CWH, interview, January 19, 1979.

CHAPTER 7. NOW THEY KNOW, AND THEY AIN'T GONNA DO

1 JWC, interview, January 9, 1979; WJG, interview, January 23, 1979.

2 BEA, interview, February 13, 1979.

3 BCB, interview, December 13, 1978; CLB, interview, April 19, 2017 (Brown joined).

4 BEA, interview, March 3, 2017; WCT, interview, April 17, 2017.

5 CWH, interview, January 19, 1979.

6 Williamson, *Black Power on Campus*, 25, 26; Rogers [Kendi], *Black Campus Movement*, 97.

7 Knight, *Street of Dreams*, 125; JWC, interview, January 9, 1979.

8 CWH, interview, January 19, 1979; BEA, interview, February 13, 1979; Williamson, *Black Power on Campus*, 33.

9 Williamson, *Black Power on Campus*, 25–26, 33; BEA, interview, February 13, March 3, 2017.

10 Rogers [Kendi], *Black Campus Movement*, 83; CWH, interview, January 19, 1979.

11 Fuller, *No Struggle, No Progress*, 92; Hopkins, "Malcolm X University," 40.

12 Fuller, *No Struggle, No Progress*, 83; Korstad and Leloudis, *To Right These Wrongs*, 337.

13 ACK, interview, November 6, 1978; Pye, interview, March 2, 1985, ABTOHC.

14 CLB, interview, December 16, 1978, April 19, 2017; CWH, interview, January 19, 1979. Moreover, Fuller was hardly the radical agitator his critics believed. David Henderson, who encountered Fuller during the vigil, described him as a "very pacifying force." Fuller was, according to Henderson, "never very radical, . . . never an instigator, [and] never a bomb thrower." DMH, interview, January 14, 1977. Further, Durham mayor Wensell Grabarek credited Fuller with preventing a riot in Durham on the night of King's assassination. Fuller, *No Struggle, No Progress*, 90.

15 Sokol, *There Goes My Everything*, 92–93.

16 BEA, interview, December 5, 2017.

17 Rogers [Kendi], *Black Campus Movement*, 82; CLB, interview, December 16, 1978, April 19, 2017; WCT, interview, November 8, 1978.

18 CWH, interview, January 19, 1979; WCT, interview, April 17, 2017.

19 Biondi, *Black Revolution on Campus*, 25; Rogers [Kendi], *Black Campus Movement*, 86.

20 BEA, interview, December 5, 2017; WCT, interview, April 17, 2017.

21 Joe Martin, "Statement to Board of Homeland Ministries, United Church of Christ," April 28, 1969, Box 72, Allen Building Takeover by Black Students: 1969, VPSA Records; RHP to William G. Anlyan et al., "Memorandum on Administrative Council Meeting," January 30, 1969, Box 7, Administrative Council: 1967–1969, DMK Records.

22 BRH, interview, January 7, 1979; BEA, interview, December 17, 1978; CWH, interview, January 19, 1979; CWH quoted in Sarah Xu and Rachel Rubin, "'Water Boiling': An Oral History of the Allen Building Takeover, Part 1," DC, May 14, 2019.

23 CWH, interview, January 19, 1979; CWH, "Interim Report," 40; BCB, interview, December 13, 1978; WCT, interview, January 23, 1985, ABTOHC.

24 JW, interview, February 13, 1985, ABTOHC; Bair, "Early Years of Negro History Week."

25 Richard Smurthwaite, "'Black Week' Approaches," DC, January 30, 1969; "Action Taken on Items Identified at Meeting of October 4, 1968."

26 Duke University Afro-American Society, "Ten-Point Program: What We Want and Why We Want It," *Harambee*, February 5, 1969, Box 1, Folder 2, ABTC. The percentage was chosen to correspond to the approximate percentage of Blacks in the population in the Southeast.

27 Duke University Afro-American Society, "Ten-Point Program"; Ballard, *Education of Black Folk*, 73–74, 75; Knight, *Street of Dreams*, 134.

28 WJG, interview, January 16, 1979.

29 RHP to Anlyan et al., "Memorandum on Administrative Council Meeting."

30 RHP to Anlyan et al., "Memorandum on Administrative Council Meeting"; RHP to MEH, memorandum, January 30, 1969, Box 23, Dean's Office—Trinity College, OP Records.

31 RHP to Anlyan et al., "Memorandum on Administrative Council Meeting."

32 "Afros Talk Grades at Forum," DC, February 1, 1969.

33 WJG, interview, January 16, 1979.

34 MEH, interview, November 1979; WJG, interview, January 23, 1979; JWC, interview, January 9, 1979.

35 BEA, interview, December 17, 1978.

36 DMK, response to AAS 12 demands, October 1968, Box 72, Afro-American Society Demonstration: 1969, VPSA Records.

37 DMK to Board of Trustees, memorandum, February 3, 1969, Box 1, Miscellany, DMK Records.

38 DMK, "Knight's Statement," DC, February 4, 1969

39 DMK, "Knight's Statement"; DMK to Dillard Teer, February 4, 1969, Box 16, Hope Valley Country Club, DMK Records; DMK, interview, April 16, 1979.

40 DMK, interview, April 16, 1979.

41 WJG, interview, January 23, 1979.

42 DMK, interview, April 16, 1979.

43 WJG to DMK, January 9, 1969, Box 16, Hope Valley Country Club, DMK Records.

44 DMK to WJG, January 14, 1969, Box 16, Hope Valley Country Club, DMK Records.

45 DMK, interview, April 16, 1979.

46 Steve Emerson, "Afros Decry Lack of Action by Knight," DC, February 5, 1969.

47 Chuck Hopkins, "Why Duke Is Racist," DC, February 4, 1969.

48 DMK to Stephen Glenn Hoffius et al., memorandum, February 14, 1969, Box 1, Afro-American Situation: 1969—Letters Concerning, DMK Records; Pat Black, "Knight Warns against Campus Revolt," DC, February 5, 1969.

49 "Black Week Calendar, *Harambee*, February 5, 1969.

50 "Statement of Purpose—To Educate the White Masses," *Harambee*, February 5, 1969.

51 Chuck Hopkins, "Black Rap," *Harambee*, February 5, 1969.

52 Larry Weston, "Epiphany," *Harambee*, February 5, 1969.

53 Michael McBride, "A New Language," *Harambee*, February 5, 1969. Despite this violent imagery, the vast majority of AAS members remained committed to non-violent protest. Indeed, *Harambee* was dedicated to "the memory of Dr. Martin Luther King and his principles." BRH, interview, January 7, 1979; BEA, interview, February 13, 1979; BCB, interview, December 13, 1978.

54 Tom A. Finch to DMK, February 21, 1969, Box 1, Afro-American Situation: 1969—Letters Concerning, DMK Records; William M. Werber to DMK, April 3, 1969, Box 26, William Werber: 1967–1969, DMK Records; Sim A. DeLapp to Howard Wilkinson, February 14, 1969, Box 71, Afro-American Society: 1968–1969, VPSA Records.

55 Michael Kopen, "Fuller Urges Blacks Join 'Fight for Dignity,'" DC, February 7, 1969.

56 WCT, interview, January 23, 1985, ABTOHC.

57 JWC, interview, January 9, 1979.

58 Gregory quoted in Rogers [Kendi], *Black Campus Movement*, 81.

59 DMK, interview, April 16, 1979; Knight, *Street of Dreams*, 135.

60 CWH, interview, January 19, 1979.

61 "Afros Present Demands, Discuss Them at Knight's," DC, February 11, 1969.

62 CWH, interview, January 19, 1979; "Afros Present Demands."

63 "Allen Building Takeover, 1969 February 10–1969 March 12," tape 6, Box 6, Audio Tapes: 1956–1973, WDBS Collection, DUA.

64 DMK, "The Complete Text of the Statement by Dr. Knight," DC, February 12, 1969. Knight was not alone in his negative reaction to the term *demands*. Kendi

wrote that "almost all administrators despised the term 'demand' which asserted a level of black student power they were unwilling to concede in highly hierarchical academia." Rogers [Kendi], *Black Campus Movement*, 112.

65 "Minutes of Joint Meeting of the Administrative Council and the Executive Committee of the Academic Council," February 12, 1969, Box 7, Administrative Council, DMK Records; BCB, interview, December 13, 1978.

66 DMK, interview, November 21, 1978; CLB, interview, December 16, 1978.

67 Mark Pinsky, "Hamer, Jackson Tell of Anguish of Blacks," DC, February 12, 1969; "Black Week Calendar," *Harambee*, February 5, 1969.

68 Julie Logan and Gary Wein, "'Black Week' Spurs Greater Afro Unity," DC, February 13, 1969.

69 JW, interview, February 13, 1985, ABTOHC; BEA, interview, December 17, 1978.

70 BEA, interview, February 13, 1979.

71 WCT, interview, November 8, 1978, April 17, 2017; BEA, interview, December 17, 1978; BRH quoted in Rogers [Kendi], *Black Campus Movement*, 81.

72 BRH, interview, January 7, 1979.

73 BEA, interview, December 17, 1978; BCB, interview, December 13, 1978; CWH, interview, January 19, 1979.

74 BEA, interview, December 17, 1978, February 13, 1979; BCB, interview, December 13, 1978.

75 BEA, interview, December 17, 1978.

76 BEA, interview, February 13, 1979.

77 CLB, interview, December 16, 1978; BCB, interview, December 13, 1978; CWH, interview, January 19, 1979; WCT, interview, November 8, 1978.

78 BEA, interview, March 3, 2017. Armstrong explained how the Black students were able to determine where the Allen Building was most vulnerable. "We had classes in the building," she commented. "Every time we had a class, we would get a piece of information about where a door was, where a transom was, where the windows were, what time they opened, and what time they closed. We had a little tiny office and we had drawn a map of the interior of the first floor. We knew they were most vulnerable on the most eastward part of the first floor because that is where the doors locked. . . . That is how we had detailed plans." BEA, interview, March 3, 2017.

79 BEA, interview, December 17, 1978.

80 CWH, interview, January 19, 1979.

81 CWH, interview, January 19, 1979; McBride in "Allen Building Takeover 50th"; LeBlanc, interview, February 9, 2019. Armstrong explained the internal dynamics. "There was a spectrum of reactions," she recalled. "There were people [who were] more militant or angry, and their reactions were angrier." Some of them said, "Burn the building down." In Armstrong's view, "that was totally unrealistic." BEA, interview, February 13, 1979.

82 Traver, interview, December 7, 1978.

83 CLB, interview, December 16, 1978.

84 BRH, interview, January 7, 1979; BEA, interview, February 13, 1979.

85 BCB, interview, December 13, 1978.

86 CWH, interview, January 19, 1979; BEA, interview, February 13, 1979.

87 BEA, interview, February 13, 1979.

88 "Minutes of Joint Meeting of the Administrative Council and the Executive Committee of the Academic Council," February 12, 1969, Box 7, Administrative Council, DMK Records.

89 JWC, interview, January 9, 1979; "Minutes of Joint Meeting of the Administrative Council and the Executive Committee of the Academic Council," February 12, 1969.

90 JWC, interview, January 9, 1979.

91 MEH, "Handwritten Notes of Ground Rules for Consideration of AAS Demands," February 11, 1969, Box 1, Afro-American Studies: 1969–1970, OP Records.

92 BCB, interview, December 13, 1978; MEH, interview, November 1979.

CHAPTER 8. NO OPTION TO NEGOTIATE

1 BEA, interview, December 17, 1978.

2 BEA, interview, January 31, 1985, ABTOHC, quoted in Yannella, "Race Relations," 26; BEA, interview, December 17, 1978; BRH, interview, January 7, 1979.

3 CLB, interview, December 16, 1978; CWH, interview, January 19, 1979. In fact, the truck first arrived on campus a few minutes before 8:00 a.m. and circled Chapel Drive to get the timing right. When the truck did not stop initially in front of the Allen Building, some students assumed, according to Becton, that the takeover must have been called off. Not all takeover participants were on the truck from Becton's house. Some stayed on campus Monday night, knowing that, according to Brown, if all the Black students "disappeared [from campus] at the same time," someone would get concerned about "where did all the Black folks go all of a sudden?"

4 JW, interview, February 13, 1985, ABTOHC; Cahow, interview, October 23, 1984, ABTOHC.

5 Joyce M. Siler, letter, n.d., Box 5, Campus Unrest: 1969, DMK Records; Harry R. Jackson, "Account of Events of February 13–March 19," May 27, 1969, Box 1, Folder 18, ABTC. The Black students insisted that the building was vacated peacefully and denied any allegations to the contrary. "There wasn't any physical violence," Brenda Armstrong told WDBS radio during the takeover. "We escorted them out. They walked on their own two feet." "Allen Building Takeover, 1969 February 10–1969 March 12," tape 7, Box 6, Audio Tapes: 1956–1973, WDBS Collection, DUA.

6 Jackson, "Account of Events," 2–3.

7 WJG, interview, January 23, 1979; "Bill Griffith on the 1969 Allen Building Takeover."

8 Rogers [Kendi], *Black Campus Movement*, 2. As Kendi noted, Black student protests started or were ongoing in the Midwest (Illinois and Wisconsin), the Northeast (New York), the Upper South (North Carolina), the Deep South (Mississippi), and the West Coast (Bay Area). Rogers [Kendi], *Black Campus Movement*, 2.

9 CWH, interview, January 19, 1979; Campbell, interview, February 8, 1985, ABTOHC; CWH in "Allen Building Takeover 50th."

10 "The Black Demands," February 13, 1969, Box 1, February 13, 1969, ABTC; CWH in "Allen Building Takeover 50th." The demands largely tracked the issues presented to Knight at his home on February 10, 1969. At a meeting in Page Auditorium on February 15, 1969, Michael McBride, president of the AAS, explained that negotiations on "specific demands" had been ongoing since October 1968 but that the Black students had been "negotiating for the past two and a half years on general things that affect Black students on this campus . . . ever since the Afro American Society has been formed." "Allen Building Takeover," tape 10.

11 Yannella, "Race Relations," 31–32; Jackson, "Account of Events," 2–3.

12 BEA, interview, December 17, 1978; "Blacks Occupy Allen, Ask Demands Action," DC, February 13, 1969. Howard recalled a safety issue. "We ended up being in a relatively enclosed part of the building," she recounted, giving rise to a concern that a fire might occur if tear gas mixed with kerosene. BRH, interview, January 7, 1979.

13 "Blacks Occupy Allen"; Josie Knowlin to parents, February 13, 1969, https://exhibits.library.duke.edu/exhibits/show/black-students-matter--allen-/item/1855; "Photographs of Allen Building Following Takeover," February 13, 1969, Box 5, Campus Unrest: 1969, DMK Records; CWH, interview, January 19, 1979.

14 Fuller, *No Struggle, No Progress*, 93.

15 BEA, interview, December 17, 1978; BCB, interview, December 13, 1978; Josie Knowlin to parents, February 13, 1969; JW, interview, February 13, 1985, ABTOHC, quoted in Yannella, "Race Relations," 27.

16 SDC, interview, March 1, 1985, ABTOHC; Cahow, interview, October 23, 1984, ABTOHC; Watson, interview, November 16, 1978; Pye, interview, March 2, 1985.

17 RHP, "Handwritten Minutes of Meeting in Board Room—February 13, 1969," February 13, 1969, Box 1, Occupation of Allen Building: 2/13/69—And Related Material, OP Records. Present during the day, among others, were administrators Hobbs, Woodhall, Ashmore, Huestis, Griffith, Lewis, Powell, and Price; legal counsel Edwin Bryson; vice provost Frederic Joerg; faculty members Kerckhoff, William H. Cartwright, Craufurd Goodwin, and George Williams; and student leaders Wade Norris (ASDU president) and Steve Johnson. "Blacks Occupy Allen"; Jackson, "Account of Events," 40.

18 MEH, interview, March 4, 1985, ABTOHC; RHP, "Handwritten Minutes," 1, 3; WJG, interview, February 15, 1979. The threat of setting fire to the records was later withdrawn. "Blacks Leave Peacefully," DC, February 14, 1969.

19 RHP, "Handwritten Minutes," 1–2; Ken Vickery, "Administrators React to Feb. 13," DC, March 11, 1969.

20 Cahow, interview, October 23, 1984, ABTOHC; RHP, "Handwritten Minutes," 4.

21 MEH, interview, March 4, 1985, ABTOHC; Tuthill quoted in Yannella, "Race Relations."

22 RHP, "Handwritten Minutes," 6–7, 8.

23 "Minutes of General Faculty Meeting; February 13, 1969," February 13, 1969, Box 1, Afro-American Studies: 1969–1970, OP Records; RHP, "Handwritten Minutes," 5.

24 RHP, "Handwritten Minutes," 5, 6.

25 "Minutes of General Faculty Meeting"; RHP, "Handwritten Minutes," 10.

26 WJG, interview, January 23, 1979; JWC, interview, January 9, 1979. Moreover, Cell was not the only faculty member who advocated restraint. "My vote was toward waiting it out," commented Louis Budd, who served as the initial chair of the Afro-American studies program at Duke. "It was clearly a symbolic gesture so you back off and let them symbolize." Budd, interview, March 1, 1985, ABTOHC.

27 SDC, interview, March 1, 1985, ABTOHC.

28 WJG, interview, February 15, 1979.

29 RHP, "Handwritten Minutes," 9.

30 "Allen Building Takeover," tape 1.

31 "Allen Building Takeover," tape 1.

32 "Allen Building Takeover," tape 1. Hoping to communicate the urgency the faculty now felt, Cartwright announced the formation of the Kerckhoff Committee, which, he told the crowd, had been done at the recommendation of the Executive Committee of the Academic Council acting in its role as the "committee on committees of the university faculty." "Allen Building Takeover," tape 2.

33 "WDBS 1:00 p.m. Press Release," quoted in "Chronology of Confrontation," working paper, n.d., Box 72, Afro-American Society Demonstration: 1969, VPSA Records.

34 "Allen Building Takeover," tape 1.

35 "Allen Building Takeover," tape 1.

36 RHP, "Handwritten Minutes," 9, 7; WJG, interview, January 23, 1979.

37 RHP, "Handwritten Minutes," 9.

38 RHP, "Handwritten Minutes," 10. Hobbs, Fairbank, and Wilson were also joined by Cletis Pride, director, news service, Office of Information Services, and Bob Ashley, who was reporting for the DC. Tom Wilson and Henry Fairbank, "Report of Events Occurring during the Takeover of Allen Building," February 17, 1969, Box 1, Occupation of Allen Building: 2/13/69—And Related Material, OP Records.

39 Wilson and Fairbank, "Report of Events"; Tuthill quoted in Yannella, "Race Relations"; "First Conversation between Dr. Hobbs and Black Students, at Window of Allen Building, about 12:15 p.m.," n.d., Box 1, Folder 3, Documents, February 13, 1969, ABTC.

40 Cahow, interview, October 23, 1984, ABTOHC; MEH, interview, March 4, 1985, ABTOHC; Tuthill quoted in Yannella, "Race Relations."

41 "Allen Building Takeover," tape 3. "We all took shifts answering the phones," Janice Williams remembered. "Friends were calling, other schools were calling, the news-people were calling, the *Chronicle* was calling . . . so there was a lot of phone calls that had to be answered." JW quoted in Sarah Xu and Rachel Rubin, "'Too Young to Be Afraid': An Oral History of the Allen Building Takeover, Part 2," DC, May 15, 2019.

42 BEA, interview, December 17, 1978.

43 CWH, interview, January 19, 1979.

44 JWC, interview, January 9, 1979.

45 RHP, "Handwritten Minutes," 11; MEH, "February 13, 1969: Primary Actions by M. E. Hobbs, Allen Building, Duke University," February 17, 1969, Box 1, Folder 4, Documents, February 14–19, 1969, ABTC.

46 RHP, "Handwritten Minutes," 11.

47 RHP, "Handwritten Minutes," 11; MEH, interview, March 4, 1985, ABTOHC. Griffith had informal communications with the students during the day, first by passing notes and later in conversations through a window. "Bill Griffith on the 1969 Allen Building Takeover." According to Armstrong, Black students saw Griffith as lacking the authority to speak on behalf of the university, calling him "a middleman with no power." BEA, interview, February 13, 1979.

48 RHP, "Handwritten Minutes," 11–12.

49 RHP, "Handwritten Minutes," 12; Jackson, "Account of Events," 44.

50 Jackson, "Account of Events," 46; RHP, "Handwritten Minutes," 12. According to the *Duke Chronicle*, one faction of the group "wished to avoid the emotional upsurge and prepare for long range commitment to achieve the thirteen demands of the blacks." David Smallen, "Whites Help Blacks in Allen," DC, February 14, 1969.

51 BEA, interview, March 3, 2017; "Allen Building Takeover," tape 2; Fuller, *No Struggle, No Progress*, 93.

52 "Blacks Occupy Allen;" DeMik, interview, February 12, 1985, ABTOHC.

53 DMK, interview, November 21, 1978; Knight, *Street of Dreams*, 135, 138.

54 MEH, interview, November 1979; BRH, interview, January 7, 1979; BEA, interview, December 17, 1978. "He knew what he was going to precipitate," Armstrong said. "We were going to be forcibly put out of the building. That would have ignited just a terrible situation." Roger Marshall heard Knight talk to alumni about the potential for violence from whites in Durham. For support, according to Marshall,

the Duke president always pointed out that "every pickup truck [owned] by every redneck bum had a gun rack in the back." Marshall dismissed the concern. The men Knight worried about were likely hunters, Marshall thought. They weren't "Ku Klux Klan members looking for a race riot just because they had a gun rack in their truck." Marshall, interview, January 13, 1977.

55 These included Durham police and members of the North Carolina Highway Patrol. "Chronology of Confrontation"; WCT, interview, November 8, 1978.

56 BEA, interview, December 17, 1978; Jacobs, *Across the Line*, 72.

57 MEH, "First Statement to Black Students," February 13, 1969, Box 1, Afro-American Situation: February 1969, Miscellaneous Material: 1968–1969, DMK Records.

58 MEH, "First Statement to Black Students"; "WDBS 3:30 p.m. Press Release," quoted in "Chronology of Confrontation"; MEH, "February 13, 1969: Primary Actions"; WJG, interview, February 15, 1979.

59 Smallen, "Whites Help Blacks in Allen"; "Chronology of Confrontation."

60 RHP, "Handwritten Minutes," 13–14.

61 "Minutes of General Faculty Meeting."

62 "Minutes of General Faculty Meeting."

63 "Allen Building Takeover," tape 2.

64 MEH, interview, March 4, 1985; Watson, interview, November 16, 1978.

65 "Minutes of General Faculty Meeting."

66 "WDBS 1:00 p.m. Press Release," quoted in "Chronology of Confrontation."

67 "Allen Building Takeover," tape 2.

68 BEA, interview, December 17, 1978; JW, interview, February 13, 1985, ABTOHC. Howard viewed the potential for the use of force differently. "I didn't have any doubt that they would call out the fire department and the police," she commented. BRH, interview, January 7, 1979.

69 SDC, interview, March 1, 1985, ABTOHC.

70 Watson, interview, November 16, 1978.

71 Joe Martin to WJG, memorandum, February 19, 1969, Box 72, Afro-American Society Demonstration: 1969, VPSA Records; RHP, "Handwritten Minutes," 15.

72 RHP, "Handwritten Minutes," 15.

73 RHP, "Handwritten Minutes," 15; Alan Ray, "Knight Explains Use of Police," DC, February 14, 1969.

74 DMK, interview, April 16, 1979.

75 DMK, interview, November 21, 1978. Knight was clear that this complicated feeling was not the reason he invoked force. DMK, interview, November 21, 1978. Kerckhoff understood the sense of relief Knight must have felt. "At a psycho-dynamic level," Kerckhoff speculated, "it may be that someone in a position of harried responsibility can say, 'Thank God it's out of my hands.'" ACK, interview, November 6, 1978.

76 CWH, interview, January 19, 1979.

77 DeMik, interview, February 12, 1985, ABTOHC.

78 JWC, interview, January 9, 1979.

79 RHP, "Handwritten Minutes," 16; WJG, interview, January 23, 1979.

80 "Second Statement to Students from Marcus Hobbs," quoted in "Chronology of Confrontation"; Wilson and Fairbank, "Report of Events"; "Allen Building Takeover," tape 2.

81 RHP, "Handwritten Minutes," 16; "Allen Building Takeover," tape 1.

82 "Allen Building Takeover," tape 2.

83 WCT, interview, January 23, 1985, ABTOHC; Xu and Rubin, "Too Young to Be Afraid."

84 Fuller, *No Struggle, No Progress*, 94.

85 CLB, interview, December 16, 1978; CWH, interview, January 19, 1979; JW, interview, February 13, 1985, ABTOHC.

86 CWH, interview, January 19, 1979; JW, interview, February 13, 1985, ABTOHC; JW in "Allen Building Takeover 50th"; BRH, interview, January 7, 1979.

87 JW in "Allen Building Takeover 50th"; "Allen Building Takeover," tape 2.

88 CWH, interview, January 19, 1979; Catherine LeBlanc in "Allen Building Takeover 50th"; Michael LeBlanc quoted in Xu and Rubin, "Too Young to Be Afraid."

89 JW, interview, February 13, 1985, ABTOHC; "Allen Building Takeover," tape 2.

90 Fuller, *No Struggle, No Progress*, 93; BEA, interview, December 17, 1978.

91 CWH, interview, January 19, 1979; CLB, interview, December 16, 1978; LeBlanc in "Allen Building Takeover 50th."

92 WCT, interview, November 8, 1978; BCB, interview, December 13, 1978; BRH, interview, January 7, 1979; BEA, interview, December 17, 1978; JW, interview, February 13, 1985, ABTOHC.

93 WJG, interview, January 23, 1979.

94 CWH, interview, January 19, 1979. Griffith explained that the likely reason the door had been chained from the outside was to prevent additional people from entering the building, including football players and others who might want to attack the protesters. It was "something of a mutual protection situation," he recalled. WJG, interview, February 15, 1979.

95 Wilson and Fairbank, "Report of Events."

96 CWH, interview, January 19, 1979; CLB, interview, December 16, 1978; LeBlanc quoted in Sarah Xu and Rachel Rubin, "'We're the Enemy': An Oral History of the Allen Building Takeover, Part 3," DC, May 16, 2019. Some accounts of these moments have the police arriving at the Allen Building only after the students had departed.

97 WCT, interview, April 17, 2017.

98 "Allen Building Takeover," tape 2; Joe Martin to WJG, memorandum, February 19, 1969. Asked why the Black students had vacated the Allen Building, one

marcher responded incredulously, "Did you see those bad boys out there?" "Allen Building Takeover," tape 1.

99   JW, interview, February 13, 1985, ABTOHC.

100   "Allen Building Takeover," tape 2; "Chronology of Confrontation"; Jackson, "Account of Events," 50; Joe Martin to WJG, memorandum, February 19, 1969. At this time, Joe Martin approached a police car on the quad, telling the officer inside that the Allen Building had been vacated and secured. According to Martin, the officer replied that "he knew and was having difficulty finding Captain Seagroves and getting authorization to leave." Joe Martin to WJG, memorandum, February 19, 1969.

101   "Allen Building Takeover," tape 7. One student reported seeing paper cups, wet towels, and at least "two rather large, flat stones approximately 4–5 inches in length, three inches in width and an inch thick" thrown at the police. John M. Bowers to WJG, February 16, 1969, Box 72, Afro-American Society Demonstration: 1969, VPSA Records. Another student saw events differently. "I, who was no more than ten feet from the police," Mark Stancato reported, "did not see a single object hit the policemen." Mark E. Stancato to WJG, n.d., Box 72, Afro-American Society Demonstration: 1969, VPSA Records.

102   DeMik, interview, February 12, 1985, ABTOHC; Campbell, interview, February 8, 1985, ABTOHC; "Police and Students Clash on Main Quad," DC, February 14, 1969; WJG, interview, March 5, 1985, ABTOHC.

103   Joe Martin to WJG, memorandum, February 19, 1969; Mark E. Stancato to WJG, February 16, 1969, Box 72, Afro-American Society Demonstration: 1969, VPSA Records; DeMik, interview, February 12, 1985, ABTOHC.

104   Wilson and Fairbank, "Report of Events."

105   SDC, interview, March 1, 1985, ABTOHC.

106   JWC, interview, January 9, 1979; Campbell, interview, February 8, 1985, ABTOHC; Gulley quoted in Erin Williams, "In 1969, Black Students Took Over a Duke University Building: A New Exhibit Reminds Us Why That Event Mattered," Indy Week, March 6, 2019; BRH, interview, January 7, 1979. On May 4, 1970, members of the Ohio National Guard shot unarmed students at Ohio's Kent State University during a mass protest against the bombing of Cambodia by U.S. military forces.

107   Cahow, interview, October 23, 1984, ABTOHC; MEH, interview, March 4, 1985, ABTOHC.

108   RHP, "Handwritten Minutes," 17; WJG, interview, January 23, 1979; Cahow, interview, October 23, 1984, ABTOHC.

109   Cahow, interview, October 23, 1984, ABTOHC; JWC, interview, January 9, 1979.

110   Stuart M. Sessoms to RHP, February 14, 1969, Box 71, Afro-American Society: 1968–1969, VPSA Records.

111   JW in "Allen Building Takeover 50th"; McBride, interview, May 21, 2019; BEA, interview, December 17, 1978.

112 BRH, interview, January 7, 1979; CWH, interview, January 19, 1979.

113 "Allen Building Takeover," tape 5.

114 "Allen Building Takeover," tape 5.

115 Richard Smurthwaite and Heloise Merrill, "Students Ask Amnesty, Strike," DC, February 14, 1969.

116 Knight, *Street of Dreams*, 137.

117 WJG, interview, February 5, 1977; CBH, interview, February 9, 1977.

118 One student commented with appropriate dismay that "nowhere else in the country, at the many schools facing the same situation, was police force called so quickly and with such lack of forethought." Robert B. Entman to MEH, February 16, 1969, Box 72, Afro-American Society Demonstration: 1969, VPSA Records.

119 DMK, interview, November 21, 1978; Charles Becton, "Why Give Up on Duke?," DC, March 11, 1969.

120 DMK, interview, November 21, 1978.

CHAPTER 9. WE SHALL HAVE COCKTAILS IN THE GLOAMING

1 DMK to Kenneth A. Menken, March 3, 1969, Box 1, Afro-American Situation: 1969—Letters Concerning, DMK Records.

2 Henry E. Rauch to MEH, February 15, 1969, Box 1, Occupation of the Allen Building: 2/13/69—And Related Materials, OP Records; Tom A. Finch to DMK, February 21, 1969, Box 1, Afro-American Situation: 1969—Letters Concerning, DMK Records.

3 Allan Kornberg and Kurt Black to CBH, April 3, 1969, Box 5, Pickets and Protests, A. Kenneth Pye, Chancellor, Records and Papers, DUA; Knight, *Street of Dreams*, 141; L. C. Biedenharn to DMK, February 14, 1969, Box 1, Occupation of the Allen Building: 2/13/69—And Related Materials, OP Records; Irwin Fridovich to DMK, February 13, 1969, Robert M. Jackson to DMK, telegram, February 13, 1969, both in Box 5, Campus Unrest: 1969—Letters, DMK Records.

4 "Editorial: The Invasion," DC, February 14, 1969; James Huntley Grayson to DMK, n.d., Ray Winton to DMK, February 14, 1969, both in Box 5, Campus Unrest: 1969—Letters, DMK Records.

5 Allan Kornberg and Kurt Black to CBH, April 3, 1969, Box 5, Pickets and Protests, A. Kenneth Pye, Chancellor, Records and Papers, DUA; SDC, interview, March 1, 1985, ABTOHC; BEA quoted in Sarah Xu and Rachel Rubin, "'We're the Enemy': An Oral History of the Allen Building Takeover, Part 3," DC, May 16, 2019.

6 Bernard H. Thomas to DMK, February 14, 1969, William J. Massey and Jeanne Kelly to DMK, February 14, 1969, John A. Radford, letter, February 14, 1969, Jane

Stroud Mellon to DMK, n.d., all in Box 7, Vigil and Allen Building Takeover Files, 1968–1969, AARC.

7   Winston-Salem alumnus to DMK, February 14, 1969, G. F. Smart, MD, to DMK, February 14, 1969, Bob Stewart to DMK, February 14, 1969, C. B. Falls Jr. to DMK, February 15, 1969, all in Box 7, Vigil and Allen Building Takeover Files, 1968–1969, AARC.

8   DMK, interview, November 21, 1978.

9   R. W. Grabarek to Robert Scott, telegram, February 14, 1969, Box 5, Campus Unrest: 1969—Letters, DMK Records; "State Requests Knight to Cancel Students' Plan for Convocation," DC, February 15, 1969.

10 Richard Smurthwaite, "Students Convene in Page: Knight Absent," DC, February 16, 1969; "Some Agreement Indicated: Knight, Blacks Meet," DC, February 16, 1969.

11 "Allen Building Takeover, 1969 February 10–1969 March 12," tape 10, Box 6, Audio Tapes: 1956–1973, WDBS Collection, DUA.

12 "Some Agreement Indicated"; Ralph Karpinos and Clay Steinman, "1000 Confront Knight," DC, February 16, 1969.

13 "Comments at University House," February 15, 1969, Box 5, Campus Unrest, DMK Records.

14 "Comments at University House."

15 "Comments at University House."

16 "Comments at University House."

17 "Comments at University House."

18 DMK, "Statement by Dr. Douglas Knight for WDBS Radio," February 15, 1969, Box 72, Afro-American Society Demonstration: 1969, VPSA Records.

19 Watson, interview, November 16, 1978; Richard Smurthwaite, "Fuller Served as Spokesman for Blacks, Whites in Crisis," DC, March 7, 1969.

20 "Allen Building Takeover," tape 16.

21 ACK, "Report on Faculty Committee on Student Concerns," February 16, 1969, Box 1, Occupation of the Allen Building: 2/13/69—And Related Materials, OP Records. A second example in this category was the "African Studies living-learning arrangement." Kerckhoff confirmed that the university was "fully committed" to such an arrangement (subject to Black student involvement in its organization and receipt of any required governmental approvals) and targeted fall 1969 for its implementation.

22 "Allen Building Takeover," tape 16.

23 "Allen Building Takeover," tape 16. Also in this category was review of the records of Black students who had been dismissed after the fall semester for academic reasons. Efforts would be made to involve as many as possible in the recently announced summer transitional program as a pathway to readmission.

24 "Allen Building Takeover," tape 16.

25 ACK, "Report on Faculty Committee on Student Concerns," February 16, 1969, Box 1, Occupation of the Allen Building: 2/13/69—And Related Materials, OP Records; "Allen Building Takeover," tape 16.

26 DMK, "Statement"; "Duke Claims Militants Not Given Concessions," press clipping, n.d., Box 5, Campus Unrest, DMK Records.

27 Jean Cary, "University to Meet Most Afro Demands," DC, February 17, 1969; "Black Students Say Duke Now Committed," DC, February 17, 1969.

28 "'Understanding' at Duke," *Charleston Evening Post*, February 18, 1969; "Shape Up or Ship Out," *Richmond News Leader*, February 19, 1969.

29 Douglas Holt to DMK, February 27, 1969, Leonard H. Craver Jr., letter, February 18, 1969, both in Box 7, Files of Roger Marshall Concerning the Vigil and Allen Building Takeover: 1968–1969, AARC.

30 Don S. Garber to DMK, n.d., William C. Sienicles to Roger Marshall, February 24, 1969, both in Box 7, Files of Roger Marshall Concerning the Vigil and Allen Building Takeover: 1968–1969, AARC.

31 J. M. Hunt Jr. to DMK, February 19, 1969, "A Durham Alumnus," letter, n.d., Dewey H. Huffines Jr. to Charles B. Wade, February 24, 1969, all in Box 7, Files of Roger Marshall Concerning the Vigil and Allen Building Takeover: 1968–1969, AARC.

32 "Board of Trustees Minutes," March 7, 1969, vol. 13, BoT Records.

33 Alexander T. Davison to DMK, March 12, 1969, DMK to Alexander T. Davison, March 18, 1969, both in Box 1, Afro-American Situation: 1969—Letters Concerning, DMK Records.

34 "Knight Denies Duke Conceded to Blacks," DC, February 21, 1969.

35 Ed Harrison, "McBride Derides Knight's Statement," DC, February 25, 1969.

36 I. Harding Hughes Jr. to DMK, February 17, 1969, Box 72, Afro-American Society Demonstration: 1969, VPSA Records.

37 I. Harding Hughes Jr. to DMK, February 17, 1969, DMK to I. Harding Hughes Jr., February 17, 1969, DMK to William W. Pleasants, February 18, 1969, all in Box 72, Afro-American Society Demonstration: 1969, VPSA Records.

38 "Editorial: A New Provocation," DC, February 25, 1969; Campus Student Leaders to DMK, February 24, 1969, Box 1, Afro-American Situation: 1969—Letters Concerning, DMK Records; Harrison, "McBride Derides Knight's Statement"; Faculty Committee on Student Concerns to DMK, February 21, 1969, Box 7, Faculty Committee on Student Concerns, DMK Records.

39 DMK to Robert J. Sheheen, March 3, 1969, Box 1, Afro-American Situation: 1969—Letters Concerning, DMK Records; "Board of Trustees Minutes," March 7, 1969.

40 Duke University Afro-American Society, "Ten-Point Program: What We Want and Why We Want It," *Harambee*, February 5, 1969.

41 SDC, interview, March 1, 1985, ABTOHC; Budd, interview, March 1, 1985, ABTOHC; JWC, interview, January 9, 1979; ACK, interview, November 6, 1978.

42 Tom Campbell, "Afros, Profs Plan Studies," DC, March 1, 1969.

43 JWC, interview, January 9, 1979; Mark Stancato, "Faculty Acts, Afros Say No," DC, March 4, 1969; SDC, interview, March 1, 1985, ABTOHC.

44 CLB, "Why Give Up on Duke?," DC, March 11, 1969.

45 "Conference Report from the Afro-Americans," DC, March 4, 1969; Stancato, "Faculty Acts."

46 Alan Kerckhoff, "Conference Report," DC, March 4, 1969.

47 Harris Proctor et al., "Proctor Committee Report to the Provost of Duke University," March 4, 1969, Box 72, Afro-American Society Demonstration: 1969, VPSA Records.

48 "Conference Report from the Afro-Americans" (emphasis added).

49 ACK to MEH, March 3, 1969, Box 5, Faculty Committee on Student Concerns, OP Records.

50 MEH to Duke University Afro-American Society, March 5, 1969, Box 1, Afro-American Studies: 1969–1970, OP Records.

51 Michael R. McBride, "Black Students Demands Concerning African-American Studies," March 5, 1969, Box 1, Afro-American Situation: 1969—Miscellaneous Material, DMK Records.

52 Jim Pou, "Blacks May Leave if Committee Not Revised," DC, March 6, 1969.

53 "Torchlit March Misses Trustees," DC, March 7, 1969; "Restoring Faith," DC, March 7, 1969.

54 "FAS and SFAC Act; Blacks Refuse Meeting: Afros Refuse Talk Offer by Provost," DC, March 8, 1969.

55 Harold W. Lewis to Louis J. Budd et al., memorandum, March 10, 1969, Box 1, Afro-American Studies, DMK Records. The other members of the committee were Cell, Cook, Joel Smith, and John J. TePaske.

56 JWC, interview, January 9, 1979.

57 ACK, interview, November 6, 1978; Budd, interview, March 1, 1985, ABTOHC.

58 ACK, interview, November 6, 1978; JWC, interview, January 9, 1979.

59 Andy Parker, "Blacks to Leave Duke; No Settlement Reached," DC, March 11, 1969.

60 Fuller, *No Struggle, No Progress*, 97; Parker, "Blacks to Leave Duke." Founded by Fuller and others in October 1969, Malcolm X Liberation University was an independent Black university located initially in Durham. The mission of the university, as set forth in its organizational documents, was to "produce scholars and workers totally committed to the liberation of all African people throughout the Diaspora." Quoted in Fuller, *No Struggle, No Progress*, 99. The school moved to Greensboro, North Carolina, in October 1970 and ceased operations due to lack of funding in June 1973. Bertie Howard, among other members of the AAS, was active in the creation and operation of the university. Malcolm X Liberation University was seen by some as a response to the failure of Duke to implement a curriculum that was meaningful and relevant to its Black students.

61 CWH, interview, January 19, 1979; SDC, interview, March 1, 1985, ABTOHC.

62 Becton, "Why Give Up on Duke?"

63 "To Trust Tomorrow," DC, March 12, 1969.

64 BRH, interview, January 7, 1979.

65 DMK and Barnes Woodhall to members of the Duke University community, "Relations with Our Black Students with Respect to African and Afro-American Studies," March 11, 1969, Box 1, Afro-American Studies: 1969–1970, OP Records.

66 ACK to all members of the Afro-American Society, memorandum, March 13, 1969, Box 5, Faculty Committee on Student Concerns, OP Records.

67 Michael R. McBride to ACK, March 14, 1969, Box 7, Faculty Committee on Student Concerns, DMK Records.

68 MEH to ACK, March 20, 1969, Box 5, Faculty Committee on Student Concerns, OP Records.

69 Gretchen Wolf, "Violence Flares Up after Durham Rally," DC, March 12, 1969; Julie Logan, "Budd Group Meets, Silent; Curfew Imposed on City," DC, March 13, 1969; Jerome Katz, "Blacks Decide to Stay at Duke," DC, March 18, 1969.

70 "Afro Statement," DC, March 18, 1969.

71 Louis J. Budd to Michael R. McBride, March 18, 1969, Box 1, Afro-American Studies: 1969–1970, OP Records.

72 MEH, interview, March 4, 1985, ABTOHC.

73 J. Harris Proctor to MEH, May 26, 1969, Box 1, Afro-American Studies: 1969–1970, OP Records.

74 MEH to J. Harris Proctor, June 18, 1969, Box 1, Afro-American Studies: 1969–1970, OP Records.

75 DMK, interview, April 16, 1979.

76 Harold Lewis to Search Committee, December 6, 1969, Box 1, Afro-American Studies: 1969–1970, OP Records; Committee of Twelve, "Draft Report," December 31, 1969, Box 68, Committee of Twelve, VPSA Records.

77 Maxwell Berry, MD, to DMK, February 14, 1969, Russell Price to DMK, February 15, 1969, George B. Johnson to DMK, February 13, 1969, all in Box 7, Files of Roger Marshall Concerning the Vigil and Allen Building Takeover: 1968–1969, AARC.

78 F. W. Dennerline Jr. to DMK, February 14, 1969, Box 7, Files of Roger Marshall Concerning the Vigil and Allen Building Takeover: 1968–1969, AARC; DMK, interview, November 21, 1978; Knight, *Street of Dreams*, 137.

79 CLB, interview, December 16, 1978; Faculty Committee on Student Concerns to DMK, memorandum, February 15, 1969, Box 7, Faculty Committee on Student Concerns, DMK Records.

80 BRH in "Allen Building Takeover 50th"; BEA, interview, December 17, 1978; Tom McBride and Ruth D. McBride to DMK, March 2, 1969, DMK to Tom McBride and Ruth D. McBride, March 13, 1969, both in Box 1, Afro-American Situation: 1969—Letters Concerning, DMK Records.

81 Newsome quoted in Saurav, "Allen Building Takeover"; John Howell, "Blacks Are Charged; Trials Could Begin in Two Weeks," DC, March 6, 1969.

82 Afro-American Society, "Blacks File Petition Asking Speedy Trial," DC, February 27, 1969; BEA, interview, December 17, 1978; BCB, interview, December 13, 1978.

83 Doug Hastings, "Afro Trials Begin Today," DC, March 19, 1969; "Pickets, Protest Procedures," DC, March 19, 1969; "Blacks Get Probation for Building Takeover," DC, March 20, 1969.

84 "Pickets, Protest Procedures."

85 Unless otherwise noted, all descriptions of the disciplinary hearing are drawn from "Handwritten Notes of Disciplinary Hearing," March 19, 1969, Pickets and Protests Policy, ABTC.

86 "Handwritten Notes of Disciplinary Hearing" (emphasis added); BEA, interview, December 17, 1978.

87 BEA, interview, December 17, 1978.

88 BEA, interview, December 17, 1978.

89 University Hearing Committee, "Findings and Sentence of University Hearing Committee," n.d., Box 1, Occupation of the Allen Building: 2/13/69—and Related Materials, OP Records; CWH in "Allen Building Takeover 50th."

90 BEA, interview, December 17, 1978.

91 Michael Kopen, "Blacks React to Verdict," DC, March 21, 1969.

92 Pye, interview, March 2, 1985, ABTOHC. Prior to the hearing, Pye alerted Knight that he would be asking the university's counsel what sentence the school thought was appropriate for the defendants. After the defendants concluded their case, Pye asked the university's lawyer what direction he had from the university on the "appropriate sanction that should be placed against the students." Pye was shocked when Spears said he "had no instructions from the university on this point." After Pye pressed him, Spears explained that Knight had said "it was up to the tribunal" to determine the appropriate punishment. "Frankly, in my mind," Pye related, "nothing could be crazier than the university not having any position on what in the hell they thought ought to be done to sixty students after it had preferred charges against the sixty students." Despite his professed desire to "protect" the students, Knight appears to have been attempting to keep as much distance as possible between himself and the outcome of the disciplinary hearing. Pye, interview, March 2, 1985, ABTOHC.

93 Knight, *Dancer and the Dance*, 134; Knight, *Street of Dreams*, 138–39.

94 Knight, *Street of Dreams*, 139.

95 Knight, *Dancer and the Dance*, 128; DMK, interview, November 21, 1978, April 16, 1979.

96 DMK, interview, April 16, 1979.

97 Durden, *Lasting Legacy*, 256; DMK, interview, April 16, 1979.

98 DMK to members of the Duke University community, March 27, 1969, Box 16, Knight, Douglas M.—Misc.—1966–1969, DMK Records; Durden, *Lasting Legacy*, 256.

99 "... To Embody It," DC, March 31, 1969; DMK, interview, April 16, 1979.

100 DMK, interview, November 21, 1978, April 16, 1979; DMK quoted in "Remembering the Vigil"; Knight, *Dancer and the Dance*, 135.

101 "Douglas M. Knight, Fifth Duke President."

102 SDC, interview, March 1, 1985, ABTOHC.

103 Various administrators and staff, "A Protest," n.d., Box 16, Knight, Douglas M.—Misc.—1966–1969, DMK Records.

104 Barnes Woodhall and Frances Woodhall to DMK and Grace Knight, April 23, 1969, Box 16, Knight, Douglas M.—Misc.—1966–1969, DMK Records.

105 This version of the "aims" of Duke University, in effect in 1963, was initially drafted in 1903 after the board of Trinity College asked that a major revision of the college's bylaws be prepared. The wording was changed in 1924 when Duke University was organized. "Charter, Bylaws, Aims, and Mission Statement," University Archives, accessed October 17, 2019, https://library.duke.edu/rubenstein/uarchives/history/articles/charter-bylaws-aims-mission/.

106 Faculty Committee on Student Concerns, "Final Report of the Faculty Committee on Student Concerns," June 3, 1969, Box 5, Faculty Committee on Student Concerns, OP Records.

107 WJG, interview, January 23, 1979.

108 DMK, interview, April 16, 1979.

EPILOGUE

1 CLB, interview, April 19, 2017; LeBlanc in "Allen Building Takeover 50th"; BEA, interview, December 17, 1978.

2 BEA, interview, March 3, 2017.

3 Vincent E. Price, "Remarks Honoring the 50th Anniversary of the Allen Building Takeover," Office of the President, February 9, 2019, https://president.duke.edu/2019/02/09/remarks-honoring-the-50th-anniversary-of-the-allen-building-takeover/; Armstrong and Booher, "Let's Talk about Race"; Armstrong, interview, March 3, 2017.

4 Bob Entman, "Sanford 'Meets All' Standards," DC, December 15, 1969; Cook, interview, March 1, 1985, ABTOHC; Ralph Karpinos, "Sanford Named President: Cites Community Responsibility," DC, December 15, 1969; Jacob Goldman, "Union Approved by 491–100 Vote," DC, January 28, 1972; WCT, interview, April 17, 2017. As one indication of his commitment, Sanford had sent his children to desegregated public schools while serving as governor of North Carolina.

5 "Low Student Debt"; Stefanie Pousoulides, "Duke University Hospital Falls Out of Nation's Top 20 Hospitals," DC, August 1, 2019; Lexi Kadis, "Duke Graduate Programs Earn High Rankings in 2020 U.S. News and World Report List," DC, March 18, 2019; "Duke Facts," Duke University, accessed April 16, 2019, https://facts.duke.edu; "Duke University Hospital."

6 "Duke Facts"; "Our Students by the Numbers," Office of Undergraduate Admissions, accessed November 13, 2019, https://admissions.duke.edu.

7 Duke has adopted a statement of diversity and inclusion: "Duke aspires to create a community built on collaboration, innovation, creativity, and belonging. Our collective success depends on the robust exchange of ideas—an exchange that is best when the rich diversity of our perspectives, backgrounds, and experiences flourishes. To achieve this exchange, it is essential that all members of the community feel secure and welcome, that the contributions of all individuals are respected, and that all voices are heard. All members of our community have a responsibility to uphold these values." "Duke's Commitment to Diversity and Inclusion," Office of the Provost, Duke University, accessed September 22, 2019, https://provost.duke.edu/initiatives/commitment-to-diversity-and-inclusion.

8 This followed what director Chandra Guinn described as fourteen years of "more protests, more demands, more discussion, and more pushing" by Duke students. "Pivot Point: The Allen Building Takeover at Duke Fifty Years Later; Part 3—Aftermath," *The Devils' Share: The Podcast of Duke Magazine*, 2019, https://sites.duke.edu/devilsshare/pivot-point-the-allen-building-takeover-at-duke-fifty-years-later/.

9 "Our Students by the Numbers"; "Duke Facts."

10 "Duke Names Quad in Honor of Julian Abele"; "Duke Removes Robert E. Lee Statue"; "Carr Building to Be Renamed."

11 Walk, interview, February 27, 2019.

12 Amrith Ramkumar and Rachel Chason, "Duke's Executive Vice President Tallman Trask Hit Parking Attendant with Car, Accused of Using Racial Slur," DC, February 29, 2016.

13 Amrith Ramkumar and Rachel Chason, "Employees Describe Hostile, Discriminatory Environment in Parking and Transportation Services Department," DC, March 1, 2016.

14 Gautam Hathi and Rachel Chason, "Latest Coverage of the Allen Building Sit-In," DC, April 1, 2016; "Duke to Move to $15 Minimum Wage."

15 Roberts, interview, February 27, 2019.

16 Sydney Roberts, "Activism Then and Now: An Intergenerational Conversation," address, Washington Duke Inn and Golf Club, Durham, NC, February 9, 2019.

17 Jeremy Bauer-Wolf, "Hate Incidents on Campus Still Rising," *Inside Higher Ed*, February 25, 2019, https://www.insidehighered.com/news/2019/02/25/hate

-incidents-still-rise-college-campuses/; "Ignorance, Bad Judgment Cause of Noose Incident"; Steven Petrow, "Civilities: A Gay Duke Student Threatened with Death Speaks Up," *Washington Post*, November 16, 2015; Samantha Neal and Amrith Ramkumar, "Students Gather at Chapel Steps Friday Afternoon after Vandalism to Black Lives Matter Flyer," DC, October 23, 2015.

18 Petrow, "How Talking to Undergraduates Changed My Mind."

19 Nick Chiles, "Black Ministry Students at Duke Say They Face Unequal Treatment and Racism," *Code Switch*, NPR, May 24, 2017, https://www.npr.org/sections/codeswitch/2017/05/24/467233031/black-ministry-students-at-duke-say-they-face-unequal-treatment-and-racism/.

20 "Year in Review: Top Stories of 2018," DC, December 31, 2018; Ben Leonard, "Students, Alumni Express Frustration with Larry Moneta's Tweet on Hate Speech, Freedom of Expression," DC, April 27, 2018; Ben Leonard, "How the Recent Racially Charged Incidents at Duke Relate to Previous Ones," DC, April 30, 2018. Moneta retired as student affairs vice president in 2019 after an eighteen-year career at the university.

21 Sarah Krueger, "Duke Students Deliver Petition Calling for Anti-Hate Policy," WRAL: Local News, April 30, 2018, https://www.wral.com/duke-students-deliver-petition-calling-for-anti-hate-policy-/17521025/; Nathan Luzum, "Administrators Open Discussions about Changes to Hate and Bias Policy," DC, May 18, 2018.

22 Ben Leonard, "Here's Everything You Need to Know about the Joe Van Gogh Firings—And the Questions That Still Remain," DC, May 10, 2018.

23 Katie Jane Fernelius, "A Duke University VP Walked into the Campus Joe Van Gogh, Heard a Rap Song, Demanded That the Employees Be Fired," *Indy Week*, May 8, 2018.

24 "Duke, Joe Van Gogh Release Statements on Employees' Termination," DC, May 9, 2018; Allison Hussey, "Joe Van Gogh Cuts Ties with Duke after Controversial Firing of Two Employees," *Indy Week*, May 11, 2018.

25 "New Year, Same Problems?," DC, August 27, 2018; Bre Bradham, Ben Leonard, and Nathan Luzum, "Latinx Heritage Month Mural Found Defaced on East Campus Bridge," DC, September 22, 2018; Jake Sheridan, "Incidents on Campus Part of National Trend, Says Southern Poverty Law Center," DC, November 26, 2018.

26 Amy B. Wang, "Duke Professor Apologizes for Telling Chinese Students to Speak English on Campus," *Washington Post*, January 28, 2019.

27 Walk, interview, February 27, 2019.

28 Sean Cho, "Price Addresses Biostatistics Email Controversy in Statement to Duke Community," DC, February 4, 2019.

29 Nayoung Aimee Kwon, "Statement to Duke's Leadership and Faculty from the Director of the Asian American Studies Program," DC, February 21, 2019;

Sheridan, "Incidents on Campus." Kwon cited the Duke University Task Force on Bias and Hate Issues (2016), Duke University Task Force on Diversity (2015), Duke University Task Force on Gender (2018), and Duke University Task Force on Reimagining Doctoral Education (2018).

30 Jake Satisky, "Price Outlines Five Values at Academic Council," DC, September 23, 2019; Walk, interview, February 27, 2019; Armstrong and Booher, "Let's Talk about Race"; Carter Forinash, "Protesters Reflect on Allen Building Takeover at 50th Anniversary Event," DC, February 13, 2019; Cameron Oglesby, "'We Belong Here': Students Build Unity at 5th Black Convocation," DC, September 5, 2019.

31 "President Price: 'We Have More Work to Do.'"

32 "President Price: 'We Have More Work to Do.'"

33 "Statement from President Price."

34 "Statement from President Price."

BIBLIOGRAPHY

‒‒‒‒‒

ARCHIVAL SOURCES

Duke University Archives, David M. Rubenstein Rare Book and Manuscript Library, Duke University, Durham, NC

Allen Building Takeover Collection

Allen Building Takeover Oral History Collection

   All interviews conducted by Don Yannella in Durham, NC.

   Armstrong, Brenda. January 31, 1985.

   Budd, Louis. March 1, 1985.

   Cahow, Clark. October 23, 1984.

   Campbell, Tom. February 8, 1985.

   Cook, Samuel. March 1, 1985.

   DeMik, Harry. February 12, 1985.

   Griffith, William. March 5, 1985.

   Hobbs, Marcus. March 4, 1985 (mislabeled as A. Kenneth Pye, part 1).

   Pye, A. Kenneth. March 2, 1985.

   Turner, William C., Jr. January 23, 1985.

   Williams, Janice. February 13, 1985.

Alumni Affairs Reference Collection

Black History at Duke Reference Collection

Board of Trustees Records

Duke Vigil Collection

A. Hollis Edens Papers

J. Deryl Hart Records

Barney Lee Jones Papers

Douglas M. Knight Records

Labor Unions Reference Collection

Office of the Provost Records

A. Kenneth Pye, Chancellor, Records and Papers

Radio TV Services Records

Terry Sanford Papers

Student Papers Reference Collection

Trinity College of Arts and Sciences, Office of the Dean Records

University Archives Photographs Collection

Vice President for Business and Finance Records

Vice President for Student Affairs Records

WDBS Collection

Bunyan S. Womble Papers

Southern Oral History Program Collection, Southern Historical Collection, Wilson Library, University of North Carolina at Chapel Hill

Becton, Charles. Interview by Pamela Foster. February 20, 1994. Durham, NC. #J-0009.

Forte, Minnie. Interview by Gerrelyn Patterson. February 10, 2005. Durham, NC. #U-0117.

Holt, Sterlin. Interview by Gerrelyn C. Patterson. February 18, 2005. Durham, NC. #U-0119.

Lucas, Jeanne Hopkins. Interview by Gerrelyn Patterson. April 15, 2005. Raleigh, NC. #U-0122.

Williams, Jacqueline. Interview by Gerrelyn Patterson. February 9, 2005. Durham, NC. #U-0132.

INTERVIEWS

All interviews conducted by the author in Durham, NC, unless otherwise noted.

Armstrong, Brenda. December 17, 1978, February 13, 1979, March 3, December 5, 2017.

Ashley, Robert. August 29, 2018.

Beach, W. Waldo. Interview by Jorge Kotelanski. January 26, 1990. Transcript in Kotelanski, "Prolonged and Patient Efforts."

Becton, Charles. December 16, 1978, April 19, 2017.

Brown, Brenda. December 13, 1978, April 19, 2017.

Burke, Steven. February 6, 1977.

Cell, John W. January 18, 1977, January 9, 1979.

Cole, R. Taylor. Interview by Jorge Kotelanski. March 1, 1990. Transcript in Kotelanski, "Prolonged and Patient Efforts."

Cushman, Robert. Interview by Jorge Kotelanski. February 28, 1990. Transcript in Kotelanski, "Prolonged and Patient Efforts."

Griffith, William J. January 20, February 5, 1977, January 16, 23, February 15, 1979.

Gutman, Huck. April 13, 2018.

Henderson, David M. January 14, February 9, 1977.

Hobbs, Marcus E. November 1979.

Hopkins, Charles. January 19, 1979.

Howard, Bertie R. January 7, 1979.

Huestis, Charles B. February 9, 1977.

Kerckhoff, Alan. November 6, 1978.

Kinney, Jonathan C. September 12, 2017. Arlington, VA.

Klopfer, Peter. Interview by Jorge Kotelanski. February 8, 1990. Transcript in Kotelanski, "Prolonged and Patient Efforts."

Knight, Douglas M. November 21, 1978, April 16, 1979. Chadds Ford, PA.

LeBlanc, Michael. Interview by Sarah Xu and Rachel Rubin. February 9, 2019. http://livinghistory.sanford.duke.edu/interviews/michael-leblanc/.

Marshall, Roger L. January 13, 1977.

McBride, Michael. Interview by Sarah Xu and Rachel Rubin. May 21, 2019. http://livinghistory.sanford.duke.edu/interviews/michael-mcbride/.

Preiss, Jack. February 5, 1977.

Roberts, Sydney. February 27, 2019.

Simons, Serena. February 1, 1977.

Small, Margaret "Bunny." April 12, 2018.

Traver, Hutch. December 7, 1978. Creedmoor, NC.

Turner, William C., Jr. November 8, 1978, April 17, 2017.

Walk, Trey. February 27, 2019.

Watson, Richard L. November 16, 1978.

PERIODICALS

Carolina Times (Durham, NC)

Charleston Evening Post (Charleston, SC)

Charlotte News (Charlotte, NC)

Daily Times-News (Burlington, NC)

Duke Chronicle

Duke Magazine

Duke Today

Duke University Alumni Magazine

Durham Chronicle

Durham Herald

Durham Herald-Sun

Durham Morning Herald

Harambee (Durham, NC)

High Point Enterprise

Indy Week (Durham, NC)

The Lawrentian (Appleton, WI)

Richmond News Leader (Richmond, VA)

Trinity Chronicle (Durham, NC)

Washington Post

OTHER SOURCES

"Allen Building Takeover 50th: The Original Allen Building Takeover Protesters Tell Their Stories." Washington Duke Inn and Golf Club, Durham, NC, February 9, 2019. https://www.youtube.com/watch?v=a1anTB7TVxA.

Ainsworth, Tracy, and Gail A. Williams, comps. *Legacy, 1963–1993: Thirty Years of African-American Students at Duke University.* Durham, NC: Duke University Office of the University Vice President and Vice Provost, 1993.

Anderson, Elijah. "Black in White Space." Penn Institute for Urban Research, May 21, 2018. https://penniur.upenn.edu/publications/black-in-white-space.

Anderson, Elijah. "The White Space." *Journal of Race and Ethnicity* 1, no. 1 (2014): 10–21.

Anderson, James D. *The Education of Blacks in the South, 1860–1935.* Chapel Hill: University of North Carolina Press, 1988.

Anlyan, William G. *Metamorphoses: Memoirs of a Life in Medicine.* Durham, NC: Duke University Press, 2004.

Annual Catalogue of Duke University: Constitution and By-Laws. Durham, NC: Duke University, 1925.

Armstrong, Brenda E. "Allen Building Takeover: A Personal Account." In *Legacy, 1963–1993: Thirty Years of African-American Students at Duke University,* compiled by Tracy Ainsworth and Gail A. Williams, 41–45. Durham, NC: Duke University Office of the University Vice President and Vice Provost, 1993.

Armstrong, Brenda E., and Bridget Booher. "Let's Talk about Race." *Duke Magazine,* February 13, 2013. https://alumni.duke.edu/magazine/articles/lets-talk-about-race.

Bair, Sarah. "Early Years of Negro History Week, 1926–1950." In *Histories of Social Studies and Race: 1865–2000,* edited by Christine Woyshner and Chara Haeussler Bohan, 57–77. New York: Palgrave Macmillan, 2012.

Ballard, Allen B. *The Education of Black Folk.* Lincoln, NE: iUniverse, 2004.

Batchelor, John E. *Race and Education in North Carolina: From Segregation to Desegregation.* Baton Rouge: Louisiana State University Press, 2015.

Beezer, Bruce. "North Carolina's Rationale for Mandating Separate Schools: A Legal History." *Journal of Negro Education* 52 (1983): 213–26.

Bermanzohn, Sally Avery. *Through Survivors' Eyes: From the Sixties to the Greensboro Massacre.* Nashville, TN: Vanderbilt University Press, 2003.

"Bill Griffith on the 1969 Allen Building Takeover." *Duke Today,* September 11, 2013. https://today.duke.edu/2013/09/griffithallenbuilding.

"Black History at Duke." Accessed June 18, 2020. https://spotlight.duke.edu/50years/timeline-2/.

Biondi, Martha. *The Black Revolution on Campus.* Berkeley: University of California Press, 2012.

Booher, Bridget. "Duke Desegregates: The First Five." *Duke Magazine,* September 1992.

Brown, Leslie. *Upbuilding Black Durham: Gender, Class, and Black Community Development in the Jim Crow South.* Chapel Hill: University of North Carolina Press, 2008.

Bulletin of Duke University: Catalogue Number 1962–1963, Announcements for 1963–1964. Durham, NC: Duke University, 1963.

Carmichael, Stokely. "Toward Black Liberation." 1966. Reprinted in *Black Fire: An Anthology of Afro-American Writing,* edited by Amiri Baraka and Larry Neal, 119–32. Baltimore: Black Classic Press, 2007.

"Carr Building to Be Renamed." *Duke Today*, September 1, 2018. https://today.duke
.edu/2018/12/carr-building-be-renamed/.

Carter, Luther J. "Duke University: Students Demand New Deal for Negro Workers."
Science 160, no. 3827 (May 3, 1968): 513–17.

Chafe, William H. *Civilities and Civil Rights: Greensboro, North Carolina, and the
Black Struggle for Freedom.* New York: Oxford University Press, 1980.

Chafe, William H. *The Unfinished Journey: America since World War II.* 7th ed.
Oxford: Oxford University Press, 2015.

Cole, R. Taylor. *The Recollections of R. Taylor Cole: Educator, Emissary, Development
Planner.* Durham, NC: Duke University Press, 1983.

Crow, Jeffrey J., Paul D. Escott, and Flora J. Hatley. *A History of African Americans
in North Carolina.* Raleigh, NC: Office of Archives and History, North Carolina
Department of Cultural Resources, 2008.

"Douglas M. Knight, Fifth Duke President, Dies at 83." *Duke Today*, January 23, 2005.
https://today.duke.edu/2005/01/knight_0105.html.

Du Bois, W. E. B. "The Upbuilding of Black Durham: The Success of the Negroes and
Their Value to a Tolerant and Helpful Southern City." *World's Work* 23 (January 1912). Available at Documenting the American South. Accessed October 17,
2019. http://docsouth.unc.edu/nc/dubois/summary.html.

"Duke Names Quad in Honor of Julian Abele." *Duke Today*, March 1, 2016. https://
today.duke.edu/2016/03/abele/.

"Duke Removes Robert E. Lee Statue from Chapel Entrance." *Duke Today*, August 19, 2017.
https://today.duke.edu/2017/08/duke-removes-robert-e-lee-statue-chapel-entrance/.

"Duke to Move to $15 Minimum Wage by 2019." *Duke Today*, August 25, 2017. https://
today.duke.edu/2017/08/duke-move-15-minimum-wage-2019.

Duke University. "50 Years of Black Students at Duke." YouTube, January 26, 2013.
https://www.youtube.com/watch?v=HpFEZcwpMOA.

"Duke University Hospital." *U.S. News and World Report.* Accessed April 16, 2019. https://
health.usnews.com/best-hospitals/area/nc/duke-university-medical-center-6360355.

Durden, Robert F. *Bold Entrepreneur: A Life of James B. Duke.* Durham, NC: Carolina
Academic Press, 2003.

Durden, Robert F. *Lasting Legacy to the Carolinas: The Duke Endowment, 1924–1994.*
Durham, NC: Duke University Press, 1998.

Durden, Robert F. *The Launching of Duke University, 1924–1949.* Durham, NC: Duke
University Press, 1993.

Egerton, John. *Speak Now against the Day: The Generation before the Civil Rights
Movement in the South.* Chapel Hill: University of North Carolina Press, 1994.

Exum, William H. *Paradoxes of Protest: Black Student Activism in a White University.*
Philadelphia, PA: Temple University Press, 1985.

Farnham, Christie Anne. *The Education of the Southern Belle: Higher Education and Student Socialization in the Antebellum South*. New York: New York University Press, 1994.

Fuller, Howard. *No Struggle, No Progress: A Warrior's Life from Black Power to Education Reform*. Milwaukee, WI: Marquette University Press, 2014.

Gaines, Patrice. "Faces of Hope: Integrating Duke." Black America Web, February 27, 2013. https://blackamericaweb.com/2013/02/27/faces-of-hope-integrating-duke/.

Goodwyn, Lawrence. *The Populist Moment: A Short History of the Agrarian Revolt in America*. New York: Oxford University Press, 1978.

Greene, Christina. *Our Separate Ways: Women and the Black Freedom Movement in Durham, North Carolina*. Chapel Hill: University of North Carolina Press, 2005.

Hendrick, Lydia. "The Silent Vigil 1968: A First Step." YouTube, February 26, 2020. https://www.youtube.com/watch?v=-UAhyyJdH44&list=PL-P-8DrC8BRIOpLjtcm q9DiltIhkdNAvB&index=19&t=0s.

Hicks, Sally. "Talkin 'bout My Generation." *Duke Magazine*, June 1, 2005. https://alumni.duke.edu/magazine/articles/talking-bout-my-generation.

"Honoring His Legacy." *Duke Today*, January 21, 2015. https://today.duke.edu/2015/01/jhf100.

Hope Valley Country Club Yearbook. Durham, NC: Hope Valley Country Club, 1966.

Hopkins, Chuck. "Malcolm X University: Interim Report." *Negro Digest* 19, no. 5 (March 1970): 39–42.

"Ignorance, Bad Judgment Cause of Noose Incident, Investigation Finds." *Duke Today*, May 1, 2015. https://today.duke.edu/2015/05/nooseinvestigation/.

Jacobs, Barry. *Across the Line: Profiles in Basketball Courage—Tales of the First Black Players in the ACC and SEC*. Guilford, CT: Lyons, 2008.

Johnson, James Weldon. *God's Trombones: Seven Negro Sermons in Verse*. New York: Viking, 1927.

Johnson, William. "The Timid Generation." *Sports Illustrated*, March 11, 1968, 69–78.

Jones, Alison. "How the 1968 Silent Vigil Marked a Turning Point for Duke." *Duke Today*, April 2, 2018. https://today.duke.edu/2018/04/how-1968-silent-vigil -marked-turning-point-duke/.

Kean, Melissa. *Desegregating Private Higher Education in the South: Duke, Emory, Rice, Tulane, and Vanderbilt*. Baton Rouge: Louisiana State University Press, 2008.

Kendi, Ibram X. *Stamped from the Beginning: The Definitive History of Racist Ideas in America*. New York: Nation Books, 2016.

King, Martin Luther, Jr. "'Facing the Challenge of a New Age': Martin Luther King, Jr., Booker T. Washington High School Gymnasium, Rocky Mount, North Carolina." Edited by W. Jason Miller. http://kingsfirstdream.com/wp-content/uploads/2015 /11/Martin-Luther-King-Jr.-speech-NOT-annotated-transcript-Rocky-Mount-NC -November-27-1962.pdf.

Klopfer, Peter H. "Duke: Repressive Labor Policies." *Science* 160, no. 3835 (June 28, 1968): 1397.

Knight, Douglas M. *The Dancer and the Dance*. New York: Separate Star, 2003.

Knight, Douglas M. *Street of Dreams*. Durham, NC: Duke University Press, 1989.

Kornberg, Allan, and Joel Smith. "It Ain't Over Yet: Activism in a Southern University." In *Black Power and Student Rebellion*, edited by James McEvoy and Abraham Miller, 100–121. Belmont, CA: Wadsworth, 1969.

Korstad, Robert R., and James L. Leloudis. *To Right These Wrongs: The North Carolina Fund and the Battle to End Poverty and Inequality in 1960s America*. Chapel Hill: University of North Carolina Press, 2010.

Kotelanski, Jorge. "Prolonged and Patient Efforts: The Desegregation of Duke University, 1948–1963." Bachelor's thesis, Duke University, 1990.

Litwack, Leon F. *Been in the Storm So Long: The Aftermath of Slavery*. New York: Vintage, 1980.

Litwack, Leon F. *Trouble in Mind: Black Southerners in the Age of Jim Crow*. New York: Knopf, 1975.

Litwack, Leon F. *Trouble in Mind: Black Southerners in the Age of Jim Crow*. New York: Vintage, 1999.

"Low Student Debt at Duke Cited in New Rankings." *Duke Today*, September 10, 2019. https://today.duke.edu/2019/09/low-student-debt-duke-cited-new-rankings.

Ludwig, Erik. "Closing In on the 'Plantation': Coalition Building and the Role of Black Women's Grievances in Duke University Labor Disputes, 1965–1968." *Feminist Studies* 25, no. 1 (Spring 1999): 79–94.

McConville, Ed. "Oliver Harvey: 'Gotta Take Some Risks.'" *Southern Justice* 6, no. 2 (Summer 1978): 24–28.

McWhirter, Christian. *Battle Hymns: The Power and Popularity of Music in the Civil War*. Chapel Hill: University of North Carolina Press, 2012.

McWhirter, Christian. "The Birth of 'Dixie.'" *New York Times*, March 31, 2012.

Milligan, Joy. "Subsidizing Segregation." *Virginia Law Review* 104 (2018): 847–932.

Murray, Peter C. *Methodists and the Crucible of Race, 1930–1975*. Columbia: University of Missouri Press, 2004.

Partner, Simon, and Emma Johnston. *Bull City Survivor: Standing Up to a Hard Life in a Southern City*. Jefferson, NC: McFarland, 2013.

Petrow, Steven. "How Talking to Undergraduates Changed My Mind." *The Atlantic*, November 30, 2015.

Porter, Earl W. *Trinity and Duke, 1892–1924: Foundations of Duke University*. Durham, NC: Duke University Press, 1964.

"President Price: 'We Have More Work to Do.'" *Duke Today*, May 10, 2018. https://today.duke.edu/2018/05/president-price-we-have-more-work-do.

Proctor, Samuel DeWitt. *The Substance of Things Hoped For: A Memoir of African-American Faith*. Valley Forge, PA: Judson Press, 1995.

Rabinowitz, Howard. *Race Relations in the Urban South, 1865–1890*. New York: Oxford University Press, 1978.

"Remembering the Vigil: A University Milestone." *Duke Magazine*, March 31, 1998. https://alumni.duke.edu/magazine/articles/remembering-vigil-university-milestone.

Rogers, Ibram H. [Ibram X. Kendi]. *The Black Campus Movement: Black Students and the Racial Reconstitution of Higher Education, 1965–1972*. New York: Palgrave Macmillan, 2012.

Sacks, Karen Brodkin. *Caring by the Hour: Women, Work, and Organizing at Duke Medical Center*. Urbana: University of Illinois Press, 1988.

Saurav, Sanjay. "The Allen Building Takeover: Transforming Students into Activists." YouTube, February 27, 2020. https://www.youtube.com/watch?v=DRz93KsD2iU&list=PL-P-8DrC8BRIOpLjtcmq9DiltIhkdNAvB&index=20&t=0s.

Smith, H. Shelton. *In His Image, but . . . : Racism in Southern Religion, 1780–1910*. Durham, NC: Duke University Press, 1972.

Sokol, Jason. *There Goes My Everything: White Southerners in the Age of Civil Rights, 1945–1975*. New York: Vintage, 2007.

"Statement from President Price on Juneteenth Celebration and Next Steps on Addressing Racism," *Duke Today*, June 17, 2020. https://today.duke.edu/2020/06/statement-president-price-juneteenth-celebration-and-next-steps-addressing-racism.

Tindall, George Brown. *The Emergence of the New South, 1913–1945*. Baton Rouge: Louisiana State University Press, 1967.

Tumin, Melvin M. *Desegregation: Resistance and Readiness*. Princeton, NJ: Princeton University Press, 1958.

Ture, Kwame, and Charles V. Hamilton. *Black Power: The Politics of Liberation*. New York: Vintage, 1992.

Van Deburg, William L. *New Day in Babylon: The Black Power Movement and American Culture, 1965–1975*. Chicago: University of Chicago Press, 1992.

Walker, Vanessa Siddle. *Their Highest Potential: An African American School Community in the Segregated South*. Chapel Hill: University of North Carolina Press, 1996.

Williamson, Joy Ann. *Black Power on Campus: The University of Illinois, 1965–75*. Urbana: University of Illinois Press, 2003.

Yannella, Don. "Race Relations at Duke University and the Allen Building Takeover." Bachelor's thesis, Duke University, 1985.

INDEX

Brovard, T. F., 66, 70

Brown, Brenda C.: and AAS, 91, 93, 100, 190; background, 40, 43, 45; on administration attitudes, 52, 54; on Allen Building takeover, 183, 202; on Black student enrollment, 169; on community-building, 85; and isolation, 51; on Knight, 201; and segregated facilities controversy, 91, 93, 100; and Silent Vigil, 137; and student organizations, 81, 83

Brown, Leslie, 9, 291n23

Brown v. Board of Education, 9

Bryan, T. Conn, 20

Bryce-Laporte, Roy, 254

Bryson, Edwin, 118, 165, 215, 227

Bubas, Vic, 70

Budd, Louis, 254, 258, 262

Budd, W. P., 70

budget, 167

Burch, Mary Jane, 67

Burke, Steven, 112

Burns, E. J., 19

Cahow, Clark R., 180, 209, 213–14, 220, 236–37, 266

Campbell, Tom, 211, 235–36

campus security, 45

Cannon, James, III, 19

Carmichael, Stokely (Kwame Ture), 77–80, 185, 306n53

Carr, Julian, 279

Carter, Constance Jackson, 41

Cartwright, William, 215–17, 225, 238

Cell, John W.: and ad hoc committee, 169, 171, 174, 177–79, 181; and Allen Building takeover, 213, 216, 221, 229, 236–37, 240; on Black militancy, 161–62, 182; on Black student activism, 184–85, 193; and Black studies program, 254, 258; and Black Week, 199; on desegregation, 161; funding proposals, 177–78, 181, 248; on Hobbs, 206–7; on Knight, 30, 174; on Silent Vigil, 133, 155–56, 160

Chafe, William H., 17, 78, 105

Chicken Box restaurant, 132

civil rights movement, 28, 38, 60–61, 77. *See also* Black Power; Carmichael, Stokely (Kwame Ture); King, Martin Luther, Jr.

Claiborne, Claudius, 43, 56–57, 64–65

Cleland, James T., 13

Cole, R. Taylor, 18; on Black students, 40; and desegregation, 21, 23, 54, 300n56; and Knight, 173; on May Queen, 75; and segregated facilities controversy, 89; and Silent Vigil, 133–34, 138; and Special Committee, 149; and University House occupation, 118, 120–21, 313n46

collective bargaining: administration and, 151–54; demands for, 108, 125–26; and Silent Vigil, 125, 137–39, 142–43; trustees and, 143, 145–47, 153, 158

community: and activism, 87, 202; and Allen Building takeover, 222, 231–32, 241, 245, 247, 259; Black, 33–41, 53, 56–58, 64, 88, 106, 127, 140, 211, 222; and Black Power, 78; and education, 35–39; students and, 51, 55, 58–59, 77, 82, 85–87, 151, 186; and Silent Vigil, 130, 133, 140, 159; views on, 98–99. *See also* Afro-American Society (AAS)

Confederate flag, 13, 46–47, 161, 171–72, 175

Cook, Samuel DuBois: on administration, 180; and Allen Building takeover, 213, 216–17, 226, 235–36, 240; and Black studies program, 176, 253–54, 262; hiring of, 65; and King, 135; and Knight, 64, 174, 271; on police, 243; and Silent Vigil, 132–33, 140–41, 154, 159; on Sanford, 278; on student withdrawals, 259; on white teachers, 44

Cooley, Harold, 20

Cooper, Otis, 37–38

Couch, William, Jr., 254

Cousin, Philip R., 56, 302n67

Cox, Robert B., 67, 69–70, 304n32

Creamer, Bob, 151–52

Creed, George, 37

Cuninggim, Merrimon, 304n26

Cushman, Robert, 17, 54

Davis, Guion C., 38

Day, Bobbie Jean, 266

Ture, Kwame. *See* Carmichael, Stokely (Kwame Ture)

Turner, William C., Jr.: adjustment to Duke, 51, 52, 57, 59, 77, 179; and Allen Building takeover, 204, 230, 232–33; background and family, 40–41, 43–44, 50, 183, 276; on Black students, 33; on Black Week, 202; on concerns, 164; on Durham, 56; on education, 35; and *God's Trombones*, 198–99; and home community, 298n22; and racial consciousness, 188–89; and racism, 46, 48–49; on Sanford, 278; on segregation, 10, 32

Tuthill, Richard L., 215, 219–20, 266

University Caucus, 69

University House, 271; occupation, 104–5, 110–13, 115–24, 157, 239–40, 313n28, 313n46, 313–14nn47–48, 314n56

University of North Carolina, 9, 63

University Policy and Planning Advisory Committee, 89, 94

Upchurch, Walter M., 147

Van Deburg, William, 78

Van Pelt, Jeff, 113, 115–16, 133, 155

Vigil Strategy Committee, 144–45, 150–51, 154

Wade, Charles B., Jr., 147, 215, 250, 269–70

Walk, Trey, 280, 284

Wallace, George, 28

Washington, Booker T., 34, 301n65

Washington, Booker T., High School, 37–39, 298n13

Washington, Henry, 282

Watson, Brantley, 153

Watson, Katherine, 169, 174, 176, 179, 181

Watson, Richard L., Jr., 55, 169, 213, 226, 247

Wells, Bill, 17

Werber, William M., 68, 198, 304n26

Werner, Bill, 201

West Campus, 279–80

Weston, Larry, 197

White, Nathaniel, Jr., 35, 42–44, 46

Whitfield, Clarence, 118, 251–52

Wilkinson, Howard, 135

Williams, Jacqueline, 36–37

Williams, Janice, 34, 276; and Allen Building takeover, 209, 213, 226–27, 231–32, 332n41; on Black History Month, 190; on Black student activism, 185; on Black Week, 201; on cultural negation, 77; on Duke's attitudes, 179; social life, 51, 300n51; on student community, 82

Williams, Mary Lou, Center for Black Culture, 279, 283

Williamson, Joy Ann, 81, 175, 184, 323n34

Wilson, Clint, 70

Wilson, Mary Grace, 50, 74–75

Wilson, Thomas G., 219, 229, 235

Winton, Ray, 243

withdrawal (from university), 257, 259–62

Woman's College, 5, 8, 20, 69. *See also* May Queen

Womble, Bunyan S., 22–23

women: and Allen Building takeover, 231–32; harassment of, 47–48; progressiveness of, 89; sign-out rules, 116, 122, 160; student quality, 8

Women's Student Government Association, 65–66, 69–70

Woodhall, Barnes, 21, 118, 260–61, 294n51